# NARRATIVE SOJOURNER T

Written by Olive Gilbert, based on
Sojourner Truth, 1850

---

## INCIDENTS IN THE LIFE OF A SLAVE GIRL, Written by Herself.

By Harriet A. Jacobs, 1861

---

## THE HISTORY OF MARY PRINCE, A WEST INDIAN SLAVE. RELATED BY HERSELF.
WITH A SUPPLEMENT BY THE EDITOR, 1831

To which is added,
THE NARRATIVE OF ASA-ASA, A CAPTURED AFRICAN.

---

## THE STORY OF Mattie J. Jackson;

Her Parentage—Experience of Eighteen Years in Slavery—
Incidents During the War—Her Escape from Slavery.
A TRUE STORY.

WRITTEN AND ARRANGED BY
DR. L. S. THOMPSON, (FORMERLY MRS. SCHUYLER,)
AS GIVEN BY MATTIE.

# BOOK CONTENTS

NARRATIVE OF SOJOURNER TRUTH     3

INCIDENTS IN THE LIFE OF A SLAVE GIRL,
Written by Herself.     95

THE HISTORY OF MARY PRINCE,
A WEST INDIAN SLAVE.
RELATED BY HERSELF.     279

THE STORY OF Mattie J. Jackson;     339

# NARRATIVE OF SOJOURNER TRUTH

Written by Olive Gilbert, based on information provided by Sojourner Truth.

1850

# CONTENTS

| | |
|---|---|
| SHORT BIOGRAPHY of SOJOURNER TRUTH | 5 |
| HER BIRTH AND PARENTAGE | 7 |
| ACCOMMODATIONS | 8 |
| HER BROTHERS AND SISTERS | 9 |
| HER RELIGIOUS INSTRUCTION | 10 |
| THE AUCTION | 11 |
| DEATH OF MAU-MAU BETT | 13 |
| LAST DAYS OF BOMEFREE | 14 |
| DEATH OF BOMEFREE | 16 |
| COMMENCEMENT OF ISABELLA'S TRIALS IN LIFE | 17 |
| TRIALS CONTINUED | 19 |
| HER STANDING WITH HER NEW | 21 |
| MASTER AND MISTRESS | 25 |
| ISABELLA'S MARRIAGE | 26 |
| ISABELLA AS A MOTHER | 27 |
| SLAVEHOLDER'S PROMISES HER ESCAPE | 29 |
| ILLEGAL SALE OF HER SON | 31 |
| IT IS OFTEN DARKEST JUST BEFORE DAWN | 33 |
| DEATH OF MRS. ELIZA FOWLER | 39 |
| ISABELLA'S RELIGIOUS EXPERIENCE | 42 |
| NEW TRIALS | 51 |
| FINDING A BROTHER AND SISTER | 56 |
| GLEANINGS | 58 |
| THE MATTHIAS DELUSION | 62 |
| FASTING | 68 |
| THE CAUSE OF HER LEAVING THE CITY | 69 |
| THE CONSEQUENCES OF REFUSING A TRAVELLER A NIGHT'S LODGING | 73 |
| SOME OF HER VIEWS AND REASONINGS | 76 |
| THE SECOND ADVENT DOCTRINES | 78 |
| ANOTHER CAMP-MEETING | 82 |
| LAST INTERVIEW WITH HER MASTER | 88 |
| CERTIFICATES OF CHARACTER | 89 |
| "AIN'T I A WOMAN?" SPEECH | 90 |

# SHORT BIOGRAPHY of SOJOURNER TRUTH

Soujourner Truth was born as Isabella Baumfree around 1797, in New York. In 1806, after her slaveowner died, Truth was sold to a new owner with a flock of sheep for $100. She was sold two more times in the next four years, and although her 4th slaveowner was kind to her, his wife was not.

She fell in love with a slave named Robert, who was a slave at a nearby farm. When Robert's owner found out about their relationship, he forbade it. When Robert was caught sneaking over to see Truth, Robert's owner beat him savagely until Truth's master intervened. After this, Truth never saw Robert again and he died a few years later.

Later, Truth married an older slave named Thomas. Together, they had four children; one which died during childbirth. Truth also had a child as a result from being raped by her master.

While slavery was in the process of being abolished in New York, Truth left the farm where she was enslaved, with her baby daughter, Sophia, in 1826. She found refuge with a man and his wife named Isaac and Maria Van Wagenen, who paid $20 to Truth's master to enable her to live with them until the Emancipation Proclamation took effect in July 4, 1827.

While Truth lived with the Van Wagenen family, she learned that her old master had illegally sold her 5-year-old son Peter another slaveowner. With the help of the Van Wagenens, Truth took Peter's masters to court and after months of legal proceedings, took back custody of him. Unfortunately, he had been abused badly by his master. Truth was one of the first black women to win a court case against a white man.

While living with the Van Wagenen family, and after an amazing spiritual experience, Truth became a Christian woman. She moved to New York City in 1829, where she met many people, and experienced new things.

In 1839, her son Peter took a job on a whaling ship. He never received any of the letters Truth sent to him, and although he sent five letters to Truth, she only received three of them. When the whaling ship returned to port, Peter was not on the ship and Truth never saw him again.

1843 was the year Baumfree changed her name to Sojourner Truth, after she heard the spirit of God tell her to go forth and preach the truth. She told her friends, "The Spirit calls me, and I must go."

After this, she became *very* involved in slavery abolition work and she became a women's right activist. She spoke at conventions, and meetings. She gave a famous, extemporaneous speech called "Ain't I A Woman?" of which two recollected versions exist (they're both found at the end of this book).

Sojourner Truth continued to live a remarkable life. She continued to advocate for slaves and for women throughout the remainder of her life.

Truth died on November 26, 1883. For more than a century, Truth has been honored and recognized for her advocacy and bravery.

# NARRATIVE OF SOJOURNER TRUTH

## HER BIRTH AND PARENTAGE.

THE subject of this biography, SOJOURNER TRUTH, as she now calls herself-but whose name, originally, was Isabella-was born, as near as she can now calculate, between the years 1797 and 1800. She was the daughter of James and Betsey, slaves of one Colonel Ardinburgh, Hurley, Ulster County, New York.

Colonel Ardinburgh belonged to that class of people called Low Dutch.

Of her first master, she can give no account, as she must have been a mere infant when he died; and she, with her parents and some ten or twelve other fellow human chattels, became the legal property of his son, Charles Ardinburgh. She distinctly remembers hearing her father and mother say, that their lot was a fortunate one, as Master Charles was the best of the family,- being, comparatively speaking, a kind master to his slaves.

James and Betsey having, by their faithfulness, docility, and respectful behavior, won his particular regard, received from him particular favors- among which was a lot of land, lying back on the slope of a mountain, where, by improving the pleasant evenings and Sundays, they managed to raise a little tobacco, corn, or flax; which they exchanged for extras, in the articles of food or clothing for themselves and children. She has no remembrance that Saturday afternoon was ever added to their own time, as it is by some masters in the Southern States.

# ACCOMMODATIONS.

Among Isabella's earliest recollections was the removal of her master, Charles Ardinburgh, into his new house, which he had built for a hotel, soon after the decease of his father. A cellar, under this hotel, was assigned to his slaves, as their sleeping apartment,-all the slaves he possessed, of both sexes, sleeping (as is quite common in a state of slavery) in the same room. She carries in her mind, to this day, a vivid picture of this dismal chamber; its only lights consisting of a few panes of glass, through which she thinks the sun never shone, but with thrice reflected rays; and the space between the loose boards of the floor, and the uneven earth below, was often filled with mud and water, the uncomfortable splashings of which were as annoying as its noxious vapors must have been chilling and fatal to health. She shudders, even now, as she goes back in memory, and revisits this cellar, and sees its inmates, of both sexes and all ages, sleeping on those damp boards, like the horse, with a little straw and a blanket; and she wonders not at the rheumatisms, and fever-sores, and palsies, that distorted the limbs and racked the bodies of those fellow-slaves in after-life. Still, she does not attribute this cruelty-for cruelty it certainly is, to be so unmindful of the health and comfort of any being, leaving entirely out of sight his more important part, his everlasting interests,-so much to any innate or constitutional cruelty of the master, as to that gigantic inconsistency, that inherited habit among slaveholders, of expecting a willing and intelligent obedience from the slave, because he is a MAN-at the same time every thing belonging to the soul-harrowing system does its best to crush the last vestige of a man within him; and when it is crushed, and often before, he is denied the comforts of life, on the plea that he knows neither the want nor the use of them, and because he is considered to be little more or little less than a beast.

# HER BROTHERS AND SISTERS.

Isabella's father was very tall and straight, when young, which gave him the name of 'Bomefree'-low Dutch for tree-at least, this is SOJOURNER's pronunciation of it-and by this name he usually went. The most familiar appellation of her mother was 'Mau-mau Bett.' She was the mother of some ten or twelve children; though Sojourner is far from knowing the exact number of her brothers and sisters; she being the youngest, save one, and all older than herself having been sold before her remembrance. She was privileged to behold six of them while she remained a slave.

Of the two that immediately preceded her in age, a boy of five years, and a girl of three, who were sold when she was an infant, she heard much; and she wishes that all who would fain believe that slave parents have not natural affection for their offspring could have listened as she did, while Bomefree and Mau-mau Bett,-their dark cellar lighted by a blazing pine-knot,-would sit for hours, recalling and recounting every endearing, as well as harrowing circumstance that taxed memory could supply, from the histories of those dear departed ones, of whom they had been robbed, and for whom their hearts still bled. Among the rest, they would relate how the little boy, on the last morning he was with them, arose with the birds, kindled a fire, calling for his Mau-mau to 'come, for all was now ready for her'-little dreaming of the dreadful separation which was so near at hand, but of which his parents had an uncertain, but all the more cruel foreboding. There was snow on the ground, at the time of which we are speaking; and a large old-fashioned sleigh was seen to drive up to the door of the late Col. Ardinburgh. This event was noticed with childish pleasure by the unsuspicious boy; but when he was taken and put into the sleigh, and saw his little sister actually shut and locked into the sleigh box, his eyes were at once opened to their intentions; and, like a frightened deer he sprang from the sleigh, and running into the house, concealed himself under a bed. But this availed him little. He was re-conveyed to the sleigh, and separated for ever from those whom God had constituted his natural guardians and protectors, and who should have found him, in return, a stay and a staff to them in their declining years. But I make no comments on facts like these, knowing that the heart of every slave parent will make its own comments, involuntarily and correctly, as soon as each heart shall make the case its own. Those who are not parents will draw their conclusions from the promptings of humanity and philanthropy:-these, enlightened by reason and revelation, are also unerring.

# HER RELIGIOUS INSTRUCTION.

Isabella and Peter, her youngest brother, remained, with their parents, the legal property of Charles Ardinburgh till his decease, which took place when Isabella was near nine years old.

After this event, she was often surprised to find her mother in tears; and when, in her simplicity, she inquired, 'Mau-mau, what makes you cry?' she would answer, 'Oh, my child, I am thinking of your brothers and sisters that have been sold away from me.' And she would proceed to detail many circumstances respecting them. But Isabella long since concluded that it was the impending fate of her only remaining children, which her mother but too well understood, even then, that called up those memories from the past, and made them crucify her heart afresh.

In the evening, when her mother's work was done, she would sit down under the sparkling vault of heaven, and calling her children to her, would talk to them of the only Being that could effectually aid or protect them. Her teachings were delivered in Low Dutch, her only language, and, translated into English, ran nearly as follows:-

'My children, there is a God, who hears and sees you.' 'A God, mau-mau! Where does he live?' asked the children. 'He lives in the sky,' she replied; 'and when you are beaten, or cruelly treated, or fall into any trouble, you must ask help of him, and he will always hear and help you.' She taught them to kneel and say the Lord's Prayer. She entreated them to refrain from lying and stealing, and to strive to obey their masters.

At times, a groan would escape her, and she would break out in the language of the Psalmist-'Oh Lord, how long?' 'Oh Lord, how long?' And in reply to Isabella's question-'What ails you, mau-mau?' her only answer was, 'Oh, a good deal ails me'-'Enough ails me.' Then again, she would point them to the stars, and say, in her peculiar language, 'Those are the same stars, and that is the same moon, that look down upon your brothers and sisters, and which they see as they look up to them, though they are ever so far away from us, and each other.'

Thus, in her humble way, did she endeavor to show them their Heavenly Father, as the only being who could protect them in their perilous condition; at the same time, she would strengthen and brighten the chain of family affection, which she trusted extended itself sufficiently to connect the widely scattered members of her precious flock. These instructions of the mother were treasured up and held sacred by Isabella, as our future narrative will show.

# THE AUCTION.

At length, the never-to-be-forgotten day of the terrible auction arrived, when the 'slaves, horses, and other cattle' of Charles Ardinburgh, deceased, were to be put under the hammer, and again change masters. Not only Isabella and Peter, but their mother, were now destined to the auction block, and would have been struck off with the rest to the highest bidder, but for the following circumstance: A question arose among the heirs, 'Who shall be burdened with Bomefree, when we have sent away his faithful Mau-mau Bett?' He was becoming weak and infirm; his limbs were painfully rheumatic and distorted-more from exposure and hardship than from old age, though he was several years older than Mau-mau Bett: he was no longer considered of value, but must soon be a burden and care to some one. After some contention on the point at issue, none being willing to be burdened with him, it was finally agreed, as most expedient for the heirs, that the price of Mau-mau Bett should be sacrificed, and she receive her freedom, on condition that she take care of and support her faithful James,- faithful, not only to her as a husband, but proverbially faithful as a slave to those who would not willingly sacrifice a dollar for his comfort, now that he had commenced his descent into the dark vale of decrepitude and suffering. This important decision was received as joyful news indeed to our ancient couple, who were the objects of it, and who were trying to prepare their hearts for a severe struggle, and one altogether new to them, as they had never before been separated; for, though ignorant, helpless, crushed in spirit, and weighed down with hardship and cruel bereavement, they were still human, and their human hearts beat within them with as true an affection as ever caused a human heart to beat. And their anticipated separation now, in the decline of life, after the last child had been torn from them, must have been truly appalling. Another privilege was granted them-that of remaining occupants of the same dark, humid cellar I have before described: otherwise, they were to support themselves as they best could. And as her mother was still able to do considerable work, and her father a little, they got on for some time very comfortably. The strangers who rented the house were humane people, and very kind to them; they were not rich, and owned no slaves. How long this state of things continued, we are unable to say, as Isabella had not then sufficiently cultivated her organ of time to calculate years, or even weeks or hours. But she thinks her mother must have lived several years after the death of Master Charles. She remembers going to visit her parents some three or four times before the death of her mother, and a good deal of time seemed to her to intervene between each visit.

At length her mother's health began to decline-a fever-sore made its ravages on one of her limbs, and the palsy began to shake her frame; still, she and James tottered about, picking up a little here and there, which, added to the mites contributed by their kind neighbors, sufficed to sustain life, and drive famine from the door.

# DEATH OF MAU-MAU BETT.

One morning, in early autumn, (from the reason above mentioned, we cannot tell what year,) Mau-mau Bett told James she would make him a loaf of rye-bread, and get Mrs. Simmons, their kind neighbor, to bake it for them, as she would bake that forenoon. James told her he had engaged to rake after the cart for his neighbors that morning; but before he commenced, he would pole off some apples from a tree near, which they were allowed to gather; and if she could get some of them baked with the bread, it would give a nice relish for their dinner. He beat off the apples, and soon after, saw Mau-mau Bett come out and gather them up.

At the blowing of the horn for dinner, he groped his way into his cellar, anticipating his humble, but warm and nourishing meal; when, lo! instead of being cheered by the sight and odor of fresh-baked bread and the savory apples, his cellar seemed more cheerless than usual, and at first neither sight nor sound met eye or ear. But, on groping his way through the room, his staff, which he used as a pioneer to go before, and warn him of danger, seemed to be impeded in its progress, and a low, gurgling, choking sound proceeded from the object before him, giving him the first intimation of the truth as it was, that Mau-mau Bett, his bosom companion, the only remaining member of his large family, had fallen in a fit of the palsy, and lay helpless and senseless on the earth! Who among us, located in pleasant homes, surrounded with every comfort, and so many kind and sympathizing friends, can picture to ourselves the dark and desolate state of poor old James-penniless, weak, lame, and nearly blind, as he was at the moment he found his companion was removed from him, and he was left alone in the world, with no one to aid, comfort, or console him? for she never revived again, and lived only a few hours after being discovered senseless by her poor bereaved James.

# LAST DAYS OF BOMEFREE.

Isabella and Peter were permitted to see the remains of their mother laid in their last narrow dwelling, and to make their bereaved father a little visit, ere they returned to their servitude. And most piteous were the lamentations of the poor old man, when, at last, they also were obliged to bid him "Farewell!" Juan Fernandes, on his desolate island, was not so pitiable an object as this poor lame man. Blind and crippled, he was too superannuated to think for a moment of taking care of himself, and he greatly feared no persons would interest themselves in his behalf. 'Oh,' he would exclaim, 'I had thought God would take me first,-Mau-mau was so much smarter than I, and could get about and take care of herself;-and I am so old, and so helpless. What is to become of me? I can't do anything any more-my children are all gone, and here I am left helpless and alone.' 'And then, as I was taking leave of him,' said his daughter, in relating it, 'he raised his voice, and cried aloud like a child-Oh, how he DID cry! I HEAR it now -and remember it as well as if it were but yesterday-poor old man!!! He thought God had done it all-and my heart bled within me at the sight of his misery. He begged me to get permission to come and see him sometimes, which I readily and heartily promised him.' But when all had left him, the Ardinburghs, having some feeling left for their faithful and favorite slave, 'took turns about' in keeping him- permitting him to stay a few weeks at one house, and then a while at another, and so around. If, when he made a removal, the place where he was going was not too far off, he took up his line of march, staff in hand, and asked for no assistance. If it was twelve or twenty miles, they gave him a ride. While he was living in this way, Isabella was twice permitted to visit him. Another time she walked twelve miles, and carried her infant in her arms to see him, but when she reached the place where she hoped to find him, he had just left for a place some twenty miles distant, and she never saw him more. The last time she did see him, she found him seated on a rock, by the road side, alone, and far from any house. He was then migrating from the house of one Ardinburgh to that of another, several miles distant. His hair was white like wool-he was almost blind-and his gait was more a creep than a walk-but the weather was warm and pleasant, and he did not dislike the journey. When Isabella addressed him, he recognized her voice, and was exceeding glad to see her. He was assisted to mount the wagon, was carried back to the famous cellar of which we have spoken, and there they held their last earthly conversation. He again, as usual, bewailed his loneliness,-spoke in tones of anguish of his many children, saying, "They are all taken away from me! I have now not one to give me a cup of cold water-why should I live and not die?" Isabella, whose heart yearned over her father, and who would have made any sacrifice to have been able to be with, and take care of him, tried to comfort, by telling him that 'she had heard the white folks say, that all the slaves in the State would be freed in ten years, and that then she would come and take care of him.' 'I would take just as good care of you as Mau-mau would, if she was here'-continued Isabel. 'Oh, my child,' replied he, 'I cannot live that long.' 'Oh, do, daddy, do live, and I will take such good care of you,' was her rejoinder. She now says, 'Why, I thought then, in my ignorance, that he could live, if he would. I just as much thought so, as I ever thought any thing in my life-and I insisted on his living: but he shook his head, and insisted he could not.'

But before Bomefree's good constitution would yield either to age, exposure, or a strong desire to die, the Ardinburghs again tired of him, and offered freedom to two old slaves-Caesar, brother of Mau-mau Bett, and his wife Betsy-on condition that they should take care of James. (I was about to say, 'their brother-in-law'-but as slaves are neither husbands nor wives in law, the idea of their being brothers-in-law is truly ludicrous.) And although they were too old and infirm to take care of themselves, (Caesar having been afflicted for a long time with fever-sores, and his wife with the jaundice), they eagerly accepted the boon of freedom, which had been the life-long desire of their souls-though at a time when emancipation was to them little more than destitution, and was a freedom more to be desired by the master than the slave. Sojourner declares of the slaves in their ignorance, that 'their thoughts are no longer than her finger.'

# DEATH OF BOMEFREE.

A rude cabin, in a lone wood, far from any neighbors, was granted to our freed friends, as the only assistance they were now to expect. Bomefree, from this time, found his poor needs hardly supplied, as his new providers were scarce able to administer to their own wants. However, the time drew near when things were to be decidedly worse rather than better; for they had not been together long, before Betty died, and shortly after, Caesar followed her to 'that bourne from whence no traveller returns'-leaving poor James again desolate, and more helpless than ever before; as, this time, there was no kind family in the house, and the Ardinburghs no longer invited him to their homes. Yet, lone, blind and helpless as he was, James for a time lived on. One day, an aged colored woman, named Soan, called at his shanty, and James besought her, in the most moving manner, even with tears, to tarry awhile and wash and mend him up, so that he might once more be decent and comfortable; for he was suffering dreadfully with the filth and vermin that had collected upon him.

Soan was herself an emancipated slave, old and weak, with no one to care for her; and she lacked the courage to undertake a job of such seeming magnitude, fearing she might herself get sick, and perish there without assistance; and with great reluctance, and a heart swelling with pity, as she afterwards declared, she felt obliged to leave him in his wretchedness and filth. And shortly after her visit, this faithful slave, this deserted wreck of humanity, was found on his miserable pallet, frozen and stiff in death. The kind angel had come at last, and relieved him of the many miseries that his fellow-man had heaped upon him. Yes, he had died, chilled and starved, with none to speak a kindly word, or do a kindly deed for him, in that last dread of hour of need!

The news of his death reached the ears of John Ardinburgh, a grandson of the old Colonel; and he declared that 'Bomefree, who had ever been a kind and faithful slave, should now have a good funeral.' And now, gentle reader, what think you constituted a good funeral? Answer-some black paint for the coffin, and-a jug of ardent spirits! What a compensation for a life of toil, of patient submission to repeated robberies of the most aggravated kind, and, also, far more than murderous neglect!! Mankind often vainly attempts to atone for unkindness or cruelty to the living, by honoring the same after death; but John Ardinburgh undoubtably meant his pot of paint and jug of whisky should act as an opiate on his slaves, rather than on his own seared conscience.

# COMMENCEMENT OF ISABELLA'S TRIALS IN LIFE.

Having seen the sad end of her parents, so far as it relates to this earthly life, we will return with Isabella to that memorable auction which threatened to separate her father and mother. A slave auction is a terrible affair to its victims, and its incidents and consequences are graven on their hearts as with a pen of burning steel.

At this memorable time, Isabella was struck off, for the sum of one hundred dollars, to one John Nealy, of Ulster County, New York; and she has an impression that in this sale she was connected with a lot of sheep. She was now nine years of age, and her trials in life may be dated from this period. She says, with emphasis, 'Now the war begun. ' She could only talk Dutch-and the Nealys could only talk English. Mr. Nealy could understand Dutch, but Isabel and her mistress could neither of them understand the language of the other-and this, of itself, was a formidable obstacle in the way of a good understanding between them, and for some time was a fruitful source of dissatisfaction to the mistress, and of punishment and suffering to Isabella. She says, 'If they sent me for a frying-pan, not knowing what they meant, perhaps I carried them pot-hooks and trammels. Then, oh! how angry mistress would be with me!' Then she suffered 'terribly-terribly ', with the cold. During the winter her feet were badly frozen, for want of proper covering. They gave her a plenty to eat, and also a plenty of whippings. One Sunday morning, in particular, she was told to go to the barn; on going there, she found her master with a bundle of rods, prepared in the embers, and bound together with cords. When he had tied her hands together before her, he gave her the most cruel whipping she was ever tortured with. He whipped her till the flesh was deeply lacerated, and the blood streamed from her wounds-and the scars remain to the present day, to testify to the fact. 'And now,' she says, 'when I hear 'em tell of whipping women on the bare flesh, it makes my flesh crawl, and my very hair rise on my head! Oh! my God!' she continues, 'what a way is this of treating human beings?' In those hours of her extremity, she did not forget the instructions of her mother, to go to God in all her trials, and every affliction; and she not only remembered, but obeyed: going to him, 'and telling him all-and asking Him if He thought it was right,' and begging him to protect and shield her from her persecutors.

She always asked with an unwavering faith that she should receive just what she pleaded for,-'And now,' she says, 'though it seems curious, I do not remember ever asking for any thing but what I got it. And I always received it as an answer to my prayers. When I got beaten, I never knew it long enough to go beforehand to pray; and I always thought that if I only had had time to pray to God for help, I should have escaped the beating.' She had no idea God had any knowledge of her thoughts, save what she told him; or heard her prayers, unless they were spoken audibly. And consequently, she could not pray unless she had time and opportunity to go by herself, where she could talk to God without being overheard.

# TRIALS CONTINUED.

When she had been at Mr. Nealy's several months, she began to beg God most earnestly to send her father to her, and as soon as she commenced to pray, she began as confidently to look for his coming, and, ere it was long, to her great joy, he came. She had no opportunity to speak to him of the troubles that weighed so heavily on her spirit, while he remained; but when he left, she followed him to the gate, and unburdened her heart to him, inquiring if he could not do something to get her a new and better place. In this way the slaves often assist each other, by ascertaining who are kind to their slaves, comparatively; and then using their influence to get such an one to hire or buy their friends; and masters, often from policy, as well as from latent humanity, allow those they are about to sell or let, to choose their own places, if the persons they happen to select for masters are considered safe pay. He promised to do all he could, and they parted. But, every day, as long as the snow lasted, (for there was snow on the ground at the time,) she returned to the spot where they separated, and walking in the tracks her father had made in the snow, repeated her prayer that 'God would help her father get her a new and better place.'

A long time had not elapsed, when a fisherman by the name of Scriver appeared at Mr. Nealy's, and inquired of Isabel 'if she would like to go and live with him.' She eagerly answered 'Yes,' and nothing doubting but he was sent in answer to her prayer; and she soon started off with him, walking while he rode; for he had bought her at the suggestion of her father, paying one hundred and five dollars for her. He also lived in Ulster County, but some five or six miles from Mr. Nealy's.

Scriver, besides being a fisherman, kept a tavern for the accommodation of people of his own class-for his was a rude, uneducated family, exceedingly profane in their language, but, on the whole, an honest, kind and well-disposed people.

They owned a large farm, but left it wholly unimproved; attending mainly to their vocations of fishing and inn-keeping. Isabella declares she can ill describe the kind of life she led with them. It was a wild, out-of-door kind of lief. She was expected to carry fish, to hoe corn, to bring roots and herbs from the woods for beers, go to the Strand for a gallon of molasses or liquor as the case might require, and 'browse around,' as she expresses it. It was a life that suited her well for the time-being as devoid of hardship or terror as it was of improvement; a need which had not yet become a want. Instead of improving at this place, morally, she retrograded, as their example taught her to curse;

and it was here that she took her first oath. After living with them for about a year and a half, she was sold to one John J. Dumont, for the sum of seventy pounds. This was in 1810. Mr. Dumont lived in the same county as her former masters, in the town of New Paltz, and she remained with him till a short time previous to her emancipation by the State, in 1828.

# HER STANDING WITH HER NEW MASTER AND MISTRESS.

Had Mrs. Dumont possessed that vein of kindness and consideration for the slaves, so perceptible in her husband's character, Isabella would have been as comfortable here, as one had best be, if one must be a slave. Mr. Dumont had been nursed in the very lap of slavery, and being naturally a man of kind feelings, treated his slaves with all the consideration he did his other animals, and more, perhaps. But Mrs. Dumont, who had been born and educated in a non-slaveholding family, and, like many others, used only to work-people, who, under the most stimulating of human motives, were willing to put forth their every energy, could not have patience with the creeping gait, the dull understanding, or see any cause for the listless manners and careless, slovenly habits of the poor down-trodden outcast-entirely forgetting that every high and efficient motive had been removed far from him; and that, had not his very intellect been crushed out of him, the slave would find little ground for aught but hopeless despondency. From this source arose a long series of trials in the life of our heroine, which we must pass over in silence; some from motives of delicacy, and others, because the relation of them might inflict undeserved pain on some now living, whom Isabel remembers only with esteem and love; therefore, the reader will not be surprised if our narrative appears somewhat tame at this point, and may rest assured that it is not for want of facts, as the most thrilling incidents of this portion of her life are from various motives suppressed.

One comparatively trifling incident she wishes related, as it made a deep impression on her mind at the time-showing, as she thinks, how God shields the innocent, and causes them to triumph over their enemies, and also how she stood between master and mistress. In her family, Mrs. Dumont employed two white girls, one of whom, named Kate, evinced a disposition to 'lord it over' Isabel, and, in her emphatic language, 'to grind her down '. Her master often shielded her from the attacks and accusations of others, praising her for her readiness and ability to work, and these praises seemed to foster a spirit of hostility to her, in the minds of Mrs. Dumont and her white servant, the latter of whom took every opportunity to cry up her faults, lessen her in the esteem of her master and increase against her the displeasure of her mistress, which was already more than sufficient for Isabel's comfort. Her master insisted that she could do as much work as half a dozen common people, and do it well, too; whilst her mistress insisted that the first was true, only because it ever came from her hand but half performed. A good deal of feeling arose from this difference of opinion, which was getting to rather an uncomfortable height, when, all at once, the potatoes that Isabel cooked for breakfast assumed a dingy, dirty look. Her mistress blamed her severely, asking her master to observe 'a fine specimen of Bell's work!'-adding, 'it is the way all her work is done.' Her master scolded also this time, and commanded her to be more careful in future. Kate joined with zest in the censures, and was very hard upon her. Isabella thought that she had done all she well could to have them nice; and became quite distressed at their appearances, and wondered what she should do to avoid them. In this dilemma, Gertrude Dumont (Mr. D.'s eldest child, a good, kind-hearted girl of ten years, who pitied Isabel sincerely), when she heard them all blame her so unsparingly, came forward, offering her sympathy and assistance; and when about to retire to bed, on the night of Isabella's humiliation, she advanced to Isabel, and told her, if she would wake her early next morning, she would get up and attend to her potatoes for her, while she (Isabella) went to milking, and they would see if they could not have them nice, and not have 'Poppee,' her word for father, and 'Matty,' her word for mother, and all of 'em, scolding so terribly.

Isabella gladly availed herself of this kindness, which touched her to the heart, amid so much of an opposite spirit. When Isabella had put the potatoes over to boil, Getty told her she would herself tend the fire, while Isabel milked. She had not long been seated by the fire, in performance of her promise, when Kate entered, and requested Gertrude to go out of the room and do something for her, which she refused, still keeping her place in the corner. While there, Kate came sweeping about the fire, caught up a chip, lifted some ashes with it, and dashed them into the kettle. Now the mystery was solved, the plot discovered! Kate was working a little too fast at making her mistress's words good, at showing that Mrs. Dumont and herself were on the right side of the dispute, and consequently at gaining power over Isabella. Yes, she was quite too fast, inasmuch as she had overlooked the little figure of justice, which sat in the comer, with scales nicely balanced, waiting to give all their dues.

But the time had come when she was to be overlooked no longer. It was Getty's turn to speak now. 'Oh Poppee! oh Poppee!' said she, 'Kate has been putting ashes in among the potatoes! I saw her do it! Look at those that fell on the outside of the kettle! You can now see what made the potatoes so dingy every morning, though Bell washed them clean!' And she repeated her story to every new comer, till the fraud was made as public as the censure of Isabella had been. Her mistress looked blank, and remained dumb-her master muttered something which sounded very like an oath-and poor Kate was so chop-fallen, she looked like a convicted criminal, who would gladly have hid herself, (now that the baseness was out,) to conceal her mortified pride and deep chagrin.

It was a fine triumph for Isabella and her master, and she became more ambitious than ever to please him; and he stimulated her ambition by his commendation, and by boasting of her to his friends, telling them that 'that wench' (pointing to Isabel) 'is better to me than a man-for she will do a good family's washing in the night, and be ready in the morning to go into the field, where she will do as much at raking and binding as my best hands.' Her ambition and desire to please were so great, that she often worked several nights in succession, sleeping only short snatches, as she sat in her chair; and some nights she would not allow herself to take any sleep, save what she could get resting herself against the wall, fearing that if she sat down, she would sleep too long. These extra exertions to please, and the praises consequent upon them, brought upon her head the envy of her fellow-slaves, and they taunted her with being the 'white folks' nigger.' On the other hand, she received the larger share of the confidence of her master, and many small favors that were by them unattainable. I asked her if her master, Dumont, ever whipped her? She answered, 'Oh yes, he sometimes whipped me soundly, though never cruelly. And the most severe whipping he ever give me was because I was cruel to a cat.' At this time she looked upon her master as a God; and believed that he knew of and could see her at all times, even as God himself. And she used sometimes to confess her delinquencies, from the conviction that he already knew them, and that she should fare better if she confessed voluntarily: and if any one talked to her of the injustice of her being a slave, she answered them with contempt, and immediately told her master. She then firmly believed that slavery was right and honorable. Yet she now sees very clearly the false position they were all in, both masters and slaves; and she looks back, with utter astonishment, at the absurdity of the claims so arrogantly set up by the masters, over beings designed by God to be as free as kings; and at the perfect stupidity of the slave, in admitting for one moment the validity of these claims.

In obedience to her mother's instructions, she had educated herself to such a sense of honesty, that, when she had become a mother, she would sometimes whip her child when it cried to her for bread, rather than give it a piece secretly, lest it should learn to take what was not its own! And the writer of this knows, from personal observation, that the slaveholders of the South feel it to be a religious duty to teach their slaves to be honest, and never to take what is not their own! Oh consistency, art thou not a jewel? Yet Isabella glories in the fact that she was faithful and true to her master; she says, 'It made me true to my God'-meaning, that it helped to form in her a character that loved truth, and hated a lie, and had saved her from the bitter pains and fears that are sure to follow in the wake of insincerity and hypocrisy.

As she advanced in years, an attachment sprung up between herself and a slave named Robert. But his master, an Englishman by the name of Catlin, anxious that no one's property but his own should be enhanced by the increase of his slaves, forbade Robert's visits to Isabella, and commanded him to take a wife among his fellow-servants. Notwithstanding this interdiction, Robert, following the bent of his inclinations, continued his visits to Isabel, though very stealthily, and, as he believed, without exciting the suspicion of his master; but one Saturday afternoon, hearing that Bell was ill, he took the liberty to go and see her. The first intimation she had of his visit was the appearance of her master, inquiring 'if she had seen Bob.' On her answering in the negative, he said to her, 'If you see him, tell him to take care of himself, for the Catlins are after him.' Almost at that instant, Bob made his appearance; and the first people he met were his old and his young masters. They were terribly enraged at finding him there, and the eldest began cursing, and calling upon his son to 'Knock down the d-d black rascal'; at the same time, they both fell upon him like tigers, beating him with the heavy ends of their canes, bruising and mangling his head and face in the most awful manner, and causing the blood, which streamed from his wounds, to cover him like a slaughtered beast, constituting him a most shocking spectacle. Mr. Dumont interposed at this point, telling the ruffians they could no longer thus spill human blood on his premises-he would have 'no niggers killed there.' The Catlins then took a rope they had taken with them for the purpose, and tied Bob's hands behind him in such a manner, that Mr. Dumont insisted on loosening the cord, declaring that no brute should be tied in that manner, where he was. And as they led him away, like the greatest of criminals, the more humane Dumont followed them to their homes, as Robert's protector; and when he returned, he kindly went to Bell, as he called her, telling her he did not think they would strike him any more, as their wrath had greatly cooled before he left them. Isabella had witnessed this scene from her window, and was greatly shocked at the murderous treatment of poor Robert, whom she truly loved, and whose only crime, in the eye of his persecutors, was his affection for her. This beating, and we know not what after treatment, completely subdued the spirit of its victim, for Robert ventured no more to visit Isabella, but like an obedient and faithful chattel, took himself a wife from the house of his master. Robert did not live many years after his last visit to Isabel, but took his departure to that country, where 'they neither marry nor are given in marriage,' and where the oppressor cannot molest.

# ISABELLA'S MARRIAGE.

Subsequently, Isabella was married to a fellow-slave, named Thomas, who had previously had two wives, one of whom, if not both, had been torn from him and sold far away. And it is more than probable, that he was not only allowed but encouraged to take another at each successive sale. I say it is probable, because the writer of this knows from personal observation, that such is the custom among slaveholders at the present day; and that in a twenty months' residence among them, we never knew any one to open the lip against the practice; and when we severely censured it, the slaveholder had nothing to say; and the slave pleaded that, under existing circumstances, he could do no better.

Such an abominable state of things is silently tolerated, to say the least, by slaveholders-deny it who may. And what is that religion that sanctions, even by its silence, all that is embraced in the 'Peculiar Institution? ' If there can be any thing more diametrically opposed to the religion of Jesus, than the working of this soul-killing system-which is as truly sanctioned by the religion of America as are her ministers and churches-we wish to be shown where it can be found.

We have said, Isabella was married to Thomas-she was, after the fashion of slavery, one of the slaves performing the ceremony for them; as no true minister of Christ can perform, as in the presence of God, what he knows to be a mere farce, a mock marriage, unrecognised by any civil law, and liable to be annulled any moment, when the interest or caprice of the master should dictate.

With what feelings must slaveholders expect us to listen to their horror of amalgamation in prospect, while they are well aware that we know how calmly and quietly they contemplate the present state of licentiousness their own wicked laws have created, not only as it regards the slave, but as it regards the more privileged portion of the population of the South?

Slaveholders appear to me to take the same notice of the vices of the slave, as one does of the vicious disposition of his horse. They are often an inconvenience; further than that, they care not to trouble themselves about the matter.

# ISABELLA AS A MOTHER.

In process of time, Isabella found herself the mother of five children, and she rejoiced in being permitted to be the instrument of increasing the property of her oppressors! Think, dear reader, without a blush, if you can, for one moment, of a mother thus willingly, and with pride, laying her own children, the 'flesh of her flesh,' on the altar of slavery-a sacrifice to the bloody Moloch! But we must remember that beings capable of such sacrifices are not mothers; they are only 'things,' 'chattels,' 'property.'

But since that time, the subject of this narrative has made some advances from a state of chattelism towards that of a woman and a mother; and she now looks back upon her thoughts and feelings there, in her state of ignorance and degradation, as one does on the dark imagery of a fitful dream. One moment it seems but a frightful illusion; again it appears a terrible reality. I would to God it were but a dreamy myth, and not, as it now stands, a horrid reality to some three millions of chattelized human beings.

I have already alluded to her care not to teach her children to steal, by her example; and she says, with groanings that cannot be written, 'The Lord only knows how many times I let my children go hungry, rather than take secretly the bread I liked not to ask for.' All parents who annul their preceptive teachings by their daily practices would do well to profit by her example.

Another proof of her master's kindness of heart is found in the following fact. If her master came into the house and found her infant crying, (as she could not always attend to its wants and the commands of her mistress at the same time,) he would turn to his wife with a look of reproof, and ask her why she did not see the child taken care of; saying, most earnestly, 'I will not hear this crying; I can't bear it, and I will not hear any child cry so. Here, Bell, take care of this child, if no more work is done for a week.' And he would linger to see if his orders were obeyed, and not countermanded.

When Isabella went to the field to work, she used to put her infant in a basket, tying a rope to each handle, and suspending the basket to a branch of a tree, set another small child to swing it. It was thus secure from reptiles and was easily administered to, and even lulled to sleep, by a child too young for other labors. I was quite struck with the ingenuity of such a baby-tender, as I have sometimes been with the swinging hammock the native mother prepares for her sick infant-apparently so much easier than aught we have in our more civilized homes; easier for the child, because it gets the motion without the least jar; and easier for the nurse, because the hammock is strung so high as to supersede the necessity of stooping.

# SLAVEHOLDER'S PROMISES.

After emancipation had been decreed by the State, some years before the time fixed for its consummation, Isabella's master told her if she would do well, and be faithful, he would give her 'free papers,' one year before she was legally free by statute. In the year 1826, she had a badly diseased hand, which greatly diminished her usefulness; but on the arrival of July 4, 1827, the time specified for her receiving her 'free papers,' she claimed the fulfilment of her master's promise; but he refused granting it, on account (as he alleged) of the loss he had sustained by her hand. She plead that she had worked all the time, and done many things she was not wholly able to do, although she knew she had been less useful than formerly; but her master remained inflexible. Her very faithfulness probably operated against her now, and he found it less easy than he thought to give up the profits of his faithful Bell, who had so long done him efficient service.

But Isabella inwardly determined that she would remain quietly with him only until she had spun his wool-about one hundred pounds-and then she would leave him, taking the rest of the time to herself. 'Ah!' she says, with emphasis that cannot be written, 'the slaveholders are TERRIBLE for promising to give you this or that, or such and such a privilege, if you will do thus and so; and when the time of fulfilment comes, and one claims the promise, they, forsooth, recollect nothing of the kind: and you are, like as not, taunted with being a LIAR; or, at best, the slave is accused of not having performed his part or condition of the contract.' 'Oh!' said she, 'I have felt as if I could not live through the operation sometimes. Just think of us! so eager for our pleasures, and just foolish enough to keep feeding and feeding ourselves up with the idea that we should get what had been thus fairly promised; and when we think it is almost in our hands, find ourselves flatly denied! Just think! how could we bear it? Why, there was Charles Brodhead promised his slave Ned, that when harvesting was over, he might go and see his wife, who lived some twenty or thirty miles off. So Ned worked early and late, and as soon as the harvest was all in, he claimed the promised boon. His master said, he had merely told him he 'would see if he could go, when the harvest was over; but now he saw that he could not go.' But Ned, who still claimed a positive promise, on which he had fully depended, went on cleaning his shoes. His master asked him if he intended going, and on his replying 'yes,' took up a sled-stick that lay near him, and gave him such a blow on the head as broke his skull, killing him dead on the spot. The poor colored people all felt struck down by the blow.' Ah! and well they might. Yet it was but one of a long series of bloody, and other most effectual blows, struck against their liberty and their lives. * But to return from our digression.

The subject of this narrative was to have been free July 4, 1827, but she continued with her master till the wool was spun, and the heaviest of the 'fall's work' closed up, when she concluded to take her freedom into her own hands, and seek her fortune in some other place.

Note:
*Yet no official notice was taken of his more than brutal murder.

# HER ESCAPE.

The question in her mind, and one not easily solved, now was, 'How can I get away?' So, as was her usual custom, she 'told God she was afraid to go in the night, and in the day every body would see her.' At length, the thought came to her that she could leave just before the day dawned, and get out of the neighborhood where she was known before the people were much astir. 'Yes,' said she, fervently, 'that's a good thought! Thank you, God, for that thought!' So, receiving it as coming direct from God, she acted upon it, and one fine morning, a little before day-break, she might have been seen stepping stealthily away from the rear of Master Dumont's house, her infant on one arm and her wardrobe on the other; the bulk and weight of which, probably, she never found so convenient as on the present occasion, a cotton handkerchief containing both her clothes and her provisions.

As she gained the summit of a high hill, a considerable distance from her master's, the sun offended her by coming forth in all his pristine splendor. She thought it never was so light before; indeed, she thought it much too light. She stopped to look about her, and ascertain if her pursuers were yet in sight. No one appeared, and, for the first time, the question came up for settlement, 'Where, and to whom, shall I go?' In all her thoughts of getting away, she had not once asked herself whither she should direct her steps. She sat down, fed her infant, and again turning her thoughts to God, her only help, she prayed him to direct her to some safe asylum. And soon it occurred to her, that there was a man living somewhere in the direction she had been pursuing, by the name of Levi Rowe, whom she had known, and who, she thought, would be likely to befriend her. She accordingly pursued her way to his house, where she found him ready to entertain and assist her, though he was then on his death-bed. He bade her partake of the hospitalities of his house, said he knew of two good places where she might get in, and requested his wife to show her where they were to be found. As soon as she came in sight of the first house, she recollected having seen it and its inhabitants before, and instantly exclaimed, 'That's the place for me; I shall stop there.' She went there, and found the good people of the house, Mr. and Mrs. Van Wagener, absent, but was kindly received and hospitably entertained by their excellent mother, till the return of her children. When they arrived, she made her case known to them. They listened to her story, assuring her they never turned the needy away, and willingly gave her employment.

She had not been there long before her old master, Dumont, appeared, as she had anticipated; for when she took French leave of him, she resolved not to go too far from him, and not put him to as much trouble in looking her up-for the latter he was sure to do-as Tom and Jack had done when they ran away from him, a short time before. This was very considerate in her, to say the least, and a proof that 'like begets like.' He had often considered her feelings, though not always, and she was equally considerate.

When her master saw her, he said, 'Well, Bell, so you've run away from me.' 'No, I did not run away; I walked away by day-light, and all because you had promised me a year of my time.' His reply was, 'You must go back with me.' Her decisive answer was, 'No, I won't go back with you.' He said, 'Well, I shall take the child.' This also was as stoutly negatived.

Mr. Isaac S. Van Wagener then interposed, saying, he had never been in the practice of buying and selling slaves; he did not believe in slavery; but, rather than have Isabella taken back by force, he would buy her services for the balance of the year-for which her master charged twenty dollars, and five in addition for the child. The sum was paid, and her master Dumont departed; but not till he had heard Mr. Van Wagener tell her not to call him master-adding, 'there is but one master; and he who is your master is my master.' Isabella inquired what she should call him? He answered, 'call me Isaac Van Wagener, and my wife is Maria Van Wagener.' Isabella could not understand this, and thought it a mighty change, as it most truly was from a master whose word was law, to simple Isaac S. Van Wagener, who was master to no one. With these noble people, who, though they could not be the masters of slaves, were undoubtedly a portion of God's nobility, she resided one year, and from them she derived the name of Van Wagener; he being her last master in the eye of the law, and a slave's surname is ever the same as his master; that is, if he is allowed to have any other name than Tom, Jack, or Guffin. Slaves have sometimes been severely punished for adding their master's name to their own. But when they have no particular title to it, it is no particular offence.

# ILLEGAL SALE OF HER SON.

A little previous to Isabel's leaving her old master, he had sold her child, a boy of five years, to a Dr. Gedney, who took him with him as far as New York city, on his way to England; but finding the boy too small for his service, he sent him back to his brother, Solomon Gedney. This man disposed of him to his sister's husband, a wealthy planter, by the name of Fowler, who took him to his own home in Alabama.

This illegal and fraudulent transaction had been perpetrated some months before Isabella knew of it, as she was now living at Mr. Van Wagener's. The law expressly prohibited the sale of any slave out of the State,-and all minors were to be free at twenty-one years of age; and Mr. Dumont had sold Peter with the express understanding, that he was soon to return to the State of New York, and be emancipated at the specified time.

When Isabel heard that her son had been sold South, she immediately started on foot and alone, to find the man who had thus dared, in the face of all law, human and divine, to sell her child out of the State; and if possible, to bring him to account for the deed.

Arriving at New Paltz, she went directly to her former mistress, Dumont, complaining bitterly of the removal of her son. Her mistress heard her through, and then replied-'Ugh! a fine fuss to make about a little nigger! Why, haven't you as many of 'em left as you can see to, and take care of? A pity 'tis, the niggers are not all in Guinea!! Making such a halloo-balloo about the neighborhood; and all for a paltry nigger!!!' Isabella heard her through, and after a moment's hesitation, answered, in tones of deep determination-'I'll have my child again.' 'Have your child again!' repeated her mistress-her tones big with contempt, and scorning the absurd idea of her getting him. 'How can you get him? And what have you to support him with, if you could? Have you any money?' 'No,' answered Bell, 'I have no money, but God has enough, or what's better! And I'll have my child again.' These words were pronounced in the most slow, solemn, and determined measure and manner. And in speaking of it, she says, 'Oh my God! I know'd I'd have him agin. I was sure God would help me to get him. Why, I felt so tall within-I felt as if the power of a nation was with me!'

The impressions made by Isabella on her auditors, when moved by lofty or deep feeling, can never be transmitted to paper, (to use the words of another,) till by some Daguerrian act, we are enabled to transfer the look, the gesture, the tones of voice, in connection with the quaint, yet fit expressions used, and the spirit-stirring animation that, at such a time, pervades all she says.

After leaving her mistress, she called on Mrs. Gedney, mother of him who had sold her boy; who, after listening to her lamentations, her grief being mingled with indignation at the sale of her son, and her declaration that she would have him again-said, 'Dear me! What a disturbance to make about your child! What, is your child, better than my child? My child is gone out there, and yours is gone to live with her, to have enough of every thing, and be treated like a gentleman!' And here she laughed at Isabel's absurd fears, as she would represent them to be. 'Yes,' said Isabel, 'your child has gone there, but she is married, and my boy has gone as a slave, and he is too little to go so far from his mother. Oh, I must have my child.' And here the continued laugh of Mrs. G. seemed to Isabel, in this time of anguish and distress, almost demoniacal. And well it was for Mrs. Gedney, that, at that time, she could not even dream of the awful fate awaiting her own beloved daughter, at the hands of him whom she had chosen as worthy the wealth of her love and confidence, and in whose society her young heart had calculated on a happiness, purer and more elevated than was ever conferred by a kingly crown. But, alas! she was doomed to disappointment, as we shall relate by and by. At this point, Isabella earnestly begged of God that he would show to those about her that He was her helper; and she adds, in narrating, 'And He did; or, if He did not show them, he did me.'

# IT IS OFTEN DARKEST JUST BEFORE DAWN.

This homely proverb was illustrated in the case of our sufferer; for, at the period at which we have arrived in our narrative, to her the darkness seemed palpable, and the waters of affliction covered her soul; yet light was about to break in upon her.

Soon after the scenes related in our last chapter, which had harrowed up her very soul to agony, she met a man, (we would like to tell you who, dear reader, but it would be doing him no kindness, even at the present day, to do so,) who evidently sympathized with her, and counselled her to go to the Quakers, telling her they were already feeling very indignant at the fraudulent sale of her son, and assuring her that they would readily assist her, and direct her what to do. He pointed out to her two houses, where lived some of those people, who formerly, more than any other sect, perhaps, lived out the principles of the gospel of Christ. She wended her way to their dwellings, was listened to, unknown as she personally was to them, with patience, and soon gained their sympathies and active co-operation.

They gave her lodgings for the night; and it is very amusing to hear her tell of the 'nice, high, clean, white, beautiful bed' assigned her to sleep in, which contrasted so strangely with her former pallets, that she sat down and contemplated it, perfectly absorbed in wonder that such a bed should have been appropriated to one like herself. For some time she thought that she would lie down beneath it, on her usual bedstead, the floor. 'I did, indeed,' says she, laughing heartily at her former self. However, she finally concluded to make use of the bed, for fear that not to do so might injure the feelings of her good hostess. In the morning, the Quaker saw that she was taken and set down near Kingston, with directions to go to the Court House, and enter complaint to the Grand Jury.

By a little inquiry, she found which was the building she sought, went into the door, and taking the first man she saw of imposing appearance for the grand jury, she commenced her complaint. But he very civilly informed her there was no Grand Jury there; she must go up stairs. When she had with some difficulty ascended the flight through the crowd that filled them, she again turned to the 'grandest' looking man she could select, telling him she had come to enter a complaint to the Grand Jury. For his own amusement, he inquired what her complaint was; but, when he saw it was a serious matter, he said to her, 'This is no place to enter a complaint-go in there,' pointing in a particular direction.

She then went in, where she found the Grand Jurors indeed sitting, and again commenced to relate her injuries. After holding some conversation among themselves, one of them rose, and bidding her follow him, led the way to a side office, where he heard her story, and asked her 'if she could swear that the child she spoke of was her son?' 'Yes,' she answered, 'I swear it's my son.' 'Stop, stop!' said the lawyer, 'you must swear by this book'-giving her a book, which she thinks must have been the Bible. She took it, and putting it to her lips, began again to swear it was her child. The clerks, unable to preserve their gravity any longer, burst into an uproarious laugh; and one of them inquired of lawyer Chip of what use it could be to make her swear. 'It will answer the law,' replied the officer. He then made her comprehend just what he wished her to do, and she took a lawful oath, as far as the outward ceremony could make it one. All can judge how far she understood its spirit and meaning.

He now gave her a writ, directing her to take it to the constable at New Paltz, and have him serve it on Solomon Gedney. She obeyed, walking, or rather trotting, in her haste, some eight or nine miles

But while the constable, through mistake, served the writ on a brother of the real culprit, Solomon Gedney slipped into a boat, and was nearly across the North River, on whose banks they were standing, before the dull Dutch constable was aware of his mistake. Solomon Gedney, meanwhile, consulted a lawyer, who advised him to go to Alabama and bring back the boy, otherwise it might cost him fourteen years' imprisonment, and a thousand dollars in cash. By this time, it is hoped he began to feel that selling slaves unlawfully was not so good a business as he had wished to find it. He secreted himself till due preparations could be made, and soon set sail for Alabama. Steamboats and railroads had not then annihilated distance to the extent they now have, and although he left in the fall of the year, spring came ere he returned, bringing the boy with him-but holding on to him as his property. It had ever been Isabella's prayer, not only that her son might be returned, but that he should be delivered from bondage, and into her own hands, lest he should be punished out of mere spite to her, who was so greatly annoying and irritating to her oppressors; and if her suit was gained, her very triumph would add vastly to their irritation.

She again sought advice of Esquire Chip, whose counsel was, that the aforesaid constable serve the before-mentioned writ upon the right person. This being done, soon brought Solomon Gedney up to Kingston, where he gave bonds for his appearance at court, in the sum of $600.

Esquire Chip next informed his client, that her case must now lie over till the next session of the court, some months in the future. 'The law must take its course,' said he.

'What! wait another court! wait months?' said the persevering mother. 'Why, long before that time, he can go clear off, and take my child with him-no one knows where. I cannot wait; I must have him now, whilst he is to be had.' 'Well,' said the lawyer, very coolly, 'if he puts the boy out of the way, he must pay the $600-one half of which will be yours'; supposing, perhaps, that $300 would pay for a 'heap of children,' in the eye of a slave who never, in all her life, called a dollar her own. But in this instance, he was mistaken in his reckoning. She assured him, that she had not been seeking money, neither would money satisfy her; it was her son, and her son alone she wanted, and her son she must have. Neither could she wait court, not she. The lawyer used his every argument to convince her, that she ought to be very thankful for what they had done for her; that it was a great deal, and it was but reasonable that she should now wait patiently the time of the court.

Yet she never felt, for a moment, like being influenced by these suggestions. She felt confident she was to receive a full and literal answer to her prayer, the burden of which had been-'O Lord, give my son into my hands, and that speedily! Let not the spoilers have him any longer.' Notwithstanding, she very distinctly saw that those who had thus far helped her on so kindly were wearied of her, and she feared God was wearied also. She had a short time previous learned that Jesus was a Saviour, and an intercessor; and she thought that if Jesus could but be induced to plead for her in the present trial, God would listen to him, though he were wearied of her importunities. To him, of course, she applied. As she was walking about, scarcely knowing whither she went, asking within herself, 'Who will show me any good, and lend a helping hand in this matter,' she was accosted by a perfect stranger, and one whose name she has never learned, in the following terms: 'Halloo, there; how do you get along with your boy? do they give him up to you?' She told him all, adding that now every body was tired, and she had none to help her. He said, 'Look here! I'll tell you what you'd better do. Do you see that stone house yonder?' pointing in a particular direction. 'Well, lawyer Demain lives there, and do you go to him, and lay your case before him; I think he'll help you. Stick to him. Don't give him peace till he does. I feel sure if you press him, he'll do it for you.' She needed no further urging, but trotted off at her peculiar gait in the direction of his house, as fast as possible,-and she was not encumbered with stockings, shoes, or any other heavy article of dress. When she had told him her story, in her impassioned manner, he looked at her a few moments, as if to ascertain if he were contemplating a new variety of the genus homo, and then told her, if she would give him five dollars, he would get her son for her, in twenty-four hours. 'Why,' she replied, 'I have no money, and never had a dollar in my life!' Said he, 'If you will go to those Quakers in Poppletown, who carried you to court, they will help you to five dollars in cash, I have no doubt; and you shall have your son in twenty-four hours, from the time you bring me that sum.' She performed the journey to Poppletown, a distance of some ten miles, very expeditiously; collected considerable more than the sum specified by the barrister; then, shutting the money tightly in her hand, she trotted back, and paid the lawyer a larger fee than he had demanded. When inquired of by people what she had done with the overplus, she answered, 'Oh, I got it for lawyer Demain, and I gave it to him. ' They assured her she was a fool to do so; that she should have kept all over five dollars, and purchased herself shoes with it. 'Oh, I do not want money or clothes now, I only want my son; and if five dollars will get him, more will surely get him. ' And if the lawyer had returned it to her, she avers she would not have accepted it. She was perfectly willing he should have every coin she could raise, if he would but restore her lost son to her. Moreover, the five dollars he required were for the remuneration of him who should go after her son and his master, and not for his own services.

The lawyer now renewed his promise, that she should have her son in twenty-four hours. But Isabella, having no idea of this space of time, went several times in a day, to ascertain if her son had come. Once, when the servant opened the door and saw her, she said, in a tone expressive of much surprise, 'Why, this woman's come again!' She then wondered if she went too often. When the lawyer appeared, he told her the twenty-four hours would not expire till the next morning; if she would call then, she would see her son. The next morning saw Isabel at the lawyer's door, while he was yet in his bed. He now assured her it was morning till noon; and that before noon her son would be there, for he had sent the famous 'Matty Styles' after him, who would not fail to have the boy and his master on hand in due season, either dead or alive; of that he was sure. Telling her she need not come again; he would himself inform her of their arrival.

After dinner, he appeared at Mr. Rutzer's, (a place the lawyer had procured for her, while she awaited the arrival of her boy,) assuring her, her son had come; but that he stoutly denied having any mother, or any relatives in that place; and said, 'she must go over and identify him.' She went to the office, but at sight of her the boy cried aloud, and regarded her as some terrible being, who was about to take him away from a kind and loving friend. He knelt, even, and begged them, with tears, not to take him away from his dear master, who had brought him from the dreadful South, and been so kind to him.

When he was questioned relative to the bad scar on his forehead, he said, 'Fowler's horse hove him.' And of the one on his cheek, 'That was done by running against the carriage.' In answering these questions, he looked imploringly at his master, as much as to say, 'If they are falsehoods, you bade me say them; may they be satisfactory to you, at least.'

The justice, noting his appearance, bade him forget his master and attend only to him. But the boy persisted in denying his mother, and clinging to his master, saying his mother did not live in such a place as that. However, they allowed the mother to identify her son; and Esquire Demain pleaded that he claimed the boy for her, on the ground that he had been sold out of the State, contrary to the laws in such cases made and provided-spoke of the penalties annexed to said crime, and of the sum of money the delinquent was to pay, in case any one chose to prosecute him for the offence he had committed. Isabella, who was sitting in a corner, scarcely daring to breathe, thought within herself, 'If I can but get the boy, the $200 may remain for whoever else chooses to prosecute-I have done enough to make myself enemies already'-and she trembled at the thought of the formidable enemies she had probably arrayed against herself-helpless and despised as she was. When the pleading was at an end, Isabella understood the Judge to declare, as the sentence of the Court, that the 'boy be delivered into the hands of the mother-having no other master, no other controller, no other conductor, but his mother.' This sentence was obeyed; he was delivered into her hands, the boy meanwhile begging, most piteously, not to be taken from his dear master, saying she was not his mother, and that his mother did not live in such a place as that. And it was some time before lawyer Demain, the clerks, and Isabella, could collectively succeed in calming the child's fears, and in convincing him that Isabella was not some terrible monster, as he had for the last months, probably, been trained to believe; and who, in taking him away from his master, was taking him from all good, and consigning him to all evil.

When at last kind words and bon-bons had quieted his fears, and he could listen to their explanations, he said to Isabella- 'Well, you do look like my mother used to'; and she was soon able to make him comprehend some of the obligations he was under, and the relation he stood in, both to herself and his master. She commenced as soon as practicable to examine the boy, and found, to her utter astonishment, that from the crown of his head to the sole of his foot, the callosities and indurations on his entire body were most frightful to behold. His back she described as being like her fingers, as she laid them side by side.

'Heavens! what is all this? ' said Isabel. He answered, 'It is where Fowler whipped, kicked, and beat me.' She exclaimed, 'Oh, Lord Jesus, look! see my poor child! Oh Lord, "render unto them double" for all this! Oh my God! Pete, how did you bear it?'

'Oh, this is nothing, mammy-if you should see Phillis, I guess you'd scare! She had a little baby, and Fowler cut her till the milk as well as blood ran down her body. You would scare to see Phillis, mammy.'

When Isabella inquired, 'What did Miss Eliza * say, Pete, when you were treated so badly?' he replied, 'Oh, mammy, she said she wished I was with Bell.

Sometimes I crawled under the stoop, mammy, the blood running all about me, and my back would stick to the boards; and sometimes Miss Eliza would come and grease my sores, when all were abed and asleep.'

Note:
*Meaning Mrs. Eliza Fowler.

# DEATH OF MRS. ELIZA FOWLER.

As soon as possible she procured a place for Peter, as tender of locks, at a place called Wahkendall, near Greenkills. After he was thus disposed of, she visited her sister Sophia, who resided at Newberg, and spent the winter in several different families where she was acquainted. She remained some time in the family of a Mr. Latin, who was a relative of Solomon Gedney; and the latter, when he found Isabel with his cousin, used all his influence to persuade him she was a great mischief-maker and a very troublesome person,-that she had put him to some hundreds of dollars expense, by fabricating lies about him, and especially his sister and her family, concerning her boy, when the latter was living so like a gentleman with them; and, for his part, he would not advise his friends to harbor or encourage her. However, his cousins, the Latins, could not see with the eyes of his feelings, and consequently his words fell powerless on them, and they retained her in their service as long as they had aught for her to do.

She then went to visit her former master, Dumont. She had scarcely arrived there, when Mr. Fred. Waring entered, and seeing Isabel, pleasantly accosted her, and asked her 'what she was driving at now-a-days.' On her answering 'nothing particular,' he requested her to go over to his place, and assist his folks, as some of them were sick, and they needed an extra hand. She very gladly assented. When Mr. W. retired, her master wanted to know why she wished to help people, that called her the 'worst of devils,' as Mr. Waring had done in the courthouse-for he was the uncle of Solomon Gedney, and attended the trial we have described-and declared 'that she was a fool to; he wouldn't do it.' 'Oh,' she told him, 'she would not mind that, but was very glad to have people forget their anger towards her.' She went over, but too happy to feel that their resentment was passed, and commenced her work with a light heart and a strong will. She had not worked long in this frame of mind, before a young daughter of Mr. Waring rushed into the rooms exclaiming, with uplifted hands-'Heavens and earth, Isabella! Fowler's murdered Cousin Eliza!' 'Ho,' said Isabel, 'that's nothing-he liked to have killed my child; nothing saved him but God.' Meaning, that she was not at all surprised at it, for a man whose heart was sufficiently hardened to treat a mere child as hers had been treated, was, in her opinion, more fiend than human, and prepared for the commission of any crime that his passions might prompt him to. The child further informed her that a letter had arrived by mail bringing the news.

Immediately after this announcement, Solomon Gedney and his mother came in, going direct to Mrs. Waring's room, where she soon heard tones as of some one reading. She thought something said to her inwardly, 'Go up stairs and hear.' At first she hesitated, but it seemed to press her the more-'Go up and hear!' She went up, unusual as it is for slaves to leave their work and enter unbidden their mistress's room, for the sole purpose of seeing or hearing what may be seen or heard there. But on this occasion, Isabella says, she walked in at the door, shut it, placed her back against it, and listened. She saw them and heard them read-'He knocked her down with his fist, jumped on her with his knees, broke her collar-bone, and tore out her wind-pipe! He then attempted his escape, but was pursued and arrested, and put in an iron bank for safe-keeping!' And the friends were requested to go down and take away the poor innocent children who had thus been made in one short day more than orphans.

If this narrative should ever meet the eye of those innocent sufferers for another's guilt, let them not be too deeply affected by the relation; but, placing their confidence in Him who sees the end from the beginning, and controls the results, rest secure in the faith, that, although they may physically suffer for the sins of others, if they remain but true to themselves, their highest and more enduring interests can never suffer from such a cause. This relation should be suppressed for their sakes, were it not even now so often denied, that slavery is fast undermining all true regard for human life. We know this one instance is not a demonstration to the contrary; but, adding this to the lists of tragedies that weekly come up to us through the Southern mails, may we not admit them as proofs irrefragable? The newspapers confirmed this account of the terrible affair.

When Isabella had heard the letter, all being too much absorbed in their own feelings to take note of her, she returned to her work, her heart swelling with conflicting emotions. She was awed at the dreadful deed; she mourned the fate of the loved Eliza, who had in such an undeserved and barbarous manner been put away from her labors and watchings as a tender mother; and, 'last though not least,' in the development of her character and spirit, her heart bled for the afflicted relatives; even those of them who 'laughed at her calamity, and mocked when her fear came.' Her thoughts dwelt long and intently on the subject, and the wonderful chain of events that had conspired to bring her that day to that house, to listen to that piece of intelligence-to that house, where she never was before or afterwards in her life, and invited there by people who had so lately been hotly incensed against her. It all seemed very remarkable to her, and she viewed it as flowing from a special providence of God. She thought she saw clearly, that their unnatural bereavement was a blow dealt in retributive justice; but she found it not in her heart to exult or rejoice over them. She felt as if God had more than answered her petition, when she ejaculated, in her anguish of mind, 'Oh, Lord, render unto them double!' She said, 'I dared not find fault with God, exactly; but the language of my heart was, 'Oh, my God! that's too much-I did not mean quite so much, God!' It was a terrible blow to the friends of the deceased; and her selfish mother (who, said Isabella, made such a 'to-do about her boy, not from affection, but to have her own will and way') went deranged, and walking to and fro in her delirium, called aloud for her poor murdered daughter-'Eliza! Eliza! '

The derangement of Mrs. G. was a matter of hearsay, as Isabella saw her not after the trial; but she has no reason to doubt the truth of what she heard. Isabel could never learn the subsequent fate of Fowler, but heard, in the spring of '49, that his children had been seen in Kingston-one of whom was spoken of as a fine, interesting girl, albeit a halo of sadness fell like a veil about her.

# ISABELLA'S RELIGIOUS EXPERIENCE.

We will now turn from the outward and temporal to the inward and spiritual life of our subject. It is ever both interesting and instructive to trace the exercises of a human mind, through the trials and mysteries of life; and especially a naturally powerful mind, left as hers was almost entirely to its own workings, and the chance influences it met on its way; and especially to note its reception of that divine 'light, that lighteth every man that cometh into the world.'

We see, as knowledge dawns upon it, truth and error strangely commingled; here, a bright spot illuminated by truth-and there, one darkened and distorted by error; and the state of such a soul may be compared to a landscape at early dawn, where the sun is seen superbly gilding some objects, and causing others to send forth their lengthened, distorted, and sometimes hideous shadows.

Her mother, as we have already said, talked to her of God. From these conversations, her incipient mind drew the conclusion, that God was 'a great man'; greatly superior to other men in power; and being located 'high in the sky,' could see all that transpired on the earth. She believed he not only saw, but noted down all her actions in a great book, even as her master kept a record of whatever he wished not to forget. But she had no idea that God knew a thought of hers till she had uttered it aloud.

As we have before mentioned, she had ever been mindful of her mother's injunctions, spreading out in detail all her troubles before God, imploring and firmly trusting him to send her deliverance from them. Whilst yet a child, she listened to a story of a wounded soldier, left alone in the trail of a flying army, helpless and starving, who hardened the very ground about him with kneeling in his supplications to God for relief, until it arrived. From this narrative, she was deeply impressed with the idea, that if she also were to present her petitions under the open canopy of heaven, speaking very loud, she should the more readily be heard; consequently, she sought a fitting spot for this, her rural sanctuary. The place she selected, in which to offer up her daily orisons, was a small island in a small stream, covered with large willow shrubbery, beneath which the sheep had made their pleasant winding paths; and sheltering themselves from the scorching rays of a noon-tide sun, luxuriated in the cool shadows of the graceful willows, as they listened to the tiny falls of the silver waters. It was a lonely spot, and chosen by her for its beauty, its retirement, and because she thought that there, in the noise of those waters, she could speak louder to God, without being overheard by any who might pass that way. When she had made choice of her sanctum, at a point of the island where the stream met, after having been separated, she improved it by pulling away the branches of the shrubs from the centre, and weaving them together for a wall on the outside, forming a circular arched alcove, made entirely of the graceful willow. To this place she resorted daily, and in pressing times much more frequently.

At this time, her prayers, or, more appropriately, 'talks with God,' were perfectly original and unique, and would be well worth preserving, were it possible to give the tones and manner with the words; but no adequate idea of them can be written while the tones and manner remain inexpressible.

She would sometimes repeat, 'Our Father in heaven,' in her Low Dutch, as taught her by her mother; after that, all was from the suggestions of her own rude mind. She related to God, in minute detail, all her troubles and sufferings, inquiring, as she proceeded, 'Do you think that's right, God?' and closed by begging to be delivered from the evil, whatever it might be.

She talked to God as familiarly as if he had been a creature like herself; and a thousand times more so, than if she had been in the presence of some earthly potentate. She demanded, with little expenditure of reverence or fear, a supply of all her more pressing wants, and at times her demands approached very near to commands. She felt as if God was under obligation to her, much more than she was to him. He seemed to her benighted vision in some manner bound to do her bidding.

Her heart recoils now, with very dread, when she recalls those shocking, almost blasphemous conversations with great Jehovah. And well for herself did she deem it, that, unlike earthly potentates, his infinite character combined the tender father with the omniscient and omnipotent Creator of the universe.

She at first commenced promising God, that if he would help her out of all her difficulties, she would pay him by being very good; and this goodness she intended as a remuneration to God. She could think of no benefit that was to accrue to herself or her fellow-creatures, from her leading a life of purity and generous self-sacrifice for the good of others; as far as any but God was concerned, she saw nothing in it but heart-trying penance, sustained by the sternest exertion; and this she soon found much more easily promised than performed.

Days wore away-new trials came-God's aid was invoked, and the same promises repeated; and every successive night found her part of the contract unfulfilled. She now began to excuse herself, by telling God she could not be good in her present circumstances; but if he would give her a new place, and a good master and mistress, she could and would be good; and she expressly stipulated, that she would be good one day to show God how good she would be all of the time, when he should surround her with the right influences, and she should be delivered from the temptations that then so sorely beset her. But, alas! when night came, and she became conscious that she had yielded to all her temptations, and entirely failed of keeping her word with God, having prayed and promised one hour, and fallen into the sins of anger and profanity the next, the mortifying reflection weighed on her mind, and blunted her enjoyment. Still, she did not lay it deeply to heart, but continued to repeat her demands for aid, and her promises of pay, with full purpose of heart, at each particular time, that that day she would not fail to keep her plighted word.

Thus perished the inward spark, like a flame just igniting, when one waits to see whether it will burn on or die out, till the long desired change came, and she found herself in a new place, with a good mistress, and one who never instigated an otherwise kind master to be unkind to her; in short, a place where she had literally nothing to complain of, and where, for a time, she was more happy than she could well express. 'Oh, every thing there was so pleasant, and kind, and good, and all so comfortable; enough of every thing; indeed, it was beautiful!' she exclaimed.

Here, at Mr. Van Wagener's,-as the reader will readily perceive she must have been,-she was so happy and satisfied, that God was entirely forgotten. Why should her thoughts turn to him, who was only known to her as a help in trouble? She had no trouble now; her every prayer had been answered in every minute particular. She had been delivered from her persecutors and temptations, her youngest child had been given her, and the others she knew she had no means of sustaining if she had them with her, and was content to leave them behind. Their father, who was much older than Isabel, and who preferred serving his time out in slavery, to the trouble and dangers of the course she pursued, remained with and could keep an eye on them-though it is comparatively little that they can do for each other while they remain in slavery; and this little the slave, like persons in every other situation of life, is not always disposed to perform. There are slaves, who, copying the selfishness of their superiors in power, in their conduct towards their fellows who may be thrown upon their mercy, by infirmity or illness, allow them to suffer for want of that kindness and care which it is fully in their power to render them.

The slaves in this country have ever been allowed to celebrate the principal, if not some of the lesser festivals observed by the Catholics and Church of England;-many of them not being required to do the least service for several days, and at Christmas they have almost universally an entire week to themselves, except, perhaps, the attending to a few duties, which are absolutely required for the comfort of the families they belong to. If much service is desired, they are hired to do it, and paid for it as if they were free. The more sober portion of them spend these holidays in earning a little money. Most of them visit and attend parties and balls, and not a few of them spend it in the lowest dissipation. This respite from toil is granted them by all religionists, of whatever persuasion, and probably originated from the fact that many of the first slaveholders were members of the Church of England.

Frederick Douglass, who has devoted his great heart and noble talents entirely to the furtherance of the cause of his down-trodden race, has said-'From what I know of the effect of their holidays upon the slave, I believe them to be among the most effective means, in the hands of the slaveholder, in keeping down the spirit of insurrection. Were the slaveholders at once to abandon this practice, I have not the slightest doubt it would lead to an immediate insurrection among the slaves. These holidays serve as conductors, or safety-valves, to carry off the rebellious spirit of enslaved humanity. But for these, the slave would be forced up to the wildest desperation; and woe betide the slaveholder, the day he ventures to remove or hinder the operation of those conductors! I warn him that, in such an event, a spirit will go forth in their midst, more to be dreaded than the most appalling earthquake.'

When Isabella had been at Mr. Van Wagener's a few months, she saw in prospect one of the festivals approaching. She knows it by none but the Dutch name, Pingster, as she calls it-but I think it must have been Whitsuntide, in English. She says she 'looked back into Egypt,' and every thing looked 'so pleasant there,' as she saw retrospectively all her former companions enjoying their freedom for at least a little space, as well as their wonted convivialities, and in her heart she longed to be with them. With this picture before her mind's eye, she contrasted the quiet, peaceful life she was living with the excellent people of Wahkendall, and it seemed so dull and void of incident, that the very contrast served but to heighten her desire to return, that, at least, she might enjoy with them, once more, the coming festivities. These feelings had occupied a secret corner of her breast for some time, when, one morning, she told Mrs. Van Wagener that her old master Dumont would come that day, and that she should go home with him on his return. They expressed some surprise, and asked her where she obtained her information. She replied, that no one had told her, but she felt that he would come.

It seemed to have been one of those 'events that cast their shadows before'; for, before night, Mr. Dumont made his appearance. She informed him of her intention to accompany him home. He answered, with a smile, 'I shall not take you back again; you ran away from me.' Thinking his manner contradicted his words, she did not feel repulsed, but made herself and child ready; and when her former master had seated himself in the open dearborn, she walked towards it, intending to place herself and child in the rear, and go with him. But, ere she reached the vehicle, she says that God revealed himself to her, with all the suddenness of a flash of lightning, showing her, 'in the twinkling of an eye, that he was all over'-that he pervaded the universe-'and that there was no place where God was not.' She became instantly conscious of her great sin in forgetting her almighty Friend and 'ever-present help in time of trouble.' All her unfulfilled promises arose before her, like a vexed sea whose waves run mountains high; and her soul, which seemed but one mass of lies, shrunk back aghast from the 'awful look' of him whom she had formerly talked to, as if he had been a being like herself; and she would now fain have hid herself in the bowels of the earth, to have escaped his dread presence. But she plainly saw there was no place, not even in hell, where he was not; and where could she flee? Another such 'a look,' as she expressed it, and she felt that she must be extinguished forever, even as one, with the breath of his mouth, 'blows out a lamp,' so that no spark remains.

A dire dread of annihilation now seized her, and she waited to see if, by 'another look,' she was to be stricken from existence,-swallowed up, even as the fire licketh up the oil with which it comes in contact.

When at last the second look came not, and her attention was once more called to outward things, she observed her master had left, and exclaiming aloud, 'Oh, God, I did not know you were so big,' walked into the house, and made an effort to resume her work. But the workings of the inward man were too absorbing to admit of much attention to her avocations. She desired to talk to God, but her vileness utterly forbade it, and she was not able to prefer a petition. 'What!' said she, 'shall I lie again to God? I have told him nothing but lies; and shall I speak again, and tell another lie to God?' She could not; and now she began to wish for some one to speak to God for her. Then a space seemed opening between her and God, and she felt that if some one, who was worthy in the sight of heaven, would but plead for her in their own name, and not let God know it came from her, who was so unworthy, God might grant it. At length a friend appeared to stand between herself and an insulted Deity; and she felt as sensibly refreshed as when, on a hot day, an umbrella had been interposed between her scorching head and a burning sun. But who was this friend? became the next inquiry. Was it Deencia, who had so often befriended her? She looked at her, with her new power of sight-and, lo! she, too, seemed all 'bruises and putrifying sores,' like herself. No, it was some one very different from Deencia.

'Who are you?' she exclaimed, as the vision brightened into a form distinct, beaming with the beauty of holiness, and radiant with love. She then said, audibly addressing the mysterious visitant-'I know you, and I don't know you.' Meaning, 'You seem perfectly familiar; I feel that you not only love me, but that you always have loved me-yet I know you not-I cannot call you by name.' When she said, 'I know you,' the subject of the vision remained distinct and quiet. When she said, 'I don't know you,' it moved restlessly about, like agitated waters. So while she repeated, without intermission, 'I know you, I know you,' that the vision might remain-'Who are you?' was the cry of her heart, and her whole soul was in one deep prayer that this heavenly personage might be revealed to her, and remain with her. At length, after bending both soul and body with the intensity of this desire, till breath and strength seemed failing, and she could maintain her position no longer, an answer came to her, saying distinctly, 'It is Jesus.' 'Yes,' she responded, 'it is Jesus.'

Previous to these exercises of mind, she heard Jesus mentioned in reading or speaking, but had received from what she heard no impression that he was any other than an eminent man, like a Washington or a Lafayette. Now he appeared to her delighted mental vision as so mild, so good, and so every way lovely, and he loved her so much! And, how strange that he had always loved her, and she had never known it! And how great a blessing he conferred, in that he should stand between her and God! And God was no longer a terror and a dread to her.

She stopped not to argue the point, even in her own mind, whether he had reconciled her to God, or God to herself, (though she thinks the former now,) being but too happy that God was no longer to her as a consuming fire, and Jesus was 'altogether lovely.' Her heart was now full of joy and gladness, as it had been of terror, and at one time of despair. In the light of her great happiness, the world was clad in new beauty, the very air sparkled as with diamonds, and was redolent of heaven. She contemplated the unapproachable barriers that existed between herself and the great of this world, as the world calls greatness, and made surprising comparisons between them, and the union existing between herself and Jesus-Jesus, the transcendently lovely as well as great and powerful; for so he appeared to her, though he seemed but human; and she watched for his bodily appearance, feeling that she should know him, if she saw him; and when he came, she would go and dwell with him, as with a dear friend.

It was not given to her to see that he loved any other; and she thought if others came to know and love him, as she did, she should be thrust aside and forgotten, being herself but a poor ignorant slave, with little to recommend her to his notice. And when she heard him spoken off, she said mentally-'What! others know Jesus! I thought no one knew Jesus but me!' and she felt a sort of jealousy, lest she should be robbed of her newly found treasure.

She conceived, one day, as she listened to reading, that she heard an intimation that Jesus was married, and hastily inquired if Jesus had a wife. 'What!' said the reader, 'God have a wife?' 'Is Jesus God? ' inquired Isabella. 'Yes, to be sure he is,' was the answer returned. From this time, her conceptions of Jesus became more elevated and spiritual; and she sometimes spoke of him as God, in accordance with the teaching she had received.

But when she was simply told, that the Christian world was much divided on the subject of Christ's nature-some believing him to be coequal with the Father-to be God in and of himself, 'very God, of very God;'-some, that he is the 'well-beloved,' 'only begotten Son of God;'-and others, that he is, or was, rather, but a mere man-she said, 'Of that I only know as I saw. I did not see him to be God; else, how could he stand between me and God? I saw him as a friend, standing between me and God, through whom, love flowed as from a fountain.' Now, so far from expressing her views of Christ's character and office in accordance with any system of theology extant, she says she believes Jesus is the same spirit that was in our first parents, Adam and Eve, in the beginning, when they came from the hand of their Creator. When they sinned through disobedience, this pure spirit forsook them, and fled to heaven; that there it remained, until it returned again in the person of Jesus; and that, previous to a personal union with him, man is but a brute, possessing only the spirit of an animal.

She avers that, in her darkest hours, she had no fear of any worse hell than the one she then carried in her bosom; though it had ever been pictured to her in its deepest colors, and threatened her as a reward for all her misdemeanors. Her vileness and God's holiness and all-pervading presence, which filled immensity, and threatened her with constant annihilation, composed the burden of her vision of terror. Her faith in prayer is equal to her faith in the love of Jesus. Her language is, 'Let others say what they will of the efficacy of prayer, I believe in it, and I shall pray. Thank God! Yes, I shall always pray,' she exclaims, putting her hands together with the greatest enthusiasm.

For some time subsequent to the happy change we have spoken off, Isabella's prayers partook largely of their former character; and while, in deep affliction, she labored for the recovery of her son, she prayed with constancy and fervor; and the following may be taken as a specimen:-'Oh, God, you know how much I am distressed, for I have told you again and again. Now, God, help me get my son. If you were in trouble, as I am, and I could help you, as you can me, think I would n't do it? Yes, God, you know I would do it.' 'Oh, God, you know I have no money, but you can make the people do for me, and you must make the people do for me. I will never give you peace till you do, God.' 'Oh, God, make the people hear me-don't let them turn me off, without hearing and helping me.' And she has not a particle of doubt, that God heard her, and especially disposed the hearts of thoughtless clerks, eminent lawyers, and grave judges and others-between whom and herself there seemed to her almost an infinite remove-to listen to her suit with patient and respectful attention, backing it up with all needed aid. The sense of her nothingness in the eyes of those with whom she contended for her rights, sometimes fell on her like a heavy weight, which nothing but her unwavering confidence in an arm which she believed to be stronger than all others combined could have raised from her sinking spirit. 'Oh! how little did I feel,' she repeated, with a powerful emphasis. 'Neither would you wonder, if you could have seen me, in my ignorance and destitution, trotting about the streets, meanly clad, bare-headed, and bare-footed! Oh, God only could have made such people hear me; and he did it in answer to my prayers.' And this perfect trust, based on the rock of Deity, was a soul-protecting fortress, which, raising her above the battlements of fear, and shielding her from the machinations of the enemy, impelled her onward in the struggle, till the foe was vanquished, and the victory gained.

We have now seen Isabella, her youngest daughter, and her only son, in possession of, at least, their nominal freedom. It has been said that the freedom of the most free of the colored people of this country is but nominal; but stinted and limited as it is, at best, it is an immense remove from chattel slavery. This fact is disputed, I know; but I have no confidence in the honesty of such questionings. If they are made in sincerity, I honor not the judgment that thus decides.

Her husband, quite advanced in age, and infirm of health, was emancipated, with the balance of the adult slaves of the State, according to law, the following summer, July 4, 1828.

For a few years after this event, he was able to earn a scanty living, and when he failed to do that, he was dependent on the 'world's cold charity,' and died in a poorhouse. Isabella had herself and two children to provide for; her wages were trifling, for at that time the wages of females were at a small advance from nothing; and she doubtless had to learn the first elements of economy-for what slaves, that were never allowed to make any stipulations or calculations for themselves, ever possessed an adequate idea of the true value of time, or, in fact, of any material thing in the universe? To such, 'prudent using' is meanness-and 'saving' is a word to be sneered at. Of course, it was not in her power to make to herself a home, around whose sacred hearth-stone she could collect her family, as they gradually emerged from their prison-house of bondage; a home, where she could cultivate their affection, administer to their wants, and instil into the opening minds of her children those principles of virtue, and that love of purity, truth and benevolence, which must for ever form the foundation of a life of usefulness and happiness. No-all this was far beyond her power or means, in more senses than one; and it should be taken into the account, whenever a comparison is instituted between the progress made by her children in virtue and goodness, and the progress of those who have been nurtured in the genial warmth of a sunny home, where good influences cluster, and bad ones are carefully excluded-where 'line upon line, and precept upon precept,' are daily brought to their quotidian tasks-and where, in short, every appliance is brought in requisition, that self-denying parents can bring to bear on one of the dearest objects of a parent's life, the promotion of the welfare of their children. But God forbid that this suggestion should be wrested from its original intent, and made to shield any one from merited rebuke! Isabella's children are now of an age to know good from evil, and may easily inform themselves on any point where they may yet be in doubt; and if they now suffer themselves to be drawn by temptation into the paths of the destroyer, or forget what is due to the mother who has done and suffered so much for them, and who, now that she is descending into the vale of years, and feels her health and strength declining, will turn her expecting eyes to them for aid and comfort, just as instinctively as the child turns its confiding eye to its fond parent, when it seeks for succor or sympathy-(for it is now their turn to do the work, and bear the burdens of life, so all must bear them in turn, as the wheel of life rolls on)- if, I say, they forget this, their duty and their happiness, and pursue an opposite course of sin and folly, they must lose the respect of the wise and good, and find, when too late, that 'the way of the transgressor is hard.'

# NEW TRIALS.

The reader will pardon this passing homily, while we return to our narrative.

We were saying that the day-dreams of Isabella and her husband-the plan they drew of what they would do, and the comforts they thought to have, when they should obtain their freedom, and a little home of their own- had all turned to 'thin air,' by the postponement of their freedom to so late a day. These delusive hopes were never to be realized, and a new set of trials was gradually to open before her. These were the heart-wasting trials of watching over her children, scattered, and imminently exposed to the temptations of the adversary, with few, if any, fixed principles to sustain them.

'Oh,' she says, 'how little did I know myself of the best way to instruct and counsel them! Yet I did the best I then knew, when with them. I took them to the religious meetings; I talked to, and prayed for and with them; when they did wrong, I scolded at and whipped them.'

Isabella and her son had been free about a year, when they went to reside in the city of New York; a place which she would doubtless have avoided, could she have foreseen what was there in store for her; for this view into the future would have taught her what she only learned by bitter experience, that the baneful influences going up from such a city were not the best helps to education, commenced as the education of her children had been.

Her son Peter was, at the time of which we are speaking, just at that age when no lad should be subjected to the temptations of such a place, unprotected as he was, save by the feeble arm of a mother, herself a servant there. He was growing up to be a tall, well-formed, active lad, of quick perceptions, mild and cheerful in his disposition, with much that was open, generous and winning about him, but with little power to withstand temptation, and a ready ingenuity to provide himself with ways and means to carry out his plans, and conceal from his mother and her friends, all such as he knew would not meet their approbation. As will be readily believed, he was soon drawn into a circle of associates who did not improve either his habits or his morals.

Two years passed before Isabella knew what character Peter was establishing for himself among his low and worthless comrades-passing under the assumed name of Peter Williams; and she began to feel a parent's pride in the promising appearance of her only son. But, alas! this pride and pleasure were shortly dissipated, as distressing facts relative to him came one by one to her astonished ear. A friend of Isabella's, a lady, who was much pleased with the good humor, ingenuity, and open confessions of Peter, when driven into a corner, and who, she said, 'was so smart, he ought to have an education, if any one ought,'-paid ten dollars, as tuition fee, for him to attend a navigation school. But Peter, little inclined to spend his leisure hours in study, when he might be enjoying himself in the dance, or otherwise, with his boon companions, went regularly and made some plausible excuses to the teacher, who received them as genuine, along with the ten dollars of Mrs -, and while his mother and her friend believed him improving at school, he was, to their latent sorrow, improving in a very different place or places, and on entirely opposite principles. They also procured him an excellent place as a coachman. But, wanting money, he sold his livery, and other things belonging to his master; who, having conceived a kind regard for him, considered his youth, and prevented the law from falling, with all its rigor, upon his head. Still he continued to abuse his privileges, and to involve himself in repeated difficulties, from which his mother as often extricated him. At each time, she talked much, and reasoned and remonstrated with him; and he would, with such perfect frankness, lay open his whole soul to her, telling her he had never intended doing harm,-how he had been led along, little by little, till, before he was aware, he found himself in trouble-how he had tried to be good-and how, when he would have been so, 'evil was present with him,'-indeed he knew not how it was.

His mother, beginning to feel that the city was no place for him, urged his going to sea, and would have shipped him on board a man-of-war; but Peter was not disposed to consent to that proposition, while the city and its pleasures were accessible to him. Isabella now became a prey to distressing fears, dreading lest the next day or hour come fraught with the report of some dreadful crime, committed or abetted by her son. She thanks the Lord for sparing her that giant sorrow, as all his wrong doings never ranked higher, in the eye of the law, than misdemeanors. But as she could see no improvement in Peter, as a last resort, she resolved to leave him, for a time, unassisted, to bear the penalty of his conduct, and see what effect that would have on him. In the trial hour, she remained firm in her resolution. Peter again fell into the hands of the police, and sent for his mother, as usual; but she went not to his relief. In his extremity, he sent for Peter Williams, a respectable colored barber, whose name he had been wearing, and who sometimes helped young culprits out of their troubles, and sent them from city dangers, by shipping them on board of whaling vessels.

The curiosity of this man was awakened by the culprit's bearing his own name. He went to the Tombs and inquired into his case, but could not believe what Peter told him respecting his mother and family. Yet he redeemed him, and Peter promised to leave New York in a vessel that was to sail in the course of a week. He went to see his mother, and informed her of what had happened to him. She listened incredulously, as to an idle tale. He asked her to go with him and see for herself. She went, giving no credence to his story till she found herself in the presence of Mr. Williams, and heard him saying to her, 'I am very glad I have assisted your son; he stood in great need of sympathy and assistance; but I could not think he had such a mother here, although he assured me he had.'

Isabella's great trouble now was, a fear lest her son should deceive his benefactor, and be missing when the vessel sailed; but he begged her earnestly to trust him, for he said he had resolved to do better, and meant to abide by the resolve. Isabella's heart gave her no peace till the time of sailing, when Peter sent Mr. Williams and another messenger whom she knew, to tell her he had sailed. But for a month afterwards, she looked to see him emerging from some by-place in the city, and appearing before her; so afraid was she that he was still unfaithful, and doing wrong. But he did not appear, and at length she believed him really gone. He left in the summer of 1839, and his friends heard nothing further from him till his mother received the following letter, dated 'October 17 1840';-

MY DEAR AND BELOVED MOTHER:

'I take this opportunity to write to you and inform you that I am well, and in hopes for to find you the same. I am got on board the same unlucky ship Done, of Nantucket. I am sorry for to say, that I have been punished once severely, by shoving my head in the fire for other folks. We have had bad luck, but in hopes to have better. We have about 230 on board, but in hopes, if do n't kave good luck, that my parents will receive me with thanks. I would like to know how my sisters are. Does my cousins live in New York yet? Have you got my letter? If not, inquire to Mr. Pierce Whiting's. I wish you would write me an answer as soon as possible. I am your only son, that is so far from your home, in the wide briny ocean. I have seen more of the world than ever I expected, and if I ever should return home safe, I will tell you all my troubles and hardships. Mother, I hope you do not forget me, your dear and only son. I should like to know how Sophia, and Betsey, and Hannah, come on. I hope you all will forgive me for all that I have done.

'Your son, PETER VAN WAGENER.'

Another letter reads as follows, dated 'March 22, 1841':-

'MY DEAR MOTHER:

'I take this opportunity to write to you, and inform you that I have been well and in good health. I have wrote you a letter before, but have received no answer from you, and was very anxious to see you. I hope to see you in a short time. I have had very hard luck, but are in hopes to have better in time to come. I should like if my sisters are well, and all the people round the neighborhood. I expect to be home in twenty-two months or thereabouts. I have seen Samuel Laterett. Beware! There has happened very bad news to tell you, that Peter Jackson is dead. He died within two days' sail of Otaheite, one of the Society Islands. The Peter Jackson that used to live at Laterett's; he died on board the ship Done, of Nantucket, Captain Miller, in the latitude 15 53, and longitude 148 30 W. I have no more to say at present, but write as soon as possible.

'Your only son,
'PETER VAN WAGENER.'

Another, containing the last intelligence she has had from her son, reads as follows, and was dated 'Sept. 19, 1841':-

'DEAR MOTHER:

'I take the opportunity to write to you and inform you that I am well and in good health, and in hopes to find you in the same. This is the fifth letter that I have wrote to you, and have received no answer, and it makes me very uneasy. So pray write as quick as you can, and tell me how all the people is about the neighborhood. We are out from home twenty-three months, and in hope to be home in fifteen months. I have not much to say; but tell me if you have been up home since I left or not. I want to know what sort of a time is at home. We had very bad luck when we first came out, but since we have had very good; so I am in hopes to do well yet; but if I do n't do well, you need not expect me home these five years. So write as quick as you can, won't you? So now I am going to put an end to my writing, at present. Notice-when this you see, remember me, and place me in your mind.

> Get me to my home, that's in the far distant west,
> To the scenes of my childhood, that I like the best;
> There the tall cedars grow, and the bright waters flow,
> Where my parents will greet me, white man, let me go!
> Let me go to the spot where the cateract plays,
> Where oft I have sported in my boyish days;
> And there is my poor mother, whose heart ever flows,
> At the sight of her poor child, to her let me go, let me go!

'Your only son,
'PETER VAN WAGENER.'

Since the date of the last letter, Isabella has heard no tidings from her long-absent son, though ardently does her mother's heart long for such tidings, as her thoughts follow him around the world, in his perilous vocation, saying within herself-'He is good now, I have no doubt; I feel sure that he has persevered, and kept the resolve he made before he left home;-he seemed so different before he went, so determined to do better.' His letters are inserted here for preservation, in case they prove the last she ever hears from him in this world.

# FINDING A BROTHER AND SISTER.

When Isabella had obtained the freedom of her son, she remained in Kingston, where she had been drawn by the judicial process, about a year, during which time she became a member of the Methodist Church there: and when she went to New York, she took a letter missive from that church to the Methodist Church in John street. Afterwards, she withdrew her connection with that church, and joined Zion's Church in Church street, composed entirely of colored people. With the latter church she remained until she went to reside with Mr. Pierson, after which, she was gradually drawn into the 'kingdom' set up by the prophet Matthias, in the name of God the Father; for he said the spirit of God the Father dwelt in him.

While Isabella was in New York, her sister Sophia came from Newburg to reside in the former place. Isabel had been favored with occasional interviews with this sister, although at one time she lost sight of her for the space of seventeen years-almost the entire period of her being at Mr. Dumont's-and when she appeared before her again, handsomely dressed, she did not recognize her, till informed who she was. Sophia informed her that her brother Michael-a brother she had never seen-was in the city; and when she introduced him to Isabella, he informed her that their sister Nancy had been living in the city, and had deceased a few months before. He described her features, her dress, her manner, and said she had for some time been a member in Zion's Church, naming the class she belonged to. Isabella almost instantly recognized her as a sister in the church, with whom she had knelt at the altar, and with whom she had exchanged the speaking pressure of the hand, in recognition of their spiritual sisterhood; little thinking, at the time, that they were also children of the same earthly parents-even Bomefree and Mau-mau Bett. As inquiries and answers rapidly passed, and the conviction deepened that this was their sister, the very sister they had heard so much of, but had never seen, (for she was the self-same sister that had been locked in the great old fashioned sleigh-box, when she was taken away, never to behold her mother's face again this side the spirit-land, and Michael, the narrator, was the brother who had shared her fate,) Isabella thought, 'D-h! here she was; we met; and was I not, at the time, struck with the peculiar feeling of her hand-the bony hardness so just like mine? and yet I could not know she was my sister; and now I see she looked so like my mother.' And Isabella wept, and not alone; Sophia wept, and the strong man, Michael, mingled his tears with theirs. 'Oh Lord,' inquired Isabella, 'what is this slavery, that it can do such dreadful things? what evil can it not do?' Well may she ask, for surely the evils it can and does do, daily and hourly, can never be summed up, till we can see them as they are recorded by him who writes no errors, and reckons without mistake. This account, which now varies so widely in the estimate of different minds, will be viewed alike by all.

Think you, dear reader, when that day comes, the most 'rapid abolitionist' will say-'Behold, I saw all this while on the earth?' Will he not rather say, 'Oh, who has conceived the breadth and depth of this moral malaria, this putrescent plague-spot?' Perhaps the pioneers in the slave's cause will be as much surprised as any to find that with all their looking, there remained so much unseen.

# GLEANINGS.

There are some hard things that crossed Isabella's life while in slavery, that she has no desire to publish, for various reasons. First, because the parties from whose hands she suffered them have rendered up their account to a higher tribunal, and their innocent friends alone are living, to have their feelings injured by the recital; secondly, because they are not all for the public ear, from their very nature; thirdly, and not least, because, she says, were she to tell all that happened to her as a slave-all that she knows is 'God's truth'-it would seem to others, especially the uninitiated, so unaccountable, so unreasonable, and what is usually called so unnatural, (though it may be questioned whether people do not always act naturally,) they would not easily believe it. 'Why, no!' she says, 'they'd call me a liar! they would, indeed! and I do not wish to say anything to destroy my own character for veracity, though what I say is strictly true.' Some things have been omitted through forgetfulness, which not having been mentioned in their places, can only be briefly spoken of here;-such as, that her father Bomefree had had two wives before he took Mau mau Bett; one of whom, if not both, were torn from him by the iron hand of the ruthless trafficker in human flesh;-that her husband, Thomas, after one of his wives had been sold away from him, ran away to New York City, where he remained a year or two, before he was discovered and taken back to the prison-house of slavery;-that her master Dumont, when he promised Isabella one year of her time, before the State should make her free, made the same promise to her husband, and in addition to freedom, they were promised a log cabin for a home of their own; all of which, with the one-thousand-and-one day-dreams resulting therefrom, went into the repository of unfulfilled promises and unrealized hopes;-that she had often heard her father repeat a thrilling story of a little slave-child, which, because it annoyed the family with its cries, was caught up by a white man, who dashed its brains out against the wall. An Indian (for Indians were plenty in that region then) passed along as the bereaved mother washed the bloody corpse of her murdered child, and learning the cause of its death, said, with characteristic vehemence, 'If I had been here, I would have put my tomahawk in his head!' meaning the murderer's.

Of the cruelty of one Hasbrouck.-He had a sick slave-woman, who was lingering with a slow consumption, whom he made to spin, regardless of her weakness and suffering; and this woman had a child, that was unable to walk or talk, at the age of five years, neither could it cry like other children, but made a constant, piteous moaning sound. This exhibition of helplessness and imbecility, instead of exciting the master's pity, stung his cupidity, and so enraged him, that he would kick the poor thing about like a foot-ball.

Isabella's informant had seen this brute of a man, when the child was curled up under a chair, innocently amusing itself with a few sticks, drag it hence, that he might have the pleasure of tormenting it. She had see him, with one blow of his foot, send it rolling quite across the room, and down the steps at the door. Oh, how she wished it might instantly die! 'But,' she said, 'it seemed as tough as a moccasin.' Though it did die at last, and made glad the heart of its friends; and its persecutor, no doubt, rejoiced with them, but from very different motives. But the day of his retribution was not far off-for he sickened, and his reason fled. It was fearful to hear his old slave soon tell how, in the day of his calamity, she treated him.

She was very strong, and was therefore selected to support her master, as he sat up in bed, by putting her arms around, while she stood behind him. It was then that she did her best to wreak her vengeance on him. She would clutch his feeble frame in her iron grasp, as in a vice; and, when her mistress did not see, would give him a squeeze, a shake, and lifting him up, set him down again, as hard as possible. If his breathing betrayed too tight a grasp, and her mistress said, 'Be careful, don't hurt him, Soan!' her every-ready answer was, 'Oh no, Missus, no,' in her most pleasant tone-and then, as soon as Missus's eyes and ears were engaged away, another grasp-another shake-another bounce. She was afraid the disease alone would let him recover,-an event she dreaded more than to do wrong herself. Isabella asked her, if she were not afraid his spirit would haunt her. 'Oh, no,' says Soan; 'he was so wicked, the devil will never let him out of hell long enough for that.'

Many slaveholders boast of the love of their slaves. How would it freeze the blood of some of them to know what kind of love rankles in the bosoms of slaves for them! Witness the attempt to poison Mrs. Calhoun, and hundreds of similar cases. Most 'surprising ' to every body, because committed by slaves supposed to be so grateful for their chains.

These reflections bring to mind a discussion on this point, between the writer and a slaveholding friend in Kentucky, on Christmas morning, 1846. We had asserted, that until mankind were far in advance of what they are now, irresponsible power over our fellow-beings would be, as it is, abused. Our friend declared it was his conviction, that the cruelties of slavery existed chiefly in imagination, and that no person in D- County, where we then were, but would be above ill-treating a helpless slave. We answered, that if his belief was well-founded, the people in Kentucky were greatly in advance of the people of New England-for we would not dare say as much as that of any school-district there, letting alone counties. No, we would not answer for our own conduct even on so delicate a point.

The next evening, he very magnanimously overthrew his own position and established ours, by informing us that, on the morning previous, and as near as we could learn, at the very hour in which we were earnestly discussing the probabilities of the case, a young woman of fine appearance, and high standing in society, the pride of her husband, and the mother of an infant daughter, only a few miles from us, ay, in D- County, too, was actually beating in the skull of a slave-woman called Tabby; and not content with that, had her tied up and whipped, after her skull was broken, and she died hanging to the bedstead, to which she had been fastened. When informed that Tabby was dead, she answered, 'I am glad of it, for she has worried my life out of me.' But Tabby's highest good was probably not the end proposed by Mrs. M-, for no one supposed she meant to kill her. Tabby was considered quite lacking in good sense, and no doubt belonged to that class at the South, that are silly enough to 'die of moderate correction.'

A mob collected around the house for an hour or two, in that manner expressing a momentary indignation. But was she treated as a murderess? Not at all! She was allowed to take boat (for her residence was near the beautiful Ohio) that evening, to spend a few months with her absent friends, after which she returned and remained with her husband, no one to 'molest or make her afraid.'

Had she been left to the punishment of an outraged conscience from right motives, I would have 'rejoiced with exceeding joy'. But to see the life of one woman, and she a murderess, put in the balance against the lives of three millions of innocent slaves, and to contrast her punishment with what I felt would be the punishment of one who was merely suspected of being an equal friend of all mankind, regardless of color or condition, caused my blood to stir within me, and my heart to sicken at the thought. The husband of Mrs. M- was absent from home, at the time alluded to; and when he arrived, some weeks afterwards, bringing beautiful presents to his cherished companion, he beheld his once happy home deserted, Tabby murdered and buried in the garden, and the wife of his bosom, and the mother of his child, the doer of a dreadful deed, a murderess!

When Isabella went to New York City, she went in company with a Miss Grear, who introduced her to the family of Mr. James Latourette, a wealthy merchant, and a Methodist in religion; but who, the latter part of his life, felt that he had outgrown ordinances, and advocated free meetings, holding them at his own dwelling-house for several years previous to his death. She worked for them, and they generously gave her a home while she labored for others, and in their kindness made her as one of their own.

At that time, the 'moral reform' movement was awakening the attention of the benevolent in that city. Many women, among whom were Mrs. Latourette and Miss Grear, became deeply interested in making an attempt to reform their fallen sisters, even the most degraded of them; and in this enterprise of labor and danger, they enlisted Isabella and others, who for a time put forth their most zealous efforts, and performed the work of missionaries with much apparent success. Isabella accompanied those ladies to the most wretched abodes of vice and misery, and sometimes she went where they dared not follow. They even succeeded in establishing prayer-meetings in several places, where such a thing might least have been expected.

But these meetings soon became the most noisy, shouting, ranting, and boisterous of gatherings; where they became delirious with excitement, and then exhausted from over-action. Such meetings Isabel had not much sympathy with, at best. But one evening she attended one of them, where the members of it, in a fit of ecstasy, jumped upon her cloak in such a manner as to drag her to the floor-and then, thinking she had fallen in a spiritual trance, they increased their glorifications on her account,-jumping, shouting, stamping, and clapping of hands; rejoicing so much over her spirit, and so entirely overlooking her body, that she suffered much, both from fear and bruises; and ever after refused to attend any more such meetings, doubting much whether God had any thing to do with such worship.

# THE MATTHIAS DELUSION.

We now come to an eventful period in the life of Isabella, as identified with one of the most extraordinary religious delusions of modern times; but the limits prescribed for the present work forbid a minute narration of all the occurrences that transpired in relation to it.

After she had joined the African Church in Church street, and during her membership there, she frequently attended Mr. Latourette's meetings, at one of which, Mr. Smith invited her to go to a prayer-meeting, or to instruct the girls at the Magdalene Asylum, Bowery Hill, then under the protection of Mr. Pierson, and some other persons, chiefly respectable females. To reach the Asylum, Isabella called on Katy, Mr. Pierson's colored servant, of whom she had some knowledge. Mr. Pierson saw her there, conversed with her, asked her if she had been baptized, and was answered, characteristically, 'by the Holy Ghost.' After this, Isabella saw Katy several times, and occasionally Mr. Pierson, who engaged her to keep his house while Katy went to Virginia to see her children. This engagement was considered an answer to a prayer by Mr. Pierson, who had both fasted and prayed on the subject, while Katy and Isabella appeared to see in it the hand of God.

Mr. Pierson was characterized by a strong devotional spirit, which finally became highly fanatical. He assumed the title of Prophet, asserting that God had called him in an omnibus, in these words:-'Thou are Elijah, the Tishbite. Gather unto me all the members of Israel at the foot of Mount Carmel'; which he understood as meaning the gathering of his friends at Bowery Hill. Not long afterward, he became acquainted with the notorious Matthias, whose career was as extraordinary as it was brief. Robert Matthews, or Matthias (as he was usually called), was of Scotch extraction, but a native of Washington County, New York, and at that time about forty-seven years of age. He was religiously brought up, among the Anti-Burghers, a sect of Presbyterians; the clergyman, the Rev. Mr. Bevridge, visiting the family after the manner of the church, and being pleased with Robert, put his hand on his head, when a boy, and pronounced a blessing, and this blessing, with his natural qualities, determined his character; for he ever after thought he should be a distinguished man. Matthias was brought up a farmer till nearly eighteen years of age, but acquired indirectly the art of a carpenter, without any regular apprenticeship, and showed considerable mechanical skill. He obtained property from his uncle, Robert Thompson, and then he went into business as a store-keeper, was considered respectable, and became a member of the Scotch Presbyterian Church. He married in 1813, and continued in business in Cambridge. In 1816, he ruined himself by a building speculation, and the derangement of the currency which denied bank facilities, and soon after he came to New York with his family, and worked at his trade. He afterwards removed to Albany, and became a hearer at the Dutch Reformed Church, then under Dr. Ludlow's charge. He was frequently much excited on religious subjects.

In 1829, he was well known, if not for street preaching, for loud discussions and pavement exhortations, but he did not make set sermons. In the beginning of 1830, he was only considered zealous; but in the same year he prophesied the destruction of the Albanians and their capital, and while preparing to shave, with the Bible before him, he suddenly put down the soap and exclaimed, 'I have found it! I have found a text which proves that no man who shaves his beard can be a true Christian;' and shortly afterwards, without shaving, he went to the Mission House to deliver an address which he had promised, and in this address, he proclaimed his new character, pronounced vengeance on the land, and that the law of God was the only rule of government, and that he was commanded to take possession of the world in the name of the King of kings. His harangue was cut short by the trustees putting out the lights. About this time, Matthias laid by his implements of industry, and in June, he advised his wife to fly with him from the destruction which awaited them in the city; and on her refusal, partly on account of Matthias calling himself a Jew, whom she was unwilling to retain as a husband, he left her, taking some of the children to his sister in Argyle, forty miles from Albany. At Argyle he entered the church and interrupted the minister, declaring the congregation in darkness, and warning them to repentance. He was, of course, taken out of the church, and as he was advertised in the Albany papers, he was sent back to his family. His beard had now obtained a respectable length, and thus he attracted attention, and easily obtained an audience in the streets. For this he was sometimes arrested, once by mistake for Adam Paine, who collected the crowd, and then left Matthias with it on the approach of the officers. He repeatedly urged his wife to accompany him on a mission to convert the world, declaring that food could be obtained from the roots of the forest, if not administered otherwise. At this time he assumed the name of Matthias, called himself a Jew, and set out on a mission, taking a western course, and visiting a brother at Rochester, a skillful mechanic, since dead. Leaving his brother, he proceeded on his mission over the Northern States, occasionally returning to Albany.

After visiting Washington, and passing through Pennsylvania, he came to New York. His appearance at that time was mean, but grotesque, and his sentiments were but little known.

On May the 5th, 1832, he first called on Mr. Pierson, in Fourth street, in his absence. Isabella was alone in the house, in which she had lived since the previous autumn. On opening the door, she, for the first time, beheld Matthias, and her early impression of seeing Jesus in the flesh rushed to her mind. She heard his inquiry, and invited him into the parlor; and being naturally curious, and much excited, and possessing a good deal of tact, she drew him into conversation, stated her own opinions, and heard his replies and explanations. Her faith was at first staggered by his declaring himself a Jew; but on this point she was relieved by his saying, 'Do you not remember how Jesus prayed?' and repeated part of the Lord's Prayer, in proof that the Father's kingdom was to come, and not the Son's. She then understood him to be a converted Jew, and in the conclusion she says she 'felt as if God had sent him to set up the kingdom.' Thus Matthias at once secured the good will of Isabella, and we may supposed obtained from her some information in relation to Mr. Pierson, especially that Mrs. Pierson declared there was no true church, and approved of Mr. Pierson's preaching. Matthias left the house, promising to return on Saturday evening. Mr. P. at this time had not seen Matthias.

Isabella, desirous of hearing the expected conversation between Matthias and Mr. Pierson on Saturday, hurried her work, got it finished, and was permitted to be present. Indeed, the sameness of belief made her familiar with her employer, while her attention to her work, and characteristic faithfulness, increased his confidence. This intimacy, the result of holding the same faith, and the principle afterwards adopted of having but one table, and all things in common, made her at once the domestic and the equal, and the depositary of very curious, if not valuable information. To this object, even her color assisted. Persons who have traveled in the South know the manner in which the colored people, and especially slaves, are treated; they are scarcely regarded as being present. This trait in our American character has been frequently noticed by foreign travelers. One English lady remarks that she discovered, in course of conversation with a Southern married gentleman, that a colored girl slept in his bedroom, in which also was his wife; and when he saw that it occasioned some surprise, he remarked, 'What would he do if he wanted a glass of water in the night?' Other travelers have remarked that the presence of colored people never seemed to interrupt a conversation of any kind for one moment. Isabella, then, was present at the first interview between Matthias and Pierson. At this interview, Mr. Pierson asked Matthias if he had a family, to which he replied in the affirmative; he asked him about his beard, and he gave a scriptural reason, asserting also that the Jews did not shave, and that Adam had a beard. Mr. Pierson detailed to Matthias his experience, and Matthias gave his, and they mutually discovered that they held the same sentiments, both admitting the direct influence of the Spirit, and the transmission of spirits from one body to another. Matthias admitted the call of Mr. Pierson, in the omnibus in Wall street, which, on this occasion, he gave in these words:-'Thou art Elijah the

Tishbite, and thou shalt go before me in the spirit and power of Elias, to prepare my way before me.' And Mr. Pierson admitted Matthias' call, who completed his declaration on the 20th of June, in Argyle, which, by a curious coincidence, was the very day on which Pierson had received his call in the omnibus. Such singular coincidences have a powerful effect on excited minds. From that discovery, Pierson and Matthias rejoiced in each other, and became kindred spirits-Matthias, however, claiming to be the Father, or to possess the spirit of the Father-he was God upon the earth, because the spirit of God dwelt in him; while Pierson then understood that his mission was like that of John the Baptist, which the name Elias meant. This conference ended with an invitation to supper, and Matthias and Pierson washing each other's feet. Mr. Pierson preached on the following Sunday, but after which, he declined in favor of Matthias, and some of the party believed that the 'kingdom had then come.'

As a specimen of Matthias' preaching and sentiments, the following is said to be reliable:

'The spirit that built the Tower of Babel is now in the world-it is the spirit of the devil. The spirit of man never goes upon the clouds; all who think so are Babylonians. The only heaven is on earth. All who are ignorant of truth are Ninevites. The Jews did not crucify Christ- it was the Gentiles. Every Jew has his guardian angel attending him in this world. God don't speak through preachers; he speaks through me, his prophet.

' " John the Baptist," (addressing Mr. Pierson), "read the tenth chapter of Revelations." After the reading of the chapter, the prophet resumed speaking, as follows:-

'Ours is the mustard-seed kingdom which is to spread all over the earth. Our creed is truth, and no man can find truth unless he obeys John the Baptist, and comes clean into the church.

'All real men will be saved; all mock men will be damned. When a person has the Holy Ghost, then he is a man, and not till then. They who teach women are of the wicked. The communion is all nonsense; so is prayer. Eating a nip of bread and drinking a little wine won't do any good. All who admit members into their church, and suffer them to hold their lands and houses, their sentence is, "Depart, ye wicked, I know you not." All females who lecture their husbands, their sentence is the same. The sons of truth are to enjoy all the good things of this world, and must use their means to bring it about. Every thing that has the smell of woman will be destroyed. Woman is the capsheaf of the abomination of desolation-full of all deviltry. In a short time, the world will take fire and dissolve; it is combustible already. All women, not obedient, had better become so as soon as possible, and let the wicked spirit depart, and become temples of truth. Praying is all mocking. When you see any one wring the neck of a fowl, instead of cutting off its head, he has not got the Holy Ghost. (Cutting gives the least pain.)

'All who eat swine's flesh are of the devil; and just as certain as he eats it, he will tell a lie in less than half an hour. If you eat a piece of pork, it will go crooked through you, and the Holy Ghost will not stay in you, but one or the other must leave the house pretty soon. The pork will be as crooked in you as ram's horns, and as great a nuisance as the hogs in the street.

'The cholera is not the right word; it is choler, which means God's wrath. Abraham, Isaac, and Jacob are now in this world; they did not go up in the clouds, as some believe-why should they go there? They don't want to go there to box the compass from one place to another. The Christians now-a-days are for setting up the Son's kingdom. It is not his; it is the Father's kingdom. It puts me in mind of a man in the country, who took his son in business, and had his sign made, "Hitchcock & Son;" but the son wanted it "Hitchcock & Father"-and that is the way with your Christians. They talk of the Son's kingdom first, and not the Father's kingdom.'

Matthias and his disciples at this time did not believe in a resurrection of the body, but that the spirits of the former saints would enter the bodies of the present generation, and thus begin heaven on earth, of which he and Mr. Pierson were the first fruits.

Matthias made the residence of Mr. Pierson his own; but the latter, being apprehensive of popular violence in his house, if Matthias remained there, proposed a monthly allowance to him, and advised him to occupy another dwelling. Matthias accordingly took a house in Clarkson street, and then sent for his family at Albany, but they declined coming to the city. However, his brother George complied with a similar offer, bringing his family with him, where they found very comfortable quarters. Isabella was employed to do the housework. In May, 1833, Matthias left his house, and placed the furniture, part of which was Isabella's, elsewhere, living himself at the hotel corner of Marketfield and West streets. Isabella found employment at Mr. Whiting's, Canal street, and did the washing for Matthias by Mrs. Whiting's permission.

Of the subsequent removal of Matthias to the farm and residence of Mr. B. Folger, at Sing Sing, where he was joined by Mr. Pierson, and others laboring under a similar religious delusion-the sudden, melancholy and somewhat suspicious death of Mr. Pierson, and the arrest of Matthias on the charge of his murder, ending in a verdict of not guilty-the criminal connection that subsisted between Matthias, Mrs. Folger, and other members of the 'Kingdom,' as 'match-spirits'-the final dispersion of this deluded company, and the voluntary exilement of Matthias in the far West, after his release-&c. &c., we do not deem it useful or necessary to give any particulars. Those who are curious to know what there transpired are referred to a work published in New York in 1835, entitled 'Fanaticism; its Sources and Influence; illustrated by the simple Narrative of Isabella, in the case of Matthias, Mr. and Mrs. B. Folger, Mr. Pierson, Mr. Mills, Catharine, Isabella, &c. &c. By G. Vale, 84 Roosevelt street.' Suffice it to say, that while Isabella was a member of the household at Sing Sing, doing much laborious service in the spirit of religious disinterestedness, and gradually getting her vision purged and her mind cured of its illusions, she happily escaped the contamination that surrounded her,-assiduously endeavoring to discharge all her duties in a becoming manner.

# FASTING.

When Isabella resided with Mr. Pierson, he was in the habit of fasting every Friday; not eating or drinking anything from Thursday evening to six o'clock on Friday evening.

Then, again, he would fast two nights and three days, neither eating nor drinking; refusing himself even a cup of cold water till the third day at night, when he took supper again, as usual.

Isabella asked him why he fasted. He answered, that fasting gave him great light in the things of God; which answer gave birth to the following train of thought in the mind of his auditor:-'Well, if fasting will give light inwardly and spiritually, I need it as much as any body,-and I'll fast too. If Mr. Pierson needs to fast two nights and three days, then I, who need light more than he does, ought to fast more, and I will fast three nights and three days.'

This resolution she carried out to the letter, putting not so much as a drop of water in her mouth for three whole days and nights. The fourth morning, as she arose to her feet, not having the power to stand, she fell to the floor; but recovering herself sufficiently, she made her way to the pantry, and feeling herself quite voracious, and fearing that she might now offend God by her voracity, compelled herself to breakfast on dry bread and water-eating a large six-penny loaf before she felt at all stayed or satisfied. She says she did get light, but it was all in her body and none in her mind-and this lightness of body lasted a long time. Oh! she was so light, and felt so well, she could 'skim around like a gull.'

# THE CAUSE OF HER LEAVING THE CITY.

The first years spent by Isabella in the city, she accumulated more than enough to satisfy all her wants, and she placed all the overplus in the Savings' Bank. Afterwards, while living with Mr. Pierson, he prevailed on her to take it all thence, and invest it in a common fund which he was about establishing, as a fund to be drawn from by all the faithful; the faithful, of course, were the handful that should subscribe to his peculiar creed. This fund, commenced by Mr. Pierson, afterwards became part and parcel of the kingdom of which Matthias assumed to be head; and at the breaking up of the kingdom, her little property was merged in the general ruin-or went to enrich those who profited by the loss of others, if any such there were. Mr. Pierson and others had so assured her, that the fund would supply all her wants, at all times, and in all emergencies, and to the end of life, that she became perfectly careless on the subject-asking for no interest when she drew her money from the bank, and taking no account of the sum she placed in the fund. She recovered a few articles of the furniture from the wreck of the kingdom, and received a small sum of money from Mr. B. Folger, as the price of Mrs. Folger's attempt to convict her of murder. With this to start upon, she commenced anew her labors, in the hope of yet being able to accumulate a sufficiency to make a little home for herself, in her advancing age. With this stimulus before her, she toiled hard, working early and late, doing a great deal for a little money, and turning her hand to almost anything that promised good pay. Still, she did not prosper, and somehow, could not contrive to lay by a single dollar for a 'rainy day.'

When this had been the state of her affairs some time, she suddenly paused, and taking a retrospective view of what had passed, inquired within herself, why it was that, for all her unwearied labors, she had nothing to show; why it was that others, with much less care and labor, could hoard up treasures for themselves and children? She became more and more convinced, as she reasoned, that every thing she had undertaken in the city of New York had finally proved a failure; and where her hopes had been raised the highest, there she felt the failure had been the greatest, and the disappointment most severe.

After turning it in her mind for some time, she came to the conclusion, that she had been taking part in a great drama, which was, in itself, but one great system of robbery and wrong. 'Yes,' she said, 'the rich rob the poor, and the poor rob one another.' True, she had not received labor from others, and stinted their pay, as she felt had been practised against her; but she had taken their work from them, which was their only means to get money, and was the same to them in the end. For instance-a gentleman where she lived would give her a dollar to hire a poor man to clear the new-fallen snow from the steps and sidewalks. She would arise early, and perform the labor herself, putting the money into her own pocket. A poor man would come along, saying she ought to have let him have the job; he was poor, and needed the pay for his family. She would harden her heart against him, and answer-'I am poor too, and I need it for mine.' But, in her retrospection, she thought of all the misery she might have been adding to, in her selfish grasping, and it troubled her conscience sorely; and this insensibility to the claims of human brotherhood, and the wants of the destitute and wretched poor, she now saw, as she never had done before, to be unfeeling, selfish and wicked. These reflections and convictions gave rise to a sudden revulsion of feeling in the heart of Isabella, and she began to look upon money and property with great indifference, if not contempt-being at that time unable, probably, to discern any difference between a miserly grasping at and hoarding of money and means, and a true use of the good things of this life for one's own comfort, and the relief of such as she might be enabled to befriend and assist. One thing she was sure of-that the precepts, 'Do unto others as ye would that others should do unto you,' 'Love your neighbor as yourself,' and so forth, were maxims that had been but little thought of by herself, or practised by those about her.

Her next decision was, that she must leave the city; it was no place for her; yea, she felt called in spirit to leave it, and to travel east and lecture. She had never been further east than the city, neither had she any friends there of whom she had particular reason to expect any thing; yet to her it was plain that her mission lay in the east, and that she would find friends there. She determined on leaving; but these determinations and convictions she kept close locked in her own breast, knowing that if her children and friends were aware of it, they would make such an ado about it as would render it very unpleasant, if not distressing to all parties. Having made what preparations for leaving she deemed necessary,-which was, to put up a few articles of clothing in a pillowcase, all else being deemed an unnecessary incumbrance,-about an hour before she left, she informed Mrs. Whiting, the woman of the house where she was stopping, that her name was no longer Isabella, but SOJOURNER; and that she was going east. And to her inquiry, 'What are you going east for?' her answer was, 'The Spirit calls me there, and I must go.'

She left the city on the morning of the 1st of June, 1843, crossing over to Brooklyn, L.I.; and taking the rising sun for her only compass and guide, she 'remembered Lot's wife,' and hoping to avoid her fate, she resolved not to look back till she felt sure the wicked city from which she was fleeing was left too far behind to be visible in the distance; and when she first ventured to look back, she could just discern the blue cloud of smoke that hung over it, and she thanked the Lord that she was thus far removed from what seemed to her a second Sodom.

She was now fairly started on her pilgrimage; her bundle in one hand, and a little basket of provisions in the other, and two York shillings in her purse-her heart strong in the faith that her true work lay before her, and that the Lord was her director; and she doubted not he would provide for and protect her, and that it would be very censurable in her to burden herself with any thing more than a moderate supply for her then present needs. Her mission was not merely to travel east, but to 'lecture,' as she designated it; 'testifying of the hope that was in her'-exhorting the people to embrace Jesus, and refrain from sin, the nature and origin of which she explained to them in accordance with her own most curious and original views. Through her life, and all its chequered changes, she has ever clung fast to her first permanent impressions on religious subjects.

Wherever night overtook her, there she sought for lodgings-free, if she might-if not, she paid; at a tavern, if she chanced to be at one-if not, at a private dwelling; with the rich, if they would receive her-if not, with the poor.

But she soon discovered that the largest houses were nearly always full; if not quite full, company was soon expected; and that it was much easier to find an unoccupied corner in a small house than in a large one; and if a person possessed but a miserable roof over his head, you might be sure of a welcome to part of it.

But this, she had penetration enough to see, was quite as much the effect of a want of sympathy as of benevolence; and this was also very apparent in her religious conversations with people who were strangers to her. She said, 'she never could find out that the rich had any religion. If I had been rich and accomplished, I could; for the rich could always find religion in the rich, and I could find it among the poor.'

At first, she attended such meetings as she heard of, in the vicinity of her travels, and spoke to the people as she found them assembled. Afterwards, she advertised meetings of her own, and held forth to large audiences, having, as she said, 'a good time.'

When she became weary of travelling, and wished a place to stop a while and rest herself, she said some opening for her was always near at hand; and the first time she needed rest, a man accosted her as she was walking, inquiring if she was looking for work. She told him that was not the object of her travels, but that she would willingly work a few days, if any one wanted. He requested her to go to his family, who were sadly in want of assistance, which he had been thus far unable to supply. She went to the house where she was directed, and was received by his family, one of whom was ill, as a 'Godsend;' and when she felt constrained to resume her journey, they were very sorry, and would fain have detained her longer; but as she urged the necessity of leaving, they offered her what seemed in her eyes a great deal of money as a remuneration for her labor, and an expression of their gratitude for her opportune assistance; but she would only receive a very little of it; enough, as she says, to enable her to pay tribute to Caesar, if it was demanded of her; and two or three York shillings at a time were all she allowed herself to take; and then, with purse replenished, and strength renewed, she would once more set out to perform her mission.

# THE CONSEQUENCES OF REFUSING A TRAVELLER A NIGHT'S LODGING.

As she drew near the center of the Island, she commenced, one evening at nightfall, to solicit the favor of a night's lodging. She had repeated her request a great many, it seemed to her some twenty times, and as many times she received a negative answer. She walked on, the stars and the tiny horns of the new moon shed but a dim light on her lonely way, when she was familiarly accosted by two Indians, who took her for an acquaintance. She told them they were mistaken in the person; she was a stranger there, and asked them the direction to a tavern. They informed her it was yet a long way-some two miles or so; and inquired if she were alone. Not wishing for their protection, or knowing what might be the character of their kindness, she answered, 'No, not exactly,' and passed on. At the end of a weary way, she came to the tavern,-or rather, to a large building, which was occupied as a court-house, tavern, and jail,-and on asking for a night's lodging, was informed she could stay, if she would consent to be locked in. This to her mind was an insuperable objection. To have a key turned on her was a thing not to be thought of, at least not to be endured, and she again took up her line of march, preferring to walk beneath the open sky, to being locked up by a stranger in such a place. She had not walked far, before she heard the voice of a woman under an open shed;

She ventured to accost her, and inquired if she knew where she could get in for the night. The woman answered, that she did not, unless she went home with them; and turning to her 'good man,' asked him if the stranger could not share their home for the night, to which he cheerfully assented. Sojourner thought it evident he had been taking a drop too much, but as he was civil and good-natured, and she did not feel inclined to spend the night alone in the open air, she felt driven to the necessity of accepting their hospitality, whatever it might prove to be. The woman soon informed her that there was a ball in the place, at which they would like to drop in a while, before they went to their home.

Balls being no part of Sojourner's mission, she was not desirous of attending; but her hostess could be satisfied with nothing short of a taste of it, and she was forced to go with her, or relinquish their company at once, in which move there might be more exposure than in accompanying her. She went, and soon found herself surrounded by an assemblage of people, collected from the very dregs of society, too ignorant and degraded to understand, much less entertain, a high or bright idea,-in a dirty hovel, destitute of every comfort, and where the fumes of whiskey were abundant and powerful.

Sojourner's guide there was too much charmed with the combined entertainments of the place to be able to tear herself away, till she found her faculties for enjoyment failing her, from a too free use of liquor; and she betook herself to bed till she could recover them. Sojourner, seated in a corner, had time for many reflections, and refrained from lecturing them, in obedience to the recommendation, 'Cast not your pearls,' &c. When the night was far spent, the husband of the sleeping woman aroused the sleeper, and reminded her that she was not very polite to the woman she had invited to sleep at her house, and of the propriety of returning home. They once more emerged into the pure air, which to our friend Sojourner, after so long breathing the noisome air of the ball-room, was most refreshing and grateful. Just as day dawned, they reached the place they called their home. Sojourner now saw that she had lost nothing in the shape of rest by remaining so long at the ball, as their miserable cabin afforded but one bunk or pallet for sleeping; and had there been many such, she would have preferred sitting up all night to occupying one like it. They very politely offered her the bed, if she would use it; but civilly declining, she waited for morning with an eagerness of desire she never felt before on the subject, and was never more happy than when the eye of day shed its golden light once more over the earth. She was once more free, and while daylight should last, independent, and needed no invitation to pursue her journey. Let these facts teach us, that every pedestrian in the world is not a vagabond, and that it is a dangerous thing to compel any one to receive that hospitality from the vicious and abandoned which they should have received from us,-as thousands can testify, who have thus been caught in the snares of the wicked.

The fourth of July, Isabella arrived at Huntingdon; from thence she went to Cold Springs, where she found the people making preparations for a mass temperance-meeting. With her usual alacrity, she entered into their labors, getting up dishes a la New York, greatly to the satisfaction of those she assisted. After remaining at Cold Springs some three weeks, she returned to Huntingdon, where she took boat for Connecticut. Landing at Bridgeport, she again resumed her travels towards the north-east, lecturing some, and working some, to get wherewith to pay tribute to Caesar, as she called it; and in this manner she presently came to the city of New Haven, where she found many meetings, which she attended-at some of which, she was allowed to express her views freely, and without reservation. She also called meetings expressly to give herself an opportunity to be heard; and found in the city many true friends of Jesus, as she judged, with whom she held communion of spirit, having no preference for one sect more than another, but being well satisfied with all who gave her evidence of having known or loved the Saviour.

After thus delivering her testimony in this pleasant city, feeling she had not as yet found an abiding place, she went from thence to Bristol, at the request of a zealous sister, who desired her to go to the latter place, and hold a religious conversation with some friends of hers there. She went as requested, found the people kindly and religiously disposed, and through them she became acquainted with several very interesting persons.

A spiritually-minded brother in Bristol, becoming interested in her new views and original opinions, requested as a favor that she would go to Hartford, to see and converse with friends of his there. Standing ready to perform any service in the Lord, she went to Hartford as desired, bearing in her hand the following note from this brother:-

'SISTER,-I send you this living messenger, as I believe her to be one that God loves. Ethiopia is stretching forth her hands unto God. You can see by this sister, that God does by his Spirit alone teach his own children things to come. Please receive her, and she will tell you some new things. Let her tell her story without interrupting her, and give close attention, and you will see she has got the lever of truth, that God helps her to pry where but few can. She cannot read or write, but the law is in her heart.

'Send her to brother -, brother -, and where she can do the most good.
'From your brother, H. L. B.'

# SOME OF HER VIEWS AND REASONINGS.

As soon as Isabella saw God as an all-powerful, all-pervading spirit, she became desirous of hearing all that had been written of him, and listened to the account of the creation of the world and its first inhabitants, as contained in the first chapters of Genesis, with peculiar interest. For some time she received it all literally, though it appeared strange to her that 'God worked by the day, got tired, and stopped to rest,' &c. But after a little time, she began to reason upon it, thus-'Why, if God works by the day, and one day's work tires him, and he is obliged to rest, either from weariness or on account of darkness, or if he waited for the "cool of the day to walk in the garden," because he was inconvenienced by the heat of the sun, why then it seems that God cannot do as much as I can; for I can bear the sun at noon, and work several days and nights in succession without being much tired. Or, if he rested nights because of the darkness, it is very queer that he should make the night so dark that he could not see himself. If I had been God, I would have made the night light enough for my own convenience, surely.' But the moment she placed this idea of God by the side of the impression she had once so suddenly received of his inconceivable greatness and entire spirituality, that moment she exclaimed mentally, 'No, God does not stop to rest, for he is a spirit, and cannot tire; he cannot want for light, for he hath all light in himself. And if "God is all in all," and "worketh all in all," as I have heard them read, then it is impossible he should rest at all; for if he did, every other thing would stop and rest too; the waters would not flow, and the fishes could not swim; and all motion must cease. God could have no pauses in his work, and he needed no Sabbaths of rest. Man might need them, and he should take them when he needed them, whenever he required rest. As it regarded the worship of God, he was to be worshipped at all times and in all places; and one portion of time never seemed to her more holy than another.'

These views, which were the results of the workings of her own mind, assisted solely by the light of her own experience and very limited knowledge, were, for a long time after their adoption, closely locked in her own breast, fearing lest their avowal might bring upon her the imputation of 'infidelity,'- the usual charge preferred by all religionists, against those who entertain religious views and feelings differing materially from their own. If, from their own sad experience, they are withheld from shouting the cry of 'infidel,' they fail not to see and to feel, ay, and to say, that the dissenters are not of the right spirit, and that their spiritual eyes have never been unsealed.

While travelling in Connecticut, she met a minister, with whom she held a long discussion on these points, as well as on various other topics, such as the origin of all things, especially the origin of evil, at the same time bearing her testimony strongly against a paid ministry. He belonged to that class, and, as a matter of course, as strongly advocated his own side of the question.

I had forgotten to mention, in its proper place, a very important fact, that when she was examining the Scriptures, she wished to hear them without comment; but if she employed adult persons to read them to her, and she asked them to read a passage over again, they invariably commenced to explain, by giving her their version of it; and in this way, they tried her feelings exceedingly. In consequence of this, she ceased to ask adult persons to read the Bible to her, and substituted children in their stead. Children, as soon as they could read distinctly, would re-read the same sentence to her, as often as she wished, and without comment; and in that way she was enabled to see what her own mind could make out of the record, and that, she said, was what she wanted, and not what others thought it to mean. She wished to compare the teachings of the Bible with the witness within her; and she came to the conclusion, that the spirit of truth spoke in those records, but that the recorders of those truths had intermingled with them ideas and suppositions of their own. This is one among the many proofs of her energy and independence of character.

When it became known to her children, that Sojourner had left New York, they were filled with wonder and alarm. Where could she have gone, and why had she left? were questions no one could answer satisfactorily. Now, their imaginations painted her as a wandering maniac-and again they feared she had been left to commit suicide; and many were the tears they shed at the loss of her.

But when she reached Berlin, Conn., she wrote to them by amanuensis, informing them of her whereabouts, and waiting an answer to her letter; thus quieting their fears, and gladdening their hearts once more with assurances of her continued life and her love.

# THE SECOND ADVENT DOCTRINES.

In Hartford and vicinity, she met with several persons who believed in the 'Second Advent' doctrines; or, the immediate personal appearance of Jesus Christ. At first she thought she had never heard of 'Second Advent.' But when it was explained to her, she recollected having once attended Mr. Miller's meeting in New York, where she saw a great many enigmatical pictures hanging on the wall, which she could not understand, and which, being out of the reach of her understanding, failed to interest her. In this section of country, she attended two camp-meetings of the believers in these doctrines-the 'second advent' excitement being then at its greatest height. The last meeting was at Windsor Lock. The people, as a matter of course, eagerly inquired of her concerning her belief, as it regarded their most important tenet. She told them it had not been revealed to her; perhaps, if she could read, she might see it differently. Sometimes, to their eager inquiry, 'Oh, don't you believe the Lord is coming?' she answered, 'I believe the Lord is as near as he can be, and not be it.' With these evasive and non-exciting answers, she kept their minds calm as it respected her unbelief, till she could have an opportunity to hear their views fairly stated, in order to judge more understandingly of this matter, and see if, in her estimation, there was any good ground for expecting an event which was, in the minds of so many, as it were, shaking the very foundations of the universe. She was invited to join them in their religious exercises, and accepted the invitation-praying, and talking in her own peculiar style, and attracting many about her by her singing.

When she had convinced the people that she was a lover of God and his cause, and had gained a good standing with them, so that she could get a hearing among them, she had become quite sure in her own mind that they were laboring under a delusion, and she commenced to use her influence to calm the fears of the people, and pour oil upon the troubled waters. In one part of the grounds, she found a knot of people greatly excited: she mounted a stump and called out, 'Hear! hear!' When the people had gathered around her, as they were in a state to listen to any thing new, she addressed them as 'children,' and asked them why they made such a 'To-do;-are you not commanded to "watch and pray?" You are neither watching nor praying.' And she bade them, with the tones of a kind mother, retire to their tents, and there watch and pray, without noise or tumult, for the Lord would not come to such a scene of confusion; 'the Lord came still and quiet.' She assured them, 'the Lord might come, move all through the camp, and go away again, and they never know it,' in the state they then were.

They seemed glad to seize upon any reason for being less agitated and distressed, and many of them suppressed their noisy terror, and retired to their tents to 'watch and pray;' begging others to do the same, and listen to the advice of the good sister. She felt she had done some good, and then went to listen further to the preachers. They appeared to her to be doing their utmost to agitate and excite the people, who were already too much excited; and when she had listened till her feelings would let her listen silently no longer, she arose and addressed the preachers. The following are specimens of her speech:-

'Here you are talking about being "changed in the twinkling of an eye." If the Lord should come, he'd change you to nothing! for there is nothing to you.

'You seem to be expecting to go to some parlor away up somewhere, and when the wicked have been burnt, you are coming back to walk in triumph over their ashes-this is to be your New Jerusalem!! Now, I can't see any thing so very nice in that, coming back to such a muss as that will be, a world covered with the ashes of the wicked! Besides, if the Lord comes and burns-as you say he will-I am not going away; I am going to stay here and stand the fire, like Shadrach, Meshach, and Abednego! And Jesus will walk with me through the fire, and keep me from harm. Nothing belonging to God can burn, any more than God himself; such shall have no need to go away to escape the fire! No, I shall remain. Do you tell me that God's children can't stand fire?' And her manner and tone spoke louder than words, saying, 'It is absurd to think so!'

The ministers were taken quite aback at so unexpected an opposer, and one of them, in the kindest possible manner, commenced a discussion with her, by asking her questions, and quoting scripture to her; concluding, finally, that although she had learned nothing of the great doctrine which was so exclusively occupying their minds at the time, she had learned much that man had never taught her.

At this meeting, she received the address of different persons, residing in various places, with an invitation to visit them. She promised to go soon to Cabotville, and started, shaping her course for that place. She arrived at Springfield one evening at six o'clock, and immediately began to search for a lodging for the night. She walked from six till past nine, and was then on the road from Springfield to Cabotville, before she found any one sufficiently hospitable to give her a night's shelter under their roof. Then a man gave her twenty-five cents, and bade her go to a tavern and stay all night. She did so, returning in the morning to thank him, assuring him she had put his money to its legitimate use. She found a number of the friends she had seen at Windsor when she reached the manufacturing town of Cabotville, (which has lately taken the name of Chicopee,) and with them she spent a pleasant week or more; after which, she left them to visit the Shaker village in Enfield. She now began to think of finding a resting place, at least, for a season; for she had performed quite a long journey, considering she had walked most of the way; and she had a mind to look in upon the Shakers, and see how things were there, and whether there was any opening there for her. But on her way back to Springfield, she called at a house and asked for a piece of bread; her request was granted, and she was kindly invited to tarry all night, as it was getting late, and she would not be able to stay at every house in that vicinity, which invitation she cheerfully accepted. When the man of the house came in, he recollected having seen her at the camp-meeting, and repeated some conversations, by which she recognized him again. He soon proposed having a meeting that evening, went out and notified his friends and neighbors, who came together, and she once more held forth to them in her peculiar style. Through the agency of this meeting, she became acquainted with several people residing in Springfield, to whose houses she was cordially invited, and with whom she spent some pleasant time.

One of these friends, writing of her arrival there, speaks as follows. After saying that she and her people belonged to that class of persons who believed in the second advent doctrines; and that this class, believing also in freedom of speech and action, often found at their meetings many singular people, who did not agree with them in their principal doctrine; and that, being thus prepared to hear new and strange things, 'They listened eagerly to Sojourner, and drank in all she said;'-and also, that she 'soon became a favorite among them; that when she arose to speak in their assemblies, her commanding figure and dignified manner hushed every trifler into silence, and her singular and sometimes uncouth modes of expression never provoked a laugh, but often were the whole audience melted into tears by her touching stories.' She also adds, 'Many were the lessons of wisdom and faith I have delighted to learn from her.' . . . . 'She continued a great favorite in our meetings, both on account of her remarkable gift in prayer, and still more remarkable talent for singing, . . . and the aptness and point of her remarks, frequently illustrated by figures the most original and expressive.

'As we were walking the other day, she said she had often thought what a beautiful world this would be, when we should see every thing right side up. Now, we see every thing topsy-turvy, and all is confusion.' For a person who knows nothing of this fact in the science of optics, this seemed quite a remarkable idea.

'We also loved her for her sincere and ardent piety, her unwavering faith in God, and her contempt of what the world calls fashion, and what we call folly.

'She was in search of a quiet place, where a way-worn traveller might rest. She had heard of Fruitlands, and was inclined to go there; but the friends she found here thought it best for her to visit Northampton. She passed her time, while with us, working wherever her work was needed, and talking where work was not needed.

'She would not receive money for her work, saying she worked for the Lord; and if her wants were supplied, she received it as from the Lord.

'She remained with us till far into winter, when we introduced her at the Northampton Association.' . . . . 'She wrote to me from thence, that she had found the quiet resting place she had so long desired. And she has remained there ever since.'

# ANOTHER CAMP MEETING.

When Sojourner had been at Northampton a few months, she attended another camp-meeting, at which she performed a very important part.

A party of wild young men, with no motive but that of entertaining themselves by annoying and injuring the feelings of others, had assembled at the meeting, hooting and yelling, and in various ways interrupting the services, and causing much disturbance. Those who had the charge of the meeting, having tried their persuasive powers in vain, grew impatient and tried threatening.

The young men, considering themselves insulted, collected their friends, to the number of a hundred or more, dispersed themselves through the grounds, making the most frightful noises, and threatening to fire the tents. It was said the authorities of the meeting sat in grave consultation, decided to have the ring-leaders arrested, and sent for the constable, to the great displeasure of some of the company, who were opposed to such an appeal to force and arms. Be that as it may, Sojourner, seeing great consternation depicted in every countenance, caught the contagion, and, ere she was aware, found herself quaking with fear.

Under the impulse of this sudden emotion, she fled to the most retired corner of a tent, and secreted herself behind a trunk. saying to herself, 'I am the only colored person here, and on me, probably, their wicked mischief will fall first, and perhaps fatally.' But feeling how great was her insecurity even there, as the very tent began to shake from its foundations, she began to soliloquise as follows:-

'Shall I run away and hide from the Devil? Me, a servant of the living God? Have I not faith enough to go out and quell that mob, when I know it is written- "One shall chase a thousand, and two put ten thousand to flight"? I know there are not a thousand here; and I know I am a servant of the living God. I'll go to the rescue, and the Lord shall go with and protect me.

'Oh,' said she, 'I felt as if I had three hearts! and that they were so large, my body could hardly hold them!'

She now came forth from her hiding-place, and invited several to go with her and see what they could do to still the raging of the moral elements. They declined, and considered her wild to think of it.

The meeting was in the open fields-the full moon shed its saddened light over all-and the woman who was that evening to address them was trembling on the preachers' stand. The noise and confusion were now terrific. Sojourner left the tent alone and unaided, and walking some thirty rods to the top of a small rise of ground, commenced to sing, in her most fervid manner, with all the strength of her most powerful voice, the hymn on the resurrection of Christ-

> It was early in the morning-it was early in the morning,
> > Just at the break of day-
>
> When he rose-when he rose-when he rose,
> > And went to heaven on a cloud.'

All who have ever heard her sing this hymn will probably remember it as long as they remember her. The hymn, the tune, the style, are each too closely associated with to be easily separated from herself, and when sung in one of her most animated moods, in the open air, with the utmost strength of her most powerful voice, must have been truly thrilling.

As she commenced to sing, the young men made a rush towards her, and she was immediately encircled by a dense body of the rioters, many of them armed with sticks or clubs as their weapons of defence, if not of attack. As the circle narrowed around her, she ceased singing, and after a short pause, inquired, in a gentle but firm tone, 'Why do you come about me with clubs and sticks? I am not doing harm to any one.' 'We ar'n't a going to hurt you, old woman; we came to hear you sing,' cried many voices, simultaneously. 'Sing to us, old woman,' cries one. 'Talk to us, old woman,' says another. 'Pray, old woman,' says a third. 'Tell us your experience,' says a fourth. 'You stand and smoke so near me, I cannot sing or talk,' she answered.

'Stand back,' said several authoritative voices, with not the most gentle or courteous accompaniments, raising their rude weapons in the air. The crowd suddenly gave back, the circle became larger, as many voices again called for singing, talking, or praying, backed by assurances that no one should be allowed to hurt her-the speakers declaring with an oath, that they would 'knock down ' any person who should offer her the least indignity.

She looked about her, and with her usual discrimination, said inwardly- 'Here must be many young men in all this assemblage, bearing within them hearts susceptible of good impressions. I will speak to them.' She did speak; they silently heard, and civilly asked her many questions. It seemed to her to be given her at the time to answer them with truth and wisdom beyond herself. Her speech had operated on the roused passions of the mob like oil on agitated waters; they were, as a whole, entirely subdued, and only clamored when she ceased to speak or sing. Those who stood in the back ground, after the circle was enlarged, cried out, 'Sing aloud, old woman, we can't hear.' Those who held the sceptre of power among them requested that she should make a pulpit of a neighboring wagon. She said, 'If I do, they'll overthrow it.' 'No, they sha'n't-he who dares hurt you, we'll knock him down instantly, d-n him,' cried the chiefs. 'No we won't, no we won't, nobody shall hurt you,' answered the many voices of the mob. They kindly assisted her to mount the wagon, from which she spoke and sung to them about an hour. Of all she said to them on the occasion, she remembers only the following:-

'Well, there are two congregations on this ground. It is written that there shall be a separation, and the sheep shall be separated from the goats. The other preachers have the sheep, I have the goats. And I have a few sheep among my goats, but they are very ragged.' This exordium produced great laughter. When she became wearied with talking, she began to cast about her to contrive some way to induce them to disperse. While she paused, they loudly clamored for 'more,' 'more,'-'sing,' 'sing more.' She motioned them to be quiet, and called out to them: 'Children, I have talked and sung to you, as you asked me; and now I have a request to make of you; will you grant it?' 'Yes, yes, yes,' resounded from every quarter. 'Well, it is this,' she answered; 'if I will sing one more hymn for you, will you then go away, and leave us this night in peace?' 'Yes, yes,' came faintly, feebly from a few. 'I repeat it,' says Sojourner, 'and I want an answer from you all, as of one accord. If I will sing you one more, will you go away, and leave us this night in peace?' 'Yes, yes, yes,' shouted many voices, with hearty emphasis. 'I repeat my request once more,' said she, 'and I want you all to answer.' And she reiterated the words again. This time a long, loud 'Yes-yes-yes,' came up, as from the multitudinous mouth of the entire mob. 'AMEN! it is SEALED,' repeated Sojourner, in the deepest and most solemn tones of her powerful and sonorous voice. Its effect ran through the multitude, like an electric shock; and the most of them considered themselves bound by their promise, as they might have failed to do under less imposing circumstances. Some of them began instantly to leave; others said, 'Are we not to have one more hymn?' 'Yes,' answered their entertainer, and she commenced to sing:

> 'I bless the Lord I've got my seal-to-day and to-day-
> To slay Goliath in the field-to-day and to-day;
> The good old way is a righteous way,
> I mean to take the kingdom in the good old way.'

While singing, she heard some enforcing obedience to their promise, while a few seemed refusing to abide by it. But before she had quite concluded, she saw them turn from her, and in the course of a few minutes, they were running as fast as they well could in a solid body; and she says she can compare them to nothing but a swarm of bees, so dense was their phalanx, so straight their course, so hurried their march. As they passed with a rush very near the stand of the other preachers, the hearts of the people were smitten with fear, thinking that their entertainer had failed to enchain them longer with her spell, and that they were coming upon them with redoubled and remorseless fury. But they found they were mistaken, and that their fears were groundless; for, before they could well recover from their surprise, every rioter was gone, and not one was left on the grounds, or seen there again during the meeting. Sojourner was informed that as her audience reached the main road, some distance from the tents, a few of the rebellious spirits refused to go on, and proposed returning; but their leaders said, 'No-we have promised to leave-all promised, and we must go, all go, and you shall none of you return again.'

She did not fall in love at first sight with the Northampton Association, for she arrived there at a time when appearances did not correspond with the ideas of associationists, as they had been spread out in their writings; for their phalanx was a factory, and they were wanting in means to carry out their ideas of beauty and elegance, as they would have done in different circumstances. But she thought she would make an effort to tarry with them one night, though that seemed to her no desirable affair. But as soon as she saw that accomplished, literary, and refined persons were living in that plain and simple manner, and submitting to the labors and privations incident to such an infant institution, she said, 'Well, if these can live here, I can.' Afterwards, she gradually became pleased with, and attached to, the place and the people, as well she might; for it must have been no small thing to have found a home in a 'Community composed of some of the choicest spirits of the age,' where all was characterized by an equality of feeling, a liberty of thought and speech, and a largeness of soul, she could not have before met with, to the same extent, in any of her wanderings.

Our first knowledge of her was derived from a friend who had resided for a time in the 'Community,' and who, after describing her, and singing one of her hymns, wished that we might see her. But we little thought, at that time, that we should ever pen these 'simple annals' of this child of nature.

When we first saw her, she was working with a hearty good will; saying she would not be induced to take regular wages, believing, as once before, that now Providence had provided her with a never-failing fount, from which her every want might be perpetually supplied through her mortal life. In this, she had calculated too fast. For the Associationists found, that, taking every thing into consideration, they would find it most expedient to act individually; and again, the subject of this sketch found her dreams unreal, and herself flung back upon her own resources for the supply of her needs. This she might have found more inconvenient at her time of life-for labor, exposure, and hardship had made sad inroads upon her iron constitution, by inducing chronic disease and premature old age-had she not remained under the shadow of one,* who never wearies in doing good, giving to the needy, and supplying the wants of the destitute. She has now set her heart upon having a little home of her own, even at this late hour of life, where she may feel a greater freedom than she can in the house of another, and where she can repose a little, after her day of action has passed by. And for such a 'home' she is now dependant on the charities of the benevolent, and to them we appeal with confidence.

Through all the scenes of her eventful life may be traced the energy of a naturally powerful mind-the fearlessness and child-like simplicity of one untrammelled by education or conventional customs-purity of character-an unflinching adherence to principle-and a native enthusiasm, which, under different circumstances, might easily have produced another Joan of Arc.

With all her fervor, and enthusiasm, and speculation, her religion is not tinctured in the least with gloom. No doubt, no hesitation, no despondency, spreads a cloud over her soul; but all is bright, clear, positive, and at times ecstatic. Her trust is in God, and from him she looks for good, and not evil. She feels that 'perfect love casteth out fear.'

Having more than once found herself awaking from a mortifying delusion,- as in the case of the Sing-Sing kingdom,-and resolving not to be thus deluded again, she has set suspicion to guard the door of her heart, and allows it perhaps to be aroused by too slight causes, on certain subjects-her vivid imagination assisting to magnify the phantoms of her fears into gigantic proportions, much beyond their real size; instead of resolutely adhering to the rule we all like best, when it is to be applied to ourselves-that of placing every thing we see to the account of the best possible motive, until time and circumstance prove that we were wrong. Where no good motive can be assigned, it may become our duty to suspend our judgment till evidence can be had.

In the application of this rule, it is an undoubted duty to exercise a commendable prudence, by refusing to repose any important trust to the keeping of persons who may be strangers to us, and whose trustworthiness we have never seen tried. But no possible good, but incalculable evil may and does arise from the too common practice of placing all conduct, the source of which we do not fully understand, to the worst of intentions. How often is the gentle, timid soul discouraged, and driven perhaps to despondency, by finding its 'good evil spoken of;' and a well-meant but mistaken action loaded with an evil design!

If the world would but sedulously set about reforming itself on this one point, who can calculate the change it would produce-the evil it would annihilate, and the happiness it would confer! None but an all-seeing eye could at once embrace so vast a result. A result, how desirable! and one that can be brought about only by the most simple process-that of every individual seeing to it that he commit not this sin himself. For why should we allow in ourselves, the very fault we most dislike, when committed against us? Shall we not at least aim at consistency?

Had she possessed less generous self-sacrifice, more knowledge of the world and of business matters in general, and had she failed to take it for granted that others were like herself, and would, when her turn came to need, do as she had done, and find it 'more blessed to give than to receive,' she might have laid by something for the future. For few, perhaps, have ever possessed the power and inclination, in the same degree, at one and the same time, to labor as she has done, both day and night, for so long a period of time. And had these energies been well-directed, and the proceeds well husbanded, since she has been her own mistress, they would have given her an independence during her natural life. But her constitutional biases, and her early training, or rather want of training, prevented this result; and it is too late now to remedy the great mistake. Shall she then be left to want? Who will not answer. 'No!'

Note:
* GEORGE W. BENSON.

# HER LAST INTERVIEW WITH HER MASTER.

In the spring of 1849, Sojourner made a visit to her eldest daughter, Diana, who has ever suffered from ill health, and remained with Mr. Dumont, Isabella's humane master. She found him still living, though advanced in age, and reduced in property, (as he had been for a number of years,) but greatly enlightened on the subject of slavery. He said he could then see that 'slavery was the wickedest thing in the world, the greatest curse the earth had ever felt-that it was then very clear to his mind that it was so, though, while he was a slaveholder himself, he did not see it so, and thought it was as right as holding any other property.' Sojourner remarked to him, that it might be the same with those who are now slaveholders. 'O, no,' replied he, with warmth, 'it cannot be. For, now, the sin of slavery is so clearly written out, and so much talked against,-(why, the whole world cries out against it!)-that if any one says he don't know, and has not heard, he must, I think, be a liar. In my slaveholding days, there were few that spoke against it, and these few made little impression on any one. Had it been as it is now, think you I could have held slaves? No! I should not have dared to do it, but should have emancipated every one of them. Now, it is very different; all may hear if they will.'

Yes, reader, if any one feels that the tocsin of alarm, or the anti-slavery trump, must sound a louder note before they can hear it, one would think they must be very hard of hearing,-yea, that they belong to that class, of whom it may be truly said, 'they have stopped their ears that they may not hear.'

She received a letter from her daughter Diana, dated Hyde Park, December 19, 1849, which informed her that Mr. Dumont had 'gone West' with some of his sons-that he had taken along with him, probably through mistake, the few articles of furniture she had left with him. 'Never mind,' says Sojourner, 'what we give to the poor, we lend to the Lord.' She thanked the Lord with fervor, that she had lived to hear her master say such blessed things! She recalled the lectures he used to give his slaves, on speaking the truth and being honest, and laughing, she says he taught us not to lie and steal, when he was stealing all the time himself, and did not know it! Oh! how sweet to my mind was this confession! And what a confession for a master to make to a slave! A slaveholding master turned to a brother! Poor old man, may the Lord bless him, and all slave-holders partake of his spirit!

# CERTIFICATES OF CHARACTER.

HURLEY, ULSTER Co., Oct. 13th, 1834

This is to certify, that I am well acquainted with Isabella, this colored woman; I have been acquainted with her from her infancy; she has been in my employ for one year, and she was a faithful servant, honest, and industrious; and have always known her to be in good report by all who employed her.

ISAAC S. VAN WAGENEN

NEW PALTZ, ULSTER Co., Oct. 13th, 1834

This is to certify, that Isabella, this colored woman, lived with me since the year 1810, and that she has always been a good and faithful servant; and the eighteen years that she was with me, I always found her to be perfectly honest. I have always heard her well spoken of by every one that has employed her.

JOHN J. DUMONT

NORTHAMPTON, March 1850

We, the undersigned having known Isabella (or Sojourner Truth) for several years, most cheerfully bear testimony to her uniform good character, her untiring industry, kind deportment, unwearied benevolence, and the many social and excellent traits which make her worthy to bear her adopted name.

GEO. W. BENSON S. L. HILL A. W. THAYER
BOSTON, March, 1850

My acquaintance with the subject of the accompanying Narrative, Sojourner Truth, for several years past, has led me to form a very high appreciation of her understanding, moral integrity, disinterested kindness, and religious sincerity and enlightenment. Any assistance or co-operation that she may receive in the sale of her Narrative, or in any other manner, I am sure will be meritoriously bestowed.

WM. LLOYD GARRISON

# "AIN'T I A WOMAN?" SPEECH

On May 29, 1851, Sojourner Truth gave an extemporaneous speech called "Ain't I A Woman?" at a Women's Convention in Akron, Ohio. There are two different versions of it, from two different people who heard her give the speech.

Marius Robinson's Version of Sojourner Truth's Speech, "Ain't I A Woman?" was published in an issue of *Anti-Slavery Bugle* on June 21, 1851:

"One of the most unique and interesting speeches of the convention was made by Sojourner Truth, an emancipated slave. It is impossible to transfer it to paper, or convey any adequate idea of the effect it produced upon the audience. Those only can appreciate it who saw her powerful form, her whole-souled, earnest gesture, and listened to her strong and truthful tones. She came forward to the platform and addressing the President said with great simplicity: "May I say a few words?" Receiving an affirmative answer, she proceeded:

"I want to say a few words about this matter. I am a woman's rights. I have as much muscle as any man, and can do as much work as any man. I have plowed and reaped and husked and chopped and mowed, and can any man do more than that? I have heard much about the sexes being equal. I can carry as much as any man, and can eat as much too, if I can get it. I am as strong as any man that is now. As for intellect, all I can say is, if a woman have a pint, and a man a quart – why can't she have her little pint full? You need not be afraid to give us our rights for fear we will take too much, – for we can't take more than our pint'll hold. The poor men seems to be all in confusion, and don't know what to do. Why children, if you have woman's rights, give it to her and you will feel better. You will have your own rights, and they won't be so much trouble. I can't read, but I can hear. I have heard the Bible and have learned that Eve caused man to sin. Well, if woman upset the world, do give her a chance to set it right side up again. The Lady has spoken about Jesus, how he never spurned woman from him, and she was right. When Lazarus died, Mary and Martha came to him with faith and love and besought him to raise their brother. And Jesus wept and Lazarus came forth. And how came Jesus into the world? Through God who created him and the woman who bore him. Man, where was your part? But the women are coming up blessed be God and a few of the men are coming up with them. But man is in a tight place, the poor slave is on him, woman is coming on him, he is surely between a hawk and a buzzard."

Frances Dana Barker Gage's Version of Sojourner Truth's Speech, "Ain't I A Woman?" was from a recollection by Gage in 1863 in *History of Woman Suffrage*:

"The leaders of the movement trembled on seeing a tall, gaunt black woman in a gray dress and white turban, surmounted with an uncouth sunbonnet, march deliberately into the church, walk with the air of a queen up the aisle, and take her seat upon the pulpit steps. A buzz of disapprobation was heard all over the house, and there fell on the listening ear, 'An abolition affair!" "Woman's rights and niggers!" "I told you so!" "Go it, darkey!" . . Again and again, timorous and trembling ones came to me and said, with earnestness, "Don't let her speak, Mrs. Gage, it will ruin us. Every newspaper in the land will have our cause mixed up with abolition and niggers, and we shall be utterly denounced." My only answer was, "We shall see when the time comes."

"The second day the work waxed warm. Methodist, Baptist, Episcopal, Presbyterian, and Universalist minister came in to hear and discuss the resolutions presented. One claimed superior rights and privileges for man, on the ground of "superior intellect"; another, because of the "manhood of Christ; if God had desired the equality of woman, He would have given some token of His will through the birth, life, and death of the Saviour." Another gave us a theological view of the "sin of our first mother."

"There were very few women in those days who dared to "speak in meeting"; and the august teachers of the people were seemingly getting the better of us, while the boys in the galleries, and the sneerers among the pews, were hugely enjoying the discomfiture as they supposed, of the "strong-minded." Some of the tender-skinned friends were on the point of losing dignity, and the atmosphere betokened a storm. When, slowly from her seat in the corner rose Sojourner Truth, who, till now, had scarcely lifted her head. "Don't let her speak!" gasped half a dozen in my ear. She moved slowly and solemnly to the front, laid her old bonnet at her feet, and turned her great speaking eyes to me. There was a hissing sound of disapprobation above and below. I rose and announced, "Sojourner Truth," and begged the audience to keep silence for a few moments.

"The tumult subsided at once, and every eye was fixed on this almost Amazon form, which stood nearly six feet high, head erect, and eyes piercing the upper air like one in a dream.

"At her first word there was a profound hush. She spoke in deep tones, which, though not loud, reached every ear in the house, and away through the throng at the doors and windows.

"'Wall, chilern, whar dar is so much racket dar must be somethin' out o' kilter. I tink dat 'twixt de niggers of de Souf and de womin at de Norf, all talkin' 'bout rights, de white men will be in a fix pretty soon. But what's all dis here talkin' 'bout?

"'Dat man ober dar say dat womin needs to be helped into carriages, and lifted ober ditches, and to hab de best place everywhar. Nobody eber helps me into carriages, or ober mud-puddles, or gibs me any best place!" And raising herself to her full height, and her voice to a pitch like rolling thunder, she asked. "And a'n't I a woman? Look at me! Look at my arm! (and she bared her right arm to the shoulder, showing her tremendous muscular power). I have ploughed, and planted, and gathered into barns, and no man could head me! And a'n't I a woman? I could work as much and eat as much as a man—when I could get it—and bear de lash as well! And a'n't, I a woman? I have borne thirteen chilern, and seen 'em mos' all sold off to slavery, and when I cried out with my mother's grief, none but Jesus heard me! And a'n't I a woman?

"'Den dey talks 'bout dis ting in de head; what dis dey call it?" ("Intellect," whispered some one near.) "Dat's it, honey. What's dat got to do wid womin's rights or nigger's rights? If my cup won't hold but a pint, and yourn holds a quart, wouldn't ye be mean not to let me have my little half-measure full?" And she pointed her significant finger, and sent a keen glance at the minister who had made the argument. The cheering was long and loud.

"'Den dat little man in black dar, he say women can't have as much rights as men, 'cause Christ wan't a woman! Whar did your Christ come from?" Rolling thunder couldn't have stilled that crowd, as did those deep, wonderful tones, as she stood there with outstretched arms and eyes of fire. Raising her voice still louder, she repeated, "Whar did your Christ come from? From God and a woman! Man had nothin' to do wid Him." Oh, what a rebuke that was to that little man.

"Turning again to another objector, she took up the defense of Mother Eve. I can not follow her through it all. It was pointed, and witty, and solemn; eliciting at almost every sentence deafening applause; and she ended by asserting: "If de fust woman God ever made was strong enough to turn de world upside down all alone, dese women togedder (and she glanced her eye over the platform) ought to be able to turn it back, and get it right side up again! And now dey is asking to do it, de men better let 'em." Long-continued cheering greeted this. "'Bleeged to ye for hearin' on me, and now ole Sojourner han't got nothin' more to say."

"Amid roars of applause, she returned to her corner, leaving more than one of us with streaming eyes, and hearts beating with gratitude. She had taken us up in her strong arms and carried us safely over the slough of difficulty turning the whole tide in our favor. I have never in my life seen anything like the magical influence that subdued the mobbish spirit of the day, and turned the sneers and jeers of an excited crowd into notes of respect and admiration. Hundreds rushed up to shake hands with her, and congratulate the glorious old mother, and bid her God-speed on her mission of 'testifyin' agin concerning the wickedness of this 'ere people.'"

# INCIDENTS IN THE LIFE OF A SLAVE GIRL, Written by Herself.

## By Harriet A. Jacobs

"Northerners know nothing at all about Slavery. They think it is perpetual bondage only. They have no conception of the depth of degradation involved in that word, SLAVERY; if they had, they would never cease their efforts until so horrible a system was overthrown."
- A Woman Of North Carolina.

"Rise up, ye women that are at ease! Hear my voice, ye careless daughters! Give ear unto my speech."   - Isaiah 32:9.

Edited By L. Maria Child.
Boston: Published For The Author.

1861.

# CONTENTS

| | |
|---|---|
| PREFACE BY THE AUTHOR | 99 |
| INTRODUCTION BY THE EDITOR | 100 |
| BIOGRAPHY of Harriet Ann Jacobs | 101 |
| PICTURE of Harriet Ann Jacobs | 103 |
| I. Childhood | 104 |
| II. The New Master And Mistress. | 107 |
| III. The Slaves' New Year's Day. | 112 |
| IV. The Slave Who Dared To Feel Like A Man. | 114 |
| V. The Trials Of Girlhood. | 123 |
| VI. The Jealous Mistress. | 126 |
| VII. The Lover. | 131 |
| VIII. What Slaves Are Taught To Think Of The North. | 137 |
| IX. Sketches Of Neighboring Slaveholders. | 139 |
| X. A Perilous Passage In The Slave Girl's Life. | 145 |
| XI. The New Tie To Life. | 150 |
| XII. Fear Of Insurrection. | 154 |
| XIII. The Church And Slavery. | 159 |
| XIV. Another Link To Life. | 166 |
| XV. Continued Persecutions. | 169 |
| XVI. Scenes At The Plantation. | 174 |
| XVII. The Flight. | 182 |
| XVIII. Months Of Peril. | 185 |
| XIX. The Children Sold. | 191 |
| XX. New Perils. | 195 |
| XXI. The Loophole Of Retreat. | 199 |
| XXII. Christmas Festivities. | 202 |
| XXIII. Still In Prison. | 204 |
| XXIV. The Candidate For Congress. | 207 |
| XXV. Competition In Cunning. | 209 |
| XXVI. Important Era In My Brother's Life. | 213 |
| XXVII. New Destination For The Children. | 217 |
| XXVIII. Aunt Nancy. | 223 |
| XXIX. Preparations For Escape. | 227 |
| XXX. Northward Bound. | 234 |
| XXXI. Incidents In Philadelphia. | 237 |
| XXXII. The Meeting Of Mother And Daughter. | 241 |
| XXXIII. A Home Found. | 244 |
| XXXIV. The Old Enemy Again. | 247 |

| | |
|---|---|
| XXXV. Prejudice Against Color. | 251 |
| XXXVI. The Hairbreadth Escape. | 253 |
| XXXVII. A Visit To England | 257 |
| XXXVIII. Renewed Invitations To Go South. | 260 |
| XXXIX. The Confession. | 262 |
| XL. The Fugitive Slave Law. | 264 |
| XLI. Free At Last. | 269 |
| APPENDIX. | 275 |

# PREFACE BY THE AUTHOR

Reader be assured this narrative is no fiction. I am aware that some of my adventures may seem incredible; but they are, nevertheless, strictly true. I have not exaggerated the wrongs inflicted by Slavery; on the contrary, my descriptions fall far short of the facts. I have concealed the names of places, and given persons fictitious names. I had no motive for secrecy on my own account, but I deemed it kind and considerate towards others to pursue this course.

I wish I were more competent to the task I have undertaken. But I trust my readers will excuse deficiencies in consideration of circumstances. I was born and reared in Slavery; and I remained in a Slave State twenty-seven years. Since I have been at the North, it has been necessary for me to work diligently for my own support, and the education of my children. This has not left me much leisure to make up for the loss of early opportunities to improve myself; and it has compelled me to write these pages at irregular intervals, whenever I could snatch an hour from household duties.

When I first arrived in Philadelphia, Bishop Paine advised me to publish a sketch of my life, but I told him I was altogether incompetent to such an undertaking. Though I have improved my mind somewhat since that time, I still remain of the same opinion; but I trust my motives will excuse what might otherwise seem presumptuous. I have not written my experiences in order to attract attention to myself; on the contrary, it would have been more pleasant to me to have been silent about my own history. Neither do I care to excite sympathy for my own sufferings. But I do earnestly desire to arouse the women of the North to a realizing sense of the condition of two millions of women at the South, still in bondage, suffering what I suffered, and most of them far worse. I want to add my testimony to that of abler pens to convince the people of the Free States what Slavery really is. Only by experience can any one realize how deep, and dark, and foul is that pit of abominations. May the blessing of God rest on this imperfect effort in behalf of my persecuted people!

—Linda Brent

# INTRODUCTION BY THE EDITOR

The author of the following autobiography is personally known to me, and her conversation and manners inspire me with confidence. During the last seventeen years, she has lived the greater part of the time with a distinguished family in New York, and has so deported herself as to be highly esteemed by them. This fact is sufficient, without further credentials of her character. I believe those who know her will not be disposed to doubt her veracity, though some incidents in her story are more romantic than fiction.

At her request, I have revised her manuscript; but such changes as I have made have been mainly for purposes of condensation and orderly arrangement. I have not added any thing to the incidents, or changed the import of her very pertinent remarks. With trifling exceptions, both the ideas and the language are her own. I pruned excrescences a little, but otherwise I had no reason for changing her lively and dramatic way of telling her own story. The names of both persons and places are known to me; but for good reasons I suppress them.

It will naturally excite surprise that a woman reared in Slavery should be able to write so well. But circumstances will explain this. In the first place, nature endowed her with quick perceptions. Secondly, the mistress, with whom she lived till she was twelve years old, was a kind, considerate friend, who taught her to read and spell. Thirdly, she was placed in favorable circumstances after she came to the North; having frequent intercourse with intelligent persons, who felt a friendly interest in her welfare, and were disposed to give her opportunities for self-improvement.

I am well aware that many will accuse me of indecorum for presenting these pages to the public; for the experiences of this intelligent and much-injured woman belong to a class which some call delicate subjects, and others indelicate. This peculiar phase of Slavery has generally been kept veiled; but the public ought to be made acquainted with its monstrous features, and I willingly take the responsibility of presenting them with the veil withdrawn. I do this for the sake of my sisters in bondage, who are suffering wrongs so foul, that our ears are too delicate to listen to them. I do it with the hope of arousing conscientious and reflecting women at the North to a sense of their duty in the exertion of moral influence on the question of Slavery, on all possible occasions. I do it with the hope that every man who reads this narrative will swear solemnly before God that, so far as he has power to prevent it, no fugitive from Slavery shall ever be sent back to suffer in that loathsome den of corruption and cruelty.    —L. Maria Child

# BIOGRAPHY OF HARRIET A. JACOBS

Harriet Jacobs was born in 1813, in Edenton, North Carolina. She was born into slavery to her father, Elijah Jacobs and her mother, Delilah Horniblow.

Harriet's mother died when she six years old and she lived with her mother's mistress, Margaret Horniblow. Margaret taught Harriet to read, write and sew. When Harriet was 11, Margaret died, and Dr. James Norcom became her new master.

Although Jacobs was still a child, Norcom sexually harassed her. When she asked permission to marry a free black slave, Norcom refused to allow it. To get away from Norcom's sexual advances, she began a consensual sexual relationship with an unmarried, white lawyer named Samuel Sawyer. He was kind and caring to Jacobs. Harriet gave birth to two children with Sawyer, Joseph and Louisa.

Norcom continued to pursue her and when Jacobs learned that he was going to force her children to work as plantation slaves, she ran away in 1835. For 7 years, she hid in her grandmother's attic, and during that time, wrote letters to Norcom to confuse him on her whereabouts. Also, during that time, Sawyer was elected as a member of the United States House of Representatives and had also purchased their children. While Jacobs hid in her grandmother's attic, her children also lived with her grandmother, and she was able to watch and listen to her children from the attic.

In 1842, Jacobs made her escape north. With the help of anti-slavery friends, she was able to make it to New York and find work as a house maid in 1845 for Mary Stace Willis. She was able to be reunited with her daughter, Louisa, who had also been sent north by Sawyer to work as a house servant. Soon after, she was reunited with her brother, John, who was a fugitive slave.

She continued to work for the Willis family after her mistress died. She accompanied Mr. Willis and his daughter to England, where she wrote that there was no prejudice against people of color. A short while later, after their return to the United States, Jacobs left her employment with the family and moved to Boston to be closer to her son, daughter and brother. Her brother was very active in the anti-slavery movement.

After her brother opened an anti-slavery reading room, Jacobs became involved with it and soon joined the American Anti-Slavery Society. She helped to support the anti-slavery reading room by giving speeches and collecting donations to help support the movement.

In 1850, The Fugitive Slave Act of 1850 was passed, and the Jacobs family feared for the freedom and safety. Harriet Jacob;s brother, John, fled to

California, where he found work in the gold mines of the Gold Rush, and her son, Joseph Jacobs joined his uncle there a few years later.

Meanwhile, in an act of immeasurable kindness, and without the knowledge of Harriet Jacobs, the second wife of Mr, Willis, Cornelia Grinnell Willis paid $300 to purchase Harriet Jacobs and then gave Jacobs her freedom.

Jacobs wrote Incidents in the Life of A Slave Girl after a friend of hers, Amy Post, convinced her to do so. It was published in 1861 under the pseudonym Linda Brent. She also changed names in her book, so people wouldn't be recognized. Mr Norcom is known as Mr Flint. Jacobs was the first woman in the United States to write a fugitive slave autobiography.

After Jacobs published her book, she devoted her time to helping former slaves who were refugees of the Civil War. She supported her daughter as she worked to educate African Americans. In 1970, Harriet Jacobs ran a boarding house with Louisa in Cambridge, Massachusetts. In her later years, she lived with her daughter Louisa in Washington D.C., where she died March 7, 1887.

# Harriet Ann Jacobs

# I. CHILDHOOD

I was born a slave; but I never knew it till six years of happy childhood had passed away. My father was a carpenter, and considered so intelligent and skilful in his trade, that, when buildings out of the common line were to be erected, he was sent for from long distances, to be head workman. On condition of paying his mistress two hundred dollars a year, and supporting himself, he was allowed to work at his trade, and manage his own affairs. His strongest wish was to purchase his children; but, though he several times offered his hard earnings for that purpose, he never succeeded. In complexion my parents were a light shade of brownish yellow, and were termed mulattoes. They lived together in a comfortable home; and, though we were all slaves, I was so fondly shielded that I never dreamed I was a piece of merchandise, trusted to them for safe keeping, and liable to be demanded of them at any moment. I had one brother, William, who was two years younger than myself—a bright, affectionate child. I had also a great treasure in my maternal grandmother, who was a remarkable woman in many respects. She was the daughter of a planter in South Carolina, who, at his death, left her mother and his three children free, with money to go to St. Augustine, where they had relatives. It was during the Revolutionary War; and they were captured on their passage, carried back, and sold to different purchasers. Such was the story my grandmother used to tell me; but I do not remember all the particulars. She was a little girl when she was captured and sold to the keeper of a large hotel. I have often heard her tell how hard she fared during childhood. But as she grew older she evinced so much intelligence, and was so faithful, that her master and mistress could not help seeing it was for their interest to take care of such a valuable piece of property. She became an indispensable personage in the household, officiating in all capacities, from cook and wet nurse to seamstress. She was much praised for her cooking; and her nice crackers became so famous in the neighborhood that many people were desirous of obtaining them. In consequence of numerous requests of this kind, she asked permission of her mistress to bake crackers at night, after all the household work was done; and she obtained leave to do it, provided she would clothe herself and her children from the profits. Upon these terms, after working hard all day for her mistress, she began her midnight bakings, assisted by her two oldest children. The business proved profitable; and each year she laid by a little, which was saved for a fund to purchase her children. Her master died, and the property was divided among his heirs. The widow had her dower in the hotel which she continued to keep open. My grandmother remained in her service as a slave; but her children were divided among her master's children. As she had five, Benjamin, the youngest one, was sold, in order that each heir might have an equal portion of dollars and cents. There was so little difference in our ages that he seemed more like my brother than my uncle. He was a bright, handsome lad, nearly white; for he inherited the complexion my grandmother had derived from Anglo-Saxon ancestors. Though only ten years old, seven hundred and twenty dollars were paid for him. His sale was a terrible blow to my grandmother, but she was naturally hopeful, and she went to work with renewed energy, trusting in time to be able to purchase some of her children. She had laid up three hundred dollars, which her mistress one day begged as a loan, promising to pay her soon. The reader probably knows that no promise or writing given to a slave is legally binding; for, according to Southern laws, a slave, being property, can hold no property. When my grandmother lent her hard earnings to her mistress, she trusted solely to her honor. The honor of a slaveholder to a slave!

To this good grandmother I was indebted for many comforts. My brother Willie and I often received portions of the crackers, cakes, and preserves, she made to sell; and after we ceased to be children we were indebted to her for many more important services.

Such were the unusually fortunate circumstances of my early childhood. When I was six years old, my mother died; and then, for the first time, I learned, by the talk around me, that I was a slave. My mother's mistress was the daughter of my grandmother's mistress. She was the foster sister of my mother; they were both nourished at my grandmother's breast. In fact, my mother had been weaned at three months old, that the babe of the mistress might obtain sufficient food. They played together as children; and, when they became women, my mother was a most faithful servant to her whiter foster sister. On her death-bed her mistress promised that her children should never suffer for any thing; and during her lifetime she kept her word. They all spoke kindly of my dead mother, who had been a slave merely in name, but in nature was noble and womanly. I grieved for her, and my young mind was troubled with the thought who would now take care of me and my little brother. I was told that my home was now to be with her mistress; and I found it a happy one. No toilsome or disagreeable duties were imposed on me. My mistress was so kind to me that I was always glad to do her bidding, and proud to labor for her as much as my young years would permit. I would sit by her side for hours, sewing diligently, with a heart as free from care as that of any free-born white child. When she thought I was tired, she would send me out to run and jump; and away I bounded, to gather berries or flowers to decorate her room. Those were happy days—too happy to last. The slave child had no thought for the morrow; but there came that blight, which too surely waits on every human being born to be a chattel.

When I was nearly twelve years old, my kind mistress sickened and died. As I saw the cheek grow paler, and the eye more glassy, how earnestly I prayed in my heart that she might live! I loved her; for she had been almost like a mother to me. My prayers were not answered. She died, and they buried her in the little churchyard, where, day after day, my tears fell upon her grave.

I was sent to spend a week with my grandmother. I was now old enough to begin to think of the future; and again and again I asked myself what they would do with me. I felt sure I should never find another mistress so kind as the one who was gone. She had promised my dying mother that her children should never suffer for any thing; and when I remembered that, and recalled her many proofs of attachment to me, I could not help having some hopes that she had left me free. My friends were almost certain it would be so. They thought she would be sure to do it, on account of my mother's love and faithful service. But, alas! we all know that the memory of a faithful slave does not avail much to save her children from the auction block.

After a brief period of suspense, the will of my mistress was read, and we learned that she had bequeathed me to her sister's daughter, a child of five years old. So vanished our hopes. My mistress had taught me the precepts of God's Word: "Thou shalt love thy neighbor as thyself." "Whatsoever ye would that men should do unto you, do ye even so unto them." But I was her slave, and I suppose she did not recognize me as her neighbor. I would give much to blot out from my memory that one great wrong. As a child, I loved my mistress; and, looking back on the happy days I spent with her, I try to think with less bitterness of this act of injustice. While I was with her, she taught me to read and spell; and for this privilege, which so rarely falls to the lot of a slave, I bless her memory.

She possessed but few slaves; and at her death those were all distributed among her relatives. Five of them were my grandmother's children, and had shared the same milk that nourished her mother's children. Notwithstanding my grandmother's long and faithful service to her owners, not one of her children escaped the auction block. These God-breathing machines are no more, in the sight of their masters, than the cotton they plant, or the horses they tend.

# II. THE NEW MASTER AND MISTRESS.

Dr. Flint, a physician in the neighborhood, had married the sister of my mistress, and I was now the property of their little daughter. It was not without murmuring that I prepared for my new home; and what added to my unhappiness, was the fact that my brother William was purchased by the same family. My father, by his nature, as well as by the habit of transacting business as a skillful mechanic, had more of the feelings of a freeman than is common among slaves. My brother was a spirited boy; and being brought up under such influences, he daily detested the name of master and mistress. One day, when his father and his mistress both happened to call him at the same time, he hesitated between the two; being perplexed to know which had the strongest claim upon his obedience. He finally concluded to go to his mistress. When my father reproved him for it, he said, "You both called me, and I didn't know which I ought to go to first."

"You are my child," replied our father, "and when I call you, you should come immediately, if you have to pass through fire and water."

Poor Willie! He was now to learn his first lesson of obedience to a master. Grandmother tried to cheer us with hopeful words, and they found an echo in the credulous hearts of youth.

When we entered our new home we encountered cold looks, cold words, and cold treatment. We were glad when the night came. On my narrow bed I moaned and wept, I felt so desolate and alone.

I had been there nearly a year, when a dear little friend of mine was buried. I heard her mother sob, as the clods fell on the coffin of her only child, and I turned away from the grave, feeling thankful that I still had something left to love. I met my grandmother, who said, "Come with me, Linda;" and from her tone I knew that something sad had happened. She led me apart from the people, and then said, "My child, your father is dead." Dead! How could I believe it? He had died so suddenly I had not even heard that he was sick. I went home with my grandmother. My heart rebelled against God, who had taken from me mother, father, mistress, and friend. The good grandmother tried to comfort me. "Who knows the ways of God?" said she. "Perhaps they have been kindly taken from the evil days to come." Years afterwards I often thought of this. She promised to be a mother to her grandchildren, so far as she might be permitted to do so; and strengthened by her love, I returned to my master's. I thought I should be allowed to go to my father's house the next morning; but I was ordered to go for flowers, that my mistress's house might be decorated for an evening party. I spent the day gathering flowers and weaving them into festoons, while the dead body of my father was lying within a mile of me. What cared my owners for that? he was merely a piece of property. Moreover, they thought he had spoiled his children, by teaching them to feel that they were human beings. This was blasphemous doctrine for a slave to teach; presumptuous in him, and dangerous to the masters.

The next day I followed his remains to a humble grave beside that of my dear mother. There were those who knew my father's worth, and respected his memory.

My home now seemed more dreary than ever. The laugh of the little slave-children sounded harsh and cruel. It was selfish to feel so about the joy of others. My brother moved about with a very grave face. I tried to comfort him, by saying, "Take courage, Willie; brighter days will come by and by."

"You don't know any thing about it, Linda," he replied. "We shall have to stay here all our days; we shall never be free."

I argued that we were growing older and stronger, and that perhaps we might, before long, be allowed to hire our own time, and then we could earn money to buy our freedom. William declared this was much easier to say than to do; moreover, he did not intend to buy his freedom. We held daily controversies upon this subject.

Little attention was paid to the slaves' meals in Dr. Flint's house. If they could catch a bit of food while it was going, well and good. I gave myself no trouble on that score, for on my various errands I passed my grandmother's house, where there was always something to spare for me. I was frequently threatened with punishment if I stopped there; and my grandmother, to avoid detaining me, often stood at the gate with something for my breakfast or dinner. I was indebted to her for all my comforts, spiritual or temporal. It was her labor that supplied my scanty wardrobe. I have a vivid recollection of the linsey-woolsey dress given me every winter by Mrs. Flint. How I hated it! It was one of the badges of slavery.

While my grandmother was thus helping to support me from her hard earnings, the three hundred dollars she had lent her mistress were never repaid. When her mistress died, her son-in-law, Dr. Flint, was appointed executor. When grandmother applied to him for payment, he said the estate was insolvent, and the law prohibited payment. It did not, however, prohibit him from retaining the silver candelabra, which had been purchased with that money. I presume they will be handed down in the family, from generation to generation.

My grandmother's mistress had always promised her that, at her death, she should be free; and it was said that in her will she made good the promise. But when the estate was settled, Dr. Flint told the faithful old servant that, under existing circumstances, it was necessary she should be sold.

On the appointed day, the customary advertisement was posted up, proclaiming that there would be a "public sale of negroes, horses, &c." Dr. Flint called to tell my grandmother that he was unwilling to wound her feelings by putting her up at auction, and that he would prefer to dispose of her at private sale. My grandmother saw through his hypocrisy; she understood very well that he was ashamed of the job. She was a very spirited woman, and if he was base enough to sell her, when her mistress intended she should be free, she was determined the public should know it. She had for a long time supplied many families with crackers and preserves; consequently, "Aunt Marthy," as she was called, was generally known, and every body who knew her respected her intelligence and good character. Her long and faithful service in the family was also well known, and the intention of her mistress to leave her free. When the day of sale came, she took her place among the chattels, and at the first call she sprang upon the auction-block. Many voices called out, "Shame! Shame! Who is going to sell you, aunt Marthy? Don't stand there! That is no place for you." Without saying a word, she quietly awaited her fate. No one bid for her. At last, a feeble voice said, "Fifty dollars." It came from a maiden lady, seventy years old, the sister of my grandmother's deceased mistress. She had lived forty years under the same roof with my grandmother; she knew how faithfully she had served her owners, and how cruelly she had been defrauded of her rights; and she resolved to protect her. The auctioneer waited for a higher bid; but her wishes were respected; no one bid above her. She could neither read nor write; and when the bill of sale was made out, she signed it with a cross. But what consequence was that, when she had a big heart overflowing with human kindness? She gave the old servant her freedom.

At that time, my grandmother was just fifty years old. Laborious years had passed since then; and now my brother and I were slaves to the man who had defrauded her of her money, and tried to defraud her of her freedom. One of my mother's sisters, called Aunt Nancy, was also a slave in his family. She was a kind, good aunt to me; and supplied the place of both housekeeper and waiting maid to her mistress. She was, in fact, at the beginning and end of every thing.

Mrs. Flint, like many southern women, was totally deficient in energy. She had not strength to superintend her household affairs; but her nerves were so strong, that she could sit in her easy chair and see a woman whipped, till the blood trickled from every stroke of the lash. She was a member of the church; but partaking of the Lord's supper did not seem to put her in a Christian frame of mind. If dinner was not served at the exact time on that particular Sunday, she would station herself in the kitchen, and wait till it was dished, and then spit in all the kettles and pans that had been used for cooking. She did this to prevent the cook and her children from eking out their meagre fare with the remains of the gravy and other scrapings. The slaves could get nothing to eat except what she chose to give them. Provisions were weighed out by the pound and ounce, three times a day. I can assure you she gave them no chance to eat wheat bread from her flour barrel. She knew how many biscuits a quart of flour would make, and exactly what size they ought to be.

Dr. Flint was an epicure. The cook never sent a dinner to his table without fear and trembling; for if there happened to be a dish not to his liking, he would either order her to be whipped, or compel her to eat every mouthful of it in his presence. The poor, hungry creature might not have objected to eating it; but she did object to having her master cram it down her throat till she choked.

They had a pet dog, that was a nuisance in the house. The cook was ordered to make some Indian mush for him. He refused to eat, and when his head was held over it, the froth flowed from his mouth into the basin. He died a few minutes after. When Dr. Flint came in, he said the mush had not been well cooked, and that was the reason the animal would not eat it. He sent for the cook, and compelled her to eat it. He thought that the woman's stomach was stronger than the dog's; but her sufferings afterwards proved that he was mistaken. This poor woman endured many cruelties from her master and mistress; sometimes she was locked up, away from her nursing baby, for a whole day and night.

When I had been in the family a few weeks, one of the plantation slaves was brought to town, by order of his master. It was near night when he arrived, and Dr. Flint ordered him to be taken to the work house, and tied up to the joist, so that his feet would just escape the ground. In that situation he was to wait till the doctor had taken his tea. I shall never forget that night. Never before, in my life, had I heard hundreds of blows fall; in succession, on a human being. His piteous groans, and his "O, pray don't, massa," rang in my ear for months afterwards. There were many conjectures as to the cause of this terrible punishment. Some said master accused him of stealing corn; others said the slave had quarrelled with his wife, in presence of the overseer, and had accused his master of being the father of her child. They were both black, and the child was very fair.

I went into the work house next morning, and saw the cowhide still wet with blood, and the boards all covered with gore. The poor man lived, and continued to quarrel with his wife. A few months afterwards Dr. Flint handed them both over to a slave-trader. The guilty man put their value into his pocket, and had the satisfaction of knowing that they were out of sight and hearing. When the mother was delivered into the trader's hands, she said. "You promised to treat me well." To which he replied, "You have let your tongue run too far; damn you!" She had forgotten that it was a crime for a slave to tell who was the father of her child.

From others than the master persecution also comes in such cases. I once saw a young slave girl dying soon after the birth of a child nearly white. In her agony she cried out, "O Lord, come and take me!" Her mistress stood by, and mocked at her like an incarnate fiend. "You suffer, do you?" she exclaimed. "I am glad of it. You deserve it all, and more too."

The girl's mother said, "The baby is dead, thank God; and I hope my poor child will soon be in heaven, too."

"Heaven!" retorted the mistress. "There is no such place for the like of her and her bastard."

The poor mother turned away, sobbing. Her dying daughter called her, feebly, and as she bent over her, I heard her say, "Don't grieve so, mother; God knows all about it; and HE will have mercy upon me."

Her sufferings, afterwards, became so intense, that her mistress felt unable to stay; but when she left the room, the scornful smile was still on her lips. Seven children called her mother. The poor black woman had but the one child, whose eyes she saw closing in death, while she thanked God for taking her away from the greater bitterness of life.

# III. THE SLAVES' NEW YEAR'S DAY.

Dr. Flint owned a fine residence in town, several farms, and about fifty slaves, besides hiring a number by the year.

Hiring-day at the south takes place on the 1st of January. On the 2d, the slaves are expected to go to their new masters. On a farm, they work until the corn and cotton are laid. They then have two holidays. Some masters give them a good dinner under the trees. This over, they work until Christmas eve. If no heavy charges are meantime brought against them, they are given four or five holidays, whichever the master or overseer may think proper. Then comes New Year's eve; and they gather together their little alls, or more properly speaking, their little nothings, and wait anxiously for the dawning of day. At the appointed hour the grounds are thronged with men, women, and children, waiting, like criminals, to hear their doom pronounced. The slave is sure to know who is the most humane, or cruel master, within forty miles of him.

It is easy to find out, on that day, who clothes and feeds his slaves well; for he is surrounded by a crowd, begging, "Please, massa, hire me this year. I will work very hard, massa."

If a slave is unwilling to go with his new master, he is whipped, or locked up in jail, until he consents to go, and promises not to run away during the year. Should he chance to change his mind, thinking it justifiable to violate an extorted promise, woe unto him if he is caught! The whip is used till the blood flows at his feet; and his stiffened limbs are put in chains, to be dragged in the field for days and days!

If he lives until the next year, perhaps the same man will hire him again, without even giving him an opportunity of going to the hiring-ground. After those for hire are disposed of, those for sale are called up.

O, you happy free women, contrast your New Year's day with that of the poor bond-woman! With you it is a pleasant season, and the light of the day is blessed. Friendly wishes meet you every where, and gifts are showered upon you. Even hearts that have been estranged from you soften at this season, and lips that have been silent echo back, "I wish you a happy New Year." Children bring their little offerings, and raise their rosy lips for a caress. They are your own, and no hand but that of death can take them from you.

But to the slave mother New Year's day comes laden with peculiar sorrows. She sits on her cold cabin floor, watching the children who may all be torn from her the next morning; and often does she wish that she and they might die before the day dawns. She may be an ignorant creature, degraded by the system that has brutalized her from childhood; but she has a mother's instincts, and is capable of feeling a mother's agonies.

On one of these sale days, I saw a mother lead seven children to the auction-block. She knew that some of them would be taken from her; but they took all. The children were sold to a slave-trader, and their mother was bought by a man in her own town. Before night her children were all far away. She begged the trader to tell her where he intended to take them; this he refused to do. How could he, when he knew he would sell them, one by one, wherever he could command the highest price? I met that mother in the street, and her wild, haggard face lives to-day in my mind. She wrung her hands in anguish, and exclaimed, "Gone! All gone! Why don't God kill me?" I had no words wherewith to comfort her. Instances of this kind are of daily, yea, of hourly occurrence.

Slaveholders have a method, peculiar to their institution, of getting rid of old slaves, whose lives have been worn out in their service. I knew an old woman, who for seventy years faithfully served her master. She had become almost helpless, from hard labor and disease. Her owners moved to Alabama, and the old black woman was left to be sold to any body who would give twenty dollars for her.

# IV. THE SLAVE WHO DARED TO FEEL LIKE A MAN.

Two years had passed since I entered Dr. Flint's family, and those years had brought much of the knowledge that comes from experience, though they had afforded little opportunity for any other kinds of knowledge.

My grandmother had, as much as possible, been a mother to her orphan grandchildren. By perseverance and unwearied industry, she was now mistress of a snug little home, surrounded with the necessaries of life. She would have been happy could her children have shared them with her. There remained but three children and two grandchildren, all slaves. Most earnestly did she strive to make us feel that it was the will of God: that He had seen fit to place us under such circumstances; and though it seemed hard, we ought to pray for contentment.

It was a beautiful faith, coming from a mother who could not call her children her own. But I, and Benjamin, her youngest boy, condemned it. We reasoned that it was much more the will of God that we should be situated as she was. We longed for a home like hers. There we always found sweet balsam for our troubles. She was so loving, so sympathizing! She always met us with a smile, and listened with patience to all our sorrows. She spoke so hopefully, that unconsciously the clouds gave place to sunshine. There was a grand big oven there, too, that baked bread and nice things for the town, and we knew there was always a choice bit in store for us.

But, alas! Even the charms of the old oven failed to reconcile us to our hard lot. Benjamin was now a tall, handsome lad, strongly and gracefully made, and with a spirit too bold and daring for a slave. My brother William, now twelve years old, had the same aversion to the word master that he had when he was an urchin of seven years. I was his confidant. He came to me with all his troubles. I remember one instance in particular. It was on a lovely spring morning, and when I marked the sunlight dancing here and there, its beauty seemed to mock my sadness. For my master, whose restless, craving, vicious nature roved about day and night, seeking whom to devour, had just left me, with stinging, scorching words; words that scathed ear and brain like fire. O, how I despised him! I thought how glad I should be, if some day when he walked the earth, it would open and swallow him up, and disencumber the world of a plague.

When he told me that I was made for his use, made to obey his command in every thing; that I was nothing but a slave, whose will must and should surrender to his, never before had my puny arm felt half so strong.

So deeply was I absorbed in painful reflections afterwards, that I neither saw nor heard the entrance of any one, till the voice of William sounded close beside me. "Linda," said he, "what makes you look so sad? I love you. O, Linda, isn't this a bad world? Every body seems so cross and unhappy. I wish I had died when poor father did."

I told him that every body was not cross, or unhappy; that those who had pleasant homes, and kind friends, and who were not afraid to love them, were happy. But we, who were slave-children, without father or mother, could not expect to be happy. We must be good; perhaps that would bring us contentment.

"Yes," he said, "I try to be good; but what's the use? They are all the time troubling me." Then he proceeded to relate his afternoon's difficulty with young master Nicholas. It seemed that the brother of master Nicholas had pleased himself with making up stories about William. Master Nicholas said he should be flogged, and he would do it. Whereupon he went to work; but William fought bravely, and the young master, finding he was getting the better of him, undertook to tie his hands behind him. He failed in that likewise. By dint of kicking and fisting, William came out of the skirmish none the worse for a few scratches.

He continued to discourse, on his young master's meanness; how he whipped the little boys, but was a perfect coward when a tussle ensued between him and white boys of his own size. On such occasions he always took to his legs. William had other charges to make against him. One was his rubbing up pennies with quicksilver, and passing them off for quarters of a dollar on an old man who kept a fruit stall. William was often sent to buy fruit, and he earnestly inquired of me what he ought to do under such circumstances. I told him it was certainly wrong to deceive the old man, and that it was his duty to tell him of the impositions practised by his young master. I assured him the old man would not be slow to comprehend the whole, and there the matter would end. William thought it might with the old man, but not with him. He said he did not mind the smart of the whip, but he did not like the idea of being whipped.

While I advised him to be good and forgiving I was not unconscious of the beam in my own eye. It was the very knowledge of my own shortcomings that urged me to retain, if possible, some sparks of my brother's God-given nature. I had not lived fourteen years in slavery for nothing. I had felt, seen, and heard enough, to read the characters, and question the motives, of those around me. The war of my life had begun; and though one of God's most powerless creatures, I resolved never to be conquered. Alas, for me!

If there was one pure, sunny spot for me, I believed it to be in Benjamin's heart, and in another's, whom I loved with all the ardor of a girl's first love. My owner knew of it, and sought in every way to render me miserable. He did not resort to corporal punishment, but to all the petty, tyrannical ways that human ingenuity could devise.

I remember the first time I was punished. It was in the month of February. My grandmother had taken my old shoes, and replaced them with a new pair. I needed them; for several inches of snow had fallen, and it still continued to fall. When I walked through Mrs. Flint's room, their creaking grated harshly on her refined nerves. She called me to her, and asked what I had about me that made such a horrid noise. I told her it was my new shoes. "Take them off," said she; "and if you put them on again, I'll throw them into the fire."

I took them off, and my stockings also. She then sent me a long distance, on an errand. As I went through the snow, my bare feet tingled. That night I was very hoarse; and I went to bed thinking the next day would find me sick, perhaps dead. What was my grief on waking to find myself quite well!

I had imagined if I died, or was laid up for some time, that my mistress would feel a twinge of remorse that she had so hated "the little imp," as she styled me. It was my ignorance of that mistress that gave rise to such extravagant imaginings.

Dr. Flint occasionally had high prices offered for me; but he always said, "She don't belong to me. She is my daughter's property, and I have no right to sell her." Good, honest man! My young mistress was still a child, and I could look for no protection from her. I loved her, and she returned my affection. I once heard her father allude to her attachment to me, and his wife promptly replied that it proceeded from fear. This put unpleasant doubts into my mind. Did the child feign what she did not feel? or was her mother jealous of the mite of love she bestowed on me? I concluded it must be the latter. I said to myself, "Surely, little children are true."

One afternoon I sat at my sewing, feeling unusual depression of spirits. My mistress had been accusing me of an offence, of which I assured her I was perfectly innocent; but I saw, by the contemptuous curl of her lip, that she believed I was telling a lie.

I wondered for what wise purpose God was leading me through such thorny paths, and whether still darker days were in store for me. As I sat musing thus, the door opened softly, and William came in. "Well, brother," said I, "what is the matter this time?"

"O Linda, Ben and his master have had a dreadful time!" said he.

My first thought was that Benjamin was killed. "Don't be frightened, Linda," said William; "I will tell you all about it."

It appeared that Benjamin's master had sent for him, and he did not immediately obey the summons. When he did, his master was angry, and began to whip him. He resisted. Master and slave fought, and finally the master was thrown. Benjamin had cause to tremble; for he had thrown to the ground his master—one of the richest men in town. I anxiously awaited the result.

That night I stole to my grandmother's house; and Benjamin also stole thither from his master's. My grandmother had gone to spend a day or two with an old friend living in the country.

"I have come," said Benjamin, "to tell you good by. I am going away."

I inquired where.

"To the north," he replied.

I looked at him to see whether he was in earnest. I saw it all in his firm, set mouth. I implored him not to go, but he paid no heed to my words. He said he was no longer a boy, and every day made his yoke more galling. He had raised his hand against his master, and was to be publicly whipped for the offence. I reminded him of the poverty and hardships he must encounter among strangers. I told him he might be caught and brought back; and that was terrible to think of.

He grew vexed, and asked if poverty and hardships with freedom, were not preferable to our treatment in slavery. "Linda," he continued, "we are dogs here; foot-balls, cattle, every thing that's mean. No, I will not stay. Let them bring me back. We don't die but once."

He was right; but it was hard to give him up. "Go," said I, "and break your mother's heart."

I repented of my words ere they were out.

"Linda," said he, speaking as I had not heard him speak that evening, "how could you say that? Poor mother! be kind to her, Linda; and you, too, cousin Fanny."

Cousin Fanny was a friend who had lived some years with us.

Farewells were exchanged, and the bright, kind boy, endeared to us by so many acts of love, vanished from our sight.

It is not necessary to state how he made his escape. Suffice it to say, he was on his way to New York when a violent storm overtook the vessel. The captain said he must put into the nearest port. This alarmed Benjamin, who was aware that he would be advertised in every port near his own town. His embarrassment was noticed by the captain. To port they went. There the advertisement met the captain's eye. Benjamin so exactly answered its description, that the captain laid hold on him, and bound him in chains. The storm passed, and they proceeded to New York. Before reaching that port

Benjamin managed to get off his chains and throw them overboard. He escaped from the vessel, but was pursued, captured, and carried back to his master.

When my grandmother returned home and found her youngest child had fled, great was her sorrow; but, with characteristic piety, she said, "God's will be done." Each morning, she inquired if any news had been heard from her boy. Yes, news was heard. The master was rejoicing over a letter, announcing the capture of his human chattel.

That day seems but as yesterday, so well do I remember it. I saw him led through the streets in chains, to jail. His face was ghastly pale, yet full of determination. He had begged one of the sailors to go to his mother's house and ask her not to meet him. He said the sight of her distress would take from him all self-control. She yearned to see him, and she went; but she screened herself in the crowd, that it might be as her child had said.

We were not allowed to visit him; but we had known the jailer for years, and he was a kind-hearted man. At midnight he opened the jail door for my grandmother and myself to enter, in disguise. When we entered the cell not a sound broke the stillness. "Benjamin, Benjamin!" whispered my grandmother. No answer. "Benjamin!" she again faltered. There was a jingle of chains. The moon had just risen, and cast an uncertain light through the bars of the window. We knelt down and took Benjamin's cold hands in ours. We did not speak. Sobs were heard, and Benjamin's lips were unsealed; for his mother was weeping on his neck. How vividly does memory bring back that sad night! Mother and son talked together. He asked her pardon for the suffering he had caused her. She said she had nothing to forgive; she could not blame his desire for freedom. He told her that when he was captured, he broke away, and was about casting himself into the river, when thoughts of her came over him, and he desisted. She asked if he did not also think of God. I fancied I saw his face grow fierce in the moonlight. He answered, "No, I did not think of him. When a man is hunted like a wild beast he forgets there is a God, a heaven. He forgets every thing in his struggle to get beyond the reach of the bloodhounds."

"Don't talk so, Benjamin," said she. "Put your trust in God. Be humble, my child, and your master will forgive you."

"Forgive me for what, mother? For not letting him treat me like a dog? No! I will never humble myself to him. I have worked for him for nothing all my life, and I am repaid with stripes and imprisonment. Here I will stay till I die, or till he sells me."

The poor mother shuddered at his words. I think he felt it; for when he next spoke, his voice was calmer. "Don't fret about me, mother. I ain't worth it," said he. "I wish I had some of your goodness. You bear every thing patiently, just as though you thought it was all right. I wish I could."

She told him she had not always been so; once, she was like him; but when sore troubles came upon her, and she had no arm to lean upon, she learned to call on God, and he lightened her burdens. She besought him to do likewise.

We overstaid our time, and were obliged to hurry from the jail.

Benjamin had been imprisoned three weeks, when my grandmother went to intercede for him with his master. He was immovable. He said Benjamin should serve as an example to the rest of his slaves; he should be kept in jail till he was subdued, or be sold if he got but one dollar for him. However, he afterwards relented in some degree. The chains were taken off, and we were allowed to visit him.

As his food was of the coarsest kind, we carried him as often as possible a warm supper, accompanied with some little luxury for the jailer.

Three months elapsed, and there was no prospect of release or of a purchaser. One day he was heard to sing and laugh. This piece of indecorum was told to his master, and the overseer was ordered to re-chain him. He was now confined in an apartment with other prisoners, who were covered with filthy rags. Benjamin was chained near them, and was soon covered with vermin. He worked at his chains till he succeeded in getting out of them. He passed them through the bars of the window, with a request that they should be taken to his master, and he should be informed that he was covered with vermin.

This audacity was punished with heavier chains, and prohibition of our visits.

My grandmother continued to send him fresh changes of clothes. The old ones were burned up. The last night we saw him in jail his mother still begged him to send for his master, and beg his pardon. Neither persuasion nor argument could turn him from his purpose. He calmly answered, "I am waiting his time."

Those chains were mournful to hear.

Another three months passed, and Benjamin left his prison walls. We that loved him waited to bid him a long and last farewell. A slave trader had bought him. You remember, I told you what price he brought when ten years of age. Now he was more than twenty years old, and sold for three hundred dollars. The master had been blind to his own interest. Long confinement had made his face too pale, his form too thin; moreover, the trader had heard something of his character, and it did not strike him as suitable for a slave. He said he would give any price if the handsome lad was a girl. We thanked God that he was not.

Could you have seen that mother clinging to her child, when they fastened the irons upon his wrists; could you have heard her heart-rending groans, and seen her bloodshot eyes wander wildly from face to face, vainly pleading for mercy; could you have witnessed that scene as I saw it, you would exclaim, Slavery is damnable! Benjamin, her youngest, her pet, was forever gone! She could not realize it. She had had an interview with the trader for the purpose of ascertaining if Benjamin could be purchased. She was told it was impossible, as he had given bonds not to sell him till he was out of the state. He promised that he would not sell him till he reached New Orleans.

With a strong arm and unvaried trust, my grandmother began her work of love. Benjamin must be free. If she succeeded, she knew they would still be separated; but the sacrifice was not too great. Day and night she labored. The trader's price would treble that he gave; but she was not discouraged.

She employed a lawyer to write to a gentleman, whom she knew, in New Orleans. She begged him to interest himself for Benjamin, and he willingly favored her request. When he saw Benjamin, and stated his business, he thanked him; but said he preferred to wait a while before making the trader an offer. He knew he had tried to obtain a high price for him, and had invariably failed. This encouraged him to make another effort for freedom. So one morning, long before day, Benjamin was missing. He was riding over the blue billows, bound for Baltimore.

For once his white face did him a kindly service. They had no suspicion that it belonged to a slave; otherwise, the law would have been followed out to the letter, and the thing rendered back to slavery. The brightest skies are often overshadowed by the darkest clouds. Benjamin was taken sick, and compelled to remain in Baltimore three weeks. His strength was slow in returning; and his desire to continue his journey seemed to retard his recovery. How could he get strength without air and exercise? He resolved to venture on a short walk. A by-street was selected, where he thought himself secure of not being met by any one that knew him; but a voice called out, "Halloo, Ben, my boy! what are you doing here!"

His first impulse was to run; but his legs trembled so that he could not stir. He turned to confront his antagonist, and behold, there stood his old master's next door neighbor! He thought it was all over with him now; but it proved otherwise. That man was a miracle. He possessed a goodly number of slaves, and yet was not quite deaf to that mystic clock, whose ticking is rarely heard in the slaveholder's breast.

"Ben, you are sick," said he. "Why, you look like a ghost. I guess I gave you something of a start. Never mind, Ben, I am not going to touch you. You had a pretty tough time of it, and you may go on your way rejoicing for all me. But I would advise you to get out of this place plaguy quick, for there are several gentlemen here from our town." He described the nearest and safest route to

New York, and added, "I shall be glad to tell your mother I have seen you. Good by, Ben."

Benjamin turned away, filled with gratitude, and surprised that the town he hated contained such a gem—a gem worthy of a purer setting.

This gentleman was a Northerner by birth, and had married a southern lady. On his return, he told my grandmother that he had seen her son, and of the service he had rendered him.

Benjamin reached New York safely, and concluded to stop there until he had gained strength enough to proceed further. It happened that my grandmother's only remaining son had sailed for the same city on business for his mistress. Through God's providence, the brothers met. You may be sure it was a happy meeting. "O Phil," exclaimed Benjamin, "I am here at last." Then he told him how near he came to dying, almost in sight of free land, and how he prayed that he might live to get one breath of free air. He said life was worth something now, and it would be hard to die. In the old jail he had not valued it; once, he was tempted to destroy it; but something, he did not know what, had prevented him; perhaps it was fear. He had heard those who profess to be religious declare there was no heaven for self-murderers; and as his life had been pretty hot here, he did not desire a continuation of the same in another world. "If I die now," he exclaimed, "thank God, I shall die a freeman!"

He begged my uncle Phillip not to return south; but stay and work with him, till they earned enough to buy those at home. His brother told him it would kill their mother if he deserted her in her trouble. She had pledged her house, and with difficulty had raised money to buy him. Would he be bought?

"No, never!" he replied. "Do you suppose, Phil, when I have got so far out of their clutches, I will give them one red cent? No! And do you suppose I would turn mother out of her home in her old age? That I would let her pay all those hard-earned dollars for me, and never to see me? For you know she will stay south as long as her other children are slaves. What a good mother! Tell her to buy you, Phil. You have been a comfort to her, and I have been a trouble. And Linda, poor Linda; what'll become of her? Phil, you don't know what a life they lead her. She has told me something about it, and I wish old Flint was dead, or a better man. When I was in jail, he asked her if she didn't want him to ask my master to forgive me, and take me home again. She told him, No; that I didn't want to go back. He got mad, and said we were all alike. I never despised my own master half as much as I do that man. There is many a worse slaveholder than my master; but for all that I would not be his slave."

While Benjamin was sick, he had parted with nearly all his clothes to pay necessary expenses. But he did not part with a little pin I fastened in his bosom when we parted. It was the most valuable thing I owned, and I thought none more worthy to wear it. He had it still.

His brother furnished him with clothes, and gave him what money he had.

They parted with moistened eyes; and as Benjamin turned away, he said, "Phil, I part with all my kindred." And so it proved. We never heard from him again.

Uncle Phillip came home; and the first words he uttered when he entered the house were, "Mother, Ben is free! I have seen him in New York." She stood looking at him with a bewildered air. "Mother, don't you believe it?" he said, laying his hand softly upon her shoulder. She raised her hands, and exclaimed, "God be praised! Let us thank him." She dropped on her knees, and poured forth her heart in prayer. Then Phillip must sit down and repeat to her every word Benjamin had said. He told her all; only he forbore to mention how sick and pale her darling looked. Why should he distress her when she could do him no good?

The brave old woman still toiled on, hoping to rescue some of her other children. After a while she succeeded in buying Phillip. She paid eight hundred dollars, and came home with the precious document that secured his freedom. The happy mother and son sat together by the old hearthstone that night, telling how proud they were of each other, and how they would prove to the world that they could take care of themselves, as they had long taken care of others. We all concluded by saying, "He that is willing to be a slave, let him be a slave."

# V. THE TRIALS OF GIRLHOOD.

During the first years of my service in Dr. Flint's family, I was accustomed to share some indulgences with the children of my mistress. Though this seemed to me no more than right, I was grateful for it, and tried to merit the kindness by the faithful discharge of my duties. But I now entered on my fifteenth year—a sad epoch in the life of a slave girl. My master began to whisper foul words in my ear. Young as I was, I could not remain ignorant of their import. I tried to treat them with indifference or contempt. The master's age, my extreme youth, and the fear that his conduct would be reported to my grandmother, made him bear this treatment for many months. He was a crafty man, and resorted to many means to accomplish his purposes. Sometimes he had stormy, terrific ways, that made his victims tremble; sometimes he assumed a gentleness that he thought must surely subdue. Of the two, I preferred his stormy moods, although they left me trembling. He tried his utmost to corrupt the pure principles my grandmother had instilled. He peopled my young mind with unclean images, such as only a vile monster could think of. I turned from him with disgust and hatred. But he was my master. I was compelled to live under the same roof with him—where I saw a man forty years my senior daily violating the most sacred commandments of nature. He told me I was his property; that I must be subject to his will in all things. My soul revolted against the mean tyranny. But where could I turn for protection? No matter whether the slave girl be as black as ebony or as fair as her mistress. In either case, there is no shadow of law to protect her from insult, from violence, or even from death; all these are inflicted by fiends who bear the shape of men. The mistress, who ought to protect the helpless victim, has no other feelings towards her but those of jealousy and rage. The degradation, the wrongs, the vices, that grow out of slavery, are more than I can describe. They are greater than you would willingly believe. Surely, if you credited one half the truths that are told you concerning the helpless millions suffering in this cruel bondage, you at the north would not help to tighten the yoke. You surely would refuse to do for the master, on your own soil, the mean and cruel work which trained bloodhounds and the lowest class of whites do for him at the south.

Every where the years bring to all enough of sin and sorrow; but in slavery the very dawn of life is darkened by these shadows. Even the little child, who is accustomed to wait on her mistress and her children, will learn, before she is twelve years old, why it is that her mistress hates such and such a one among the slaves. Perhaps the child's own mother is among those hated ones. She listens to violent outbreaks of jealous passion, and cannot help understanding what is the cause. She will become prematurely knowing in evil things. Soon she will learn to tremble when she hears her master's footfall. She will be compelled to realize that she is no longer a child. If God has bestowed beauty upon her, it will prove her greatest curse. That which commands admiration in the white woman only hastens the degradation of the female slave. I know that some are too much brutalized by slavery to feel the humiliation of their position; but many slaves feel it most acutely, and shrink from the memory of it. I cannot tell how much I suffered in the presence of these wrongs, nor how I am still pained by the retrospect. My master met me at every turn, reminding me that I belonged to him, and swearing by heaven and earth that he would compel me to submit to him. If I went out for a breath of fresh air, after a day of unwearied toil, his footsteps dogged me. If I knelt by my mother's grave, his dark shadow fell on me even there. The light heart which nature had given me became heavy with sad forebodings. The other slaves in my master's house noticed the change. Many of them pitied me; but none dared to ask the cause. They had no need to inquire. They knew too well the guilty practices under that roof; and they were aware that to speak of them was an offence that never went unpunished.

    I longed for some one to confide in. I would have given the world to have laid my head on my grandmother's faithful bosom, and told her all my troubles. But Dr. Flint swore he would kill me, if I was not as silent as the grave. Then, although my grandmother was all in all to me, I feared her as well as loved her. I had been accustomed to look up to her with a respect bordering upon awe. I was very young, and felt shamefaced about telling her such impure things, especially as I knew her to be very strict on such subjects. Moreover, she was a woman of a high spirit. She was usually very quiet in her demeanor; but if her indignation was once roused, it was not very easily quelled. I had been told that she once chased a white gentleman with a loaded pistol, because he insulted one of her daughters. I dreaded the consequences of a violent outbreak; and both pride and fear kept me silent. But though I did not confide in my grandmother, and even evaded her vigilant watchfulness and inquiry, her presence in the neighborhood was some protection to me. Though she had been a slave, Dr. Flint was afraid of her. He dreaded her scorching rebukes. Moreover, she was known and patronized by many people; and he did not wish to have his villany made public. It was lucky for me that I did not live on a distant plantation, but in a town not so large that the inhabitants were ignorant of each other's affairs. Bad as are the laws and customs in a slaveholding community, the doctor, as a professional man, deemed it prudent to keep up some outward show of decency.

O, what days and nights of fear and sorrow that man caused me! Reader, it is not to awaken sympathy for myself that I am telling you truthfully what I suffered in slavery. I do it to kindle a flame of compassion in your hearts for my sisters who are still in bondage, suffering as I once suffered.

I once saw two beautiful children playing together. One was a fair white child; the other was her slave, and also her sister. When I saw them embracing each other, and heard their joyous laughter, I turned sadly away from the lovely sight. I foresaw the inevitable blight that would fall on the little slave's heart. I knew how soon her laughter would be changed to sighs. The fair child grew up to be a still fairer woman. From childhood to womanhood her pathway was blooming with flowers, and overarched by a sunny sky. Scarcely one day of her life had been clouded when the sun rose on her happy bridal morning.

How had those years dealt with her slave sister, the little playmate of her childhood? She, also, was very beautiful; but the flowers and sunshine of love were not for her. She drank the cup of sin, and shame, and misery, whereof her persecuted race are compelled to drink.

In view of these things, why are ye silent, ye free men and women of the north? Why do your tongues falter in maintenance of the right? Would that I had more ability! But my heart is so full, and my pen is so weak! There are noble men and women who plead for us, striving to help those who cannot help themselves. God bless them! God give them strength and courage to go on! God bless those, every where, who are laboring to advance the cause of humanity!

# VI. THE JEALOUS MISTRESS.

I would ten thousand times rather that my children should be the half-starved paupers of Ireland than to be the most pampered among the slaves of America. I would rather drudge out my life on a cotton plantation, till the grave opened to give me rest, than to live with an unprincipled master and a jealous mistress. The felon's home in a penitentiary is preferable. He may repent, and turn from the error of his ways, and so find peace; but it is not so with a favorite slave. She is not allowed to have any pride of character. It is deemed a crime in her to wish to be virtuous.

Mrs. Flint possessed the key to her husband's character before I was born. She might have used this knowledge to counsel and to screen the young and the innocent among her slaves; but for them she had no sympathy. They were the objects of her constant suspicion and malevolence. She watched her husband with unceasing vigilance; but he was well practised in means to evade it. What he could not find opportunity to say in words he manifested in signs. He invented more than were ever thought of in a deaf and dumb asylum. I let them pass, as if I did not understand what he meant; and many were the curses and threats bestowed on me for my stupidity. One day he caught me teaching myself to write. He frowned, as if he was not well pleased; but I suppose he came to the conclusion that such an accomplishment might help to advance his favorite scheme. Before long, notes were often slipped into my hand. I would return them, saying, "I can't read them, sir." "Can't you?" he replied; "then I must read them to you." He always finished the reading by asking, "Do you understand?" Sometimes he would complain of the heat of the tea room, and order his supper to be placed on a small table in the piazza. He would seat himself there with a well-satisfied smile, and tell me to stand by and brush away the flies. He would eat very slowly, pausing between the mouthfuls. These intervals were employed in describing the happiness I was so foolishly throwing away, and in threatening me with the penalty that finally awaited my stubborn disobedience. He boasted much of the forbearance he had exercised towards me, and reminded me that there was a limit to his patience. When I succeeded in avoiding opportunities for him to talk to me at home, I was ordered to come to his office, to do some errand. When there, I was obliged to stand and listen to such language as he saw fit to address to me. Sometimes I so openly expressed my contempt for him that he would become violently enraged, and I wondered why he did not strike me. Circumstanced as he was, he probably thought it was better policy to be forebearing. But the state of things grew worse and worse daily. In desperation I told him that I must and would apply to my grandmother for protection. He threatened me with death, and worse than death, if I made any complaint to her. Strange to say, I did not despair. I was naturally of a buoyant disposition, and always I had a hope of somehow getting out of his clutches. Like many a poor, simple slave before me, I trusted that some threads of joy would yet be woven into my dark destiny.

    I had entered my sixteenth year, and every day it became more apparent that my presence was intolerable to Mrs. Flint. Angry words frequently passed between her and her husband. He had never punished me himself, and he would not allow any body else to punish me. In that respect, she was never satisfied; but, in her angry moods, no terms were too vile for her to bestow upon me. Yet I, whom she detested so bitterly, had far more pity for her than he had, whose duty it was to make her life happy. I never wronged her, or wished to wrong her, and one word of kindness from her would have brought me to her feet.

    After repeated quarrels between the doctor and his wife, he announced his intention to take his youngest daughter, then four years old, to sleep in his apartment. It was necessary that a servant should sleep in the same room, to be on hand if the child stirred. I was selected for that office, and informed for what purpose that arrangement had been made. By managing to keep within sight of people, as much as possible, during the day time, I had hitherto succeeded in eluding my master, though a razor was often held to my throat to force me to change this line of policy. At night I slept by the side of my great aunt, where I felt safe. He was too prudent to come into her room. She was an old woman, and had been in the family many years. Moreover, as a married man, and a professional man, he deemed it necessary to save appearances in some degree. But he resolved to remove the obstacle in the way of his scheme; and he thought he had planned it so that he should evade suspicion. He was well aware how much I prized my refuge by the side of my old aunt, and he determined to dispossess me of it. The first night the doctor had the little child in his room alone. The next morning, I was ordered to take my station as nurse the following night. A kind Providence interposed in my favor. During the day Mrs. Flint heard of this new arrangement, and a storm followed. I rejoiced to hear it rage.

    After a while my mistress sent for me to come to her room. Her first question was, "Did you know you were to sleep in the doctor's room?"

"Yes, ma'am."

"Who told you?"

"My master."

"Will you answer truly all the questions I ask?"

"Yes, ma'am."

"Tell me, then, as you hope to be forgiven, are you innocent of what I have accused you?"

"I am."

She handed me a Bible, and said, "Lay your hand on your heart, kiss this holy book, and swear before God that you tell me the truth."

I took the oath she required, and I did it with a clear conscience.

"You have taken God's holy word to testify your innocence," said she. "If you have deceived me, beware! Now take this stool, sit down, look me directly in the face, and tell me all that has passed between your master and you."

I did as she ordered. As I went on with my account her color changed frequently, she wept, and sometimes groaned. She spoke in tones so sad, that I was touched by her grief. The tears came to my eyes; but I was soon convinced that her emotions arose from anger and wounded pride. She felt that her marriage vows were desecrated, her dignity insulted; but she had no compassion for the poor victim of her husband's perfidy. She pitied herself as a martyr; but she was incapable of feeling for the condition of shame and misery in which her unfortunate, helpless slave was placed. Yet perhaps she had some touch of feeling for me; for when the conference was ended, she spoke kindly, and promised to protect me. I should have been much comforted by this assurance if I could have had confidence in it; but my experiences in slavery had filled me with distrust. She was not a very refined woman, and had not much control over her passions. I was an object of her jealousy, and, consequently, of her hatred; and I knew I could not expect kindness or confidence from her under the circumstances in which I was placed. I could not blame her. Slaveholders' wives feel as other women would under similar circumstances. The fire of her temper kindled from small-sparks, and now the flame became so intense that the doctor was obliged to give up his intended arrangement.

I knew I had ignited the torch, and I expected to suffer for it afterwards; but I felt too thankful to my mistress for the timely aid she rendered me to care much about that. She now took me to sleep in a room adjoining her own. There I was an object of her especial care, though not to her especial comfort, for she spent many a sleepless night to watch over me. Sometimes I woke up, and found her bending over me. At other times she whispered in my ear, as though it was her husband who was speaking to me, and listened to hear what I would answer. If she startled me, on such occasions, she would glide stealthily away; and the next morning she would tell me I had been talking in my sleep, and ask who I was talking to. At last, I began to be fearful for my life. It had been often threatened; and you can imagine, better than I can describe, what an unpleasant sensation it must produce to wake up in the dead of night and find a jealous woman bending over you. Terrible as this experience was, I had fears that it would give place to one more terrible.

My mistress grew weary of her vigils; they did not prove satisfactory. She changed her tactics. She now tried the trick of accusing my master of crime, in my presence, and gave my name as the author of the accusation. To my utter astonishment, he replied, "I don't believe it; but if she did acknowledge it, you tortured her into exposing me." Tortured into exposing him! Truly, Satan had no difficulty in distinguishing the color of his soul! I understood his object in making this false representation. It was to show me that I gained nothing by seeking the protection of my mistress; that the power was still all in his own hands. I pitied Mrs. Flint. She was a second wife, many years the junior of her husband; and the hoary-headed miscreant was enough to try the patience of a wiser and better woman. She was completely foiled, and knew not how to proceed. She would gladly have had me flogged for my supposed false oath; but, as I have already stated, the doctor never allowed any one to whip me. The old sinner was politic. The application of the lash might have led to remarks that would have exposed him in the eyes of his children and grandchildren. How often did I rejoice that I lived in a town where all the inhabitants knew each other! If I had been on a remote plantation, or lost among the multitude of a crowded city, I should not be a living woman at this day.

The secrets of slavery are concealed like those of the Inquisition. My master was, to my knowledge, the father of eleven slaves. But did the mothers dare to tell who was the father of their children? Did the other slaves dare to allude to it, except in whispers among themselves? No, indeed! They knew too well the terrible consequences.

My grandmother could not avoid seeing things which excited her suspicions. She was uneasy about me, and tried various ways to buy me; but the never-changing answer was always repeated: "Linda does not belong to me. She is my daughter's property, and I have no legal right to sell her." The conscientious man! He was too scrupulous to sell me; but he had no scruples whatever about committing a much greater wrong against the helpless young girl placed under his guardianship, as his daughter's property. Sometimes my persecutor would ask me whether I would like to be sold. I told him I would rather be sold to any body than to lead such a life as I did. On such occasions he would assume the air of a very injured individual, and reproach me for my ingratitude. "Did I not take you into the house, and make you the companion of my own children?" he would say. "Have I ever treated you like a negro? I have never allowed you to be punished, not even to please your mistress. And this is the recompense I get, you ungrateful girl!" I answered that he had reasons of his own for screening me from punishment, and that the course he pursued made my mistress hate me and persecute me. If I wept, he would say, "Poor child! Don't cry! don't cry! I will make peace for you with your mistress. Only let me arrange matters in my own way. Poor, foolish girl! you don't know what is for your own good. I would cherish you. I would make a lady of you. Now go, and think of all I have promised you."

I did think of it.

Reader, I draw no imaginary pictures of southern homes. I am telling you the plain truth. Yet when victims make their escape from the wild beast of Slavery, northerners consent to act the part of bloodhounds, and hunt the poor fugitive back into his den, "full of dead men's bones, and all uncleanness." Nay, more, they are not only willing, but proud, to give their daughters in marriage to slaveholders. The poor girls have romantic notions of a sunny clime, and of the flowering vines that all the year round shade a happy home. To what disappointments are they destined! The young wife soon learns that the husband in whose hands she has placed her happiness pays no regard to his marriage vows. Children of every shade of complexion play with her own fair babies, and too well she knows that they are born unto him of his own household. Jealousy and hatred enter the flowery home, and it is ravaged of its loveliness.

Southern women often marry a man knowing that he is the father of many little slaves. They do not trouble themselves about it. They regard such children as property, as marketable as the pigs on the plantation; and it is seldom that they do not make them aware of this by passing them into the slave-trader's hands as soon as possible, and thus getting them out of their sight. I am glad to say there are some honorable exceptions.

I have myself known two southern wives who exhorted their husbands to free those slaves towards whom they stood in a "parental relation;" and their request was granted. These husbands blushed before the superior nobleness of their wives' natures. Though they had only counselled them to do that which it was their duty to do, it commanded their respect, and rendered their conduct more exemplary. Concealment was at an end, and confidence took the place of distrust.

Though this bad institution deadens the moral sense, even in white women, to a fearful extent, it is not altogether extinct. I have heard southern ladies say of Mr. Such a one, "He not only thinks it no disgrace to be the father of those little niggers, but he is not ashamed to call himself their master. I declare, such things ought not to be tolerated in any decent society!"

# VII. THE LOVER.

Why does the slave ever love? Why allow the tendrils of the heart to twine around objects which may at any moment be wrenched away by the hand of violence? When separations come by the hand of death, the pious soul can bow in resignation, and say, "Not my will, but thine be done, O Lord!" But when the ruthless hand of man strikes the blow, regardless of the misery he causes, it is hard to be submissive. I did not reason thus when I was a young girl. Youth will be youth. I loved and I indulged the hope that the dark clouds around me would turn out a bright lining. I forgot that in the land of my birth the shadows are too dense for light to penetrate. A land

> Where laughter is not mirth; nor thought the mind;
> Nor words a language; nor e'en men mankind.
> Where cries reply to curses, shrieks to blows,
> And each is tortured in his separate hell.

There was in the neighborhood a young colored carpenter; a free born man. We had been well acquainted in childhood, and frequently met together afterwards. We became mutually attached, and he proposed to marry me. I loved him with all the ardor of a young girl's first love. But when I reflected that I was a slave, and that the laws gave no sanction to the marriage of such, my heart sank within me. My lover wanted to buy me; but I knew that Dr. Flint was too willful and arbitrary a man to consent to that arrangement. From him, I was sure of experiencing all sort of opposition, and I had nothing to hope from my mistress. She would have been delighted to have got rid of me, but not in that way. It would have relieved her mind of a burden if she could have seen me sold to some distant state, but if I was married near home I should be just as much in her husband's power as I had previously been,—for the husband of a slave has no power to protect her. Moreover, my mistress, like many others, seemed to think that slaves had no right to any family ties of their own; that they were created merely to wait upon the family of the mistress. I once heard her abuse a young slave girl, who told her that a colored man wanted to make her his wife. "I will have you peeled and pickled, my lady," said she, "if I ever hear you mention that subject again. Do you suppose that I will have you tending my children with the children of that nigger?" The girl to whom she said this had a mulatto child, of course not acknowledged by its father. The poor black man who loved her would have been proud to acknowledge his helpless offspring.

Many and anxious were the thoughts I revolved in my mind. I was at a loss what to do. Above all things, I was desirous to spare my lover the insults that had cut so deeply into my own soul. I talked with my grandmother about it, and partly told her my fears. I did not dare to tell her the worst. She had long suspected all was not right, and if I confirmed her suspicions I knew a storm would rise that would prove the overthrow of all my hopes.

This love-dream had been my support through many trials; and I could not bear to run the risk of having it suddenly dissipated. There was a lady in the neighborhood, a particular friend of Dr. Flint's, who often visited the house. I had a great respect for her, and she had always manifested a friendly interest in me. Grandmother thought she would have great influence with the doctor. I went to this lady, and told her my story. I told her I was aware that my lover's being a free-born man would prove a great objection; but he wanted to buy me; and if Dr. Flint would consent to that arrangement, I felt sure he would be willing to pay any reasonable price. She knew that Mrs. Flint disliked me; therefore, I ventured to suggest that perhaps my mistress would approve of my being sold, as that would rid her of me. The lady listened with kindly sympathy, and promised to do her utmost to promote my wishes. She had an interview with the doctor, and I believe she pleaded my cause earnestly; but it was all to no purpose.

How I dreaded my master now! Every minute I expected to be summoned to his presence; but the day passed, and I heard nothing from him. The next morning, a message was brought to me: "Master wants you in his study." I found the door ajar, and I stood a moment gazing at the hateful man who claimed a right to rule me, body and soul. I entered, and tried to appear calm. I did not want him to know how my heart was bleeding. He looked fixedly at me, with an expression which seemed to say, "I have half a mind to kill you on the spot." At last he broke the silence, and that was a relief to both of us.

"So you want to be married, do you?" said he, "and to a free nigger."

"Yes, sir."

"Well, I'll soon convince you whether I am your master, or the nigger fellow you honor so highly. If you must have a husband, you may take up with one of my slaves."

What a situation I should be in, as the wife of one of his slaves, even if my heart had been interested!

I replied, "Don't you suppose, sir, that a slave can have some preference about marrying? Do you suppose that all men are alike to her?"

"Do you love this nigger?" said he, abruptly.

"Yes, sir."

"How dare you tell me so!" he exclaimed, in great wrath. After a slight pause, he added, "I supposed you thought more of yourself; that you felt above the insults of such puppies."

I replied, "If he is a puppy, I am a puppy, for we are both of the negro race. It is right and honorable for us to love each other. The man you call a puppy never insulted me, sir; and he would not love me if he did not believe me to be a virtuous woman."

He sprang upon me like a tiger, and gave me a stunning blow. It was the first time he had ever struck me; and fear did not enable me to control my anger. When I had recovered a little from the effects, I exclaimed, "You have struck me for answering you honestly. How I despise you!"

There was silence for some minutes. Perhaps he was deciding what should be my punishment; or, perhaps, he wanted to give me time to reflect on what I had said, and to whom I had said it. Finally, he asked, "Do you know what you have said?"

"Yes, sir; but your treatment drove me to it."

"Do you know that I have a right to do as I like with you,—that I can kill you, if I please?"

"You have tried to kill me, and I wish you had; but you have no right to do as you like with me."

"Silence!" he exclaimed, in a thundering voice. "By heavens, girl, you forget yourself too far! Are you mad? If you are, I will soon bring you to your senses. Do you think any other master would bear what I have borne from you this morning? Many masters would have killed you on the spot. How would you like to be sent to jail for your insolence?"

"I know I have been disrespectful, sir," I replied; "but you drove me to it; I couldn't help it. As for the jail, there would be more peace for me there than there is here."

"You deserve to go there," said he, "and to be under such treatment, that you would forget the meaning of the word peace. It would do you good. It would take some of your high notions out of you. But I am not ready to send you there yet, notwithstanding your ingratitude for all my kindness and forbearance. You have been the plague of my life. I have wanted to make you happy, and I have been repaid with the basest ingratitude; but though you have proved yourself incapable of appreciating my kindness, I will be lenient towards you, Linda. I will give you one more chance to redeem your character. If you behave yourself and do as I require, I will forgive you and treat you as I always have done; but if you disobey me, I will punish you as I would the meanest slave on my plantation. Never let me hear that fellow's name mentioned again. If I ever know of your speaking to him, I will cowhide you both; and if I catch him lurking about my premises, I will shoot him as soon as I would a dog. Do you hear what I say? I'll teach you a lesson about marriage and free niggers! Now go, and let this be the last time I have occasion to speak to you on this subject."

Reader, did you ever hate? I hope not. I never did but once; and I trust I never shall again. Somebody has called it "the atmosphere of hell;" and I believe it is so.

For a fortnight the doctor did not speak to me. He thought to mortify me; to make me feel that I had disgraced myself by receiving the honorable addresses of a respectable colored man, in preference to the base proposals of a white man. But though his lips disdained to address me, his eyes were very loquacious. No animal ever watched its prey more narrowly than he watched me. He knew that I could write, though he had failed to make me read his letters; and he was now troubled lest I should exchange letters with another man. After a while he became weary of silence; and I was sorry for it. One morning, as he passed through the hall, to leave the house, he contrived to thrust a note into my hand. I thought I had better read it, and spare myself the vexation of having him read it to me. It expressed regret for the blow he had given me, and reminded me that I myself was wholly to blame for it. He hoped I had become convinced of the injury I was doing myself by incurring his displeasure. He wrote that he had made up his mind to go to Louisiana; that he should take several slaves with him, and intended I should be one of the number. My mistress would remain where she was; therefore I should have nothing to fear from that quarter. If I merited kindness from him, he assured me that it would be lavishly bestowed. He begged me to think over the matter, and answer the following day.

The next morning I was called to carry a pair of scissors to his room. I laid them on the table, with the letter beside them. He thought it was my answer, and did not call me back. I went as usual to attend my young mistress to and from school. He met me in the street, and ordered me to stop at his office on my way back. When I entered, he showed me his letter, and asked me why I had not answered it. I replied, "I am your daughter's property, and it is in your power to send me, or take me, wherever you please." He said he was very glad to find me so willing to go, and that we should start early in the autumn. He had a large practice in the town, and I rather thought he had made up the story merely to frighten me. However that might be, I was determined that I would never go to Louisiana with him.

Summer passed away, and early in the autumn Dr. Flint's eldest son was sent to Louisiana to examine the country, with a view to emigrating. That news did not disturb me. I knew very well that I should not be sent with him. That I had not been taken to the plantation before this time, was owing to the fact that his son was there. He was jealous of his son; and jealousy of the overseer had kept him from punishing me by sending me into the fields to work. Is it strange, that I was not proud of these protectors? As for the overseer, he was a man for whom I had less respect than I had for a bloodhound.

Young Mr. Flint did not bring back a favorable report of Louisiana, and I heard no more of that scheme. Soon after this, my lover met me at the corner of the street, and I stopped to speak to him. Looking up, I saw my master watching us from his window. I hurried home, trembling with fear. I was sent for, immediately, to go to his room. He met me with a blow. "When is mistress to be married?" said he, in a sneering tone. A shower of oaths and imprecations followed. How thankful I was that my lover was a free man! that my tyrant had no power to flog him for speaking to me in the street!

Again and again I revolved in my mind how all this would end. There was no hope that the doctor would consent to sell me on any terms. He had an iron will, and was determined to keep me, and to conquer me. My lover was an intelligent and religious man. Even if he could have obtained permission to marry me while I was a slave, the marriage would give him no power to protect me from my master. It would have made him miserable to witness the insults I should have been subjected to. And then, if we had children, I knew they must "follow the condition of the mother." What a terrible blight that would be on the heart of a free, intelligent father! For his sake, I felt that I ought not to link his fate with my own unhappy destiny. He was going to Savannah to see about a little property left him by an uncle; and hard as it was to bring my feelings to it, I earnestly entreated him not to come back. I advised him to go to the Free States, where his tongue would not be tied, and where his intelligence would be of more avail to him. He left me, still hoping the day would come when I could be bought. With me the lamp of hope had gone out. The dream of my girlhood was over. I felt lonely and desolate.

Still I was not stripped of all. I still had my good grandmother, and my affectionate brother. When he put his arms round my neck, and looked into my eyes, as if to read there the troubles I dared not tell, I felt that I still had something to love. But even that pleasant emotion was chilled by the reflection that he might be torn from me at any moment, by some sudden freak of my master. If he had known how we loved each other, I think he would have exulted in separating us. We often planned together how we could get to the north. But, as William remarked, such things are easier said than done. My movements were very closely watched, and we had no means of getting any money to defray our expenses. As for grandmother, she was strongly opposed to her children's undertaking any such project. She had not forgotten poor Benjamin's sufferings, and she was afraid that if another child tried to escape, he would have a similar or a worse fate. To me, nothing seemed more dreadful than my present life. I said to myself, "William must be free. He shall go to the north, and I will follow him." Many a slave sister has formed the same plans.

# VIII. WHAT SLAVES ARE TAUGHT TO THINK OF THE NORTH.

Slaveholders pride themselves upon being honorable men; but if you were to hear the enormous lies they tell their slaves, you would have small respect for their veracity. I have spoken plain English. Pardon me. I cannot use a milder term. When they visit the north, and return home, they tell their slaves of the runaways they have seen, and describe them to be in the most deplorable condition. A slaveholder once told me that he had seen a runaway friend of mine in New York, and that she besought him to take her back to her master, for she was literally dying of starvation; that many days she had only one cold potato to eat, and at other times could get nothing at all. He said he refused to take her, because he knew her master would not thank him for bringing such a miserable wretch to his house. He ended by saying to me, "This is the punishment she brought on herself for running away from a kind master."

This whole story was false. I afterwards staid with that friend in New York, and found her in comfortable circumstances. She had never thought of such a thing as wishing to go back to slavery. Many of the slaves believe such stories, and think it is not worth while to exchange slavery for such a hard kind of freedom. It is difficult to persuade such that freedom could make them useful men, and enable them to protect their wives and children. If those heathen in our Christian land had as much teaching as some Hindoos, they would think otherwise. They would know that liberty is more valuable than life. They would begin to understand their own capabilities, and exert themselves to become men and women.

But while the Free States sustain a law which hurls fugitives back into slavery, how can the slaves resolve to become men? There are some who strive to protect wives and daughters from the insults of their masters; but those who have such sentiments have had advantages above the general mass of slaves. They have been partially civilized and Christianized by favorable circumstances. Some are bold enough to utter such sentiments to their masters. O, that there were more of them!

Some poor creatures have been so brutalized by the lash that they will sneak out of the way to give their masters free access to their wives and daughters. Do you think this proves the black man to belong to an inferior order of beings? What would you be, if you had been born and brought up a slave, with generations of slaves for ancestors? I admit that the black man is inferior. But what is it that makes him so? It is the ignorance in which white men compel him to live; it is the torturing whip that lashes manhood out of him; it is the fierce bloodhounds of the South, and the scarcely less cruel human bloodhounds of the north, who enforce the Fugitive Slave Law. They do the work.

Southern gentlemen indulge in the most contemptuous expressions about the Yankees, while they, on their part, consent to do the vilest work for them, such as the ferocious bloodhounds and the despised negro-hunters are employed to do at home. When southerners go to the north, they are proud to do them honor; but the northern man is not welcome south of Mason and Dixon's line, unless he suppresses every thought and feeling at variance with their "peculiar institution." Nor is it enough to be silent. The masters are not pleased, unless they obtain a greater degree of subservience than that; and they are generally accommodated. Do they respect the northerner for this? I trow not. Even the slaves despise "a northern man with southern principles;" and that is the class they generally see. When northerners go to the south to reside, they prove very apt scholars. They soon imbibe the sentiments and disposition of their neighbors, and generally go beyond their teachers. Of the two, they are proverbially the hardest masters.

They seem to satisfy their consciences with the doctrine that God created the Africans to be slaves. What a libel upon the heavenly Father, who "made of one blood all nations of men!" And then who are Africans? Who can measure the amount of Anglo-Saxon blood coursing in the veins of American slaves?

I have spoken of the pains slaveholders take to give their slaves a bad opinion of the north; but, notwithstanding this, intelligent slaves are aware that they have many friends in the Free States. Even the most ignorant have some confused notions about it. They knew that I could read; and I was often asked if I had seen any thing in the newspapers about white folks over in the big north, who were trying to get their freedom for them. Some believe that the abolitionists have already made them free, and that it is established by law, but that their masters prevent the law from going into effect. One woman begged me to get a newspaper and read it over. She said her husband told her that the black people had sent word to the queen of 'Merica that they were all slaves; that she didn't believe it, and went to Washington city to see the president about it. They quarrelled; she drew her sword upon him, and swore that he should help her to make them all free.

That poor, ignorant woman thought that America was governed by a Queen, to whom the President was subordinate. I wish the President was subordinate to Queen Justice.

# IX. SKETCHES OF NEIGHBORING SLAVEHOLDERS.

There was a planter in the country, not far from us, whom I will call Mr. Litch. He was an ill-bred, uneducated man, but very wealthy. He had six hundred slaves, many of whom he did not know by sight. His extensive plantation was managed by well-paid overseers. There was a jail and a whipping post on his grounds; and whatever cruelties were perpetrated there, they passed without comment. He was so effectually screened by his great wealth that he was called to no account for his crimes, not even for murder.

Various were the punishments resorted to. A favorite one was to tie a rope round a man's body, and suspend him from the ground. A fire was kindled over him, from which was suspended a piece of fat pork. As this cooked, the scalding drops of fat continually fell on the bare flesh. On his own plantation, he required very strict obedience to the eighth commandment. But depredations on the neighbors were allowable, provided the culprit managed to evade detection or suspicion. If a neighbor brought a charge of theft against any of his slaves, he was browbeaten by the master, who assured him that his slaves had enough of every thing at home, and had no inducement to steal. No sooner was the neighbor's back turned, than the accused was sought out, and whipped for his lack of discretion. If a slave stole from him even a pound of meat or a peck of corn, if detection followed, he was put in chains and imprisoned, and so kept till his form was attentuated by hunger and suffering.

A freshnet once bore his wine cellar and meat house miles away from the plantation. Some slaves followed, and secured bits of meat and bottles of wine. Two were detected; a ham and some liquor being found in their huts. They were summoned by their master. No words were used, but a club felled them to the ground. A rough box was their coffin, and their interment was a dog's burial. Nothing was said.

Murder was so common on his plantation that he feared to be alone after nightfall. He might have believed in ghosts.

His brother, if not equal in wealth, was at least equal in cruelty. His bloodhounds were well trained. Their pen was spacious, and a terror to the slaves. They were let loose on a runway, and, if they tracked him, they literally tore the flesh from his bones. When this slaveholder died, his shrieks and groans were so frightful that they appalled his own friends. His last words were, "I am going to hell; bury my money with me."

After death his eyes remained open. To press the lids down, silver dollars were laid on them. These were buried with him. From this circumstance, a rumor went abroad that his coffin was filled with money. Three times his grave was opened, and his coffin taken out. The last time, his body was found on the ground, and a flock of buzzards were pecking at it. He was again interred, and a sentinel set over his grave. The perpetrators were never discovered.

Cruelty is contagious in uncivilized communities. Mr. Conant, a neighbor of Mr. Litch, returned from town one evening in a partial state of intoxication. His body servant gave him some offence. He was divested of his clothes, except his shirt, whipped, and tied to a large tree in front of the house. It was a stormy night in winter. The wind blew bitterly cold, and the boughs of the old tree crackled under falling sleet. A member of the family, fearing he would freeze to death, begged that he might be taken down; but the master would not relent. He remained there three hours; and, when he was cut down, he was more dead than alive. Another slave, who stole a pig from this master, to appease his hunger, was terribly flogged. In desperation, he tried to run away. But at the end of two miles, he was so faint with loss of blood, he thought he was dying. He had a wife, and he longed to see her once more. Too sick to walk, he crept back that long distance on his hands and knees. When he reached his master's, it was night. He had not strength to rise and open the gate. He moaned, and tried to call for help. I had a friend living in the same family. At last his cry reached her. She went out and found the prostrate man at the gate. She ran back to the house for assistance, and two men returned with her. They carried him in, and laid him on the floor. The back of his shirt was one clot of blood. By means of lard, my friend loosened it from the raw flesh. She bandaged him, gave him cool drink, and left him to rest. The master said he deserved a hundred more lashes. When his own labor was stolen from him, he had stolen food to appease his hunger. This was his crime.

Another neighbor was a Mrs. Wade. At no hour of the day was there cessation of the lash on her premises. Her labors began with the dawn, and did not cease till long after nightfall. The barn was her particular place of torture. There she lashed the slaves with the might of a man. An old slave of hers once said to me, "It is hell in missis's house. 'Pears I can never get out. Day and night I prays to die."

The mistress died before the old woman, and, when dying, entreated her husband not to permit any one of her slaves to look on her after death. A slave who had nursed her children, and had still a child in her care, watched her chance, and stole with it in her arms to the room where lay her dead mistress. She gazed a while on her, then raised her hand and dealt two blows on her face, saying, as she did so, "The devil is got you now!" She forgot that the child was looking on. She had just begun to talk; and she said to her father, "I did see ma, and mammy did strike ma, so," striking her own face with her little hand. The master was startled. He could not imagine how the nurse could obtain access to the room where the corpse lay; for he kept the door locked. He questioned her. She confessed that what the child had said was true, and told how she had procured the key. She was sold to Georgia.

In my childhood I knew a valuable slave, named Charity, and loved her, as all children did. Her young mistress married, and took her to Louisiana. Her little boy, James, was sold to a good sort of master. He became involved in debt, and James was sold again to a wealthy slaveholder, noted for his cruelty. With this man he grew up to manhood, receiving the treatment of a dog. After a severe whipping, to save himself from further infliction of the lash, with which he was threatened, he took to the woods. He was in a most miserable condition—cut by the cowskin, half naked, half starved, and without the means of procuring a crust of bread.

Some weeks after his escape, he was captured, tied, and carried back to his master's plantation. This man considered punishment in his jail, on bread and water, after receiving hundreds of lashes, too mild for the poor slave's offence. Therefore he decided, after the overseer should have whipped him to his satisfaction, to have him placed between the screws of the cotton gin, to stay as long as he had been in the woods. This wretched creature was cut with the whip from his head to his feet, then washed with strong brine, to prevent the flesh from mortifying, and make it heal sooner than it otherwise would. He was then put into the cotton gin, which was screwed down, only allowing him room to turn on his side when he could not lie on his back. Every morning a slave was sent with a piece of bread and bowl of water, which was placed within reach of the poor fellow. The slave was charged, under penalty of severe punishment, not to speak to him.

Four days passed, and the slave continued to carry the bread and water. On the second morning, he found the bread gone, but the water untouched. When he had been in the press four days and five night, the slave informed his master that the water had not been used for four mornings, and that horrible stench came from the gin house. The overseer was sent to examine into it. When the press was unscrewed, the dead body was found partly eaten by rats and vermin. Perhaps the rats that devoured his bread had gnawed him before life was extinct. Poor Charity! Grandmother and I often asked each other how her affectionate heart would bear the news, if she should ever hear of the murder of her son. We had known her husband, and knew that James was like him in manliness and intelligence. These were the qualities that made it so hard for him to be a plantation slave. They put him into a rough box, and buried him with less feeling than would have been manifested for an old house dog. Nobody asked any questions. He was a slave; and the feeling was that the master had a right to do what he pleased with his own property. And what did he care for the value of a slave? He had hundreds of them. When they had finished their daily toil, they must hurry to eat their little morsels, and be ready to extinguish their pine knots before nine o'clock, when the overseer went his patrol rounds. He entered every cabin, to see that men and their wives had gone to bed together, lest the men, from over-fatigue, should fall asleep in the chimney corner, and remain there till the morning horn called them to their daily task. Women are considered of no value, unless they continually increase their owner's stock. They are put on a par with animals. This same master shot a woman through the head, who had run away and been brought back to him. No one called him to account for it. If a slave resisted being whipped, the bloodhounds were unpacked, and set upon him, to tear his flesh from his bones. The master who did these things was highly educated, and styled a perfect gentleman. He also boasted the name and standing of a Christian, though Satan never had a truer follower.

I could tell of more slaveholders as cruel as those I have described. They are not exceptions to the general rule. I do not say there are no humane slaveholders. Such characters do exist, notwithstanding the hardening influences around them. But they are "like angels' visits—few and far between."

I knew a young lady who was one of these rare specimens. She was an orphan, and inherited as slaves a woman and her six children. Their father was a free man. They had a comfortable home of their own, parents and children living together. The mother and eldest daughter served their mistress during the day, and at night returned to their dwelling, which was on the premises. The young lady was very pious, and there was some reality in her religion. She taught her slaves to lead pure lives, and wished them to enjoy the fruit of their own industry. Her religion was not a garb put on for Sunday, and laid aside till Sunday returned again. The eldest daughter of the slave mother was promised in marriage to a free man; and the day before the wedding this good mistress emancipated her, in order that her marriage might have the sanction of law.

Report said that this young lady cherished an unrequited affection for a man who had resolved to marry for wealth. In the course of time a rich uncle of hers died. He left six thousand dollars to his two sons by a colored woman, and the remainder of his property to this orphan niece. The metal soon attracted the magnet. The lady and her weighty purse became his. She offered to manumit her slaves—telling them that her marriage might make unexpected changes in their destiny, and she wished to insure their happiness. They refused to take their freedom, saying that she had always been their best friend, and they could not be so happy any where as with her. I was not surprised. I had often seen them in their comfortable home, and thought that the whole town did not contain a happier family. They had never felt slavery; and, when it was too late, they were convinced of its reality.

When the new master claimed this family as his property, the father became furious, and went to his mistress for protection. "I can do nothing for you now, Harry," said she. "I no longer have the power I had a week ago. I have succeeded in obtaining the freedom of your wife; but I cannot obtain it for your children." The unhappy father swore that nobody should take his children from him. He concealed them in the woods for some days; but they were discovered and taken. The father was put in jail, and the two oldest boys sold to Georgia. One little girl, too young to be of service to her master, was left with the wretched mother. The other three were carried to their master's plantation. The eldest soon became a mother; and when the slaveholder's wife looked at the babe, she wept bitterly. She knew that her own husband had violated the purity she had so carefully inculcated. She had a second child by her master, and then he sold her and his offspring to his brother. She bore two children to the brother and was sold again. The next sister went crazy. The life she was compelled to lead drove her mad. The third one became the mother of five daughters. Before the birth of the fourth the pious mistress died. To the last, she rendered every kindness to the slaves that her unfortunate circumstances permitted. She passed away peacefully, glad to close her eyes on a life which had been made so wretched by the man she loved.

This man squandered the fortune he had received, and sought to retrieve his affairs by a second marriage; but, having retired after a night of drunken debauch, he was found dead in the morning. He was called a good master; for he fed and clothed his slaves better than most masters, and the lash was not heard on his plantation so frequently as on many others. Had it not been for slavery, he would have been a better man, and his wife a happier woman.

No pen can give an adequate description of the all-pervading corruption produced by slavery. The slave girl is reared in an atmosphere of licentiousness and fear. The lash and the foul talk of her master and his sons are her teachers. When she is fourteen or fifteen, her owner, or his sons, or the overseer, or perhaps all of them, begin to bribe her with presents. If these fail to accomplish their purpose, she is whipped or starved into submission to their will. She may have had religious principles inculcated by some pious mother or grandmother, or some good mistress; she may have a lover, whose good opinion and peace of mind are dear to her heart; or the profligate men who have power over her may be exceedingly odious to her. But resistance is hopeless.

> The poor worm
> Shall prove her contest vain. Life's little day
> Shall pass, and she is gone!

The slaveholder's sons are, of course, vitiated, even while boys, by the unclean influences every where around them. Nor do the master's daughters always escape. Severe retributions sometimes come upon him for the wrongs he does to the daughters of the slaves. The white daughters early hear their parents quarrelling about some female slave. Their curiosity is excited, and they soon learn the cause. They are attended by the young slave girls whom their father has corrupted; and they hear such talk as should never meet youthful ears, or any other ears. They know that the woman slaves are subject to their father's authority in all things; and in some cases they exercise the same authority over the men slaves. I have myself seen the master of such a household whose head was bowed down in shame; for it was known in the neighborhood that his daughter had selected one of the meanest slaves on his plantation to be the father of his first grandchild. She did not make her advances to her equals, nor even to her father's more intelligent servants. She selected the most brutalized, over whom her authority could be exercised with less fear of exposure. Her father, half frantic with rage, sought to revenge himself on the offending black man; but his daughter, foreseeing the storm that would arise, had given him free papers, and sent him out of the state.

In such cases the infant is smothered, or sent where it is never seen by any who know its history. But if the white parent is the father, instead of the mother, the offspring are unblushingly reared for the market. If they are girls, I have indicated plainly enough what will be their inevitable destiny.

You may believe what I say; for I write only that whereof I know. I was twenty-one years in that cage of obscene birds. I can testify, from my own experience and observation, that slavery is a curse to the whites as well as to the blacks. It makes white fathers cruel and sensual; the sons violent and licentious; it contaminates the daughters, and makes the wives wretched. And as for the colored race, it needs an abler pen than mine to describe the extremity of their sufferings, the depth of their degradation.

Yet few slaveholders seem to be aware of the widespread moral ruin occasioned by this wicked system. Their talk is of blighted cotton crops—not of the blight on their children's souls.

If you want to be fully convinced of the abominations of slavery, go on a southern plantation, and call yourself a negro trader. Then there will be no concealment; and you will see and hear things that will seem to you impossible among human beings with immortal souls.

# X. A PERILOUS PASSAGE IN THE SLAVE GIRL'S LIFE.

After my lover went away, Dr. Flint contrived a new plan. He seemed to have an idea that my fear of my mistress was his greatest obstacle. In the blandest tones, he told me that he was going to build a small house for me, in a secluded place, four miles away from the town. I shuddered; but I was constrained to listen, while he talked of his intention to give me a home of my own, and to make a lady of me. Hitherto, I had escaped my dreaded fate, by being in the midst of people. My grandmother had already had high words with my master about me. She had told him pretty plainly what she thought of his character, and there was considerable gossip in the neighborhood about our affairs, to which the open-mouthed jealousy of Mrs. Flint contributed not a little. When my master said he was going to build a house for me, and that he could do it with little trouble and expense, I was in hopes something would happen to frustrate his scheme; but I soon heard that the house was actually begun. I vowed before my Maker that I would never enter it: I had rather toil on the plantation from dawn till dark; I had rather live and die in jail, than drag on, from day to day, through such a living death. I was determined that the master, whom I so hated and loathed, who had blighted the prospects of my youth, and made my life a desert, should not, after my long struggle with him, succeed at last in trampling his victim under his feet. I would do any thing, every thing, for the sake of defeating him. What could I do? I thought and thought, till I became desperate, and made a plunge into the abyss.

And now, reader, I come to a period in my unhappy life, which I would gladly forget if I could. The remembrance fills me with sorrow and shame. It pains me to tell you of it; but I have promised to tell you the truth, and I will do it honestly, let it cost me what it may. I will not try to screen myself behind the plea of compulsion from a master; for it was not so. Neither can I plead ignorance or thoughtlessness. For years, my master had done his utmost to pollute my mind with foul images, and to destroy the pure principles inculcated by my grandmother, and the good mistress of my childhood. The influences of slavery had had the same effect on me that they had on other young girls; they had made me prematurely knowing, concerning the evil ways of the world. I knew what I did, and I did it with deliberate calculation.

But, O, ye happy women, whose purity has been sheltered from childhood, who have been free to choose the objects of your affection, whose homes are protected by law, do not judge the poor desolate slave girl too severely! If slavery had been abolished, I, also, could have married the man of my choice;

I could have had a home shielded by the laws; and I should have been spared the painful task of confessing what I am now about to relate; but all my prospects had been blighted by slavery. I wanted to keep myself pure; and, under the most adverse circumstances, I tried hard to preserve my self-respect; but I was struggling alone in the powerful grasp of the demon Slavery; and the monster proved too strong for me. I felt as if I was forsaken by God and man; as if all my efforts must be frustrated; and I became reckless in my despair.

I have told you that Dr. Flint's persecutions and his wife's jealousy had given rise to some gossip in the neighborhood. Among others, it chanced that a white unmarried gentleman had obtained some knowledge of the circumstances in which I was placed. He knew my grandmother, and often spoke to me in the street. He became interested for me, and asked questions about my master, which I answered in part. He expressed a great deal of sympathy, and a wish to aid me. He constantly sought opportunities to see me, and wrote to me frequently. I was a poor slave girl, only fifteen years old.

So much attention from a superior person was, of course, flattering; for human nature is the same in all. I also felt grateful for his sympathy, and encouraged by his kind words. It seemed to me a great thing to have such a friend. By degrees, a more tender feeling crept into my heart. He was an educated and eloquent gentleman; too eloquent, alas, for the poor slave girl who trusted in him. Of course I saw whither all this was tending. I knew the impassable gulf between us; but to be an object of interest to a man who is not married, and who is not her master, is agreeable to the pride and feelings of a slave, if her miserable situation has left her any pride or sentiment. It seems less degrading to give one's self, than to submit to compulsion. There is something akin to freedom in having a lover who has no control over you, except that which he gains by kindness and attachment. A master may treat you as rudely as he pleases, and you dare not speak; moreover, the wrong does not seem so great with an unmarried man, as with one who has a wife to be made unhappy. There may be sophistry in all this; but the condition of a slave confuses all principles of morality, and, in fact, renders the practice of them impossible.

When I found that my master had actually begun to build the lonely cottage, other feelings mixed with those I have described. Revenge, and calculations of interest, were added to flattered vanity and sincere gratitude for kindness. I knew nothing would enrage Dr. Flint so much as to know that I favored another, and it was something to triumph over my tyrant even in that small way. I thought he would revenge himself by selling me, and I was sure my friend, Mr. Sands, would buy me. He was a man of more generosity and feeling than my master, and I thought my freedom could be easily obtained from him. The crisis of my fate now came so near that I was desperate. I shuddered to think of being the mother of children that should be owned by my old tyrant. I knew that as soon as a new fancy took him, his victims were sold far off to get rid of them; especially if they had children. I had seen several women sold, with babies at the breast. He never allowed his offspring by slaves to remain long in sight of himself and his wife. Of a man who was not my master I could ask to have my children well supported; and in this case, I felt confident I should obtain the boon. I also felt quite sure that they would be made free. With all these thoughts revolving in my mind, and seeing no other way of escaping the doom I so much dreaded, I made a headlong plunge. Pity me, and pardon me, O virtuous reader! You never knew what it is to be a slave; to be entirely unprotected by law or custom; to have the laws reduce you to the condition of a chattel, entirely subject to the will of another. You never exhausted your ingenuity in avoiding the snares, and eluding the power of a hated tyrant; you never shuddered at the sound of his footsteps, and trembled within hearing of his voice. I know I did wrong. No one can feel it more sensibly than I do. The painful and humiliating memory will haunt me to my dying day. Still, in looking back, calmly, on the events of my life, I feel that the slave woman ought not to be judged by the same standard as others.

The months passed on. I had many unhappy hours. I secretly mourned over the sorrow I was bringing on my grandmother, who had so tried to shield me from harm. I knew that I was the greatest comfort of her old age, and that it was a source of pride to her that I had not degraded myself, like most of the slaves. I wanted to confess to her that I was no longer worthy of her love; but I could not utter the dreaded words.

As for Dr. Flint, I had a feeling of satisfaction and triumph in the thought of telling him. From time to time he told me of his intended arrangements, and I was silent. At last, he came and told me the cottage was completed, and ordered me to go to it. I told him I would never enter it. He said, "I have heard enough of such talk as that. You shall go, if you are carried by force; and you shall remain there."

I replied, "I will never go there. In a few months I shall be a mother."

He stood and looked at me in dumb amazement, and left the house without a word. I thought I should be happy in my triumph over him. But now that the truth was out, and my relatives would hear of it, I felt wretched. Humble as were their circumstances, they had pride in my good character. Now, how could I look at them in the face? My self-respect was gone! I had resolved that I would be virtuous, though I was a slave. I had said, "Let the storm beat! I will brave it till I die." And now, how humiliated I felt!

I went to my grandmother. My lips moved to make confession, but the words stuck in my throat. I sat down in the shade of a tree at her door and began to sew. I think she saw something unusual was the matter with me. The mother of slaves is very watchful. She knows there is no security for her children. After they have entered their teens she lives in daily expectation of trouble. This leads to many questions. If the girl is of a sensitive nature, timidity keeps her from answering truthfully, and this well-meant course has a tendency to drive her from maternal counsels. Presently, in came my mistress, like a mad woman, and accused me concerning her husband. My grandmother, whose suspicions had been previously awakened, believed what she said. She exclaimed, "O Linda! Has it come to this? I had rather see you dead than to see you as you now are. You are a disgrace to your dead mother." She tore from my fingers my mother's wedding ring and her silver thimble. "Go away!" she exclaimed, "and never come to my house, again." Her reproaches fell so hot and heavy, that they left me no chance to answer. Bitter tears, such as the eyes never shed but once, were my only answer. I rose from my seat, but fell back again, sobbing. She did not speak to me; but the tears were running down her furrowed cheeks, and they scorched me like fire. She had always been so kind to me! So kind! How I longed to throw myself at her feet, and tell her all the truth! But she had ordered me to go, and never to come there again. After a few minutes, I mustered strength, and started to obey her. With what feelings did I now close that little gate, which I used to open with such an eager hand in my childhood! It closed upon me with a sound I never heard before.

Where could I go? I was afraid to return to my master's. I walked on recklessly, not caring where I went, or what would become of me. When I had gone four or five miles, fatigue compelled me to stop. I sat down on the stump of an old tree. The stars were shining through the boughs above me. How they mocked me, with their bright, calm light! The hours passed by, and as I sat there alone a chilliness and deadly sickness came over me. I sank on the ground. My mind was full of horrid thoughts. I prayed to die; but the prayer was not answered. At last, with great effort I roused myself, and walked some distance further, to the house of a woman who had been a friend of my mother. When I told her why I was there, she spoke soothingly to me; but I could not be comforted. I thought I could bear my shame if I could only be reconciled to my grandmother. I longed to open my heart to her. I thought if she could know the real state of the case, and all I had been bearing for years, she would perhaps judge me less harshly. My friend advised me to send for her. I did so; but days of agonizing suspense passed before she came. Had she utterly forsaken me? No. She came at last. I knelt before her, and told her the things that had poisoned my life; how long I had been persecuted; that I saw no way of escape; and in an hour of extremity I had become desperate. She listened in silence. I told her I would bear any thing and do any thing, if in time I had hopes of obtaining her forgiveness. I begged of her to pity me, for my dead mother's sake. And she did pity me. She did not say, "I forgive you;" but she looked at me lovingly, with her eyes full of tears. She laid her old hand gently on my head, and murmured, "Poor child! Poor child!"

# XI. THE NEW TIE TO LIFE.

I returned to my good grandmother's house. She had an interview with Mr. Sands. When she asked him why he could not have left her one ewe lamb,—whether there were not plenty of slaves who did not care about character,—he made no answer, but he spoke kind and encouraging words. He promised to care for my child, and to buy me, be the conditions what they might.

I had not seen Dr. Flint for five days. I had never seen him since I made the avowal to him. He talked of the disgrace I had brought on myself; how I had sinned against my master, and mortified my old grandmother. He intimated that if I had accepted his proposals, he, as a physician, could have saved me from exposure. He even condescended to pity me. Could he have offered wormwood more bitter? He, whose persecutions had been the cause of my sin!

"Linda," said he, "though you have been criminal towards me, I feel for you, and I can pardon you if you obey my wishes. Tell me whether the fellow you wanted to marry is the father of your child. If you deceive me, you shall feel the fires of hell."

I did not feel as proud as I had done. My strongest weapon with him was gone. I was lowered in my own estimation, and had resolved to bear his abuse in silence. But when he spoke contemptuously of the lover who had always treated me honorably; when I remembered that but for him I might have been a virtuous, free, and happy wife, I lost my patience. "I have sinned against God and myself," I replied; "but not against you."

He clinched his teeth, and muttered, "Curse you!" He came towards me, with ill-suppressed rage, and exclaimed, "You obstinate girl! I could grind your bones to powder! You have thrown yourself away on some worthless rascal. You are weak-minded, and have been easily persuaded by those who don't care a straw for you. The future will settle accounts between us. You are blinded now; but hereafter you will be convinced that your master was your best friend. My lenity towards you is a proof of it. I might have punished you in many ways. I might have whipped till you fell dead under the lash. But I wanted you to live; I would have bettered your condition. Others cannot do it. You are my slave. Your mistress, disgusted by your conduct, forbids you to return to the house; therefore I leave you here for the present; but I shall see you often. I will call to-morrow."

He came with frowning brows, that showed a dissatisfied state of mind. After asking about my health, he inquired whether my board was paid, and who visited me. He then went on to say that he had neglected his duty; that as a physician there were certain things that he ought to have explained to me. Then followed talk such as would have made the most shameless blush. He ordered me to stand up before him. I obeyed. "I command you," said he, "to tell me whether the father of your child is white or black." I hesitated. "Answer me this instant!" he exclaimed. I did answer. He sprang upon me like a wolf, and grabbed my arm as if he would have broken it. "Do you love him?" said he, in a hissing tone.

"I am thankful that I do not despise him," I replied.

He raised his hand to strike me; but it fell again. I don't know what arrested the blow. He sat down, with lips tightly compressed. At last he spoke. "I came here," said he, "to make you a friendly proposition; but your ingratitude chafes me beyond endurance. You turn aside all my good intentions towards you. I don't know what it is that keeps me from killing you." Again he rose, as if he had a mind to strike me.

But he resumed. "On one condition I will forgive your insolence and crime. You must henceforth have no communication of any kind with the father of your child. You must not ask any thing from him, or receive any thing from him. I will take care of you and your child. You had better promise this at once, and not wait till you are deserted by him. This is the last act of mercy I shall show towards you."

I said something about being unwilling to have my child supported by a man who had cursed it and me also. He rejoined, that a woman who had sunk to my level had no right to expect any thing else. He asked, for the last time, would I accept his kindness? I answered that I would not.

"Very well," said he; "then take the consequences of your wayward course. Never look to me for help. You are my slave, and shall always be my slave. I will never sell you, that you may depend upon."

Hope died away in my heart as he closed the door after him. I had calculated that in his rage he would sell me to a slave-trader; and I knew the father of my child was on the watch to buy me.

About this time my uncle Phillip was expected to return from a voyage. The day before his departure I had officiated as bridesmaid to a young friend. My heart was then ill at ease, but my smiling countenance did not betray it. Only a year had passed; but what fearful changes it had wrought! My heart had grown gray in misery. Lives that flash in sunshine, and lives that are born in tears, receive their hue from circumstances. None of us know what a year may bring forth.

I felt no joy when they told me my uncle had come. He wanted to see me, though he knew what had happened. I shrank from him at first; but at last consented that he should come to my room. He received me as he always had done. O, how my heart smote me when I felt his tears on my burning cheeks! The words of my grandmother came to my mind,—"Perhaps your mother and father are taken from the evil days to come." My disappointed heart could now praise God that it was so. But why, thought I, did my relatives ever cherish hopes for me? What was there to save me from the usual fate of slave girls? Many more beautiful and more intelligent than I had experienced a similar fate, or a far worse one. How could they hope that I should escape?

My uncle's stay was short, and I was not sorry for it. I was too ill in mind and body to enjoy my friends as I had done. For some weeks I was unable to leave my bed. I could not have any doctor but my master, and I would not have him sent for. At last, alarmed by my increasing illness, they sent for him. I was very weak and nervous; and as soon as he entered the room, I began to scream. They told him my state was very critical. He had no wish to hasten me out of the world, and he withdrew.

When my babe was born, they said it was premature. It weighed only four pounds; but God let it live. I heard the doctor say I could not survive till morning. I had often prayed for death; but now I did not want to die, unless my child could die too. Many weeks passed before I was able to leave my bed. I was a mere wreck of my former self. For a year there was scarcely a day when I was free from chills and fever. My babe also was sickly. His little limbs were often racked with pain. Dr. Flint continued his visits, to look after my health; and he did not fail to remind me that my child was an addition to his stock of slaves.

I felt too feeble to dispute with him, and listened to his remarks in silence. His visits were less frequent; but his busy spirit could not remain quiet. He employed my brother in his office; and he was made the medium of frequent notes and messages to me. William was a bright lad, and of much use to the doctor. He had learned to put up medicines, to leech, cup, and bleed. He had taught himself to read and spell. I was proud of my brother, and the old doctor suspected as much. One day, when I had not seen him for several weeks, I heard his steps approaching the door. I dreaded the encounter, and hid myself. He inquired for me, of course; but I was nowhere to be found. He went to his office, and despatched William with a note. The color mounted to my brother's face when he gave it to me; and he said, "Don't you hate me, Linda, for bringing you these things?" I told him I could not blame him; he was a slave, and obliged to obey his master's will. The note ordered me to come to his office. I went. He demanded to know where I was when he called. I told him I was at home. He flew into a passion, and said he knew better. Then he launched out upon his usual themes,—my crimes against him, and my ingratitude for his forbearance. The laws were laid down to me anew, and I was dismissed. I felt humiliated that my brother should stand by, and listen to such language as would be addressed only to a slave. Poor boy! He was powerless to defend me; but I saw the tears, which he vainly strove to keep back. The manifestation of feeling irritated the doctor. William could do nothing to please him. One morning he did not arrive at the office so early as usual; and that circumstance afforded his master an opportunity to vent his spleen. He was put in jail. The next day my brother sent a trader to the doctor, with a request to be sold. His master was greatly incensed at what he called his insolence. He said he had put him there, to reflect upon his bad conduct, and he certainly was not giving any evidence of repentance. For two days he harassed himself to find somebody to do his office work; but every thing went wrong without William. He was released, and ordered to take his old stand, with many threats, if he was not careful about his future behavior.

As the months passed on, my boy improved in health. When he was a year old, they called him beautiful. The little vine was taking deep root in my existence, though its clinging fondness excited a mixture of love and pain. When I was most sorely oppressed I found a solace in his smiles. I loved to watch his infant slumbers; but always there was a dark cloud over my enjoyment. I could never forget that he was a slave. Sometimes I wished that he might die in infancy. God tried me. My darling became very ill. The bright eyes grew dull, and the little feet and hands were so icy cold that I thought death had already touched them. I had prayed for his death, but never so earnestly as I now prayed for his life; and my prayer was heard. Alas, what mockery it is for a slave mother to try to pray back her dying child to life! Death is better than slavery. It was a sad thought that I had no name to give my child. His father caressed him and treated him kindly, whenever he had a chance to see him. He was not unwilling that he should bear his name; but he had no legal claim to it; and if I had bestowed it upon him, my master would have regarded it as a new crime, a new piece of insolence, and would, perhaps, revenge it on the boy. O, the serpent of Slavery has many and poisonous fangs!

# XII. FEAR OF INSURRECTION.

Not far from this time Nat Turner's insurrection broke out; and the news threw our town into great commotion. Strange that they should be alarmed, when their slaves were so "contented and happy"! But so it was.

It was always the custom to have a muster every year. On that occasion every white man shouldered his musket. The citizens and the so-called country gentlemen wore military uniforms. The poor whites took their places in the ranks in every-day dress, some without shoes, some without hats. This grand occasion had already passed; and when the slaves were told there was to be another muster, they were surprised and rejoiced. Poor creatures! They thought it was going to be a holiday. I was informed of the true state of affairs, and imparted it to the few I could trust. Most gladly would I have proclaimed it to every slave; but I dared not. All could not be relied on. Mighty is the power of the torturing lash.

By sunrise, people were pouring in from every quarter within twenty miles of the town. I knew the houses were to be searched; and I expected it would be done by country bullies and the poor whites. I knew nothing annoyed them so much as to see colored people living in comfort and respectability; so I made arrangements for them with especial care. I arranged every thing in my grandmother's house as neatly as possible. I put white quilts on the beds, and decorated some of the rooms with flowers. When all was arranged, I sat down at the window to watch. Far as my eye could reach, it rested on a motley crowd of soldiers. Drums and fifes were discoursing martial music. The men were divided into companies of sixteen, each headed by a captain. Orders were given, and the wild scouts rushed in every direction, wherever a colored face was to be found.

It was a grand opportunity for the low whites, who had no negroes of their own to scourge. They exulted in such a chance to exercise a little brief authority, and show their subserviency to the slaveholders; not reflecting that the power which trampled on the colored people also kept themselves in poverty, ignorance, and moral degradation. Those who never witnessed such scenes can hardly believe what I know was inflicted at this time on innocent men, women, and children, against whom there was not the slightest ground for suspicion. Colored people and slaves who lived in remote parts of the town suffered in an especial manner. In some cases the searchers scattered powder and shot among their clothes, and then sent other parties to find them, and bring them forward as proof that they were plotting insurrection. Every where men, women, and children were whipped till the blood stood in puddles at their feet. Some received five hundred lashes; others were tied hands and feet, and tortured with a bucking paddle, which blisters the skin terribly. The dwellings of the colored people, unless they happened to be protected by some influential white person, who was nigh at hand, were robbed of clothing and every thing else the marauders thought worth carrying away. All day long these unfeeling wretches went round, like a troop of demons, terrifying and tormenting the helpless. At night, they formed themselves into patrol bands, and went wherever they chose among the colored people, acting out their brutal will. Many women hid themselves in woods and swamps, to keep out of their way. If any of the husbands or fathers told of these outrages, they were tied up to the public whipping post, and cruelly scourged for telling lies about white men. The consternation was universal. No two people that had the slightest tinge of color in their faces dared to be seen talking together.

I entertained no positive fears about our household, because we were in the midst of white families who would protect us. We were ready to receive the soldiers whenever they came. It was not long before we heard the tramp of feet and the sound of voices. The door was rudely pushed open; and in they tumbled, like a pack of hungry wolves. They snatched at every thing within their reach. Every box, trunk, closet, and corner underwent a thorough examination. A box in one of the drawers containing some silver change was eagerly pounced upon. When I stepped forward to take it from them, one of the soldiers turned and said angrily, "What d'ye foller us fur? D'ye s'pose white folks is come to steal?"

I replied, "You have come to search; but you have searched that box, and I will take it, if you please."

At that moment I saw a white gentleman who was friendly to us; and I called to him, and asked him to have the goodness to come in and stay till the search was over. He readily complied. His entrance into the house brought in the captain of the company, whose business it was to guard the outside of the house, and see that none of the inmates left it. This officer was Mr. Litch, the wealthy slaveholder whom I mentioned, in the account of neighboring planters, as being notorious for his cruelty. He felt above soiling his hands with the search. He merely gave orders; and, if a bit of writing was discovered, it was carried to him by his ignorant followers, who were unable to read.

My grandmother had a large trunk of bedding and table cloths. When that was opened, there was a great shout of surprise; and one exclaimed, "Where'd the damned niggers git all dis sheet an' table clarf?"

My grandmother, emboldened by the presence of our white protector said, "You may be sure we didn't pilfer 'em from your houses."

"Look here, mammy," said a grim-looking fellow without any coat, "you seem to feel mighty gran' 'cause you got all them 'ere fixens. White folks oughter have 'em all."

His remarks were interrupted by a chorus of voices shouting, "We's got 'em! We's got 'em! Dis 'ere yaller gal's got letters!"

There was a general rush for the supposed letter, which, upon examination, proved to be some verses written to me by a friend. In packing away my things, I had overlooked them. When their captain informed them of their contents, they seemed much disappointed. He inquired of me who wrote them. I told him it was one of my friends. "Can you read them?" he asked. When I told him I could, he swore, and raved, and tore the paper into bits. "Bring me all your letters!" said he, in commanding tone. I told him I had none. "Don't be afraid," he continued, in an insinuating way. "Bring them all to me. Nobody shall do you any harm." Seeing I did not move to obey him, his pleasant tone changed to oaths and threats. "Who writes to you? half free niggers?" inquired he. I replied, "O, no; most of my letters are from white people. Some request me to burn them after they are read, and some I destroy without reading."

An exclamation of surprise from some of the company put a stop to our conversation. Some silver spoons which ornamented an old-fashioned buffet had just been discovered. My grandmother was in the habit of preserving fruit for many ladies in the town, and of preparing suppers for parties; consequently she had many jars of preserves. The closet that contained these was next invaded, and the contents tasted. One of them, who was helping himself freely, tapped his neighbor on the shoulder, and said, "Wal done! Don't wonder de niggers want to kill all de white folks, when dey live on 'sarves" [meaning preserves]. I stretched out my hand to take the jar, saying, "You were not sent here to search for sweetmeats."

"And what were we sent for?" said the captain, bristling up to me. I evaded the question.

The search of the house was completed, and nothing found to condemn us. They next proceeded to the garden, and knocked about every bush and vine, with no better success. The captain called his men together, and, after a short consultation, the order to march was given. As they passed out of the gate, the captain turned back, and pronounced a malediction on the house. He said it ought to be burned to the ground, and each of its inmates receive thirty-nine lashes. We came out of this affair very fortunately; not losing any thing except some wearing apparel.

Towards evening the turbulence increased. The soldiers, stimulated by drink, committed still greater cruelties. Shrieks and shouts continually rent the air. Not daring to go to the door, I peeped under the window curtain. I saw a mob dragging along a number of colored people, each white man, with his musket upraised, threatening instant death if they did not stop their shrieks. Among the prisoners was a respectable old colored minister. They had found a few parcels of shot in his house, which his wife had for years used to balance her scales. For this they were going to shoot him on Court House Green. What a spectacle was that for a civilized country! A rabble, staggering under intoxication, assuming to be the administrators of justice!

The better class of the community exerted their influence to save the innocent, persecuted people; and in several instances they succeeded, by keeping them shut up in jail till the excitement abated. At last the white citizens found that their own property was not safe from the lawless rabble they had summoned to protect them. They rallied the drunken swarm, drove them back into the country, and set a guard over the town.

The next day, the town patrols were commissioned to search colored people that lived out of the city; and the most shocking outrages were committed with perfect impunity. Every day for a fortnight, if I looked out, I saw horsemen with some poor panting negro tied to their saddles, and compelled by the lash to keep up with their speed, till they arrived at the jail yard. Those who had been whipped too unmercifully to walk were washed with brine, tossed into a cart, and carried to jail. One black man, who had not fortitude to endure scourging, promised to give information about the conspiracy. But it turned out that he knew nothing at all. He had not even heard the name of Nat Turner. The poor fellow had, however, made up a story, which augmented his own sufferings and those of the colored people.

The day patrol continued for some weeks, and at sundown a night guard was substituted. Nothing at all was proved against the colored people, bond or free. The wrath of the slaveholders was somewhat appeased by the capture of Nat Turner. The imprisoned were released. The slaves were sent to their masters, and the free were permitted to return to their ravaged homes. Visiting was strictly forbidden on the plantations. The slaves begged the privilege of again meeting at their little church in the woods, with their burying ground around it. It was built by the colored people, and they had no higher happiness than to meet there and sing hymns together, and pour out their hearts in spontaneous prayer. Their request was denied, and the church was demolished. They were permitted to attend the white churches, a certain portion of the galleries being appropriated to their use. There, when every body else had partaken of the communion, and the benediction had been pronounced, the minister said, "Come down, now, my colored friends." They obeyed the summons, and partook of the bread and wine, in commemoration of the meek and lowly Jesus, who said, "God is your Father, and all ye are brethren."

# XIII. THE CHURCH AND SLAVERY.

After the alarm caused by Nat Turner's insurrection had subsided, the slaveholders came to the conclusion that it would be well to give the slaves enough of religious instruction to keep them from murdering their masters. The Episcopal clergyman offered to hold a separate service on Sundays for their benefit. His colored members were very few, and also very respectable—a fact which I presume had some weight with him. The difficulty was to decide on a suitable place for them to worship. The Methodist and Baptist churches admitted them in the afternoon; but their carpets and cushions were not so costly as those at the Episcopal church. It was at last decided that they should meet at the house of a free colored man, who was a member.

I was invited to attend, because I could read. Sunday evening came, and, trusting to the cover of night, I ventured out. I rarely ventured out by daylight, for I always went with fear, expecting at every turn to encounter Dr. Flint, who was sure to turn me back, or order me to his office to inquire where I got my bonnet, or some other article of dress. When the Rev. Mr. Pike came, there were some twenty persons present. The reverend gentleman knelt in prayer, then seated himself, and requested all present, who could read, to open their books, while he gave out the portions he wished them to repeat or respond to.

His text was, "Servants, be obedient to them that are your masters according to the flesh, with fear and trembling, in singleness of your heart, as unto Christ."

Pious Mr. Pike brushed up his hair till it stood upright, and, in deep, solemn tones, began: "Hearken, ye servants! Give strict heed unto my words. You are rebellious sinners. Your hearts are filled with all manner of evil. 'Tis the devil who tempts you. God is angry with you, and will surely punish you, if you don't forsake your wicked ways. You that live in town are eyeservants behind your master's back. Instead of serving your masters faithfully, which is pleasing in the sight of your heavenly Master, you are idle, and shirk your work. God sees you. You tell lies. God hears you. Instead of being engaged in worshipping him, you are hidden away somewhere, feasting on your master's substance; tossing coffee-grounds with some wicked fortuneteller, or cutting cards with another old hag. Your masters may not find you out, but God sees you, and will punish you. O, the depravity of your hearts! When your master's work is done, are you quietly together, thinking of the goodness of God to such sinful creatures? No; you are quarrelling, and tying up little bags of roots to bury under the doorsteps to poison each other with. God sees you. You men steal away to every grog shop to sell your master's corn, that you may buy rum to drink. God sees you. You sneak into the back streets, or among the bushes, to pitch coppers. Although your masters may not find you out, God sees you;

and he will punish you. You must forsake your sinful ways, and be faithful servants. Obey your old master and your young master—your old mistress and your young mistress. If you disobey your earthly master, you offend your heavenly Master. You must obey God's commandments. When you go from here, don't stop at the corners of the streets to talk, but go directly home, and let your master and mistress see that you have come."

The benediction was pronounced. We went home, highly amused at brother Pike's gospel teaching, and we determined to hear him again. I went the next Sabbath evening, and heard pretty much a repetition of the last discourse. At the close of the meeting, Mr. Pike informed us that he found it very inconvenient to meet at the friend's house, and he should be glad to see us, every Sunday evening, at his own kitchen.

I went home with the feeling that I had heard the Reverend Mr. Pike for the last time. Some of his members repaired to his house, and found that the kitchen sported two tallow candles; the first time, I am sure, since its present occupant owned it, for the servants never had any thing but pine knots. It was so long before the reverend gentleman descended from his comfortable parlor that the slaves left, and went to enjoy a Methodist shout. They never seem so happy as when shouting and singing at religious meetings. Many of them are sincere, and nearer to the gate of heaven than sanctimonious Mr. Pike, and other long-faced Christians, who see wounded Samaritans, and pass by on the other side.

The slaves generally compose their own songs and hymns; and they do not trouble their heads much about the measure. They often sing the following verses:

> Old Satan is one busy ole man;
> He rolls dem blocks all in my way;
> But Jesus is my bosom friend;
> He rolls dem blocks away.
>
> If I had died when I was young,
> Den how my stam'ring tongue would have sung;
> But I am ole, and now I stand
> A narrow chance for to tread dat heavenly land.

I well remember one occasion when I attended a Methodist class meeting. I went with a burdened spirit, and happened to sit next a poor, bereaved mother, whose heart was still heavier than mine. The class leader was the town constable—a man who bought and sold slaves, who whipped his brethren and sisters of the church at the public whipping post, in jail or out of jail. He was ready to perform that Christian office any where for fifty cents. This white-faced, black-hearted brother came near us, and said to the stricken woman, "Sister, can't you tell us how the Lord deals with your soul? Do you love him as you did formerly?"

She rose to her feet, and said, in piteous tones, "My Lord and Master, help me! My load is more than I can bear. God has hid himself from me, and I am left in darkness and misery." Then, striking her breast, she continued, "I can't tell you what is in here! They've got all my children. Last week they took the last one. God only knows where they've sold her. They let me have her sixteen years, and then—O! O! Pray for her brothers and sisters! I've got nothing to live for now. God make my time short!"

She sat down, quivering in every limb. I saw that constable class leader become crimson in the face with suppressed laughter, while he held up his handkerchief, that those who were weeping for the poor woman's calamity might not see his merriment. Then, with assumed gravity, he said to the bereaved mother, "Sister, pray to the Lord that every dispensation of his divine will may be sanctified to the good of your poor needy soul!"

The congregation struck up a hymn, and sung as though they were as free as the birds that warbled round us,—

> Ole Satan thought he had a mighty aim;
> He missed my soul, and caught my sins.
> Cry Amen, cry Amen, cry Amen to God!
>
> He took my sins upon his back;
> Went muttering and grumbling down to hell.
> Cry Amen, cry Amen, cry Amen to God!
>
> Ole Satan's church is here below.
> Up to God's free church I hope to go.
> Cry Amen, cry Amen, cry Amen to God!

Precious are such moments to the poor slaves. If you were to hear them at such times, you might think they were happy. But can that hour of singing and shouting sustain them through the dreary week, toiling without wages, under constant dread of the lash?

The Episcopal clergyman, who, ever since my earliest recollection, had been a sort of god among the slaveholders, concluded, as his family was large, that he must go where money was more abundant. A very different clergyman took his place. The change was very agreeable to the colored people, who said, "God has sent us a good man this time." They loved him, and their children followed him for a smile or a kind word. Even the slaveholders felt his influence. He brought to the rectory five slaves. His wife taught them to read and write, and to be useful to her and themselves. As soon as he was settled, he turned his attention to the needy slaves around him. He urged upon his parishioners the duty of having a meeting expressly for them every Sunday, with a sermon adapted to their comprehension. After much argument and importunity, it was finally agreed that they might occupy the gallery of the church on Sunday evenings. Many colored people, hitherto unaccustomed to attend church, now gladly went to hear the gospel preached. The sermons were simple, and they understood them. Moreover, it was the first time they had ever been addressed as human beings. It was not long before his white parishioners began to be dissatisfied. He was accused of preaching better sermons to the negroes than he did to them. He honestly confessed that he bestowed more pains upon those sermons than upon any others; for the slaves were reared in such ignorance that it was a difficult task to adapt himself to their comprehension. Dissensions arose in the parish. Some wanted he should preach to them in the evening, and to the slaves in the afternoon. In the midst of these disputings his wife died, after a very short illness. Her slaves gathered round her dying bed in great sorrow. She said, "I have tried to do you good and promote your happiness; and if I have failed, it has not been for want of interest in your welfare. Do not weep for me; but prepare for the new duties that lie before you. I leave you all free. May we meet in a better world." Her liberated slaves were sent away, with funds to establish them comfortably. The colored people will long bless the memory of that truly Christian woman. Soon after her death her husband preached his farewell sermon, and many tears were shed at his departure.

Several years after, he passed through our town and preached to his former congregation. In his afternoon sermon he addressed the colored people. "My friends," said he, "it affords me great happiness to have an opportunity of speaking to you again. For two years I have been striving to do something for the colored people of my own parish; but nothing is yet accomplished. I have not even preached a sermon to them. Try to live according to the word of God, my friends. Your skin is darker than mine; but God judges men by their hearts, not by the color of their skins." This was strange doctrine from a southern pulpit. It was very offensive to slaveholders. They said he and his wife had made fools of their slaves, and that he preached like a fool to the negroes.

I knew an old black man, whose piety and childlike trust in God were beautiful to witness. At fifty-three years old he joined the Baptist church. He had a most earnest desire to learn to read. He thought he should know how to serve God better if he could only read the Bible. He came to me, and begged me to teach him. He said he could not pay me, for he had no money; but he would bring me nice fruit when the season for it came. I asked him if he didn't know it was contrary to law; and that slaves were whipped and imprisoned for teaching each other to read. This brought the tears into his eyes. "Don't be troubled, uncle Fred," said I. "I have no thoughts of refusing to teach you. I only told you of the law, that you might know the danger, and be on your guard." He thought he could plan to come three times a week without its being suspected. I selected a quiet nook, where no intruder was likely to penetrate, and there I taught him his A, B, C. Considering his age, his progress was astonishing. As soon as he could spell in two syllables he wanted to spell out words in the Bible. The happy smile that illuminated his face put joy into my heart. After spelling out a few words, he paused, and said, "Honey, it 'pears when I can read dis good book I shall be nearer to God. White man is got all de sense. He can larn easy. It ain't easy for ole black man like me. I only wants to read dis book, dat I may know how to live; den I hab no fear 'bout dying."

I tried to encourage him by speaking of the rapid progress he had made. "Hab patience, child," he replied. "I larns slow."

I had no need of patience. His gratitude, and the happiness imparted, were more than a recompense for all my trouble.

At the end of six months he had read through the New Testament, and could find any text in it. One day, when he had recited unusually well, I said, "Uncle Fred, how do you manage to get your lessons so well?"

"Lord bress you, chile," he replied. "You nebber gibs me a lesson dat I don't pray to God to help me to understan' what I spells and what I reads. And he does help me, chile. Bress his holy name!"

There are thousands, who, like good uncle Fred, are thirsting for the water of life; but the law forbids it, and the churches withhold it. They send the Bible to heathen abroad, and neglect the heathen at home. I am glad that missionaries go out to the dark corners of the earth; but I ask them not to overlook the dark corners at home. Talk to American slaveholders as you talk to savages in Africa. Tell them it was wrong to traffic in men. Tell them it is sinful to sell their own children, and atrocious to violate their own daughters. Tell them that all men are brethren, and that man has no right to shut out the light of knowledge from his brother. Tell them they are answerable to God for sealing up the Fountain of Life from souls that are thirsting for it.

There are men who would gladly undertake such missionary work as this; but, alas! their number is small. They are hated by the south, and would be driven from its soil, or dragged to prison to die, as others have been before them. The field is ripe for the harvest, and awaits the reapers. Perhaps the great grandchildren of uncle Fred may have freely imparted to them the divine treasures, which he sought by stealth, at the risk of the prison and the scourge.

Are doctors of divinity blind, or are they hypocrites? I suppose some are the one, and some the other; but I think if they felt the interest in the poor and the lowly, that they ought to feel, they would not be so easily blinded. A clergyman who goes to the south, for the first time, has usually some feeling, however vague, that slavery is wrong. The slaveholder suspects this, and plays his game accordingly. He makes himself as agreeable as possible; talks on theology, and other kindred topics. The reverend gentleman is asked to invoke a blessing on a table loaded with luxuries. After dinner he walks round the premises, and sees the beautiful groves and flowering vines, and the comfortable huts of favored household slaves. The southerner invites him to talk with those slaves. He asks them if they want to be free, and they say, "O, no, massa." This is sufficient to satisfy him. He comes home to publish a "South Side View of Slavery," and to complain of the exaggerations of abolitionists. He assures people that he has been to the south, and seen slavery for himself; that it is a beautiful "patriarchal institution;" that the slaves don't want their freedom; that they have hallelujah meetings and other religious privileges.

What does he know of the half-starved wretches toiling from dawn till dark on the plantations? of mothers shrieking for their children, torn from their arms by slave traders? of young girls dragged down into moral filth? of pools of blood around the whipping post? of hounds trained to tear human flesh? of men screwed into cotton gins to die? The slaveholder showed him none of these things, and the slaves dared not tell of them if he had asked them.

There is a great difference between Christianity and religion at the south. If a man goes to the communion table, and pays money into the treasury of the church, no matter if it be the price of blood, he is called religious. If a pastor has offspring by a woman not his wife, the church dismiss him, if she is a white woman; but if she is colored, it does not hinder his continuing to be their good shepherd.

When I was told that Dr. Flint had joined the Episcopal church, I was much surprised. I supposed that religion had a purifying effect on the character of men; but the worst persecutions I endured from him were after he was a communicant. The conversation of the doctor, the day after he had been confirmed, certainly gave me no indication that he had "renounced the devil and all his works." In answer to some of his usual talk, I reminded him that he had just joined the church. "Yes, Linda," said he. "It was proper for me to do so. I am getting in years, and my position in society requires it, and it puts an end to all the damned slang. You would do well to join the church, too, Linda."

"There are sinners enough in it already," rejoined I. "If I could be allowed to live like a Christian, I should be glad."

"You can do what I require; and if you are faithful to me, you will be as virtuous as my wife," he replied.

I answered that the Bible didn't say so.

His voice became hoarse with rage. "How dare you preach to me about your infernal Bible!" he exclaimed. "What right have you, who are my negro, to talk to me about what you would like and what you wouldn't like? I am your master, and you shall obey me."

No wonder the slaves sing, —
   Ole Satan's church is here below;
   Up to God's free church I hope to go.

# XIV. ANOTHER LINK TO LIFE.

I had not returned to my master's house since the birth of my child. The old man raved to have me thus removed from his immediate power; but his wife vowed, by all that was good and great, she would kill me if I came back; and he did not doubt her word. Sometimes he would stay away for a season. Then he would come and renew the old threadbare discourse about his forbearance and my ingratitude. He labored, most unnecessarily, to convince me that I had lowered myself. The venomous old reprobate had no need of descanting on that theme. I felt humiliated enough. My unconscious babe was the ever-present witness of my shame. I listened with silent contempt when he talked about my having forfeited his good opinion; but I shed bitter tears that I was no longer worthy of being respected by the good and pure. Alas! slavery still held me in its poisonous grasp. There was no chance for me to be respectable. There was no prospect of being able to lead a better life.

Sometimes, when my master found that I still refused to accept what he called his kind offers, he would threaten to sell my child. "Perhaps that will humble you," said he.

Humble me! Was I not already in the dust? But his threat lacerated my heart. I knew the law gave him power to fulfil it; for slaveholders have been cunning enough to enact that "the child shall follow the condition of the mother," not of the father, thus taking care that licentiousness shall not interfere with avarice. This reflection made me clasp my innocent babe all the more firmly to my heart. Horrid visions passed through my mind when I thought of his liability to fall into the slave trader's hands. I wept over him, and said, "O my child! perhaps they will leave you in some cold cabin to die, and then throw you into a hole, as if you were a dog."

When Dr. Flint learned that I was again to be a mother, he was exasperated beyond measure. He rushed from the house, and returned with a pair of shears. I had a fine head of hair; and he often railed about my pride of arranging it nicely. He cut every hair close to my head, storming and swearing all the time. I replied to some of his abuse, and he struck me. Some months before, he had pitched me down stairs in a fit of passion; and the injury I received was so serious that I was unable to turn myself in bed for many days. He then said, "Linda, I swear by God I will never raise my hand against you again;" but I knew that he would forget his promise.

After he discovered my situation, he was like a restless spirit from the pit. He came every day; and I was subjected to such insults as no pen can describe. I would not describe them if I could; they were too low, too revolting. I tried to keep them from my grandmother's knowledge as much as I could. I knew she had enough to sadden her life, without having my troubles to bear. When she saw the doctor treat me with violence, and heard him utter oaths terrible enough to palsy a man's tongue, she could not always hold her peace. It was natural and motherlike that she should try to defend me; but it only made matters worse.

When they told me my new-born babe was a girl, my heart was heavier than it had ever been before. Slavery is terrible for men; but it is far more terrible for women. Superadded to the burden common to all, they have wrongs, and sufferings, and mortifications peculiarly their own.

Dr. Flint had sworn that he would make me suffer, to my last day, for this new crime against him, as he called it; and as long as he had me in his power he kept his word. On the fourth day after the birth of my babe, he entered my room suddenly, and commanded me to rise and bring my baby to him. The nurse who took care of me had gone out of the room to prepare some nourishment, and I was alone. There was no alternative. I rose, took up my babe, and crossed the room to where he sat. "Now stand there," said he, "till I tell you to go back!" My child bore a strong resemblance to her father, and to the deceased Mrs. Sands, her grandmother. He noticed this; and while I stood before him, trembling with weakness, he heaped upon me and my little one every vile epithet he could think of. Even the grandmother in her grave did not escape his curses. In the midst of his vituperations I fainted at his feet. This recalled him to his senses. He took the baby from my arms, laid it on the bed, dashed cold water in my face, took me up, and shook me violently, to restore my consciousness before any one entered the room. Just then my grandmother came in, and he hurried out of the house. I suffered in consequence of this treatment; but I begged my friends to let me die, rather than send for the doctor. There was nothing I dreaded so much as his presence. My life was spared; and I was glad for the sake of my little ones. Had it not been for these ties to life, I should have been glad to be released by death, though I had lived only nineteen years.

Always it gave me a pang that my children had no lawful claim to a name. Their father offered his; but, if I had wished to accept the offer, I dared not while my master lived. Moreover, I knew it would not be accepted at their baptism. A Christian name they were at least entitled to; and we resolved to call my boy for our dear good Benjamin, who had gone far away from us.

My grandmother belonged to the church; and she was very desirous of having the children christened. I knew Dr. Flint would forbid it, and I did not venture to attempt it. But chance favored me. He was called to visit a patient out of town, and was obliged to be absent during Sunday. "Now is the time," said my grandmother; "we will take the children to church, and have them christened."

When I entered the church, recollections of my mother came over me, and I felt subdued in spirit. There she had presented me for baptism, without any reason to feel ashamed. She had been married, and had such legal rights as slavery allows to a slave. The vows had at least been sacred to her, and she had never violated them. I was glad she was not alive, to know under what different circumstances her grandchildren were presented for baptism. Why had my lot been so different from my mother's? Her master had died when she was a child; and she remained with her mistress till she married. She was never in the power of any master; and thus she escaped one class of the evils that generally fall upon slaves.

When my baby was about to be christened, the former mistress of my father stepped up to me, and proposed to give it her Christian name. To this I added the surname of my father, who had himself no legal right to it; for my grandfather on the paternal side was a white gentleman. What tangled skeins are the genealogies of slavery! I loved my father; but it mortified me to be obliged to bestow his name on my children.

When we left the church, my father's old mistress invited me to go home with her. She clasped a gold chain round my baby's neck. I thanked her for this kindness; but I did not like the emblem. I wanted no chain to be fastened on my daughter, not even if its links were of gold. How earnestly I prayed that she might never feel the weight of slavery's chain, whose iron entereth into the soul!

# XV. CONTINUED PERSECUTIONS.

My children grew finely; and Dr. Flint would often say to me, with an exulting smile. "These brats will bring me a handsome sum of money one of these days."

I thought to myself that, God being my helper, they should never pass into his hands. It seemed to me I would rather see them killed than have them given up to his power. The money for the freedom of myself and my children could be obtained; but I derived no advantage from that circumstance. Dr. Flint loved money, but he loved power more. After much discussion, my friends resolved on making another trial. There was a slaveholder about to leave for Texas, and he was commissioned to buy me. He was to begin with nine hundred dollars, and go up to twelve. My master refused his offers. "Sir," said he, "she don't belong to me. She is my daughter's property, and I have no right to sell her. I mistrust that you come from her paramour. If so, you may tell him that he cannot buy her for any money; neither can he buy her children."

The doctor came to see me the next day, and my heart beat quicker as he entered. I never had seen the old man tread with so majestic a step. He seated himself and looked at me with withering scorn. My children had learned to be afraid of him. The little one would shut her eyes and hide her face on my shoulder whenever she saw him; and Benny, who was now nearly five years old, often inquired, "What makes that bad man come here so many times? Does he want to hurt us?" I would clasp the dear boy in my arms, trusting that he would be free before he was old enough to solve the problem. And now, as the doctor sat there so grim and silent, the child left his play and came and nestled up by me. At last my tormentor spoke. "So you are left in disgust, are you?" said he. "It is no more than I expected. You remember I told you years ago that you would be treated so. So he is tired of you? Ha! ha! ha! The virtuous madam don't like to hear about it, does she? Ha! ha! ha!" There was a sting in his calling me virtuous madam. I no longer had the power of answering him as I had formerly done. He continued: "So it seems you are trying to get up another intrigue. Your new paramour came to me, and offered to buy you; but you may be assured you will not succeed. You are mine; and you shall be mine for life. There lives no human being that can take you out of slavery. I would have done it; but you rejected my kind offer."

I told him I did not wish to get up any intrigue; that I had never seen the man who offered to buy me.

"Do you tell me I lie?" exclaimed he, dragging me from my chair. "Will you say again that you never saw that man?"

I answered, "I do say so."

He clinched my arm with a volley of oaths. Ben began to scream, and I told him to go to his grandmother.

"Don't you stir a step, you little wretch!" said he. The child drew nearer to me, and put his arms round me, as if he wanted to protect me. This was too much for my enraged master. He caught him up and hurled him across the room. I thought he was dead, and rushed towards him to take him up.

"Not yet!" exclaimed the doctor. "Let him lie there till he comes to."

"Let me go! Let me go!" I screamed, "or I will raise the whole house." I struggled and got away; but he clinched me again. Somebody opened the door, and he released me. I picked up my insensible child, and when I turned my tormentor was gone. Anxiously, I bent over the little form, so pale and still; and when the brown eyes at last opened, I don't know whether I was very happy. All the doctor's former persecutions were renewed. He came morning, noon, and night. No jealous lover ever watched a rival more closely than he watched me and the unknown slaveholder, with whom he accused me of wishing to get up an intrigue. When my grandmother was out of the way he searched every room to find him.

In one of his visits, he happened to find a young girl, whom he had sold to a trader a few days previous. His statement was, that he sold her because she had been too familiar with the overseer. She had had a bitter life with him, and was glad to be sold. She had no mother, and no near ties. She had been torn from all her family years before. A few friends had entered into bonds for her safety, if the trader would allow her to spend with them the time that intervened between her sale and the gathering up of his human stock. Such a favor was rarely granted. It saved the trader the expense of board and jail fees, and though the amount was small, it was a weighty consideration in a slavetrader's mind.

Dr. Flint always had an aversion to meeting slaves after he had sold them. He ordered Rose out of the house; but he was no longer her master, and she took no notice of him. For once the crushed Rose was the conqueror. His gray eyes flashed angrily upon her; but that was the extent of his power. "How came this girl here?" he exclaimed. "What right had you to allow it, when you knew I had sold her?"

I answered, "This is my grandmother's house, and Rose came to see her. I have no right to turn any body out of doors, that comes here for honest purposes."

He gave me the blow that would have fallen upon Rose if she had still been his slave. My grandmother's attention had been attracted by loud voices, and she entered in time to see a second blow dealt. She was not a woman to let such an outrage, in her own house, go unrebuked. The doctor undertook to explain that I had been insolent. Her indignant feelings rose higher and higher, and finally boiled over in words. "Get out of my house!" she exclaimed. "Go home, and take care of your wife and children, and you will have enough to do, without watching my family."

He threw the birth of my children in her face, and accused her of sanctioning the life I was leading. She told him I was living with her by compulsion of his wife; that he needn't accuse her, for he was the one to blame; he was the one who had caused all the trouble. She grew more and more excited as she went on. "I tell you what, Dr. Flint," said she, "you ain't got many more years to live, and you'd better be saying your prayers. It will take 'em all, and more too, to wash the dirt off your soul."

"Do you know whom you are talking to?" he exclaimed.

She replied, "Yes, I know very well who I am talking to."

He left the house in a great rage. I looked at my grandmother. Our eyes met. Their angry expression had passed away, but she looked sorrowful and weary—weary of incessant strife. I wondered that it did not lessen her love for me; but if it did she never showed it. She was always kind, always ready to sympathize with my troubles. There might have been peace and contentment in that humble home if it had not been for the demon Slavery.

The winter passed undisturbed by the doctor. The beautiful spring came; and when Nature resumes her loveliness, the human soul is apt to revive also. My drooping hopes came to life again with the flowers. I was dreaming of freedom again; more for my children's sake than my own. I planned and I planned. Obstacles hit against plans. There seemed no way of overcoming them; and yet I hoped.

Back came the wily doctor. I was not at home when he called. A friend had invited me to a small party, and to gratify her I went. To my great consternation, a messenger came in haste to say that Dr. Flint was at my grandmother's, and insisted on seeing me. They did not tell him where I was, or he would have come and raised a disturbance in my friend's house. They sent me a dark wrapper, I threw it on and hurried home. My speed did not save me; the doctor had gone away in anger. I dreaded the morning, but I could not delay it; it came, warm and bright. At an early hour the doctor came and asked me where I had been last night. I told him. He did not believe me, and sent to my friend's house to ascertain the facts. He came in the afternoon to assure me he was satisfied that I had spoken the truth. He seemed to be in a facetious mood, and I expected some jeers were coming. "I suppose you need some recreation," said he, "but I am surprised at your being there, among those negroes. It was not the place for you. Are you allowed to visit such people?"

I understood this covert fling at the white gentleman who was my friend; but I merely replied, "I went to visit my friends, and any company they keep is good enough for me."

He went on to say, "I have seen very little of you of late, but my interest in you is unchanged. When I said I would have no more mercy on you I was rash. I recall my words. Linda, you desire freedom for yourself and your children, and you can obtain it only through me. If you agree to what I am about to propose, you and they shall be free. There must be no communication of any kind between you and their father. I will procure a cottage, where you and the children can live together. Your labor shall be light, such as sewing for my family. Think what is offered you, Linda—a home and freedom! Let the past be forgotten. If I have been harsh with you at times, your willfulness drove me to it. You know I exact obedience from my own children, and I consider you as yet a child."

He paused for an answer, but I remained silent. "Why don't you speak?" said he. "What more do you wait for?"

"Nothing, sir."

"Then you accept my offer?"

"No, sir."

His anger was ready to break loose; but he succeeded in curbing it, and replied, "You have answered without thought. But I must let you know there are two sides to my proposition; if you reject the bright side, you will be obliged to take the dark one. You must either accept my offer, or you and your children shall be sent to your young master's plantation, there to remain till your young mistress is married; and your children shall fare like the rest of the negro children. I give you a week to consider it."

He was shrewd; but I knew he was not to be trusted. I told him I was ready to give my answer now.

"I will not receive it now," he replied. "You act too much from impulse. Remember that you and your children can be free a week from to-day if you choose."

On what a monstrous chance hung the destiny of my children! I knew that my master's offer was a snare, and that if I entered it escape would be impossible. As for his promise, I knew him so well that I was sure if he gave me free papers, they would be so managed as to have no legal value. The alternative was inevitable. I resolved to go to the plantation. But then I thought how completely I should be in his power, and the prospect was appalling. Even if I should kneel before him, and implore him to spare me, for the sake of my children, I knew he would spurn me with his foot, and my weakness would be his triumph.

Before the week expired, I heard that young Mr. Flint was about to be married to a lady of his own stamp. I foresaw the position I should occupy in his establishment. I had once been sent to the plantation for punishment, and fear of the son had induced the father to recall me very soon. My mind was made up; I was resolved that I would foil my master and save my children, or I would perish in the attempt. I kept my plans to myself; I knew that friends would try to dissuade me from them, and I would not wound their feelings by rejecting their advice.

On the decisive day the doctor came, and said he hoped I had made a wise choice.

"I am ready to go to the plantation, sir," I replied.

"Have you thought how important your decision is to your children?" said he.

I told him I had.

"Very well. Go to the plantation, and my curse go with you," he replied. "Your boy shall be put to work, and he shall soon be sold; and your girl shall be raised for the purpose of selling well. Go your own ways!" He left the room with curses, not to be repeated.

As I stood rooted to the spot, my grandmother came and said, "Linda, child, what did you tell him?"

I answered that I was going to the plantation.

"Must you go?" said she. "Can't something be done to stop it?"

I told her it was useless to try; but she begged me not to give up. She said she would go to the doctor, and remind him how long and how faithfully she had served in the family, and how she had taken her own baby from her breast to nourish his wife. She would tell him I had been out of the family so long they would not miss me; that she would pay them for my time, and the money would procure a woman who had more strength for the situation than I had. I begged her not to go; but she persisted in saying, "He will listen to me, Linda." She went, and was treated as I expected. He coolly listened to what she said, but denied her request. He told her that what he did was for my good, that my feelings were entirely above my situation, and that on the plantation I would receive treatment that was suitable to my behavior.

My grandmother was much cast down. I had my secret hopes; but I must fight my battle alone. I had a woman's pride, and a mother's love for my children; and I resolved that out of the darkness of this hour a brighter dawn should rise for them. My master had power and law on his side; I had a determined will. There is might in each.

# XVI. SCENES AT THE PLANTATION.

Early the next morning I left my grandmother's with my youngest child. My boy was ill, and I left him behind. I had many sad thoughts as the old wagon jolted on. Hitherto, I had suffered alone; now, my little one was to be treated as a slave. As we drew near the great house, I thought of the time when I was formerly sent there out of revenge. I wondered for what purpose I was now sent. I could not tell. I resolved to obey orders so far as duty required; but within myself, I determined to make my stay as short as possible. Mr. Flint was waiting to receive us, and told me to follow him up stairs to receive orders for the day. My little Ellen was left below in the kitchen. It was a change for her, who had always been so carefully tended. My young master said she might amuse herself in the yard. This was kind of him, since the child was hateful to his sight. My task was to fit up the house for the reception of the bride. In the midst of sheets, tablecloths, towels, drapery, and carpeting, my head was as busy planning, as were my fingers with the needle. At noon I was allowed to go to Ellen. She had sobbed herself to sleep. I heard Mr. Flint say to a neighbor, "I've got her down here, and I'll soon take the town notions out of her head. My father is partly to blame for her nonsense. He ought to have broke her in long ago." The remark was made within my hearing, and it would have been quite as manly to have made it to my face. He had said things to my face which might, or might not, have surprised his neighbor if he had known of them. He was "a chip of the old block."

I resolved to give him no cause to accuse me of being too much of a lady, so far as work was concerned. I worked day and night, with wretchedness before me. When I lay down beside my child, I felt how much easier it would be to see her die than to see her master beat her about, as I daily saw him beat other little ones. The spirit of the mothers was so crushed by the lash, that they stood by, without courage to remonstrate. How much more must I suffer, before I should be "broke in" to that degree?

I wished to appear as contented as possible. Sometimes I had an opportunity to send a few lines home; and this brought up recollections that made it difficult, for a time, to seem calm and indifferent to my lot. Notwithstanding my efforts, I saw that Mr. Flint regarded me with a suspicious eye. Ellen broke down under the trials of her new life. Separated from me, with no one to look after her, she wandered about, and in a few days cried herself sick. One day, she sat under the window where I was at work, crying that weary cry which makes a mother's heart bleed. I was obliged to steel myself to bear it. After a while it ceased. I looked out, and she was gone. As it was near noon, I ventured to go down in search of her. The great house was raised two feet above the ground. I looked under it, and saw her about midway, fast asleep. I crept under and drew her out. As I held her in my arms, I thought how well it would be for her if she never waked up; and I uttered my thought aloud. I was startled to hear some one say, "Did you speak to me?" I looked up, and saw Mr. Flint standing beside me. He said nothing further, but turned, frowning, away. That night he sent Ellen a biscuit and a cup of sweetened milk. This generosity surprised me. I learned afterwards, that in the afternoon he had killed a large snake, which crept from under the house; and I supposed that incident had prompted his unusual kindness.

The next morning the old cart was loaded with shingles for town. I put Ellen into it, and sent her to her grandmother. Mr. Flint said I ought to have asked his permission. I told him the child was sick, and required attention which I had no time to give. He let it pass; for he was aware that I had accomplished much work in a little time.

I had been three weeks on the plantation, when I planned a visit home. It must be at night, after every body was in bed. I was six miles from town, and the road was very dreary. I was to go with a young man, who, I knew, often stole to town to see his mother. One night, when all was quiet, we started. Fear gave speed to our steps, and we were not long in performing the journey. I arrived at my grandmother's. Her bed room was on the first floor, and the window was open, the weather being warm. I spoke to her and she awoke. She let me in and closed the window, lest some late passer-by should see me. A light was brought, and the whole household gathered round me, some smiling and some crying. I went to look at my children, and thanked God for their happy sleep. The tears fell as I leaned over them. As I moved to leave, Benny stirred. I turned back, and whispered, "Mother is here." After digging at his eyes with his little fist, they opened, and he sat up in bed, looking at me curiously. Having satisfied himself that it was I, he exclaimed, "O mother! you ain't dad, are you? They didn't cut off your head at the plantation, did they?"

My time was up too soon, and my guide was waiting for me. I laid Benny back in his bed, and dried his tears by a promise to come again soon. Rapidly we retraced our steps back to the plantation. About half way we were met by a company of four patrols. Luckily we heard their horse's hoofs before they came in sight, and we had time to hide behind a large tree. They passed, hallooing and shouting in a manner that indicated a recent carousal. How thankful we were that they had not their dogs with them! We hastened our footsteps, and when we arrived on the plantation we heard the sound of the hand-mill. The slaves were grinding their corn. We were safely in the house before the horn summoned them to their labor. I divided my little parcel of food with my guide, knowing that he had lost the chance of grinding his corn, and must toil all day in the field.

Mr. Flint often took an inspection of the house, to see that no one was idle. The entire management of the work was trusted to me, because he knew nothing about it; and rather than hire a superintendent he contented himself with my arrangements. He had often urged upon his father the necessity of having me at the plantation to take charge of his affairs, and make clothes for the slaves; but the old man knew him too well to consent to that arrangement.

When I had been working a month at the plantation, the great aunt of Mr. Flint came to make him a visit. This was the good old lady who paid fifty dollars for my grandmother, for the purpose of making her free, when she stood on the auction block. My grandmother loved this old lady, whom we all called Miss Fanny. She often came to take tea with us. On such occasions the table was spread with a snow-white cloth, and the china cups and silver spoons were taken from the old-fashioned buffet. There were hot muffins, tea rusks, and delicious sweetmeats. My grandmother kept two cows, and the fresh cream was Miss Fanny's delight. She invariably declared that it was the best in town. The old ladies had cosey times together. They would work and chat, and sometimes, while talking over old times, their spectacles would get dim with tears, and would have to be taken off and wiped. When Miss Fanny bade us good by, her bag was filled with grandmother's best cakes, and she was urged to come again soon.

There had been a time when Dr. Flint's wife came to take tea with us, and when her children were also sent to have a feast of "Aunt Marthy's" nice cooking. But after I became an object of her jealousy and spite, she was angry with grandmother for giving a shelter to me and my children. She would not even speak to her in the street. This wounded my grandmother's feelings, for she could not retain ill will against the woman whom she had nourished with her milk when a babe. The doctor's wife would gladly have prevented our intercourse with Miss Fanny if she could have done it, but fortunately she was not dependent on the bounty of the Flints. She had enough to be independent; and that is more than can ever be gained from charity, however lavish it may be.

Miss Fanny was endeared to me by many recollections, and I was rejoiced to see her at the plantation. The warmth of her large, loyal heart made the house seem pleasanter while she was in it. She staid a week, and I had many talks with her. She said her principal object in coming was to see how I was treated, and whether any thing could be done for me. She inquired whether she could help me in any way. I told her I believed not. She condoled with me in her own peculiar way; saying she wished that I and all my grandmother's family were at rest in our graves, for not until then should she feel any peace about us. The good old soul did not dream that I was planning to bestow peace upon her, with regard to myself and my children; not by death, but by securing our freedom.

Again and again I had traversed those dreary twelve miles, to and from the town; and all the way, I was meditating upon some means of escape for myself and my children. My friends had made every effort that ingenuity could devise to effect our purchase, but all their plans had proved abortive. Dr. Flint was suspicious, and determined not to loosen his grasp upon us. I could have made my escape alone; but it was more for my helpless children than for myself that I longed for freedom. Though the boon would have been precious to me, above all price, I would not have taken it at the expense of leaving them in slavery. Every trial I endured, every sacrifice I made for their sakes, drew them closer to my heart, and gave me fresh courage to beat back the dark waves that rolled and rolled over me in a seemingly endless night of storms.

The six weeks were nearly completed, when Mr. Flint's bride was expected to take possession of her new home. The arrangements were all completed, and Mr. Flint said I had done well. He expected to leave home on Saturday, and return with his bride the following Wednesday. After receiving various orders from him, I ventured to ask permission to spend Sunday in town. It was granted; for which favor I was thankful. It was the first I had ever asked of him, and I intended it should be the last. I needed more than one night to accomplish the project I had in view; but the whole of Sunday would give me an opportunity. I spent the Sabbath with my grandmother. A calmer, more beautiful day never came down out of heaven. To me it was a day of conflicting emotions. Perhaps it was the last day I should ever spend under that dear, old sheltering roof! Perhaps these were the last talks I should ever have with the faithful old friend of my whole life! Perhaps it was the last time I and my children should be together! Well, better so, I thought, than that they should be slaves. I knew the doom that awaited my fair baby in slavery, and I determined to save her from it, or perish in the attempt. I went to make this vow at the graves of my poor parents, in the burying-ground of the slaves. "There the wicked cease from troubling, and there the weary be at rest. There the prisoners rest together; they hear not the voice of the oppressor; the servant is free from his master." I knelt by the graves of my parents, and thanked God, as I had often done before, that they had not lived to witness my trials, or to mourn over my sins. I had received my mother's blessing when she died; and in many an hour of tribulation I had seemed to hear her voice, sometimes chiding me, sometimes whispering loving words into my wounded heart. I have shed many and bitter tears, to think that when I am gone from my children they cannot remember me with such entire satisfaction as I remembered my mother.

The graveyard was in the woods, and twilight was coming on. Nothing broke the death-like stillness except the occasional twitter of a bird. My spirit was overawed by the solemnity of the scene. For more than ten years I had frequented this spot, but never had it seemed to me so sacred as now. A black stump, at the head of my mother's grave, was all that remained of a tree my father had planted. His grave was marked by a small wooden board, bearing his name, the letters of which were nearly obliterated. I knelt down and kissed them, and poured forth a prayer to God for guidance and support in the perilous step I was about to take. As I passed the wreck of the old meeting house, where, before Nat Turner's time, the slaves had been allowed to meet for worship, I seemed to hear my father's voice come from it, bidding me not to tarry till I reached freedom or the grave. I rushed on with renovated hopes. My trust in God had been strengthened by that prayer among the graves.

My plan was to conceal myself at the house of a friend, and remain there a few weeks till the search was over. My hope was that the doctor would get discouraged, and, for fear of losing my value, and also of subsequently finding my children among the missing, he would consent to sell us; and I knew somebody would buy us. I had done all in my power to make my children comfortable during the time I expected to be separated from them. I was packing my things, when grandmother came into the room, and asked what I was doing. "I am putting my things in order," I replied. I tried to look and speak cheerfully; but her watchful eye detected something beneath the surface. She drew me towards her, and asked me to sit down. She looked earnestly at me, and said, "Linda, do you want to kill your old grandmother? Do you mean to leave your little, helpless children? I am old now, and cannot do for your babies as I once did for you."

I replied, that if I went away, perhaps their father would be able to secure their freedom.

"Ah, my child," said she, "don't trust too much to him. Stand by your own children, and suffer with them till death. Nobody respects a mother who forsakes her children; and if you leave them, you will never have a happy moment. If you go, you will make me miserable the short time I have to live. You would be taken and brought back, and your sufferings would be dreadful. Remember poor Benjamin. Do give it up, Linda. Try to bear a little longer. Things may turn out better than we expect."

My courage failed me, in view of the sorrow I should bring on that faithful, loving old heart. I promised that I would try longer, and that I would take nothing out of her house without her knowledge.

Whenever the children climbed on my knee, or laid their heads on my lap, she would say, "Poor little souls! what would you do without a mother? She don't love you as I do." And she would hug them to her own bosom, as if to reproach me for my want of affection; but she knew all the while that I loved them better than my life. I slept with her that night, and it was the last time. The memory of it haunted me for many a year.

On Monday I returned to the plantation, and busied myself with preparations for the important day. Wednesday came. It was a beautiful day, and the faces of the slaves were as bright as the sunshine. The poor creatures were merry. They were expecting little presents from the bride, and hoping for better times under her administration. I had no such hopes for them. I knew that the young wives of slaveholders often thought their authority and importance would be best established and maintained by cruelty; and what I had heard of young Mrs. Flint gave me no reason to expect that her rule over them would be less severe than that of the master and overseer. Truly, the colored race are the most cheerful and forgiving people on the face of the earth. That their masters sleep in safety is owing to their superabundance of heart; and yet they look upon their sufferings with less pity than they would bestow on those of a horse or a dog.

I stood at the door with others to receive the bridegroom and bride. She was a handsome, delicate-looking girl, and her face flushed with emotion at sight of her new home. I thought it likely that visions of a happy future were rising before her. It made me sad; for I knew how soon clouds would come over her sunshine. She examined every part of the house, and told me she was delighted with the arrangements I had made. I was afraid old Mrs. Flint had tried to prejudice her against me, and I did my best to please her.

All passed off smoothly for me until dinner time arrived. I did not mind the embarrassment of waiting on a dinner party, for the first time in my life, half so much as I did the meeting with Dr. Flint and his wife, who would be among the guests. It was a mystery to me why Mrs. Flint had not made her appearance at the plantation during all the time I was putting the house in order. I had not met her, face to face, for five years, and I had no wish to see her now. She was a praying woman, and, doubtless, considered my present position a special answer to her prayers. Nothing could please her better than to see me humbled and trampled upon. I was just where she would have me—in the power of a hard, unprincipled master. She did not speak to me when she took her seat at table; but her satisfied, triumphant smile, when I handed her plate, was more eloquent than words. The old doctor was not so quiet in his demonstrations. He ordered me here and there, and spoke with peculiar emphasis when he said "your mistress." I was drilled like a disgraced soldier. When all was over, and the last key turned, I sought my pillow, thankful that God had appointed a season of rest for the weary.

The next day my new mistress began her housekeeping. I was not exactly appointed maid of all work; but I was to do whatever I was told. Monday evening came. It was always a busy time. On that night the slaves received their weekly allowance of food. Three pounds of meat, a peck of corn, and perhaps a dozen herring were allowed to each man. Women received a pound and a half of meat, a peck of corn, and the same number of herring. Children over twelve years old had half the allowance of the women. The meat was cut and weighed by the foreman of the field hands, and piled on planks before the meat house. Then the second foreman went behind the building, and when the first foreman called out, "Who takes this piece of meat?" he answered by calling somebody's name. This method was resorted to as a means of preventing partiality in distributing the meat. The young mistress came out to see how things were done on her plantation, and she soon gave a specimen of her character. Among those in waiting for their allowance was a very old slave, who had faithfully served the Flint family through three generations. When he hobbled up to get his bit of meat, the mistress said he was too old to have any allowance; that when niggers were too old to work, they ought to be fed on grass. Poor old man! He suffered much before he found rest in the grave.

My mistress and I got along very well together. At the end of a week, old Mrs. Flint made us another visit, and was closeted a long time with her daughter-in-law. I had my suspicions what was the subject of the conference. The old doctor's wife had been informed that I could leave the plantation on one condition, and she was very desirous to keep me there. If she had trusted me, as I deserved to be trusted by her, she would have had no fears of my accepting that condition. When she entered her carriage to return home, she said to young Mrs. Flint, "Don't neglect to send for them as quick as possible." My heart was on the watch all the time, and I at once concluded that she spoke of my children. The doctor came the next day, and as I entered the room to spread the tea table, I heard him say, "Don't wait any longer. Send for them to-morrow." I saw through the plan. They thought my children's being there would fetter me to the spot, and that it was a good place to break us all in to abject submission to our lot as slaves. After the doctor left, a gentleman called, who had always manifested friendly feelings towards my grandmother and her family. Mr. Flint carried him over the plantation to show him the results of labor performed by men and women who were unpaid, miserably clothed, and half famished. The cotton crop was all they thought of. It was duly admired, and the gentleman returned with specimens to show his friends. I was ordered to carry water to wash his hands. As I did so, he said, "Linda, how do you like your new home?" I told him I liked it as well as I expected. He replied, "They don't think you are contented, and to-morrow they are going to bring your children to be with you. I am sorry for you, Linda. I hope they will treat you kindly." I hurried from the room, unable to thank him. My suspicions were correct. My children were to be brought to the plantation to be "broke in."

To this day I feel grateful to the gentleman who gave me this timely information. It nerved me to immediate action.

# XVII. THE FLIGHT.

Mr. Flint was hard pushed for house servants, and rather than lose me he had restrained his malice. I did my work faithfully, though not, of course, with a willing mind. They were evidently afraid I should leave them. Mr. Flint wished that I should sleep in the great house instead of the servants' quarters. His wife agreed to the proposition, but said I mustn't bring my bed into the house, because it would scatter feathers on her carpet. I knew when I went there that they would never think of such a thing as furnishing a bed of any kind for me and my little ones. I therefore carried my own bed, and now I was forbidden to use it. I did as I was ordered. But now that I was certain my children were to be put in their power, in order to give them a stronger hold on me, I resolved to leave them that night. I remembered the grief this step would bring upon my dear old grandmother, and nothing less than the freedom of my children would have induced me to disregard her advice. I went about my evening work with trembling steps. Mr. Flint twice called from his chamber door to inquire why the house was not locked up. I replied that I had not done my work. "You have had time enough to do it," said he. "Take care how you answer me!"

I shut all the windows, locked all the doors, and went up to the third story, to wait till midnight. How long those hours seemed, and how fervently I prayed that God would not forsake me in this hour of utmost need! I was about to risk every thing on the throw of a die; and if I failed, O what would become of me and my poor children? They would be made to suffer for my fault.

At half past twelve I stole softly down stairs. I stopped on the second floor, thinking I heard a noise. I felt my way down into the parlor, and looked out of the window. The night was so intensely dark that I could see nothing. I raised the window very softly and jumped out. Large drops of rain were falling, and the darkness bewildered me. I dropped on my knees, and breathed a short prayer to God for guidance and protection. I groped my way to the road, and rushed towards the town with almost lightning speed. I arrived at my grandmother's house, but dared not see her. She would say, "Linda, you are killing me;" and I knew that would unnerve me. I tapped softly at the window of a room, occupied by a woman, who had lived in the house several years. I knew she was a faithful friend, and could be trusted with my secret. I tapped several times before she heard me. At last she raised the window, and I whispered, "Sally, I have run away. Let me in, quick." She opened the door softly, and said in low tones, "For God's sake, don't. Your grandmother is trying to buy you and de chillern. Mr. Sands was here last week. He tole her he was going away on business, but he wanted her to go ahead about buying you and de chillern, and he would help her all he could. Don't run away, Linda. Your grandmother is all bowed down wid trouble now."

I replied, "Sally, they are going to carry my children to the plantation tomorrow; and they will never sell them to any body so long as they have me in their power. Now, would you advise me to go back?"

"No, chile, no," answered she. "When dey finds you is gone, dey won't want de plague ob de chillern; but where is you going to hide? Dey knows ebery inch ob dis house."

I told her I had a hiding-place, and that was all it was best for her to know. I asked her to go into my room as soon as it was light, and take all my clothes out of my trunk, and pack them in hers; for I knew Mr. Flint and the constable would be there early to search my room. I feared the sight of my children would be too much for my full heart; but I could not go into the uncertain future without one last look. I bent over the bed where lay my little Benny and baby Ellen. Poor little ones! fatherless and motherless! Memories of their father came over me. He wanted to be kind to them; but they were not all to him, as they were to my womanly heart. I knelt and prayed for the innocent little sleepers. I kissed them lightly, and turned away.

As I was about to open the street door, Sally laid her hand on my shoulder, and said, "Linda, is you gwine all alone? Let me call your uncle."

"No, Sally," I replied, "I want no one to be brought into trouble on my account."

I went forth into the darkness and rain. I ran on till I came to the house of the friend who was to conceal me.

Early the next morning Mr. Flint was at my grandmother's inquiring for me. She told him she had not seen me, and supposed I was at the plantation. He watched her face narrowly, and said, "Don't you know any thing about her running off?" She assured him that she did not. He went on to say, "Last night she ran off without the least provocation. We had treated her very kindly. My wife liked her. She will soon be found and brought back. Are her children with you?" When told that they were, he said, "I am very glad to hear that. If they are here, she cannot be far off. If I find out that any of my niggers have had any thing to do with this damned business, I'll give 'em five hundred lashes." As he started to go to his father's, he turned round and added, persuasively, "Let her be brought back, and she shall have her children to live with her."

The tidings made the old doctor rave and storm at a furious rate. It was a busy day for them. My grandmother's house was searched from top to bottom. As my trunk was empty, they concluded I had taken my clothes with me. Before ten o'clock every vessel northward bound was thoroughly examined, and the law against harboring fugitives was read to all on board. At night a watch was set over the town. Knowing how distressed my grandmother would be, I wanted to send her a message; but it could not be done. Every one who went in or out of her house was closely watched. The doctor said he would take my children, unless she became responsible for them; which of course she willingly did. The next day was spent in searching. Before night, the following advertisement was posted at every corner, and in every public place for miles round:—

$300 REWARD! Ran away from the subscriber, an intelligent, bright, mulatto girl, named Linda, 21 years of age. Five feet four inches high. Dark eyes, and black hair inclined to curl; but it can be made straight. Has a decayed spot on a front tooth. She can read and write, and in all probability will try to get to the Free States. All persons are forbidden, under penalty of law, to harbor or employ said slave. $150 will be given to whoever takes her in the state, and $300 if taken out of the state and delivered to me, or lodged in jail.

Dr. Flint.

# XVIII. MONTHS OF PERIL.

The search for me was kept up with more perseverence than I had anticipated. I began to think that escape was impossible. I was in great anxiety lest I should implicate the friend who harbored me. I knew the consequences would be frightful; and much as I dreaded being caught, even that seemed better than causing an innocent person to suffer for kindness to me. A week had passed in terrible suspense, when my pursuers came into such close vicinity that I concluded they had tracked me to my hiding-place. I flew out of the house, and concealed myself in a thicket of bushes. There I remained in an agony of fear for two hours. Suddenly, a reptile of some kind seized my leg. In my fright, I struck a blow which loosened its hold, but I could not tell whether I had killed it; it was so dark, I could not see what it was; I only knew it was something cold and slimy. The pain I felt soon indicated that the bite was poisonous. I was compelled to leave my place of concealment, and I groped my way back into the house. The pain had become intense, and my friend was startled by my look of anguish. I asked her to prepare a poultice of warm ashes and vinegar, and I applied it to my leg, which was already much swollen. The application gave me some relief, but the swelling did not abate. The dread of being disabled was greater than the physical pain I endured. My friend asked an old woman, who doctored among the slaves, what was good for the bite of a snake or a lizard. She told her to steep a dozen coppers in vinegar, over night, and apply the cankered vinegar to the inflamed part.1

Note-->

1 (return)
[ The poison of a snake is a powerful acid, and is counteracted by powerful alkalies, such as potash, ammonia, &c. The Indians are accustomed to apply wet ashes, or plunge the limb into strong lie. White men, employed to lay out railroads in snaky places, often carry ammonia with them as an antidote.— EDITOR.]

I had succeeded in cautiously conveying some messages to my relatives. They were harshly threatened, and despairing of my having a chance to escape, they advised me to return to my master, ask his forgiveness, and let him make an example of me. But such counsel had no influence with me. When I started upon this hazardous undertaking, I had resolved that, come what would, there should be no turning back. "Give me liberty, or give me death," was my motto. When my friend contrived to make known to my relatives the painful situation

I had been in for twenty-four hours, they said no more about my going back to my master. Something must be done, and that speedily; but where to return for help, they knew not. God in his mercy raised up "a friend in need."

Among the ladies who were acquainted with my grandmother, was one who had known her from childhood, and always been very friendly to her. She had also known my mother and her children, and felt interested for them. At this crisis of affairs she called to see my grandmother, as she not unfrequently did. She observed the sad and troubled expression of her face, and asked if she knew where Linda was, and whether she was safe. My grandmother shook her head, without answering. "Come, Aunt Martha," said the kind lady, "tell me all about it. Perhaps I can do something to help you." The husband of this lady held many slaves, and bought and sold slaves. She also held a number in her own name; but she treated them kindly, and would never allow any of them to be sold. She was unlike the majority of slaveholders' wives. My grandmother looked earnestly at her. Something in the expression of her face said "Trust me!" and she did trust her. She listened attentively to the details of my story, and sat thinking for a while. At last she said, "Aunt Martha, I pity you both. If you think there is any chance of Linda's getting to the Free States, I will conceal her for a time. But first you must solemnly promise that my name shall never be mentioned. If such a thing should become known, it would ruin me and my family. No one in my house must know of it, except the cook. She is so faithful that I would trust my own life with her; and I know she likes Linda. It is a great risk; but I trust no harm will come of it. Get word to Linda to be ready as soon as it is dark, before the patrols are out. I will send the housemaids on errands, and Betty shall go to meet Linda." The place where we were to meet was designated and agreed upon. My grandmother was unable to thank the lady for this noble deed; overcome by her emotions, she sank on her knees and sobbed like a child.

I received a message to leave my friend's house at such an hour, and go to a certain place where a friend would be waiting for me. As a matter of prudence no names were mentioned. I had no means of conjecturing who I was to meet, or where I was going. I did not like to move thus blindfolded, but I had no choice. It would not do for me to remain where I was. I disguised myself, summoned up courage to meet the worst, and went to the appointed place. My friend Betty was there; she was the last person I expected to see. We hurried along in silence. The pain in my leg was so intense that it seemed as if I should drop but fear gave me strength. We reached the house and entered unobserved. Her first words were: "Honey, now you is safe. Dem devils ain't coming to search dis house. When I get you into missis' safe place, I will bring some nice hot supper. I specs you need it after all dis skeering." Betty's vocation led her to think eating the most important thing in life. She did not realize that my heart was too full for me to care much about supper.

The mistress came to meet us, and led me up stairs to a small room over her own sleeping apartment. "You will be safe here, Linda," said she; "I keep this room to store away things that are out of use. The girls are not accustomed to be sent to it, and they will not suspect any thing unless they hear some noise. I always keep it locked, and Betty shall take care of the key. But you must be very careful, for my sake as well as your own; and you must never tell my secret; for it would ruin me and my family. I will keep the girls busy in the morning, that Betty may have a chance to bring your breakfast; but it will not do for her to come to you again till night. I will come to see you sometimes. Keep up your courage. I hope this state of things will not last long." Betty came with the "nice hot supper," and the mistress hastened down stairs to keep things straight till she returned. How my heart overflowed with gratitude! Words choked in my throat; but I could have kissed the feet of my benefactress. For that deed of Christian womanhood, may God forever bless her!

I went to sleep that night with the feeling that I was for the present the most fortunate slave in town. Morning came and filled my little cell with light. I thanked the heavenly Father for this safe retreat. Opposite my window was a pile of feather beds. On the top of these I could lie perfectly concealed, and command a view of the street through which Dr. Flint passed to his office. Anxious as I was, I felt a gleam of satisfaction when I saw him. Thus far I had outwitted him, and I triumphed over it. Who can blame slaves for being cunning? They are constantly compelled to resort to it. It is the only weapon of the weak and oppressed against the strength of their tyrants.

I was daily hoping to hear that my master had sold my children; for I knew who was on the watch to buy them. But Dr. Flint cared even more for revenge than he did for money. My brother William and the good aunt who had served in his family twenty years, and my little Benny, and Ellen, who was a little over two years old, were thrust into jail, as a means of compelling my relatives to give some information about me. He swore my grandmother should never see one of them again till I was brought back. They kept these facts from me for several days. When I heard that my little ones were in a loathsome jail, my first impulse was to go to them. I was encountering dangers for the sake of freeing them, and must I be the cause of their death? The thought was agonizing. My benefactress tried to soothe me by telling me that my aunt would take good care of the children while they remained in jail. But it added to my pain to think that the good old aunt, who had always been so kind to her sister's orphan children, should be shut up in prison for no other crime than loving them. I suppose my friends feared a reckless movement on my part, knowing, as they did, that my life was bound up in my children. I received a note from my brother William. It was scarcely legible, and ran thus: "Wherever you are, dear sister, I beg of you not to come here. We are all much better off than you are. If you come, you will ruin us all. They would force you to tell where you had been, or they would kill you. Take the advice of your friends; if not for the sake of me and your children, at least for the sake of those you would ruin."

Poor William! He also must suffer for being my brother. I took his advice and kept quiet. My aunt was taken out of jail at the end of a month, because Mrs. Flint could not spare her any longer. She was tired of being her own housekeeper. It was quite too fatiguing to order her dinner and eat it too. My children remained in jail, where brother William did all he could for their comfort. Betty went to see them sometimes, and brought me tidings. She was not permitted to enter the jail; but William would hold them up to the grated window while she chatted with them. When she repeated their prattle, and told me how they wanted to see their ma, my tears would flow. Old Betty would exclaim, "Lors, chile! what's you crying 'bout? Dem young uns vil kill you dead. Don't be so chick'n hearted! If you does, you vil nebber git thro' dis world."

Good old soul! She had gone through the world childless. She had never had little ones to clasp their arms round her neck; she had never seen their soft eyes looking into hers; no sweet little voices had called her mother; she had never pressed her own infants to her heart, with the feeling that even in fetters there was something to live for. How could she realize my feelings? Betty's husband loved children dearly, and wondered why God had denied them to him. He expressed great sorrow when he came to Betty with the tidings that Ellen had been taken out of jail and carried to Dr. Flint's. She had the measles a short time before they carried her to jail, and the disease had left her eyes affected. The doctor had taken her home to attend to them. My children had always been afraid of the doctor and his wife. They had never been inside of their house. Poor little Ellen cried all day to be carried back to prison. The instincts of childhood are true. She knew she was loved in the jail. Her screams and sobs annoyed Mrs. Flint. Before night she called one of the slaves, and said, "Here, Bill, carry this brat back to the jail. I can't stand her noise. If she would be quiet I should like to keep the little minx. She would make a handy waiting-maid for my daughter by and by. But if she staid here, with her white face, I suppose I should either kill her or spoil her. I hope the doctor will sell them as far as wind and water can carry them. As for their mother, her ladyship will find out yet what she gets by running away. She hasn't so much feeling for her children as a cow has for its calf. If she had, she would have come back long ago, to get them out of jail, and save all this expense and trouble. The good-for-nothing hussy! When she is caught, she shall stay in jail, in irons, for one six months, and then be sold to a sugar plantation. I shall see her broke in yet. What do you stand there for, Bill? Why don't you go off with the brat? Mind, now, that you don't let any of the niggers speak to her in the street!"

When these remarks were reported to me, I smiled at Mrs. Flint's saying that she should either kill my child or spoil her. I thought to myself there was very little danger of the latter. I have always considered it as one of God's special providences that Ellen screamed till she was carried back to jail.

That same night Dr. Flint was called to a patient, and did not return till near morning. Passing my grandmother's, he saw a light in the house, and thought to himself, "Perhaps this has something to do with Linda." He knocked, and the door was opened. "What calls you up so early?" said he. "I saw your light, and I thought I would just stop and tell you that I have found out where Linda is. I know where to put my hands on her, and I shall have her before twelve o'clock." When he had turned away, my grandmother and my uncle looked anxiously at each other. They did not know whether or not it was merely one of the doctor's tricks to frighten them. In their uncertainty, they thought it was best to have a message conveyed to my friend Betty. Unwilling to alarm her mistress, Betty resolved to dispose of me herself. She came to me, and told me to rise and dress quickly. We hurried down stairs, and across the yard, into the kitchen. She locked the door, and lifted up a plank in the floor. A buffalo skin and a bit of carpet were spread for me to lie on, and a quilt thrown over me. "Stay dar," said she, "till I sees if dey know 'bout you. Dey say dey vil put thar hans on you afore twelve o'clock. If dey did know whar you are, dey won't know now. Dey'll be disapinted dis time. Dat's all I got to say. If dey comes rummagin 'mong my tings, de'll get one bressed sarssin from dis 'ere nigger." In my shallow bed I had but just room enough to bring my hands to my face to keep the dust out of my eyes; for Betty walked over me twenty times in an hour, passing from the dresser to the fireplace. When she was alone, I could hear her pronouncing anathemas over Dr. Flint and all his tribe, every now and then saying, with a chuckling laugh, "Dis nigger's too cute for 'em dis time." When the housemaids were about, she had sly ways of drawing them out, that I might hear what they would say. She would repeat stories she had heard about my being in this, or that, or the other place. To which they would answer, that I was not fool enough to be staying round there; that I was in Philadelphia or New York before this time. When all were abed and asleep, Betty raised the plank, and said, "Come out, chile; come out. Dey don't know nottin 'bout you. Twas only white folks' lies, to skeer de niggers."

Some days after this adventure I had a much worse fright. As I sat very still in my retreat above stairs, cheerful visions floated through my mind. I thought Dr. Flint would soon get discouraged, and would be willing to sell my children, when he lost all hopes of making them the means of my discovery. I knew who was ready to buy them. Suddenly I heard a voice that chilled my blood. The sound was too familiar to me, it had been too dreadful, for me not to recognize at once my old master. He was in the house, and I at once concluded he had come to seize me. I looked round in terror. There was no way of escape. The voice receded. I supposed the constable was with him, and they were searching the house. In my alarm I did not forget the trouble I was bringing on my generous benefactress. It seemed as if I were born to bring sorrow on all who befriended me, and that was the bitterest drop in the bitter cup of my life. After a while I heard approaching footsteps; the key was turned in my door. I braced myself against the wall to keep from falling. I ventured to look up, and there stood my kind benefactress alone. I was too much overcome to speak, and sunk down upon the floor.

"I thought you would hear your master's voice," she said; "and knowing you would be terrified, I came to tell you there is nothing to fear. You may even indulge in a laugh at the old gentleman's expense. He is so sure you are in New York, that he came to borrow five hundred dollars to go in pursuit of you. My sister had some money to loan on interest. He has obtained it, and proposes to start for New York to-night. So, for the present, you see you are safe. The doctor will merely lighten his pocket hunting after the bird he has left behind."

# XIX. THE CHILDREN SOLD.

The Doctor came back from New York, of course without accomplishing his purpose. He had expended considerable money, and was rather disheartened. My brother and the children had now been in jail two months, and that also was some expense. My friends thought it was a favorable time to work on his discouraged feelings. Mr. Sands sent a speculator to offer him nine hundred dollars for my brother William, and eight hundred for the two children. These were high prices, as slaves were then selling; but the offer was rejected. If it had been merely a question of money, the doctor would have sold any boy of Benny's age for two hundred dollars; but he could not bear to give up the power of revenge. But he was hard pressed for money, and he revolved the matter in his mind. He knew that if he could keep Ellen till she was fifteen, he could sell her for a high price; but I presume he reflected that she might die, or might be stolen away. At all events, he came to the conclusion that he had better accept the slave-trader's offer. Meeting him in the street, he inquired when he would leave town. "To-day, at ten o'clock," he replied. "Ah, do you go so soon?" said the doctor. "I have been reflecting upon your proposition, and I have concluded to let you have the three negroes if you will say nineteen hundred dollars." After some parley, the trader agreed to his terms. He wanted the bill of sale drawn up and signed immediately, as he had a great deal to attend to during the short time he remained in town. The doctor went to the jail and told William he would take him back into his service if he would promise to behave himself but he replied that he would rather be sold. "And you shall be sold, you ungrateful rascal!" exclaimed the doctor. In less than an hour the money was paid, the papers were signed, sealed, and delivered, and my brother and children were in the hands of the trader.

It was a hurried transaction; and after it was over, the doctor's characteristic caution returned. He went back to the speculator, and said, "Sir, I have come to lay you under obligations of a thousand dollars not to sell any of those negroes in this state." "You come too late," replied the trader; "our bargain is closed." He had, in fact, already sold them to Mr. Sands, but he did not mention it. The doctor required him to put irons on "that rascal, Bill," and to pass through the back streets when he took his gang out of town. The trader was privately instructed to concede to his wishes. My good old aunt went to the jail to bid the children good by, supposing them to be the speculator's property, and that she should never see them again. As she held Benny in her lap, he said, "Aunt Nancy, I want to show you something." He led her to the door and showed her a long row of marks, saying, "Uncle Will taught me to count. I have made a mark for every day I have been here, and it is sixty days. It is a long time; and the speculator is going to take me and Ellen away. He's a bad man. It's wrong for him to take grandmother's children. I want to go to my mother."

My grandmother was told that the children would be restored to her, but she was requested to act as if they were really to be sent away. Accordingly, she made up a bundle of clothes and went to the jail. When she arrived, she found William handcuffed among the gang, and the children in the trader's cart. The scene seemed too much like reality. She was afraid there might have been some deception or mistake. She fainted, and was carried home.

When the wagon stopped at the hotel, several gentlemen came out and proposed to purchase William, but the trader refused their offers, without stating that he was already sold. And now came the trying hour for that drove of human beings, driven away like cattle, to be sold they knew not where. Husbands were torn from wives, parents from children, never to look upon each other again this side the grave. There was wringing of hands and cries of despair.

Dr. Flint had the supreme satisfaction of seeing the wagon leave town, and Mrs. Flint had the gratification of supposing that my children were going "as far as wind and water would carry them." According to agreement, my uncle followed the wagon some miles, until they came to an old farm house. There the trader took the irons from William, and as he did so, he said, "You are a damned clever fellow. I should like to own you myself. Them gentlemen that wanted to buy you said you was a bright, honest chap, and I must git you a good home. I guess your old master will swear to-morrow, and call himself an old fool for selling the children. I reckon he'll never git their mammy back again. I expect she's made tracks for the north. Good by, old boy. Remember, I have done you a good turn. You must thank me by coaxing all the pretty gals to go with me next fall. That's going to be my last trip. This trading in niggers is a bad business for a fellow that's got any heart. Move on, you fellows!" And the gang went on, God alone knows where.

Much as I despise and detest the class of slave-traders, whom I regard as the vilest wretches on earth, I must do this man the justice to say that he seemed to have some feeling. He took a fancy to William in the jail, and wanted to buy him. When he heard the story of my children, he was willing to aid them in getting out of Dr. Flint's power, even without charging the customary fee.

My uncle procured a wagon and carried William and the children back to town. Great was the joy in my grandmother's house! The curtains were closed, and the candles lighted. The happy grandmother cuddled the little ones to her bosom. They hugged her, and kissed her, and clapped their hands, and shouted. She knelt down and poured forth one of her heartfelt prayers of thanksgiving to God. The father was present for a while; and though such a "parental relation" as existed between him and my children takes slight hold on the hearts or consciences of slaveholders, it must be that he experienced some moments of pure joy in witnessing the happiness he had imparted.

I had no share in the rejoicings of that evening. The events of the day had not come to my knowledge. And now I will tell you something that happened to me; though you will, perhaps, think it illustrates the superstition of slaves. I sat in my usual place on the floor near the window, where I could hear much that was said in the street without being seen. The family had retired for the night, and all was still. I sat there thinking of my children, when I heard a low strain of music. A band of serenaders were under the window, playing "Home, sweet home." I listened till the sounds did not seem like music, but like the moaning of children. It seemed as if my heart would burst. I rose from my sitting posture, and knelt. A streak of moonlight was on the floor before me, and in the midst of it appeared the forms of my two children. They vanished; but I had seen them distinctly. Some will call it a dream, others a vision. I know not how to account for it, but it made a strong impression on my mind, and I felt certain something had happened to my little ones.

I had not seen Betty since morning. Now I heard her softly turning the key. As soon as she entered, I clung to her, and begged her to let me know whether my children were dead, or whether they were sold; for I had seen their spirits in my room, and I was sure something had happened to them. "Lor, chile," said she, putting her arms round me, "you's got de high-sterics. I'll sleep wid you to-night, 'cause you'll make a noise, and ruin missis. Something has stirred you up mightily. When you is done cryin, I'll talk wid you. De chillern is well, and mighty happy. I seed 'em myself. Does dat satisfy you? Dar, chile, be still! Somebody vill hear you." I tried to obey her. She lay down, and was soon sound asleep; but no sleep would come to my eyelids.

At dawn, Betty was up and off to the kitchen. The hours passed on, and the vision of the night kept constantly recurring to my thoughts. After a while I heard the voices of two women in the entry. In one of them I recognized the housemaid. The other said to her, "Did you know Linda Brent's children was sold to the speculator yesterday. They say ole massa Flint was mighty glad to see 'em drove out of town; but they say they've come back agin. I 'spect it's all their daddy's doings. They say he's bought William too. Lor! how it will take hold of ole massa Flint! I'm going roun' to aunt Marthy's to see 'bout it."

I bit my lips till the blood came to keep from crying out. Were my children with their grandmother, or had the speculator carried them off? The suspense was dreadful. Would Betty never come, and tell me the truth about it? At last she came, and I eagerly repeated what I had overheard. Her face was one broad, bright smile. "Lor, you foolish ting!" said she. "I'se gwine to tell you all 'bout it. De gals is eating thar breakfast, and missus tole me to let her tell you; but, poor creeter! t'aint right to keep you waitin', and I'se gwine to tell you. Brudder, chillern, all is bought by de daddy! I'se laugh more dan nuff, tinking 'bout ole massa Flint. Lor, how he vill swar! He's got ketched dis time, any how; but I must be getting out o' dis, or dem gals vill come and ketch me."

Betty went off laughing; and I said to myself, "Can it be true that my children are free? I have not suffered for them in vain. Thank God!"

Great surprise was expressed when it was known that my children had returned to their grandmother's. The news spread through the town, and many a kind word was bestowed on the little ones.

Dr. Flint went to my grandmother's to ascertain who was the owner of my children, and she informed him. "I expected as much," said he. "I am glad to hear it. I have had news from Linda lately, and I shall soon have her. You need never expect to see her free. She shall be my slave as long as I live, and when I am dead she shall be the slave of my children. If I ever find out that you or Phillip had anything to do with her running off I'll kill him. And if I meet William in the street, and he presumes to look at me, I'll flog him within an inch of his life. Keep those brats out of my sight!"

As he turned to leave, my grandmother said something to remind him of his own doings. He looked back upon her, as if he would have been glad to strike her to the ground.

I had my season of joy and thanksgiving. It was the first time since my childhood that I had experienced any real happiness. I heard of the old doctor's threats, but they no longer had the same power to trouble me. The darkest cloud that hung over my life had rolled away. Whatever slavery might do to me, it could not shackle my children. If I fell a sacrifice, my little ones were saved. It was well for me that my simple heart believed all that had been promised for their welfare. It is always better to trust than to doubt.

# XX. NEW PERILS.

The doctor, more exasperated than ever, again tried to revenge himself on my relatives. He arrested uncle Phillip on the charge of having aided my flight. He was carried before a court, and swore truly that he knew nothing of my intention to escape, and that he had not seen me since I left my master's plantation. The doctor then demanded that he should give bail for five hundred dollars that he would have nothing to do with me. Several gentlemen offered to be security for him; but Mr. Sands told him he had better go back to jail, and he would see that he came out without giving bail.

The news of his arrest was carried to my grandmother, who conveyed it to Betty. In the kindness of her heart, she again stowed me away under the floor; and as she walked back and forth, in the performance of her culinary duties, she talked apparently to herself, but with the intention that I should hear what was going on. I hoped that my uncle's imprisonment would last but few days; still I was anxious. I thought it likely Dr. Flint would do his utmost to taunt and insult him, and I was afraid my uncle might lose control of himself, and retort in some way that would be construed into a punishable offence; and I was well aware that in court his word would not be taken against any white man's. The search for me was renewed. Something had excited suspicions that I was in the vicinity. They searched the house I was in. I heard their steps and their voices. At night, when all were asleep, Betty came to release me from my place of confinement. The fright I had undergone, the constrained posture, and the dampness of the ground, made me ill for several days. My uncle was soon after taken out of prison; but the movements of all my relatives, and of all our friends, were very closely watched.

We all saw that I could not remain where I was much longer. I had already staid longer than was intended, and I knew my presence must be a source of perpetual anxiety to my kind benefactress. During this time, my friends had laid many plans for my escape, but the extreme vigilance of my persecutors made it impossible to carry them into effect.

One morning I was much startled by hearing somebody trying to get into my room. Several keys were tried, but none fitted. I instantly conjectured it was one of the housemaids; and I concluded she must either have heard some noise in the room, or have noticed the entrance of Betty. When my friend came, at her usual time, I told her what had happened. "I knows who it was," said she. "Tend upon it, 'twas dat Jenny. Dat nigger allers got de debble in her." I suggested that she might have seen or heard something that excited her curiosity.

"Tut! tut! chile!" exclaimed Betty, "she ain't seen notin', nor hearn notin'. She only 'spects something. Dat's all. She wants to fine out who hab cut and make my gownd. But she won't nebber know. Dat's sartin. I'll git missis to fix her."

I reflected a moment, and said, "Betty, I must leave here to-night."

"Do as you tink best, poor chile," she replied. "I'se mighty 'fraid dat 'ere nigger vill pop on you some time."

She reported the incident to her mistress, and received orders to keep Jenny busy in the kitchen till she could see my uncle Phillip. He told her he would send a friend for me that very evening. She told him she hoped I was going to the north, for it was very dangerous for me to remain any where in the vicinity. Alas, it was not an easy thing, for one in my situation, to go to the north. In order to leave the coast quite clear for me, she went into the country to spend the day with her brother, and took Jenny with her. She was afraid to come and bid me good by, but she left a kind message with Betty. I heard her carriage roll from the door, and I never again saw her who had so generously befriended the poor, trembling fugitive! Though she was a slaveholder, to this day my heart blesses her!

I had not the slightest idea where I was going. Betty brought me a suit of sailor's clothes,—jacket, trowsers, and tarpaulin hat. She gave me a small bundle, saying I might need it where I was going. In cheery tones, she exclaimed, "I'se so glad you is gwine to free parts! Don't forget ole Betty. P'raps I'll come 'long by and by."

I tried to tell her how grateful I felt for all her kindness. But she interrupted me. "I don't want no tanks, honey. I'se glad I could help you, and I hope de good Lord vill open de path for you. I'se gwine wid you to de lower gate. Put your hands in your pockets, and walk ricketty, like de sailors."

I performed to her satisfaction. At the gate I found Peter, a young colored man, waiting for me. I had known him for years. He had been an apprentice to my father, and had always borne a good character. I was not afraid to trust to him. Betty bade me a hurried good by, and we walked off. "Take courage, Linda," said my friend Peter. "I've got a dagger, and no man shall take you from me, unless he passes over my dead body."

It was a long time since I had taken a walk out of doors, and the fresh air revived me. It was also pleasant to hear a human voice speaking to me above a whisper. I passed several people whom I knew, but they did not recognize me in my disguise. I prayed internally that, for Peter's sake, as well as my own, nothing might occur to bring out his dagger. We walked on till we came to the wharf. My aunt Nancy's husband was a seafaring man, and it had been deemed necessary to let him into our secret. He took me into his boat, rowed out to a vessel not far distant, and hoisted me on board. We three were the only occupants of the vessel. I now ventured to ask what they proposed to do with me. They said I was to remain on board till near dawn, and then they would hide me in Snaky Swamp, till my uncle Phillip had prepared a place of concealment for me. If the vessel had been bound north, it would have been of no avail to me, for it would certainly have been searched. About four o'clock, we were again seated in the boat, and rowed three miles to the swamp. My fear of snakes had been increased by the venomous bite I had received, and I dreaded to enter this hiding place. But I was in no situation to choose, and I gratefully accepted the best that my poor, persecuted friends could do for me.

Peter landed first, and with a large knife cut a path through bamboos and briers of all descriptions. He came back, took me in his arms, and carried me to a seat made among the bamboos. Before we reached it, we were covered with hundreds of mosquitos. In an hour's time they had so poisoned my flesh that I was a pitiful sight to behold. As the light increased, I saw snake after snake crawling round us. I had been accustomed to the sight of snakes all my life, but these were larger than any I had ever seen. To this day I shudder when I remember that morning. As evening approached, the number of snakes increased so much that we were continually obliged to thrash them with sticks to keep them from crawling over us. The bamboos were so high and so thick that it was impossible to see beyond a very short distance. Just before it became dark we procured a seat nearer to the entrance of the swamp, being fearful of losing our way back to the boat. It was not long before we heard the paddle of oars, and the low whistle, which had been agreed upon as a signal. We made haste to enter the boat, and were rowed back to the vessel. I passed a wretched night; for the heat of the swamp, the mosquitos, and the constant terror of snakes, had brought on a burning fever. I had just dropped asleep, when they came and told me it was time to go back to that horrid swamp. I could scarcely summon courage to rise. But even those large, venomous snakes were less dreadful to my imagination than the white men in that community called civilized. This time Peter took a quantity of tobacco to burn, to keep off the mosquitos. It produced the desired effect on them, but gave me nausea and severe headache. At dark we returned to the vessel. I had been so sick during the day, that Peter declared I should go home that night, if the devil himself was on patrol. They told me a place of concealment had been provided for me at my grandmother's. I could not imagine how it was possible to hide me in her house, every nook and corner of which was known to the Flint family. They told me to wait and see. We were rowed ashore, and went boldly through the streets, to my grandmother's. I wore my sailor's clothes, and had blackened my face with charcoal. I passed several people whom I knew. The father of my children came so near that I brushed against his arm; but he had no idea who it was.

"You must make the most of this walk," said my friend Peter, "for you may not have another very soon."

I thought his voice sounded sad. It was kind of him to conceal from me what a dismal hole was to be my home for a long, long time.

# XXI. THE LOOPHOLE OF RETREAT.

A small shed had been added to my grandmother's house years ago. Some boards were laid across the joists at the top, and between these boards and the roof was a very small garret, never occupied by any thing but rats and mice. It was a pent roof, covered with nothing but shingles, according to the southern custom for such buildings. The garret was only nine feet long and seven wide. The highest part was three feet high, and sloped down abruptly to the loose board floor. There was no admission for either light or air. My uncle Phillip, who was a carpenter, had very skilfully made a concealed trap-door, which communicated with the storeroom. He had been doing this while I was waiting in the swamp. The storeroom opened upon a piazza. To this hole I was conveyed as soon as I entered the house. The air was stifling; the darkness total. A bed had been spread on the floor. I could sleep quite comfortably on one side; but the slope was so sudden that I could not turn on my other without hitting the roof. The rats and mice ran over my bed; but I was weary, and I slept such sleep as the wretched may, when a tempest has passed over them. Morning came. I knew it only by the noises I heard; for in my small den day and night were all the same. I suffered for air even more than for light. But I was not comfortless. I heard the voices of my children. There was joy and there was sadness in the sound. It made my tears flow. How I longed to speak to them! I was eager to look on their faces; but there was no hole, no crack, through which I could peep. This continued darkness was oppressive. It seemed horrible to sit or lie in a cramped position day after day, without one gleam of light. Yet I would have chosen this, rather than my lot as a slave, though white people considered it an easy one; and it was so compared with the fate of others. I was never cruelly overworked; I was never lacerated with the whip from head to foot; I was never so beaten and bruised that I could not turn from one side to the other; I never had my heel-strings cut to prevent my running away; I was never chained to a log and forced to drag it about, while I toiled in the fields from morning till night; I was never branded with hot iron, or torn by bloodhounds. On the contrary, I had always been kindly treated, and tenderly cared for, until I came into the hands of Dr. Flint. I had never wished for freedom till then. But though my life in slavery was comparatively devoid of hardships, God pity the woman who is compelled to lead such a life!

My food was passed up to me through the trap-door my uncle had contrived; and my grandmother, my uncle Phillip, and aunt Nancy would seize such opportunities as they could, to mount up there and chat with me at the opening. But of course this was not safe in the daytime. It must all be done in darkness. It was impossible for me to move in an erect position, but I crawled about my den for exercise. One day I hit my head against something, and found it was a gimlet. My uncle had left it sticking there when he made the trap-door. I was as rejoiced as Robinson Crusoe could have been at finding such a treasure. It put a lucky thought into my head. I said to myself, "Now I will have some light. Now I will see my children." I did not dare to begin my work during the daytime, for fear of attracting attention. But I groped round; and having found the side next the street, where I could frequently see my children, I stuck the gimlet in and waited for evening. I bored three rows of holes, one above another; then I bored out the interstices between. I thus succeeded in making one hole about an inch long and an inch broad. I sat by it till late into the night, to enjoy the little whiff of air that floated in. In the morning I watched for my children. The first person I saw in the street was Dr. Flint. I had a shuddering, superstitious feeling that it was a bad omen. Several familiar faces passed by. At last I heard the merry laugh of children, and presently two sweet little faces were looking up at me, as though they knew I was there, and were conscious of the joy they imparted. How I longed to tell them I was there!

My condition was now a little improved. But for weeks I was tormented by hundreds of little red insects, fine as a needle's point, that pierced through my skin, and produced an intolerable burning. The good grandmother gave me herb teas and cooling medicines, and finally I got rid of them. The heat of my den was intense, for nothing but thin shingles protected me from the scorching summer's sun. But I had my consolations. Through my peeping-hole I could watch the children, and when they were near enough, I could hear their talk. Aunt Nancy brought me all the news she could hear at Dr. Flint's. From her I learned that the doctor had written to New York to a colored woman, who had been born and raised in our neighborhood, and had breathed his contaminating atmosphere. He offered her a reward if she could find out any thing about me. I know not what was the nature of her reply; but he soon after started for New York in haste, saying to his family that he had business of importance to transact. I peeped at him as he passed on his way to the steamboat. It was a satisfaction to have miles of land and water between us, even for a little while; and it was a still greater satisfaction to know that he believed me to be in the Free States. My little den seemed less dreary than it had done. He returned, as he did from his former journey to New York, without obtaining any satisfactory information. When he passed our house next morning, Benny was standing at the gate. He had heard them say that he had gone to find me, and he called out, "Dr. Flint, did you bring my mother home? I want to see her." The doctor stamped his foot at him in a rage, and exclaimed, "Get out of the way, you little damned rascal! If you don't, I'll cut off your head."

Benny ran terrified into the house, saying, "You can't put me in jail again. I don't belong to you now." It was well that the wind carried the words away from the doctor's ear. I told my grandmother of it, when we had our next conference at the trap-door, and begged of her not to allow the children to be impertinent to the irascible old man.

Autumn came, with a pleasant abatement of heat. My eyes had become accustomed to the dim light, and by holding my book or work in a certain position near the aperture I contrived to read and sew. That was a great relief to the tedious monotony of my life. But when winter came, the cold penetrated through the thin shingle roof, and I was dreadfully chilled. The winters there are not so long, or so severe, as in northern latitudes; but the houses are not built to shelter from cold, and my little den was peculiarly comfortless. The kind grandmother brought me bedclothes and warm drinks. Often I was obliged to lie in bed all day to keep comfortable; but with all my precautions, my shoulders and feet were frostbitten. O, those long, gloomy days, with no object for my eye to rest upon, and no thoughts to occupy my mind, except the dreary past and the uncertain future! I was thankful when there came a day sufficiently mild for me to wrap myself up and sit at the loophole to watch the passers by. Southerners have the habit of stopping and talking in the streets, and I heard many conversations not intended to meet my ears. I heard slave-hunters planning how to catch some poor fugitive. Several times I heard allusions to Dr. Flint, myself, and the history of my children, who, perhaps, were playing near the gate. One would say, "I wouldn't move my little finger to catch her, as old Flint's property." Another would say, "I'll catch any nigger for the reward. A man ought to have what belongs to him, if he is a damned brute." The opinion was often expressed that I was in the Free States. Very rarely did any one suggest that I might be in the vicinity. Had the least suspicion rested on my grandmother's house, it would have been burned to the ground. But it was the last place they thought of. Yet there was no place, where slavery existed, that could have afforded me so good a place of concealment.

Dr. Flint and his family repeatedly tried to coax and bribe my children to tell something they had heard said about me. One day the doctor took them into a shop, and offered them some bright little silver pieces and gay handkerchiefs if they would tell where their mother was. Ellen shrank away from him, and would not speak; but Benny spoke up, and said, "Dr. Flint, I don't know where my mother is. I guess she's in New York; and when you go there again, I wish you'd ask her to come home, for I want to see her; but if you put her in jail, or tell her you'll cut her head off, I'll tell her to go right back."

# XXII. CHRISTMAS FESTIVITIES.

Christmas was approaching. Grandmother brought me materials, and I busied myself making some new garments and little playthings for my children. Were it not that hiring day is near at hand, and many families are fearfully looking forward to the probability of separation in a few days, Christmas might be a happy season for the poor slaves. Even slave mothers try to gladden the hearts of their little ones on that occasion. Benny and Ellen had their Christmas stockings filled. Their imprisoned mother could not have the privilege of witnessing their surprise and joy. But I had the pleasure of peeping at them as they went into the street with their new suits on. I heard Benny ask a little playmate whether Santa Claus brought him any thing. "Yes," replied the boy; "but Santa Claus ain't a real man. It's the children's mothers that put things into the stockings." "No, that can't be," replied Benny, "for Santa Claus brought Ellen and me these new clothes, and my mother has been gone this long time."

How I longed to tell him that his mother made those garments, and that many a tear fell on them while she worked!

Every child rises early on Christmas morning to see the Johnkannaus. Without them, Christmas would be shorn of its greatest attraction. They consist of companies of slaves from the plantations, generally of the lower class. Two athletic men, in calico wrappers, have a net thrown over them, covered with all manner of bright-colored stripes. Cows' tails are fastened to their backs, and their heads are decorated with horns. A box, covered with sheepskin, is called the gumbo box. A dozen beat on this, while other strike triangles and jawbones, to which bands of dancers keep time. For a month previous they are composing songs, which are sung on this occasion. These companies, of a hundred each, turn out early in the morning, and are allowed to go round till twelve o'clock, begging for contributions. Not a door is left unvisited where there is the least chance of obtaining a penny or a glass of rum. They do not drink while they are out, but carry the rum home in jugs, to have a carousal. These Christmas donations frequently amount to twenty or thirty dollars. It is seldom that any white man or child refuses to give them a trifle. If he does, they regale his ears with the following song:—

>Poor massa, so dey say;
>Down in de heel, so dey say;
>Got no money, so dey say;
>Not one shillin, so dey say;
>God A'mighty bress you, so dey say.

Christmas is a day of feasting, both with white and colored people. Slaves, who are lucky enough to have a few shillings, are sure to spend them for good eating; and many a turkey and pig is captured, without saying, "By your leave, sir." Those who cannot obtain these, cook a 'possum, or a raccoon, from which savory dishes can be made. My grandmother raised poultry and pigs for sale and it was her established custom to have both a turkey and a pig roasted for Christmas dinner.

On this occasion, I was warned to keep extremely quiet, because two guests had been invited. One was the town constable, and the other was a free colored man, who tried to pass himself off for white, and who was always ready to do any mean work for the sake of currying favor with white people. My grandmother had a motive for inviting them. She managed to take them all over the house. All the rooms on the lower floor were thrown open for them to pass in and out; and after dinner, they were invited up stairs to look at a fine mocking bird my uncle had just brought home. There, too, the rooms were all thrown open that they might look in. When I heard them talking on the piazza, my heart almost stood still. I knew this colored man had spent many nights hunting for me. Every body knew he had the blood of a slave father in his veins; but for the sake of passing himself off for white, he was ready to kiss the slaveholders' feet. How I despised him! As for the constable, he wore no false colors. The duties of his office were despicable, but he was superior to his companion, inasmuch as he did not pretend to be what he was not. Any white man, who could raise money enough to buy a slave, would have considered himself degraded by being a constable; but the office enabled its possessor to exercise authority. If he found any slave out after nine o'clock, he could whip him as much as he liked; and that was a privilege to be coveted. When the guests were ready to depart, my grandmother gave each of them some of her nice pudding, as a present for their wives. Through my peep-hole I saw them go out of the gate, and I was glad when it closed after them. So passed the first Christmas in my den.

## XXIII. STILL IN PRISON.

When spring returned, and I took in the little patch of green the aperture commanded, I asked myself how many more summers and winters I must be condemned to spend thus. I longed to draw in a plentiful draught of fresh air, to stretch my cramped limbs, to have room to stand erect, to feel the earth under my feet again. My relatives were constantly on the lookout for a chance of escape; but none offered that seemed practicable, and even tolerably safe. The hot summer came again, and made the turpentine drop from the thin roof over my head.

During the long nights I was restless for want of air, and I had no room to toss and turn. There was but one compensation; the atmosphere was so stifled that even mosquitos would not condescend to buzz in it. With all my detestation of Dr. Flint, I could hardly wish him a worse punishment, either in this world or that which is to come, than to suffer what I suffered in one single summer. Yet the laws allowed him to be out in the free air, while I, guiltless of crime, was pent up here, as the only means of avoiding the cruelties the laws allowed him to inflict upon me! I don't know what kept life within me. Again and again, I thought I should die before long; but I saw the leaves of another autumn whirl through the air, and felt the touch of another winter. In summer the most terrible thunder storms were acceptable, for the rain came through the roof, and I rolled up my bed that it might cool the hot boards under it. Later in the season, storms sometimes wet my clothes through and through, and that was not comfortable when the air grew chilly. Moderate storms I could keep out by filling the chinks with oakum.

But uncomfortable as my situation was, I had glimpses of things out of doors, which made me thankful for my wretched hiding-place. One day I saw a slave pass our gate, muttering, "It's his own, and he can kill it if he will." My grandmother told me that woman's history. Her mistress had that day seen her baby for the first time, and in the lineaments of its fair face she saw a likeness to her husband. She turned the bondwoman and her child out of doors, and forbade her ever to return. The slave went to her master, and told him what had happened. He promised to talk with her mistress, and make it all right. The next day she and her baby were sold to a Georgia trader.

Another time I saw a woman rush wildly by, pursued by two men. She was a slave, the wet nurse of her mistress's children. For some trifling offence her mistress ordered her to be stripped and whipped. To escape the degradation and the torture, she rushed to the river, jumped in, and ended her wrongs in death.

Senator Brown, of Mississippi, could not be ignorant of many such facts as these, for they are of frequent occurrence in every Southern State. Yet he stood up in the Congress of the United States, and declared that slavery was "a great moral, social, and political blessing; a blessing to the master, and a blessing to the slave!"

I suffered much more during the second winter than I did during the first. My limbs were benumbed by inaction, and the cold filled them with cramp. I had a very painful sensation of coldness in my head; even my face and tongue stiffened, and I lost the power of speech. Of course it was impossible, under the circumstances, to summon any physician. My brother William came and did all he could for me. Uncle Phillip also watched tenderly over me; and poor grandmother crept up and down to inquire whether there were any signs of returning life. I was restored to consciousness by the dashing of cold water in my face, and found myself leaning against my brother's arm, while he bent over me with streaming eyes. He afterwards told me he thought I was dying, for I had been in an unconscious state sixteen hours. I next became delirious, and was in great danger of betraying myself and my friends. To prevent this, they stupefied me with drugs. I remained in bed six weeks, weary in body and sick at heart. How to get medical advice was the question. William finally went to a Thompsonian doctor, and described himself as having all my pains and aches. He returned with herbs, roots, and ointment. He was especially charged to rub on the ointment by a fire; but how could a fire be made in my little den? Charcoal in a furnace was tried, but there was no outlet for the gas, and it nearly cost me my life. Afterwards coals, already kindled, were brought up in an iron pan, and placed on bricks. I was so weak, and it was so long since I had enjoyed the warmth of a fire, that those few coals actually made me weep. I think the medicines did me some good; but my recovery was very slow. Dark thoughts passed through my mind as I lay there day after day. I tried to be thankful for my little cell, dismal as it was, and even to love it, as part of the price I had paid for the redemption of my children. Sometimes I thought God was a compassionate Father, who would forgive my sins for the sake of my sufferings. At other times, it seemed to me there was no justice or mercy in the divine government. I asked why the curse of slavery was permitted to exist, and why I had been so persecuted and wronged from youth upward. These things took the shape of mystery, which is to this day not so clear to my soul as I trust it will be hereafter.

In the midst of my illness, grandmother broke down under the weight and anxiety and toil. The idea of losing her, who had always been my best friend and a mother to my children, was the sorest trial I had yet had. O, how earnestly

I prayed that she might recover! How hard it seemed, that I could not tend upon her, who had so long and so tenderly watched over me!

One day the screams of a child nerved me with strength to crawl to my peeping-hole, and I saw my son covered with blood. A fierce dog, usually kept chained, had seized and bitten him. A doctor was sent for, and I heard the groans and screams of my child while the wounds were being sewed up. O, what torture to a mother's heart, to listen to this and be unable to go to him!

But childhood is like a day in spring, alternately shower and sunshine. Before night Benny was bright and lively, threatening the destruction of the dog; and great was his delight when the doctor told him the next day that the dog had bitten another boy and been shot. Benny recovered from his wounds; but it was long before he could walk.

When my grandmother's illness became known, many ladies, who were her customers, called to bring her some little comforts, and to inquire whether she had every thing she wanted. Aunt Nancy one night asked permission to watch with her sick mother, and Mrs. Flint replied, "I don't see any need of your going. I can't spare you." But when she found other ladies in the neighborhood were so attentive, not wishing to be outdone in Christian charity, she also sallied forth, in magnificent condescension, and stood by the bedside of her who had loved her in her infancy, and who had been repaid by such grievous wrongs. She seemed surprised to find her so ill, and scolded uncle Phillip for not sending for Dr. Flint. She herself sent for him immediately, and he came. Secure as I was in my retreat, I should have been terrified if I had known he was so near me. He pronounced my grandmother in a very critical situation, and said if her attending physician wished it, he would visit her. Nobody wished to have him coming to the house at all hours, and we were not disposed to give him a chance to make out a long bill.

As Mrs. Flint went out, Sally told her the reason Benny was lame was, that a dog had bitten him. "I'm glad of it," replied she. "I wish he had killed him. It would be good news to send to his mother. Her day will come. The dogs will grab her yet." With these Christian words she and her husband departed, and, to my great satisfaction, returned no more.

I learned from uncle Phillip, with feelings of unspeakable joy and gratitude, that the crisis was passed and grandmother would live. I could now say from my heart, "God is merciful. He has spared me the anguish of feeling that I caused her death."

# XXIV. THE CANDIDATE FOR CONGRESS.

The summer had nearly ended, when Dr. Flint made a third visit to New York, in search of me. Two candidates were running for Congress, and he returned in season to vote. The father of my children was the Whig candidate. The doctor had hitherto been a stanch Whig; but now he exerted all his energies for the defeat of Mr. Sands. He invited large parties of men to dine in the shade of his trees, and supplied them with plenty of rum and brandy. If any poor fellow drowned his wits in the bowl, and, in the openness of his convivial heart, proclaimed that he did not mean to vote the Democratic ticket, he was shoved into the street without ceremony.

The doctor expended his liquor in vain. Mr. Sands was elected; an event which occasioned me some anxious thoughts. He had not emancipated my children, and if he should die they would be at the mercy of his heirs. Two little voices, that frequently met my ear, seemed to plead with me not to let their father depart without striving to make their freedom secure. Years had passed since I had spoken to him. I had not even seen him since the night I passed him, unrecognized, in my disguise of a sailor. I supposed he would call before he left, to say something to my grandmother concerning the children, and I resolved what course to take.

The day before his departure for Washington I made arrangements, toward evening, to get from my hiding-place into the storeroom below. I found myself so stiff and clumsy that it was with great difficulty I could hitch from one resting place to another. When I reached the storeroom my ankles gave way under me, and I sank exhausted on the floor. It seemed as if I could never use my limbs again. But the purpose I had in view roused all the strength I had. I crawled on my hands and knees to the window, and, screened behind a barrel, I waited for his coming. The clock struck nine, and I knew the steamboat would leave between ten and eleven. My hopes were failing. But presently I heard his voice, saying to some one, "Wait for me a moment. I wish to see aunt Martha." When he came out, as he passed the window, I said, "Stop one moment, and let me speak for my children." He started, hesitated, and then passed on, and went out of the gate. I closed the shutter I had partially opened, and sank down behind the barrel. I had suffered much; but seldom had I experienced a keener pang than I then felt. Had my children, then, become of so little consequence to him? And had he so little feeling for their wretched mother that he would not listen a moment while she pleaded for them? Painful memories were so busy within me, that I forgot I had not hooked the shutter, till I heard some one opening it. I looked up. He had come back. "Who called me?" said he, in a low tone. "I did," I replied. "Oh, Linda," said he, "I knew your voice; but I was afraid to answer, lest my friend should hear me. Why do you come here? Is it possible you risk yourself in this house? They are mad to allow it. I shall expect to hear that you are all ruined," I did not wish to implicate him, by letting him know my place of concealment; so I merely said, "I thought you would come to bid grandmother good by, and so I came here to speak a few words to you about emancipating my children. Many changes may take place during the six months you are gone to Washington, and it does not seem right for you to expose them to the risk of such changes. I want nothing for myself; all I ask is, that you will free my children, or authorize some friend to do it, before you go."

He promised he would do it, and also expressed a readiness; to make any arrangements whereby I could be purchased.

I heard footsteps approaching, and closed the shutter hastily. I wanted to crawl back to my den, without letting the family know what I had done; for I knew they would deem it very imprudent. But he stepped back into the house, to tell my grandmother that he had spoken with me at the storeroom window, and to beg of her not to allow me to remain in the house over night. He said it was the height of madness for me to be there; that we should certainly all be ruined. Luckily, he was in too much of a hurry to wait for a reply, or the dear old woman would surely have told him all.

I tried to go back to my den, but found it more difficult to go up than I had to come down. Now that my mission was fulfilled, the little strength that had supported me through it was gone, and I sank helpless on the floor. My grandmother, alarmed at the risk I had run, came into the storeroom in the dark, and locked the door behind her. "Linda," she whispered, "where are you?"

"I am here by the window," I replied. "I couldn't have him go away without emancipating the children. Who knows what may happen?"

"Come, come, child," said she, "it won't do for you to stay here another minute. You've done wrong; but I can't blame you, poor thing!" I told her I could not return without assistance, and she must call my uncle. Uncle Phillip came, and pity prevented him from scolding me. He carried me back to my dungeon, laid me tenderly on the bed, gave me some medicine, and asked me if there was any thing more he could do. Then he went away, and I was left with my own thoughts—starless as the midnight darkness around me.

My friends feared I should become a cripple for life; and I was so weary of my long imprisonment that, had it not been for the hope of serving my children, I should have been thankful to die; but, for their sakes, I was willing to bear on.

# XXV. COMPETITION IN CUNNING.

Dr. Flint had not given me up. Every now and then he would say to my grandmother that I would yet come back, and voluntarily surrender myself; and that when I did, I could be purchased by my relatives, or any one who wished to buy me. I knew his cunning nature too well not to perceive that this was a trap laid for me; and so all my friends understood it. I resolved to match my cunning against his cunning. In order to make him believe that I was in New York, I resolved to write him a letter dated from that place. I sent for my friend Peter, and asked him if he knew any trustworthy seafaring person, who would carry such a letter to New York, and put it in the post office there. He said he knew one that he would trust with his own life to the ends of the world. I reminded him that it was a hazardous thing for him to undertake. He said he knew it, but he was willing to do any thing to help me. I expressed a wish for a New York paper, to ascertain the names of some of the streets. He run his hand into his pocket, and said, "Here is half a one, that was round a cap I bought of a pedler yesterday." I told him the letter would be ready the next evening. He bade me good by, adding, "Keep up your spirits, Linda; brighter days will come by and by."

My uncle Phillip kept watch over the gate until our brief interview was over. Early the next morning, I seated myself near the little aperture to examine the newspaper. It was a piece of the New York Herald; and, for once, the paper that systematically abuses the colored people, was made to render them a service. Having obtained what information I wanted concerning streets and numbers, I wrote two letters, one to my grandmother, the other to Dr. Flint. I reminded him how he, a gray-headed man, had treated a helpless child, who had been placed in his power, and what years of misery he had brought upon her. To my grandmother, I expressed a wish to have my children sent to me at the north, where I could teach them to respect themselves, and set them a virtuous example; which a slave mother was not allowed to do at the south. I asked her to direct her answer to a certain street in Boston, as I did not live in New York, though I went there sometimes. I dated these letters ahead, to allow for the time it would take to carry them, and sent a memorandum of the date to the messenger. When my friend came for the letters, I said, "God bless and reward you, Peter, for this disinterested kindness. Pray be careful. If you are detected, both you and I will have to suffer dreadfully. I have not a relative who would dare to do it for me." He replied, "You may trust to me, Linda. I don't forget that your father was my best friend, and I will be a friend to his children so long as God lets me live."

It was necessary to tell my grandmother what I had done, in order that she might be ready for the letter, and prepared to hear what Dr. Flint might say about my being at the north. She was sadly troubled. She felt sure mischief would come of it. I also told my plan to aunt Nancy, in order that she might report to us what was said at Dr. Flint's house. I whispered it to her through a crack, and she whispered back, "I hope it will succeed. I shan't mind being a slave all my life, if I can only see you and the children free."

I had directed that my letters should be put into the New York post office on the 20th of the month. On the evening of the 24th my aunt came to say that Dr. Flint and his wife had been talking in a low voice about a letter he had received, and that when he went to his office he promised to bring it when he came to tea. So I concluded I should hear my letter read the next morning. I told my grandmother Dr. Flint would be sure to come, and asked her to have him sit near a certain door, and leave it open, that I might hear what he said. The next morning I took my station within sound of that door, and remained motionless as a statue. It was not long before I heard the gate slam, and the well-known footsteps enter the house. He seated himself in the chair that was placed for him, and said, "Well, Martha, I've brought you a letter from Linda. She has sent me a letter, also. I know exactly where to find her; but I don't choose to go to Boston for her. I had rather she would come back of her own accord, in a respectable manner. Her uncle Phillip is the best person to go for her. With him, she would feel perfectly free to act. I am willing to pay his expenses going and returning. She shall be sold to her friends. Her children are free; at least I suppose they are; and when you obtain her freedom, you'll make a happy family. I suppose, Martha, you have no objection to my reading to you the letter Linda has written to you."

He broke the seal, and I heard him read it. The old villain! He had suppressed the letter I wrote to grandmother, and prepared a substitute of his own, the purport of which was as follows:—

> Dear Grandmother: I have long wanted to write to you; but the disgraceful manner in which I left you and my children made me ashamed to do it. If you knew how much I have suffered since I ran away, you would pity and forgive me. I have purchased freedom at a dear rate. If any arrangement could be made for me to return to the south without being a slave, I would gladly come. If not, I beg of you to send my children to the north. I cannot live any longer without them. Let me know in time, and I will meet them in New York or Philadelphia, whichever place best suits my uncle's convenience. Write as soon as possible to your unhappy daughter, Linda.

"It is very much as I expected it would be," said the old hypocrite, rising to go. "You see the foolish girl has repented of her rashness, and wants to return. We must help her to do it, Martha. Talk with Phillip about it. If he will go for her, she will trust to him, and come back. I should like an answer to-morrow. Good morning, Martha."

As he stepped out on the piazza, he stumbled over my little girl. "Ah, Ellen, is that you?" he said, in his most gracious manner. "I didn't see you. How do you do?"

"Pretty well, sir," she replied. "I heard you tell grandmother that my mother is coming home. I want to see her."

"Yes, Ellen, I am going to bring her home very soon," rejoined he; "and you shall see her as much as you like, you little curly-headed nigger."

This was as good as a comedy to me, who had heard it all; but grandmother was frightened and distressed, because the doctor wanted my uncle to go for me.

The next evening Dr. Flint called to talk the matter over. My uncle told him that from what he had heard of Massachusetts, he judged he should be mobbed if he went there after a runaway slave. "All stuff and nonsense, Phillip!" replied the doctor. "Do you suppose I want you to kick up a row in Boston? The business can all be done quietly. Linda writes that she wants to come back. You are her relative, and she would trust you. The case would be different if I went. She might object to coming with me; and the damned abolitionists, if they knew I was her master, would not believe me, if I told them she had begged to go back. They would get up a row; and I should not like to see Linda dragged through the streets like a common negro. She has been very ungrateful to me for all my kindness; but I forgive her, and want to act the part of a friend towards her. I have no wish to hold her as my slave. Her friends can buy her as soon as she arrives here."

Finding that his arguments failed to convince my uncle, the doctor "let the cat out of the bag," by saying that he had written to the mayor of Boston, to ascertain whether there was a person of my description at the street and number from which my letter was dated. He had omitted this date in the letter he had made up to read to my grandmother. If I had dated from New York, the old man would probably have made another journey to that city. But even in that dark region, where knowledge is so carefully excluded from the slave, I had heard enough about Massachusetts to come to the conclusion that slaveholders did not consider it a comfortable place to go in search of a runaway. That was before the Fugitive Slave Law was passed; before Massachusetts had consented to become a "nigger hunter" for the south.

My grandmother, who had become skittish by seeing her family always in danger, came to me with a very distressed countenance, and said, "What will you do if the mayor of Boston sends him word that you haven't been there? Then he will suspect the letter was a trick; and maybe he'll find out something about it, and we shall all get into trouble. O Linda, I wish you had never sent the letters."

"Don't worry yourself, Grandmother," said I. "The mayor of Boston won't trouble himself to hunt niggers for Dr. Flint. The letters will do good in the end. I shall get out of this dark hole some time or other."

"I hope you will, child," replied the good, patient old friend. "You have been here a long time; almost five years; but whenever you do go, it will break your old grandmother's heart. I should be expecting every day to hear that you were brought back in irons and put in jail. God help you, poor child! Let us be thankful that some time or other we shall go 'where the wicked cease from troubling, and the weary are at rest.'" My heart responded, Amen.

The fact that Dr. Flint had written to the mayor of Boston convinced me that he believed my letter to be genuine, and of course that he had no suspicion of my being any where in the vicinity. It was a great object to keep up this delusion, for it made me and my friends feel less anxious, and it would be very convenient whenever there was a chance to escape. I resolved, therefore, to continue to write letters from the north from time to time.

Two or three weeks passed, and as no news came from the mayor of Boston, grandmother began to listen to my entreaty to be allowed to leave my cell, sometimes, and exercise my limbs to prevent my becoming a cripple. I was allowed to slip down into the small storeroom, early in the morning, and remain there a little while. The room was all filled up with barrels, except a small open space under my trap-door. This faced the door, the upper part of which was of glass, and purposely left uncurtained, that the curious might look in. The air of this place was close; but it was so much better than the atmosphere of my cell, that I dreaded to return. I came down as soon as it was light, and remained till eight o'clock, when people began to be about, and there was danger that some one might come on the piazza. I had tried various applications to bring warmth and feeling into my limbs, but without avail. They were so numb and stiff that it was a painful effort to move; and had my enemies come upon me during the first mornings I tried to exercise them a little in the small unoccupied space of the storeroom, it would have been impossible for me to have escaped.

# XXVI. IMPORTANT ERA IN MY BROTHER'S LIFE.

I missed the company and kind attentions of my brother William, who had gone to Washington with his master, Mr. Sands. We received several letters from him, written without any allusion to me, but expressed in such a manner that I knew he did not forget me. I disguised my hand, and wrote to him in the same manner. It was a long session; and when it closed, William wrote to inform us that Mr. Sands was going to the north, to be gone some time, and that he was to accompany him. I knew that his master had promised to give him his freedom, but no time had been specified. Would William trust to a slave's chances? I remembered how we used to talk together, in our young days, about obtaining our freedom, and I thought it very doubtful whether he would come back to us.

Grandmother received a letter from Mr. Sands, saying that William had proved a most faithful servant, and he would also say a valued friend; that no mother had ever trained a better boy. He said he had travelled through the Northern States and Canada; and though the abolitionists had tried to decoy him away, they had never succeeded. He ended by saying they should be at home shortly.

We expected letters from William, describing the novelties of his journey, but none came. In time, it was reported that Mr. Sands would return late in the autumn, accompanied by a bride. Still no letters from William. I felt almost sure I should never see him again on southern soil; but had he no word of comfort to send to his friends at home? to the poor captive in her dungeon? My thoughts wandered through the dark past, and over the uncertain future. Alone in my cell, where no eye but God's could see me, I wept bitter tears. How earnestly I prayed to him to restore me to my children, and enable me to be a useful woman and a good mother!

At last the day arrived for the return of the travellers. Grandmother had made loving preparations to welcome her absent boy back to the old hearthstone. When the dinner table was laid, William's place occupied its old place. The stage coach went by empty. My grandmother waited dinner. She thought perhaps he was necessarily detained by his master. In my prison I listened anxiously, expecting every moment to hear my dear brother's voice and step. In the course of the afternoon a lad was sent by Mr. Sands to tell grandmother that William did not return with him; that the abolitionists had decoyed him away. But he begged her not to feel troubled about it, for he felt confident she would see William in a few days. As soon as he had time to reflect he would come back, for he could never expect to be so well off at the north as he had been with him.

If you had seen the tears, and heard the sobs, you would have thought the messenger had brought tidings of death instead of freedom. Poor old grandmother felt that she should never see her darling boy again. And I was selfish. I thought more of what I had lost, than of what my brother had gained. A new anxiety began to trouble me. Mr. Sands had expended a good deal of money, and would naturally feel irritated by the loss he had incurred. I greatly feared this might injure the prospects of my children, who were now becoming valuable property. I longed to have their emancipation made certain. The more so, because their master and father was now married. I was too familiar with slavery not to know that promises made to slaves, though with kind intentions, and sincere at the time, depend upon many contingencies for their fulfillment.

Much as I wished William to be free, the step he had taken made me sad and anxious. The following Sabbath was calm and clear; so beautiful that it seemed like a Sabbath in the eternal world. My grandmother brought the children out on the piazza, that I might hear their voices. She thought it would comfort me in my despondency; and it did. They chatted merrily, as only children can. Benny said, "Grandmother, do you think uncle Will has gone for good? Won't he ever come back again? May be he'll find mother. If he does, won't she be glad to see him! Why don't you and uncle Phillip, and all of us, go and live where mother is? I should like it; wouldn't you, Ellen?"

"Yes, I should like it," replied Ellen; "but how could we find her? Do you know the place, grandmother? I don't remember how mother looked—do you, Benny?"

Benny was just beginning to describe me when they were interrupted by an old slave woman, a near neighbor, named Aggie. This poor creature had witnessed the sale of her children, and seen them carried off to parts unknown, without any hopes of ever hearing from them again. She saw that my grandmother had been weeping, and she said, in a sympathizing tone, "What's the matter, aunt Marthy?"

"O Aggie," she replied, "it seems as if I shouldn't have any of my children or grandchildren left to hand me a drink when I'm dying, and lay my old body in the ground. My boy didn't come back with Mr. Sands. He staid at the north."

Poor old Aggie clapped her hands for joy. "Is dat what you's crying fur?" she exclaimed. "Git down on your knees and bress de Lord! I don't know whar my poor chillern is, and I nebber 'spect to know. You don't know whar poor Linda's gone to; but you do know whar her brudder is. He's in free parts; and dat's de right place. Don't murmur at de Lord's doings but git down on your knees and tank him for his goodness."

My selfishness was rebuked by what poor Aggie said. She rejoiced over the escape of one who was merely her fellow-bondman, while his own sister was only thinking what his good fortune might cost her children. I knelt and prayed God to forgive me; and I thanked him from my heart, that one of my family was saved from the grasp of slavery.

It was not long before we received a letter from William. He wrote that Mr. Sands had always treated him kindly, and that he had tried to do his duty to him faithfully. But ever since he was a boy, he had longed to be free; and he had already gone through enough to convince him he had better not lose the chance that offered. He concluded by saying, "Don't worry about me, dear grandmother. I shall think of you always; and it will spur me on to work hard and try to do right. When I have earned money enough to give you a home, perhaps you will come to the north, and we can all live happy together."

Mr. Sands told my uncle Phillip the particulars about William's leaving him. He said, "I trusted him as if he were my own brother, and treated him as kindly. The abolitionists talked to him in several places; but I had no idea they could tempt him. However, I don't blame William. He's young and inconsiderate, and those Northern rascals decoyed him. I must confess the scamp was very bold about it. I met him coming down the steps of the Astor House with his trunk on his shoulder, and I asked him where he was going. He said he was going to change his old trunk. I told him it was rather shabby, and asked if he didn't need some money. He said, No, thanked me, and went off. He did not return so soon as I expected; but I waited patiently. At last I went to see if our trunks were packed, ready for our journey. I found them locked, and a sealed note on the table informed me where I could find the keys. The fellow even tried to be religious. He wrote that he hoped God would always bless me, and reward me for my kindness; that he was not unwilling to serve me; but he wanted to be a free man; and that if I thought he did wrong, he hoped I would forgive him. I intended to give him his freedom in five years. He might have trusted me. He has shown himself ungrateful; but I shall not go for him, or send for him. I feel confident that he will soon return to me."

I afterwards heard an account of the affair from William himself. He had not been urged away by abolitionists. He needed no information they could give him about slavery to stimulate his desire for freedom. He looked at his hands, and remembered that they were once in irons. What security had he that they would not be so again? Mr. Sands was kind to him; but he might indefinitely postpone the promise he had made to give him his freedom. He might come under pecuniary embarrassments, and his property be seized by creditors; or he might die, without making any arrangements in his favor. He had too often known such accidents to happen to slaves who had kind masters, and he wisely resolved to make sure of the present opportunity to own himself. He was scrupulous about taking any money from his master on false pretences; so he sold his best clothes to pay for his passage to Boston. The slaveholders pronounced him a base, ungrateful wretch, for thus requiting his master's indulgence. What would they have done under similar circumstances?

When Dr. Flint's family heard that William had deserted Mr. Sands, they chuckled greatly over the news. Mrs. Flint made her usual manifestations of Christian feeling, by saying, "I'm glad of it. I hope he'll never get him again. I like to see people paid back in their own coin. I reckon Linda's children will have to pay for it. I should be glad to see them in the speculator's hands again, for I'm tired of seeing those little niggers march about the streets."

# XXVII. NEW DESTINATION FOR THE CHILDREN.

Mrs. Flint proclaimed her intention of informing Mrs. Sands who was the father of my children. She likewise proposed to tell her what an artful devil I was; that I had made a great deal of trouble in her family; that when Mr. Sands was at the north, she didn't doubt I had followed him in disguise, and persuaded William to run away. She had some reason to entertain such an idea; for I had written from the north, from time to time, and I dated my letters from various places. Many of them fell into Dr. Flint's hands, as I expected they would; and he must have come to the conclusion that I travelled about a good deal. He kept a close watch over my children, thinking they would eventually lead to my detection.

A new and unexpected trial was in store for me. One day, when Mr. Sands and his wife were walking in the street, they met Benny. The lady took a fancy to him, and exclaimed, "What a pretty little negro! Whom does he belong to?"

Benny did not hear the answer; but he came home very indignant with the stranger lady, because she had called him a negro. A few days afterwards, Mr. Sands called on my grandmother, and told her he wanted her to take the children to his house. He said he had informed his wife of his relation to them, and told her they were motherless; and she wanted to see them.

When he had gone, my grandmother came and asked what I would do. The question seemed a mockery. What could I do? They were Mr. Sands's slaves, and their mother was a slave, whom he had represented to be dead. Perhaps he thought I was. I was too much pained and puzzled to come to any decision; and the children were carried without my knowledge. Mrs. Sands had a sister from Illinois staying with her. This lady, who had no children of her own, was so much pleased with Ellen, that she offered to adopt her, and bring her up as she would a daughter. Mrs. Sands wanted to take Benjamin. When grandmother reported this to me, I was tried almost beyond endurance. Was this all I was to gain by what I had suffered for the sake of having my children free? True, the prospect seemed fair; but I knew too well how lightly slaveholders held such "parental relations." If pecuniary troubles should come, or if the new wife required more money than could conveniently be spared, my children might be thought of as a convenient means of raising funds. I had no trust in thee, O Slavery! Never should I know peace till my children were emancipated with all due formalities of law.

I was too proud to ask Mr. Sands to do any thing for my own benefit; but I could bring myself to become a supplicant for my children. I resolved to remind him of the promise he had made me, and to throw myself upon his honor for the performance of it. I persuaded my grandmother to go to him, and tell him I was not dead, and that I earnestly entreated him to keep the promise he had made me; that I had heard of the recent proposals concerning my children, and did not feel easy to accept them; that he had promised to emancipate them, and it was time for him to redeem his pledge. I knew there was some risk in thus betraying that I was in the vicinity; but what will not a mother do for her children? He received the message with surprise, and said, "The children are free. I have never intended to claim them as slaves. Linda may decide their fate. In my opinion, they had better be sent to the north. I don't think they are quite safe here. Dr. Flint boasts that they are still in his power. He says they were his daughter's property, and as she was not of age when they were sold, the contract is not legally binding."

So, then, after all I had endured for their sakes, my poor children were between two fires; between my old master and their new master! And I was powerless. There was no protecting arm of the law for me to invoke. Mr. Sands proposed that Ellen should go, for the present, to some of his relatives, who had removed to Brooklyn, Long Island. It was promised that she should be well taken care of, and sent to school. I consented to it, as the best arrangement I could make for her. My grandmother, of course, negotiated it all; and Mrs. Sands knew of no other person in the transaction. She proposed that they should take Ellen with them to Washington, and keep her till they had a good chance of sending her, with friends, to Brooklyn. She had an infant daughter. I had had a glimpse of it, as the nurse passed with it in her arms. It was not a pleasant thought to me, that the bondwoman's child should tend her free-born sister; but there was no alternative. Ellen was made ready for the journey. O, how it tried my heart to send her away, so young, alone, among strangers! Without a mother's love to shelter her from the storms of life; almost without memory of a mother! I doubted whether she and Benny would have for me the natural affection that children feel for a parent. I thought to myself that I might perhaps never see my daughter again, and I had a great desire that she should look upon me, before she went, that she might take my image with her in her memory. It seemed to me cruel to have her brought to my dungeon. It was sorrow enough for her young heart to know that her mother was a victim of slavery, without seeing the wretched hiding-place to which it had driven her. I begged permission to pass the last night in one of the open chambers, with my little girl. They thought I was crazy to think of trusting such a young child with my perilous secret. I told them I had watched her character, and I felt sure she would not betray me; that I was determined to have an interview, and if they would not facilitate it, I would take my own way to obtain it. They remonstrated against the rashness of such a proceeding; but finding they could not change my purpose, they yielded. I slipped through the trap-door into the storeroom, and my uncle kept watch at the gate, while I passed into the piazza and went up stairs, to the room I used to occupy. It was more than five years since I had seen it; and how the memories crowded on me! There I had taken shelter when my mistress drove me from her house; there came my old tyrant, to mock, insult, and curse me; there my children were first laid in my arms; there I had watched over them, each day with a deeper and sadder love; there I had knelt to God, in anguish of heart, to forgive the wrong I had done. How vividly it all came back! And after this long, gloomy interval, I stood there such a wreck!

In the midst of these meditations, I heard footsteps on the stairs. The door opened, and my uncle Phillip came in, leading Ellen by the hand. I put my arms round her, and said, "Ellen, my dear child, I am your mother." She drew back a little, and looked at me; then, with sweet confidence, she laid her cheek against mine, and I folded her to the heart that had been so long desolated. She was the first to speak. Raising her head, she said, inquiringly, "You really are my mother?" I told her I really was; that during all the long time she had not seen me, I had loved her most tenderly; and that now she was going away, I wanted to see her and talk with her, that she might remember me. With a sob in her voice, she said, "I'm glad you've come to see me; but why didn't you ever come before? Benny and I have wanted so much to see you! He remembers you, and sometimes he tells me about you. Why didn't you come home when Dr. Flint went to bring you?"

I answered, "I couldn't come before, dear. But now that I am with you, tell me whether you like to go away." "I don't know," said she, crying. "Grandmother says I ought not to cry; that I am going to a good place, where I can learn to read and write, and that by and by I can write her a letter. But I shan't have Benny, or grandmother, or uncle Phillip, or any body to love me. Can't you go with me? O, do go, dear mother!"

I told her I couldn't go now; but sometime I would come to her, and then she and Benny and I would live together, and have happy times. She wanted to run and bring Benny to see me now. I told her he was going to the north, before long, with uncle Phillip, and then I would come to see him before he went away. I asked if she would like to have me stay all night and sleep with her. "O, yes," she replied. Then, turning to her uncle, she said, pleadingly, "May I stay? Please, uncle! She is my own mother." He laid his hand on her head, and said, solemnly, "Ellen, this is the secret you have promised grandmother never to tell. If you ever speak of it to any body, they will never let you see your grandmother again, and your mother can never come to Brooklyn." "Uncle," she replied, "I will never tell." He told her she might stay with me; and when he had gone, I took her in my arms and told her I was a slave, and that was the reason she must never say she had seen me. I exhorted her to be a good child, to try to please the people where she was going, and that God would raise her up friends. I told her to say her prayers, and remember always to pray for her poor mother, and that God would permit us to meet again. She wept, and I did not check her tears. Perhaps she would never again have a chance to pour her tears into a mother's bosom. All night she nestled in my arms, and I had no inclination to slumber. The moments were too precious to lose any of them. Once, when I thought she was asleep, I kissed her forehead softly, and she said, "I am not asleep, dear mother."

Before dawn they came to take me back to my den. I drew aside the window curtain, to take a last look of my child. The moonlight shone on her face, and I bent over her, as I had done years before, that wretched night when I ran away. I hugged her close to my throbbing heart; and tears, too sad for such young eyes to shed, flowed down her cheeks, as she gave her last kiss, and whispered in my ear, "Mother, I will never tell." And she never did.

When I got back to my den, I threw myself on the bed and wept there alone in the darkness. It seemed as if my heart would burst. When the time for Ellen's departure drew nigh, I could hear neighbors and friends saying to her, "Good by, Ellen. I hope your poor mother will find you out. Won't you be glad to see her!" She replied, "Yes, ma'am;" and they little dreamed of the weighty secret that weighed down her young heart. She was an affectionate child, but naturally very reserved, except with those she loved, and I felt secure that my secret would be safe with her. I heard the gate close after her, with such feelings as only a slave mother can experience. During the day my meditations were very sad. Sometimes I feared I had been very selfish not to give up all claim to her, and let her go to Illinois, to be adopted by Mrs. Sands's sister. It was my experience of slavery that decided me against it. I feared that circumstances might arise that would cause her to be sent back. I felt confident that I should go to New York myself; and then I should be able to watch over her, and in some degree protect her.

Dr. Flint's family knew nothing of the proposed arrangement till after Ellen was gone, and the news displeased them greatly. Mrs. Flint called on Mrs. Sands's sister to inquire into the matter. She expressed her opinion very freely as to the respect Mr. Sands showed for his wife, and for his own character, in acknowledging those "young niggers." And as for sending Ellen away, she pronounced it to be just as much stealing as it would be for him to come and take a piece of furniture out of her parlor. She said her daughter was not of age to sign the bill of sale, and the children were her property; and when she became of age, or was married, she could take them, wherever she could lay hands on them.

Miss Emily Flint, the little girl to whom I had been bequeathed, was now in her sixteenth year. Her mother considered it all right and honorable for her, or her future husband, to steal my children; but she did not understand how any body could hold up their heads in respectable society, after they had purchased their own children, as Mr. Sands had done. Dr. Flint said very little. Perhaps he thought that Benny would be less likely to be sent away if he kept quiet. One of my letters, that fell into his hands, was dated from Canada; and he seldom spoke of me now. This state of things enabled me to slip down into the storeroom more frequently, where I could stand upright, and move my limbs more freely.

Days, weeks, and months passed, and there came no news of Ellen. I sent a letter to Brooklyn, written in my grandmother's name, to inquire whether she had arrived there. Answer was returned that she had not. I wrote to her in Washington; but no notice was taken of it. There was one person there, who ought to have had some sympathy with the anxiety of the child's friends at home; but the links of such relations as he had formed with me, are easily broken and cast away as rubbish. Yet how protectingly and persuasively he once talked to the poor, helpless slave girl! And how entirely I trusted him! But now suspicions darkened my mind. Was my child dead, or had they deceived me, and sold her?

If the secret memoirs of many members of Congress should be published, curious details would be unfolded. I once saw a letter from a member of Congress to a slave, who was the mother of six of his children. He wrote to request that she would send her children away from the great house before his return, as he expected to be accompanied by friends. The woman could not read, and was obliged to employ another to read the letter. The existence of the colored children did not trouble this gentleman, it was only the fear that friends might recognize in their features a resemblance to him.

At the end of six months, a letter came to my grandmother, from Brooklyn. It was written by a young lady in the family, and announced that Ellen had just arrived. It contained the following message from her: "I do try to do just as you told me to, and I pray for you every night and morning." I understood that these words were meant for me; and they were a balsam to my heart. The writer closed her letter by saying, "Ellen is a nice little girl, and we shall like to have her with us. My cousin, Mr. Sands, has given her to me, to be my little waiting maid. I shall send her to school, and I hope some day she will write to you herself." This letter perplexed and troubled me. Had my child's father merely placed her there till she was old enough to support herself? Or had he given her to his cousin, as a piece of property? If the last idea was correct, his cousin might return to the south at any time, and hold Ellen as a slave. I tried to put away from me the painful thought that such a foul wrong could have been done to us. I said to myself, "Surely there must be some justice in man;" then I remembered, with a sigh, how slavery perverted all the natural feelings of the human heart. It gave me a pang to look on my light-hearted boy. He believed himself free; and to have him brought under the yoke of slavery, would be more than I could bear. How I longed to have him safely out of the reach of its power!

# XXVIII. AUNT NANCY.

I have mentioned my great-aunt, who was a slave in Dr. Flint's family, and who had been my refuge during the shameful persecutions I suffered from him. This aunt had been married at twenty years of age; that is, as far as slaves can marry. She had the consent of her master and mistress, and a clergyman performed the ceremony. But it was a mere form, without any legal value. Her master or mistress could annul it any day they pleased. She had always slept on the floor in the entry, near Mrs. Flint's chamber door, that she might be within call. When she was married, she was told she might have the use of a small room in an outhouse. Her mother and her husband furnished it. He was a seafaring man, and was allowed to sleep there when he was at home. But on the wedding evening, the bride was ordered to her old post on the entry floor.

Mrs. Flint, at that time, had no children; but she was expecting to be a mother, and if she should want a drink of water in the night, what could she do without her slave to bring it? So my aunt was compelled to lie at her door, until one midnight she was forced to leave, to give premature birth to a child. In a fortnight she was required to resume her place on the entry floor, because Mrs. Flint's babe needed her attentions. She kept her station there through summer and winter, until she had given premature birth to six children; and all the while she was employed as night-nurse to Mrs. Flint's children. Finally, toiling all day, and being deprived of rest at night, completely broke down her constitution, and Dr. Flint declared it was impossible she could ever become the mother of a living child. The fear of losing so valuable a servant by death, now induced them to allow her to sleep in her little room in the out-house, except when there was sickness in the family. She afterwards had two feeble babes, one of whom died in a few days, and the other in four weeks. I well remember her patient sorrow as she held the last dead baby in her arms. "I wish it could have lived," she said; "it is not the will of God that any of my children should live. But I will try to be fit to meet their little spirits in heaven."

Aunt Nancy was housekeeper and waiting-maid in Dr. Flint's family. Indeed, she was the factotum of the household. Nothing went on well without her. She was my mother's twin sister, and, as far as was in her power, she supplied a mother's place to us orphans. I slept with her all the time I lived in my old master's house, and the bond between us was very strong. When my friends tried to discourage me from running away; she always encouraged me. When they thought I had better return and ask my master's pardon, because there was no possibility of escape, she sent me word never to yield. She said if I persevered I might, perhaps, gain the freedom of my children; and even if I perished in doing it, that was better than to leave them to groan under the same persecutions that had blighted my own life. After I was shut up in my dark cell, she stole away, whenever she could, to bring me the news and say something cheering. How often did I kneel down to listen to her words of consolation, whispered through a crack! "I am old, and have not long to live," she used to say; "and I could die happy if I could only see you and the children free. You must pray to God, Linda, as I do for you, that he will lead you out of this darkness." I would beg her not to worry herself on my account; that there was an end of all suffering sooner or later, and that whether I lived in chains or in freedom, I should always remember her as the good friend who had been the comfort of my life. A word from her always strengthened me; and not me only. The whole family relied upon her judgement, and were guided by her advice. I had been in my cell six years when my grandmother was summoned to the bedside of this, her last remaining daughter. She was very ill, and they said she would die. Grandmother had not entered Dr. Flint's house for several years. They had treated her cruelly, but she thought nothing of that now. She was grateful for permission to watch by the death-bed of her child. They had always been devoted to each other; and now they sat looking into each other's eyes, longing to speak of the secret that had weighed so much on the hearts of both. My aunt had been stricken with paralysis. She lived but two days, and the last day she was speechless. Before she lost the power of utterance, she told her mother not to grieve if she could not speak to her; that she would try to hold up her hand; to let her know that all was well with her. Even the hard-hearted doctor was a little softened when he saw the dying woman try to smile on the aged mother, who was kneeling by her side. His eyes moistened for a moment, as he said she had always been a faithful servant, and they should never be able to supply her place. Mrs. Flint took to her bed, quite overcome by the shock. While my grandmother sat alone with the dead, the doctor came in, leading his youngest son, who had always been a great pet with aunt Nancy, and was much attached to her. "Martha," said he, "aunt Nancy loved this child, and when he comes where you are, I hope you will be kind to him, for her sake." She replied, "Your wife was my foster-child, Dr. Flint, the foster-sister of my poor Nancy, and you little know me if you think I can feel any thing but good will for her children."

"I wish the past could be forgotten, and that we might never think of it," said he; "and that Linda would come to supply her aunt's place. She would be worth more to us than all the money that could be paid for her. I wish it for your sake also, Martha. Now that Nancy is taken away from you, she would be a great comfort to your old age." He knew he was touching a tender chord. Almost choking with grief, my grandmother replied, "It was not I that drove

Linda away. My grandchildren are gone; and of my nine children only one is left. God help me!"

To me, the death of this kind relative was an inexpressible sorrow. I knew that she had been slowly murdered; and I felt that my troubles had helped to finish the work. After I heard of her illness, I listened constantly to hear what news was brought from the great house; and the thought that I could not go to her made me utterly miserable. At last, as uncle Phillip came into the house, I heard some one inquire, "How is she?" and he answered, "She is dead." My little cell seemed whirling round, and I knew nothing more till I opened my eyes and found uncle Phillip bending over me. I had no need to ask any questions. He whispered, "Linda, she died happy." I could not weep. My fixed gaze troubled him. "Don't look so" he said. "Don't add to my poor mother's trouble. Remember how much she has to bear, and that we ought to do all we can to comfort her." Ah, yes, that blessed old grandmother, who for seventy-three years had borne the pelting storms of a slave-mother's life. She did indeed need consolation!

Mrs. Flint had rendered her poor foster-sister childless, apparently without any compunction; and with cruel selfishness had ruined her health by years of incessant, unrequited toil, and broken rest. But now she became very sentimental. I suppose she thought it would be a beautiful illustration of the attachment existing between slaveholder and slave, if the body of her old worn-out servant was buried at her feet. She sent for the clergyman and asked if he had any objection to burying aunt Nancy in the doctor's family burial-place. No colored person had ever been allowed interment in the white people's burying-ground, and the minister knew that all the deceased of your family reposed together in the old graveyard of the slaves. He therefore replied, "I have no objection to complying with your wish; but perhaps aunt Nancy's mother may have some choice as to where her remains shall be deposited."

It had never occurred to Mrs. Flint that slaves could have any feelings. When my grandmother was consulted, she at once said she wanted Nancy to lie with all the rest of her family, and where her own old body would be buried. Mrs. Flint graciously complied with her wish, though she said it was painful to her to have Nancy buried away from her. She might have added with touching pathos, "I was so long used to sleep with her lying near me, on the entry floor."

My uncle Phillip asked permission to bury his sister at his own expense; and slaveholders are always ready to grant such favors to slaves and their relatives. The arrangements were very plain, but perfectly respectable. She was buried on the Sabbath, and Mrs. Flint's minister read the funeral service. There was a large concourse of colored people, bond and free, and a few white persons who had always been friendly to our family. Dr. Flint's carriage was in the procession; and when the body was deposited in its humble resting place, the mistress dropped a tear, and returned to her carriage, probably thinking she had performed her duty nobly.

It was talked of by the slaves as a mighty grand funeral. Northern travellers, passing through the place, might have described this tribute of respect to the humble dead as a beautiful feature in the "patriarchal institution;" a touching proof of the attachment between slaveholders and their servants; and tender-hearted Mrs. Flint would have confirmed this impression, with handkerchief at her eyes. We could have told them a different story. We could have given them a chapter of wrongs and sufferings, that would have touched their hearts, if they had any hearts to feel for the colored people. We could have told them how the poor old slave-mother had toiled, year after year, to earn eight hundred dollars to buy her son Phillip's right to his own earnings; and how that same Phillip paid the expenses of the funeral, which they regarded as doing so much credit to the master. We could also have told them of a poor, blighted young creature, shut up in a living grave for years, to avoid the tortures that would be inflicted on her, if she ventured to come out and look on the face of her departed friend.

All this, and much more, I thought of, as I sat at my loophole, waiting for the family to return from the grave; sometimes weeping, sometimes falling asleep, dreaming strange dreams of the dead and the living.

It was sad to witness the grief of my bereaved grandmother. She had always been strong to bear, and now, as ever, religious faith supported her. But her dark life had become still darker, and age and trouble were leaving deep traces on her withered face. She had four places to knock for me to come to the trapdoor, and each place had a different meaning. She now came oftener than she had done, and talked to me of her dead daughter, while tears trickled slowly down her furrowed cheeks. I said all I could to comfort her; but it was a sad reflection, that instead of being able to help her, I was a constant source of anxiety and trouble. The poor old back was fitted to its burden. It bent under it, but did not break.

# XXIX. PREPARATIONS FOR ESCAPE.

I hardly expect that the reader will credit me, when I affirm that I lived in that little dismal hole, almost deprived of light and air, and with no space to move my limbs, for nearly seven years. But it is a fact; and to me a sad one, even now; for my body still suffers from the effects of that long imprisonment, to say nothing of my soul. Members of my family, now living in New York and Boston, can testify to the truth of what I say.

Countless were the nights that I sat late at the little loophole scarcely large enough to give me a glimpse of one twinkling star. There, heard the patrols and slave-hunters conferring together about the capture of runaways, well knowing how rejoiced they would be to catch me.

Season after season, year after year, I peeped at my children's faces, and heard their sweet voices, with a heart yearning all the while to say, "Your mother is here." Sometimes it appeared to me as if ages had rolled away since I entered upon that gloomy, monotonous existence. At times, I was stupefied and listless; at other times I became very impatient to know when these dark years would end, and I should again be allowed to feel the sunshine, and breathe the pure air.

After Ellen left us, this feeling increased. Mr. Sands had agreed that Benny might go to the north whenever his uncle Phillip could go with him; and I was anxious to be there also, to watch over my children, and protect them so far as I was able. Moreover, I was likely to be drowned out of my den, if I remained much longer; for the slight roof was getting badly out of repair, and uncle Phillip was afraid to remove the shingles, lest some one should get a glimpse of me. When storms occurred in the night, they spread mats and bits of carpet, which in the morning appeared to have been laid out to dry; but to cover the roof in the daytime might have attracted attention. Consequently, my clothes and bedding were often drenched; a process by which the pains and aches in my cramped and stiffened limbs were greatly increased. I revolved various plans of escape in my mind, which I sometimes imparted to my grandmother, when she came to whisper with me at the trap-door. The kind-hearted old woman had an intense sympathy for runaways. She had known too much of the cruelties inflicted on those who were captured. Her memory always flew back at once to the sufferings of her bright and handsome son, Benjamin, the youngest and dearest of her flock. So, whenever I alluded to the subject, she would groan out, "O, don't think of it, child. You'll break my heart." I had no good old aunt Nancy now to encourage me; but my brother William and my children were continually beckoning me to the north.

And now I must go back a few months in my story. I have stated that the first of January was the time for selling slaves, or leasing them out to new masters. If time were counted by heart-throbs, the poor slaves might reckon years of suffering during that festival so joyous to the free. On the New Year's day preceding my aunt's death, one of my friends, named Fanny, was to be sold at auction, to pay her master's debts. My thoughts were with her during all the day, and at night I anxiously inquired what had been her fate. I was told that she had been sold to one master, and her four little girls to another master, far distant; that she had escaped from her purchaser, and was not to be found. Her mother was the old Aggie I have spoken of. She lived in a small tenement belonging to my grandmother, and built on the same lot with her own house. Her dwelling was searched and watched, and that brought the patrols so near me that I was obliged to keep very close in my den. The hunters were somehow eluded; and not long afterwards Benny accidentally caught sight of Fanny in her mother's hut. He told his grandmother, who charged him never to speak of it, explaining to him the frightful consequences; and he never betrayed the trust. Aggie little dreamed that my grandmother knew where her daughter was concealed, and that the stooping form of her old neighbor was bending under a similar burden of anxiety and fear; but these dangerous secrets deepened the sympathy between the two old persecuted mothers.

My friend Fanny and I remained many weeks hidden within call of each other; but she was unconscious of the fact. I longed to have her share my den, which seemed a more secure retreat than her own; but I had brought so much trouble on my grandmother, that it seemed wrong to ask her to incur greater risks. My restlessness increased. I had lived too long in bodily pain and anguish of spirit. Always I was in dread that by some accident, or some contrivance, slavery would succeed in snatching my children from me. This thought drove me nearly frantic, and I determined to steer for the North Star at all hazards. At this crisis, Providence opened an unexpected way for me to escape. My friend Peter came one evening, and asked to speak with me. "Your day has come, Linda," said he. "I have found a chance for you to go to the Free States. You have a fortnight to decide." The news seemed too good to be true; but Peter explained his arrangements, and told me all that was necessary was for me to say I would go. I was going to answer him with a joyful yes, when the thought of Benny came to my mind. I told him the temptation was exceedingly strong, but I was terribly afraid of Dr. Flint's alleged power over my child, and that I could not go and leave him behind. Peter remonstrated earnestly. He said such a good chance might never occur again; that Benny was free, and could be sent to me; and that for the sake of my children's welfare I ought not to hesitate a moment. I told him I would consult with uncle Phillip. My uncle rejoiced in the plan, and bade me go by all means. He promised, if his life was spared, that he would either bring or send my son to me as soon as I reached a place of safety. I resolved to go, but thought nothing had better be said to my grandmother till very near the time of departure. But my uncle thought she would feel it more keenly if I left here so suddenly. "I will reason with her," said he, "and convince her how necessary it is, not only for your sake, but for hers also. You cannot be blind to the fact that she is sinking under her burdens." I was not blind to it. I knew that my concealment was an ever-present source of anxiety, and that the older she grew the more nervously fearful she was of discovery. My uncle talked with her, and finally succeeded in persuading her that it was absolutely necessary for me to seize the chance so unexpectedly offered.

    The anticipation of being a free woman proved almost too much for my weak frame. The excitement stimulated me, and at the same time bewildered me. I made busy preparations for my journey, and for my son to follow me. I resolved to have an interview with him before I went, that I might give him cautions and advice, and tell him how anxiously I should be waiting for him at the north. Grandmother stole up to me as often as possible to whisper words of counsel. She insisted upon writing to Dr. Flint, as soon as I arrived in the Free States, and asking him to sell me to her. She said she would sacrifice her house, and all she had in the world, for the sake of having me safe with my children in any part of the world. If she could only live to know that she could die in peace. I promised the dear old faithful friend that I would write to her as soon as I arrived, and put the letter in a safe way to reach her; but in my own mind I resolved that not another cent of her hard earnings should be spent to pay rapacious slaveholders for what they called their property. And even if I had not been unwilling to buy what I had already a right to possess, common humanity would have prevented me from accepting the generous offer, at the expense of turning my aged relative out of house and home, when she was trembling on the brink of the grave.

    I was to escape in a vessel; but I forbear to mention any further particulars. I was in readiness, but the vessel was unexpectedly detained several days. Meantime, news came to town of a most horrible murder committed on a fugitive slave, named James. Charity, the mother of this unfortunate young man, had been an old acquaintance of ours. I have told the shocking particulars of his death, in my description of some of the neighboring slaveholders. My grandmother, always nervously sensitive about runaways, was terribly frightened. She felt sure that a similar fate awaited me, if I did not desist from my enterprise. She sobbed, and groaned, and entreated me not to go. Her excessive fear was somewhat contagious, and my heart was not proof against her extreme agony. I was grievously disappointed, but I promised to relinquish my project.

When my friend Peter was apprised of this, he was both disappointed and vexed. He said, that judging from our past experience, it would be a long time before I had such another chance to throw away. I told him it need not be thrown away; that I had a friend concealed near by, who would be glad enough to take the place that had been provided for me. I told him about poor Fanny, and the kind-hearted, noble fellow, who never turned his back upon any body in distress, white or black, expressed his readiness to help her. Aggie was much surprised when she found that we knew her secret. She was rejoiced to hear of such a chance for Fanny, and arrangements were made for her to go on board the vessel the next night. They both supposed that I had long been at the north, therefore my name was not mentioned in the transaction. Fanny was carried on board at the appointed time, and stowed away in a very small cabin. This accommodation had been purchased at a price that would pay for a voyage to England. But when one proposes to go to fine old England, they stop to calculate whether they can afford the cost of the pleasure; while in making a bargain to escape from slavery, the trembling victim is ready to say, "take all I have, only don't betray me!"

The next morning I peeped through my loophole, and saw that it was dark and cloudy. At night I received news that the wind was ahead, and the vessel had not sailed. I was exceedingly anxious about Fanny, and Peter too, who was running a tremendous risk at my instigation. Next day the wind and weather remained the same. Poor Fanny had been half dead with fright when they carried her on board, and I could readily imagine how she must be suffering now. Grandmother came often to my den, to say how thankful she was I did not go. On the third morning she rapped for me to come down to the storeroom. The poor old sufferer was breaking down under her weight of trouble. She was easily flurried now. I found her in a nervous, excited state, but I was not aware that she had forgotten to lock the door behind her, as usual. She was exceedingly worried about the detention of the vessel. She was afraid all would be discovered, and then Fanny, and Peter, and I, would all be tortured to death, and Phillip would be utterly ruined, and her house would be torn down. Poor Peter! If he should die such a horrible death as the poor slave James had lately done, and all for his kindness in trying to help me, how dreadful it would be for us all! Alas, the thought was familiar to me, and had sent many a sharp pang through my heart. I tried to suppress my own anxiety, and speak soothingly to her. She brought in some allusion to aunt Nancy, the dear daughter she had recently buried, and then she lost all control of herself. As she stood there, trembling and sobbing, a voice from the piazza called out,

"Whar is you, aunt Marthy?" Grandmother was startled, and in her agitation opened the door, without thinking of me. In stepped Jenny, the mischievous housemaid, who had tried to enter my room, when I was concealed in the house of my white benefactress. "I's bin huntin ebery whar for you, aunt Marthy," said she. "My missis wants you to send her some crackers." I had slunk down behind a barrel, which entirely screened me, but I imagined that Jenny was looking directly at the spot, and my heart beat violently. My grandmother immediately thought what she had done, and went out quickly with Jenny to count the crackers locking the door after her. She returned to me, in a few minutes, the perfect picture of despair. "Poor child!" she exclaimed, "my carelessness has ruined you. The boat ain't gone yet. Get ready immediately, and go with Fanny. I ain't got another word to say against it now; for there's no telling what may happen this day."

Uncle Phillip was sent for, and he agreed with his mother in thinking that Jenny would inform Dr. Flint in less than twenty-four hours. He advised getting me on board the boat, if possible; if not, I had better keep very still in my den, where they could not find me without tearing the house down. He said it would not do for him to move in the matter, because suspicion would be immediately excited; but he promised to communicate with Peter. I felt reluctant to apply to him again, having implicated him too much already; but there seemed to be no alternative. Vexed as Peter had been by my indecision, he was true to his generous nature, and said at once that he would do his best to help me, trusting I should show myself a stronger woman this time.

He immediately proceeded to the wharf, and found that the wind had shifted, and the vessel was slowly beating down stream. On some pretext of urgent necessity, he offered two boatmen a dollar apiece to catch up with her. He was of lighter complexion than the boatmen he hired, and when the captain saw them coming so rapidly, he thought officers were pursuing his vessel in search of the runaway slave he had on board. They hoisted sails, but the boat gained upon them, and the indefatigable Peter sprang on board.

The captain at once recognized him. Peter asked him to go below, to speak about a bad bill he had given him. When he told his errand, the captain replied, "Why, the woman's here already; and I've put her where you or the devil would have a tough job to find her."

"But it is another woman I want to bring," said Peter. "She is in great distress, too, and you shall be paid any thing within reason, if you'll stop and take her."

"What's her name?" inquired the captain. "Linda," he replied.

"That's the name of the woman already here," rejoined the captain. "By George! I believe you mean to betray me."

"O!" exclaimed Peter, "God knows I wouldn't harm a hair of your head. I am too grateful to you. But there really is another woman in great danger. Do have the humanity to stop and take her!"

After a while they came to an understanding. Fanny, not dreaming I was any where about in that region, had assumed my name, though she called herself Johnson. "Linda is a common name," said Peter, "and the woman I want to bring is Linda Brent."

The captain agreed to wait at a certain place till evening, being handsomely paid for his detention.

Of course, the day was an anxious one for us all. But we concluded that if Jenny had seen me, she would be too wise to let her mistress know of it; and that she probably would not get a chance to see Dr. Flint's family till evening, for I knew very well what were the rules in that household. I afterwards believed that she did not see me; for nothing ever came of it, and she was one of those base characters that would have jumped to betray a suffering fellow being for the sake of thirty pieces of silver.

I made all my arrangements to go on board as soon as it was dusk. The intervening time I resolved to spend with my son. I had not spoken to him for seven years, though I had been under the same roof, and seen him every day, when I was well enough to sit at the loophole. I did not dare to venture beyond the storeroom; so they brought him there, and locked us up together, in a place concealed from the piazza door. It was an agitating interview for both of us. After we had talked and wept together for a little while, he said, "Mother, I'm glad you're going away. I wish I could go with you. I knew you was here; and I have been so afraid they would come and catch you!" I was greatly surprised, and asked him how he had found it out.

He replied, "I was standing under the eaves, one day, before Ellen went away, and I heard somebody cough up over the wood shed. I don't know what made me think it was you, but I did think so. I missed Ellen, the night before she went away; and grandmother brought her back into the room in the night; and I thought maybe she'd been to see you, before she went, for I heard grandmother whisper to her, 'Now go to sleep; and remember never to tell.'"

I asked him if he ever mentioned his suspicions to his sister. He said he never did; but after he heard the cough, if he saw her playing with other children on that side of the house, he always tried to coax her round to the other side, for fear they would hear me cough, too. He said he had kept a close lookout for Dr. Flint, and if he saw him speak to a constable, or a patrol, he always told grandmother. I now recollected that I had seen him manifest uneasiness, when people were on that side of the house, and I had at the time been puzzled to conjecture a motive for his actions. Such prudence may seem extraordinary in a boy of twelve years, but slaves, being surrounded by mysteries, deceptions, and dangers, early learn to be suspicious and watchful, and prematurely cautious and cunning. He had never asked a question of grandmother, or uncle Phillip, and I had often heard him chime in with other children, when they spoke of my being at the north.

I told him I was now really going to the Free States, and if he was a good, honest boy, and a loving child to his dear old grandmother, the Lord would bless him, and bring him to me, and we and Ellen would live together. He began to tell me that grandmother had not eaten any thing all day. While he was speaking, the door was unlocked, and she came in with a small bag of money, which she wanted me to take. I begged her to keep a part of it, at least, to pay for Benny's being sent to the north; but she insisted, while her tears were falling fast, that I should take the whole. "You may be sick among strangers," she said, "and they would send you to the poorhouse to die." Ah, that good grandmother!

For the last time I went up to my nook. Its desolate appearance no longer chilled me, for the light of hope had risen in my soul. Yet, even with the blessed prospect of freedom before me, I felt very sad at leaving forever that old homestead, where I had been sheltered so long by the dear old grandmother; where I had dreamed my first young dream of love; and where, after that had faded away, my children came to twine themselves so closely round my desolate heart. As the hour approached for me to leave, I again descended to the storeroom. My grandmother and Benny were there. She took me by the hand, and said, "Linda, let us pray." We knelt down together, with my child pressed to my heart, and my other arm round the faithful, loving old friend I was about to leave forever. On no other occasion has it ever been my lot to listen to so fervent a supplication for mercy and protection. It thrilled through my heart, and inspired me with trust in God.

Peter was waiting for me in the street. I was soon by his side, faint in body, but strong of purpose. I did not look back upon the old place, though I felt that I should never see it again.

# XXX. NORTHWARD BOUND.

I never could tell how we reached the wharf. My brain was all of a whirl, and my limbs tottered under me. At an appointed place we met my uncle Phillip, who had started before us on a different route, that he might reach the wharf first, and give us timely warning if there was any danger. A row-boat was in readiness. As I was about to step in, I felt something pull me gently, and turning round I saw Benny, looking pale and anxious. He whispered in my ear, "I've been peeping into the doctor's window, and he's at home. Good by, mother. Don't cry; I'll come." He hastened away. I clasped the hand of my good uncle, to whom I owed so much, and of Peter, the brave, generous friend who had volunteered to run such terrible risks to secure my safety. To this day I remember how his bright face beamed with joy, when he told me he had discovered a safe method for me to escape. Yet that intelligent, enterprising, noble-hearted man was a chattel! Liable, by the laws of a country that calls itself civilized, to be sold with horses and pigs! We parted in silence. Our hearts were all too full for words!

Swiftly the boat glided over the water. After a while, one of the sailors said, "Don't be down-hearted, madam. We will take you safely to your husband, in ——." At first I could not imagine what he meant; but I had presence of mind to think that it probably referred to something the captain had told him; so I thanked him, and said I hoped we should have pleasant weather.

When I entered the vessel the captain came forward to meet me. He was an elderly man, with a pleasant countenance. He showed me to a little box of a cabin, where sat my friend Fanny. She started as if she had seen a spectre. She gazed on me in utter astonishment, and exclaimed, "Linda, can this be you? or is it your ghost?" When we were locked in each other's arms, my overwrought feelings could no longer be restrained. My sobs reached the ears of the captain, who came and very kindly reminded us, that for his safety, as well as our own, it would be prudent for us not to attract any attention. He said that when there was a sail in sight he wished us to keep below; but at other times, he had no objection to our being on deck. He assured us that he would keep a good lookout, and if we acted prudently, he thought we should be in no danger. He had represented us as women going to meet our husbands in ——. We thanked him, and promised to observe carefully all the directions he gave us.

Fanny and I now talked by ourselves, low and quietly, in our little cabin. She told me of the suffering she had gone through in making her escape, and of her terrors while she was concealed in her mother's house. Above all, she dwelt on the agony of separation from all her children on that dreadful auction day. She could scarcely credit me, when I told her of the place where I had passed nearly seven years. "We have the same sorrows," said I. "No," replied she, "you are going to see your children soon, and there is no hope that I shall ever even hear from mine."

The vessel was soon under way, but we made slow progress. The wind was against us, I should not have cared for this, if we had been out of sight of the town; but until there were miles of water between us and our enemies, we were filled with constant apprehensions that the constables would come on board. Neither could I feel quite at ease with the captain and his men. I was an entire stranger to that class of people, and I had heard that sailors were rough, and sometimes cruel. We were so completely in their power, that if they were bad men, our situation would be dreadful. Now that the captain was paid for our passage, might he not be tempted to make more money by giving us up to those who claimed us as property? I was naturally of a confiding disposition, but slavery had made me suspicious of every body. Fanny did not share my distrust of the captain or his men. She said she was afraid at first, but she had been on board three days while the vessel lay in the dock, and nobody had betrayed her, or treated her otherwise than kindly.

The captain soon came to advise us to go on deck for fresh air. His friendly and respectful manner, combined with Fanny's testimony, reassured me, and we went with him. He placed us in a comfortable seat, and occasionally entered into conversation. He told us he was a Southerner by birth, and had spent the greater part of his life in the Slave States, and that he had recently lost a brother who traded in slaves. "But," said he, "it is a pitiable and degrading business, and I always felt ashamed to acknowledge my brother in connection with it." As we passed Snaky Swamp, he pointed to it, and said, "There is a slave territory that defies all the laws." I thought of the terrible days I had spent there, and though it was not called Dismal Swamp, it made me feel very dismal as I looked at it.

I shall never forget that night. The balmy air of spring was so refreshing! And how shall I describe my sensations when we were fairly sailing on Chesapeake Bay? O, the beautiful sunshine! the exhilarating breeze! And I could enjoy them without fear or restraint. I had never realized what grand things air and sunlight are till I had been deprived of them.

Ten days after we left land we were approaching Philadelphia. The captain said we should arrive there in the night, but he thought we had better wait till morning, and go on shore in broad daylight, as the best way to avoid suspicion.

I replied, "You know best. But will you stay on board and protect us?"

He saw that I was suspicious, and he said he was sorry, now that he had brought us to the end of our voyage, to find I had so little confidence in him. Ah, if he had ever been a slave he would have known how difficult it was to trust a white man. He assured us that we might sleep through the night without fear; that he would take care we were not left unprotected. Be it said to the honor of this captain, Southerner as he was, that if Fanny and I had been white ladies, and our passage lawfully engaged, he could not have treated us more respectfully. My intelligent friend, Peter, had rightly estimated the character of the man to whose honor he had intrusted us. The next morning I was on deck as soon as the day dawned. I called Fanny to see the sun rise, for the first time in our lives, on free soil; for such I then believed it to be. We watched the reddening sky, and saw the great orb come up slowly out of the water, as it seemed. Soon the waves began to sparkle, and every thing caught the beautiful glow. Before us lay the city of strangers. We looked at each other, and the eyes of both were moistened with tears. We had escaped from slavery, and we supposed ourselves to be safe from the hunters. But we were alone in the world, and we had left dear ties behind us; ties cruelly sundered by the demon Slavery.

# XXXI. INCIDENTS IN PHILADELPHIA.

I had heard that the poor slave had many friends at the north. I trusted we should find some of them. Meantime, we would take it for granted that all were friends, till they proved to the contrary. I sought out the kind captain, thanked him for his attentions, and told him I should never cease to be grateful for the service he had rendered us. I gave him a message to the friends I had left at home, and he promised to deliver it. We were placed in a row-boat, and in about fifteen minutes were landed on a wood wharf in Philadelphia. As I stood looking round, the friendly captain touched me on the shoulder, and said, "There is a respectable-looking colored man behind you. I will speak to him about the New York trains, and tell him you wish to go directly on." I thanked him, and asked him to direct me to some shops where I could buy gloves and veils. He did so, and said he would talk with the colored man till I returned. I made what haste I could. Constant exercise on board the vessel, and frequent rubbing with salt water, had nearly restored the use of my limbs. The noise of the great city confused me, but I found the shops, and bought some double veils and gloves for Fanny and myself. The shopman told me they were so many levies. I had never heard the word before, but I did not tell him so. I thought if he knew I was a stranger he might ask me where I came from. I gave him a gold piece, and when he returned the change, I counted it, and found out how much a levy was. I made my way back to the wharf, where the captain introduced me to the colored man, as the Rev. Jeremiah Durham, minister of Bethel church. He took me by the hand, as if I had been an old friend. He told us we were too late for the morning cars to New York, and must wait until the evening, or the next morning. He invited me to go home with him, assuring me that his wife would give me a cordial welcome; and for my friend he would provide a home with one of his neighbors. I thanked him for so much kindness to strangers, and told him if I must be detained, I should like to hunt up some people who formerly went from our part of the country. Mr. Durham insisted that I should dine with him, and then he would assist me in finding my friends. The sailors came to bid us good by. I shook their hardy hands, with tears in my eyes. They had all been kind to us, and they had rendered us a greater service than they could possibly conceive of.

I had never seen so large a city, or been in contact with so many people in the streets. It seemed as if those who passed looked at us with an expression of curiosity. My face was so blistered and peeled, by sitting on deck, in wind and sunshine, that I thought they could not easily decide to what nation I belonged.

Mrs. Durham met me with a kindly welcome, without asking any questions. I was tired, and her friendly manner was a sweet refreshment. God bless her! I was sure that she had comforted other weary hearts, before I received her sympathy. She was surrounded by her husband and children, in a home made sacred by protecting laws. I thought of my own children, and sighed.

After dinner Mr. Durham went with me in quest of the friends I had spoken of. They went from my native town, and I anticipated much pleasure in looking on familiar faces. They were not at home, and we retracted our steps through streets delightfully clean. On the way, Mr. Durham observed that I had spoken to him of a daughter I expected to meet; that he was surprised, for I looked so young he had taken me for a single woman. He was approaching a subject on which I was extremely sensitive. He would ask about my husband next, I thought, and if I answered him truly, what would he think of me? I told him I had two children, one in New York the other at the south. He asked some further questions, and I frankly told him some of the most important events of my life. It was painful for me to do it; but I would not deceive him. If he was desirous of being my friend, I thought he ought to know how far I was worthy of it. "Excuse me, if I have tried your feelings," said he. "I did not question you from idle curiosity. I wanted to understand your situation, in order to know whether I could be of any service to you, or your little girl. Your straightforward answers do you credit; but don't answer every body so openly. It might give some heartless people a pretext for treating you with contempt."

That word contempt burned me like coals of fire. I replied, "God alone knows how I have suffered; and He, I trust, will forgive me. If I am permitted to have my children, I intend to be a good mother, and to live in such a manner that people cannot treat me with contempt."

"I respect your sentiments," said he. "Place your trust in God, and be governed by good principles, and you will not fail to find friends."

When we reached home, I went to my room, glad to shut out the world for a while. The words he had spoken made an indelible impression upon me. They brought up great shadows from the mournful past. In the midst of my meditations I was startled by a knock at the door. Mrs. Durham entered, her face all beaming with kindness, to say that there was an anti-slavery friend down stairs, who would like to see me. I overcame my dread of encountering strangers, and went with her. Many questions were asked concerning my experiences, and my escape from slavery; but I observed how careful they all were not to say any thing that might wound my feelings. How gratifying this was, can be fully understood only by those who have been accustomed to be treated as if they were not included within the pale of human beings. The anti-slavery friend had come to inquire into my plans, and to offer assistance, if needed. Fanny was comfortably established, for the present, with a friend of Mr. Durham. The Anti-Slavery Society agreed to pay her expenses to New

York. The same was offered to me, but I declined to accept it, telling them that my grandmother had given me sufficient to pay my expenses to the end of my journey. We were urged to remain in Philadelphia a few days, until some suitable escort could be found for us. I gladly accepted the proposition, for I had a dread of meeting slaveholders, and some dread also of railroads. I had never entered a railroad car in my life, and it seemed to me quite an important event.

That night I sought my pillow with feelings I had never carried to it before. I verily believed myself to be a free woman. I was wakeful for a long time, and I had no sooner fallen asleep, than I was roused by fire-bells. I jumped up, and hurried on my clothes. Where I came from, every body hastened to dress themselves on such occasions. The white people thought a great fire might be used as a good opportunity for insurrection, and that it was best to be in readiness; and the colored people were ordered out to labor in extinguishing the flames. There was but one engine in our town, and colored women and children were often required to drag it to the river's edge and fill it. Mrs. Durham's daughter slept in the same room with me, and seeing that she slept through all the din, I thought it was my duty to wake her. "What's the matter?" said she, rubbing her eyes.

"They're screaming fire in the streets, and the bells are ringing," I replied.

"What of that?" said she, drowsily. "We are used to it. We never get up, without the fire is very near. What good would it do?"

I was quite surprised that it was not necessary for us to go and help fill the engine. I was an ignorant child, just beginning to learn how things went on in great cities.

At daylight, I heard women crying fresh fish, berries, radishes, and various other things. All this was new to me. I dressed myself at an early hour, and sat at the window to watch that unknown tide of life. Philadelphia seemed to me a wonderfully great place. At the breakfast table, my idea of going out to drag the engine was laughed over, and I joined in the mirth.

I went to see Fanny, and found her so well contented among her new friends that she was in no haste to leave. I was also very happy with my kind hostess. She had had advantages for education, and was vastly my superior. Every day, almost every hour, I was adding to my little stock of knowledge. She took me out to see the city as much as she deemed prudent. One day she took me to an artist's room, and showed me the portraits of some of her children. I had never seen any paintings of colored people before, and they seemed to be beautiful.

At the end of five days, one of Mrs. Durham's friends offered to accompany us to New York the following morning. As I held the hand of my good hostess in a parting clasp, I longed to know whether her husband had repeated to her what I had told him. I supposed he had, but she never made any allusion to it. I presume it was the delicate silence of womanly sympathy.

When Mr. Durham handed us our tickets, he said, "I am afraid you will have a disagreeable ride; but I could not procure tickets for the first-class cars."

Supposing I had not given him money enough, I offered more. "O, no," said he, "they could not be had for any money. They don't allow colored people to go in the first-class cars."

This was the first chill to my enthusiasm about the Free States. Colored people were allowed to ride in a filthy box, behind white people, at the south, but there they were not required to pay for the privilege. It made me sad to find how the north aped the customs of slavery.

We were stowed away in a large, rough car, with windows on each side, too high for us to look out without standing up. It was crowded with people, apparently of all nations. There were plenty of beds and cradles, containing screaming and kicking babies. Every other man had a cigar or pipe in his mouth, and jugs of whiskey were handed round freely. The fumes of the whiskey and the dense tobacco smoke were sickening to my senses, and my mind was equally nauseated by the coarse jokes and ribald songs around me. It was a very disagreeable ride. Since that time there has been some improvement in these matters.

# XXXII. THE MEETING OF MOTHER AND DAUGHTER.

When we arrived in New York, I was half crazed by the crowd of coachmen calling out, "Carriage, ma'am?" We bargained with one to take us to Sullivan Street for twelve shillings. A burly Irishman stepped up and said, "I'll tak' ye for sax shillings." The reduction of half the price was an object to us, and we asked if he could take us right away. "Troth an I will, ladies," he replied. I noticed that the hackmen smiled at each other, and I inquired whether his conveyance was decent. "Yes, it's dacent it is, marm. Devil a bit would I be after takin' ladies in a cab that was not dacent." We gave him our checks. He went for the baggage, and soon reappeared, saying, "This way, if you plase, ladies." We followed, and found our trunks on a truck, and we were invited to take our seats on them. We told him that was not what we bargained for, and he must take the trunks off. He swore they should not be touched till we had paid him six shillings. In our situation it was not prudent to attract attention, and I was about to pay him what he required, when a man near by shook his head for me not to do it. After a great ado we got rid of the Irishman, and had our trunks fastened on a hack. We had been recommended to a boarding-house in Sullivan Street, and thither we drove. There Fanny and I separated. The Anti-Slavery Society provided a home for her, and I afterwards heard of her in prosperous circumstances. I sent for an old friend from my part of the country, who had for some time been doing business in New York. He came immediately. I told him I wanted to go to my daughter, and asked him to aid me in procuring an interview.

I cautioned him not to let it be known to the family that I had just arrived from the south, because they supposed I had been at the north seven years. He told me there was a colored woman in Brooklyn who came from the same town I did, and I had better go to her house, and have my daughter meet me there. I accepted the proposition thankfully, and he agreed to escort me to Brooklyn. We crossed Fulton ferry, went up Myrtle Avenue, and stopped at the house he designated. I was just about to enter, when two girls passed. My friend called my attention to them. I turned, and recognized in the eldest, Sarah, the daughter of a woman who used to live with my grandmother, but who had left the south years ago. Surprised and rejoiced at this unexpected meeting, I threw my arms round her, and inquired concerning her mother.

"You take no notice of the other girl," said my friend. I turned, and there stood my Ellen! I pressed her to my heart, then held her away from me to take a look at her. She had changed a good deal in the two years since I parted from her. Signs of neglect could be discerned by eyes less observing than a mother's. My friend invited us all to go into the house; but Ellen said she had been sent of an errand, which she would do as quickly as possible, and go home and ask Mrs. Hobbs to let her come and see me. It was agreed that I should send for her the next day. Her companion, Sarah, hastened to tell her mother of my arrival. When I entered the house, I found the mistress of it absent, and I waited for her return. Before I saw her, I heard her saying, "Where is Linda Brent? I used to know her father and mother." Soon Sarah came with her mother. So there was quite a company of us, all from my grandmother's neighborhood. These friends gathered round me and questioned me eagerly. They laughed, they cried, and they shouted. They thanked God that I had got away from my persecutors and was safe on Long Island. It was a day of great excitement. How different from the silent days I had passed in my dreary den!

The next morning was Sunday. My first waking thoughts were occupied with the note I was to send to Mrs. Hobbs, the lady with whom Ellen lived. That I had recently come into that vicinity was evident; otherwise I should have sooner inquired for my daughter. It would not do to let them know I had just arrived from the south, for that would involve the suspicion of my having been harbored there, and might bring trouble, if not ruin, on several people.

I like a straightforward course, and am always reluctant to resort to subterfuges. So far as my ways have been crooked, I charge them all upon slavery. It was that system of violence and wrong which now left me no alternative but to enact a falsehood. I began my note by stating that I had recently arrived from Canada, and was very desirous to have my daughter come and see me. She came and brought a message from Mrs. Hobbs, inviting me to her house, and assuring me that I need not have any fears. The conversation I had with my child did not leave my mind at ease. When I asked if she was well treated, she answered yes; but there was no heartiness in the tone, and it seemed to me that she said it from an unwillingness to have me troubled on her account. Before she left me, she asked very earnestly, "Mother, will you take me to live with you?" It made me sad to think that I could not give her a home till I went to work and earned the means; and that might take me a long time. When she was placed with Mrs. Hobbs, the agreement was that she should be sent to school She had been there two years, and was now nine years old, and she scarcely knew her letters. There was no excuse for this, for there were good public schools in Brooklyn, to which she could have been sent without expense.

She staid with me till dark, and I went home with her. I was received in a friendly manner by the family, and all agreed in saying that Ellen was a useful, good girl. Mrs. Hobbs looked me coolly in the face, and said, "I suppose you know that my cousin, Mr. Sands, has given her to my eldest daughter. She will make a nice waiting-maid for her when she grows up." I did not answer a word. How could she, who knew by experience the strength of a mother's love, and who was perfectly aware of the relation Mr. Sands bore to my children,—how could she look me in the face, while she thrust such a dagger into my heart?

I was no longer surprised that they had kept her in such a state of ignorance. Mr. Hobbs had formerly been wealthy, but he had failed, and afterwards obtained a subordinate situation in the Custom House. Perhaps they expected to return to the south some day; and Ellen's knowledge was quite sufficient for a slave's condition. I was impatient to go to work and earn money, that I might change the uncertain position of my children. Mr. Sands had not kept his promise to emancipate them. I had also been deceived about Ellen. What security had I with regard to Benjamin? I felt that I had none.

I returned to my friend's house in an uneasy state of mind. In order to protect my children, it was necessary that I should own myself. I called myself free, and sometimes felt so; but I knew I was insecure. I sat down that night and wrote a civil letter to Dr. Flint, asking him to state the lowest terms on which he would sell me; and as I belonged by law to his daughter, I wrote to her also, making a similar request.

Since my arrival at the north I had not been unmindful of my dear brother William. I had made diligent inquiries for him, and having heard of him in Boston, I went thither. When I arrived there, I found he had gone to New Bedford. I wrote to that place, and was informed he had gone on a whaling voyage, and would not return for some months. I went back to New York to get employment near Ellen. I received an answer from Dr. Flint, which gave me no encouragement. He advised me to return and submit myself to my rightful owners, and then any request I might make would be granted. I lent this letter to a friend, who lost it; otherwise I would present a copy to my readers.

# XXXIII. A HOME FOUND.

My greatest anxiety now was to obtain employment. My health was greatly improved, though my limbs continued to trouble me with swelling whenever I walked much. The greatest difficulty in my way was, that those who employed strangers required a recommendation; and in my peculiar position, I could, of course, obtain no certificates from the families I had so faithfully served.

One day an acquaintance told me of a lady who wanted a nurse for her babe, and I immediately applied for the situation. The lady told me she preferred to have one who had been a mother, and accustomed to the care of infants. I told her I had nursed two babes of my own. She asked me many questions, but, to my great relief, did not require a recommendation from my former employers. She told me she was an English woman, and that was a pleasant circumstance to me, because I had heard they had less prejudice against color than Americans entertained. It was agreed that we should try each other for a week. The trial proved satisfactory to both parties, and I was engaged for a month.

The heavenly Father had been most merciful to me in leading me to this place. Mrs. Bruce was a kind and gentle lady, and proved a true and sympathizing friend. Before the stipulated month expired, the necessity of passing up and down stairs frequently, caused my limbs to swell so painfully, that I became unable to perform my duties. Many ladies would have thoughtlessly discharged me; but Mrs. Bruce made arrangements to save me steps, and employed a physician to attend upon me. I had not yet told her that I was a fugitive slave. She noticed that I was often sad, and kindly inquired the cause. I spoke of being separated from my children, and from relatives who were dear to me; but I did not mention the constant feeling of insecurity which oppressed my spirits. I longed for some one to confide it; but I had been so deceived by white people, that I had lost all confidence in them. If they spoke kind words to me, I thought it was for some selfish purpose. I had entered this family with the distrustful feelings I had brought with me out of slavery; but ere six months had passed, I found that the gentle deportment of Mrs. Bruce and the smiles of her lovely babe were thawing my chilled heart. My narrow mind also began to expand under the influences of her intelligent conversation, and the opportunities for reading, which were gladly allowed me whenever I had leisure from my duties. I gradually became more energetic and more cheerful.

The old feeling of insecurity, especially with regard to my children, often threw its dark shadow across my sunshine. Mrs. Bruce offered me a home for Ellen; but pleasant as it would have been, I did not dare to accept it, for fear of offending the Hobbs family. Their knowledge of my precarious situation placed me in their power; and I felt that it was important for me to keep on the right side of them, till, by dint of labor and economy, I could make a home for my children. I was far from feeling satisfied with Ellen's situation. She was not well cared for. She sometimes came to New York to visit me; but she generally brought a request from Mrs. Hobbs that I would buy her a pair of shoes, or some article of clothing. This was accompanied by a promise of payment when Mr. Hobbs's salary at the Custom House became due; but some how or other the pay-day never came. Thus many dollars of my earnings were expended to keep my child comfortably clothed. That, however, was a slight trouble, compared with the fear that their pecuniary embarrassments might induce them to sell my precious young daughter. I knew they were in constant communication with Southerners, and had frequent opportunities to do it. I have stated that when Dr. Flint put Ellen in jail, at two years old, she had an inflammation of the eyes, occasioned by measles. This disease still troubled her; and kind Mrs. Bruce proposed that she should come to New York for a while, to be under the care of Dr. Elliott, a well known oculist. It did not occur to me that there was any thing improper in a mother's making such a request; but Mrs. Hobbs was very angry, and refused to let her go. Situated as I was, it was not politic to insist upon it. I made no complaint, but I longed to be entirely free to act a mother's part towards my children. The next time I went over to Brooklyn, Mrs. Hobbs, as if to apologize for her anger, told me she had employed her own physician to attend to Ellen's eyes, and that she had refused my request because she did not consider it safe to trust her in New York. I accepted the explanation in silence; but she had told me that my child belonged to her daughter, and I suspected that her real motive was a fear of my conveying her property away from her. Perhaps I did her injustice; but my knowledge of Southerners made it difficult for me to feel otherwise.

Sweet and bitter were mixed in the cup of my life, and I was thankful that it had ceased to be entirely bitter. I loved Mrs. Bruce's babe. When it laughed and crowed in my face, and twined its little tender arms confidingly about my neck, it made me think of the time when Benny and Ellen were babies, and my wounded heart was soothed. One bright morning, as I stood at the window, tossing baby in my arms, my attention was attracted by a young man in sailor's dress, who was closely observing every house as he passed. I looked at him earnestly. Could it be my brother William? It must be he—and yet, how changed! I placed the baby safely, flew down stairs, opened the front door, beckoned to the sailor, and in less than a minute I was clasped in my brother's arms. How much we had to tell each other! How we laughed, and how we cried, over each other's adventures! I took him to Brooklyn, and again saw him with Ellen, the dear child whom he had loved and tended so carefully, while I was shut up in my miserable den. He staid in New York a week. His old feelings of affection for me and Ellen were as lively as ever. There are no bonds so strong as those which are formed by suffering together.

# XXXIV. THE OLD ENEMY AGAIN.

My young mistress, Miss Emily Flint, did not return any answer to my letter requesting her to consent to my being sold. But after a while, I received a reply, which purported to be written by her younger brother. In order rightly to enjoy the contents of this letter, the reader must bear in mind that the Flint family supposed I had been at the north many years. They had no idea that I knew of the doctor's three excursions to New York in search of me; that I had heard his voice, when he came to borrow five hundred dollars for that purpose; and that I had seen him pass on his way to the steamboat. Neither were they aware that all the particulars of aunt Nancy's death and burial were conveyed to me at the time they occurred. I have kept the letter, of which I herewith subjoin a copy:—

> Your letter to sister was received a few days ago. I gather from it that you are desirous of returning to your native place, among your friends and relatives. We were all gratified with the contents of your letter; and let me assure you that if any members of the family have had any feeling of resentment towards you, they feel it no longer. We all sympathize with you in your unfortunate condition, and are ready to do all in our power to make you contented and happy. It is difficult for you to return home as a free person. If you were purchased by your grandmother, it is doubtful whether you would be permitted to remain, although it would be lawful for you to do so. If a servant should be allowed to purchase herself, after absenting herself so long from her owners, and return free, it would have an injurious effect. From your letter, I think your situation must be hard and uncomfortable. Come home. You have it in your power to be reinstated in our affections. We would receive you with open arms and tears of joy. You need not apprehend any unkind treatment, as we have not put ourselves to any trouble or expense to get you. Had we done so, perhaps we should feel otherwise. You know my sister was always attached to you, and that you were never treated as a slave. You were never put to hard work, nor exposed to field labor. On the contrary, you were taken into the house, and treated as one of us, and almost as free; and we, at least, felt that you were above disgracing yourself by running away. Believing you may be induced to come home voluntarily has induced me to write for my sister. The family will be rejoiced to see you; and your poor old grandmother expressed a great desire to

have you come, when she heard your letter read. In her old age she needs the consolation of having her children round her. Doubtless you have heard of the death of your aunt. She was a faithful servant, and a faithful member of the Episcopal church. In her Christian life she taught us how to live—and, O, too high the price of knowledge, she taught us how to die! Could you have seen us round her death bed, with her mother, all mingling our tears in one common stream, you would have thought the same heartfelt tie existed between a master and his servant, as between a mother and her child. But this subject is too painful to dwell upon. I must bring my letter to a close. If you are contented to stay away from your old grandmother, your child, and the friends who love you, stay where you are. We shall never trouble ourselves to apprehend you. But should you prefer to come home, we will do all that we can to make you happy. If you do not wish to remain in the family, I know that father, by our persuasion, will be induced to let you be purchased by any person you may choose in our community. You will please answer this as soon as possible, and let us know your decision. Sister sends much love to you. In the mean time believe me your sincere friend and well wisher.

This letter was signed by Emily's brother, who was as yet a mere lad. I knew, by the style, that it was not written by a person of his age, and though the writing was disguised, I had been made too unhappy by it, in former years, not to recognize at once the hand of Dr. Flint. O, the hypocrisy of slaveholders! Did the old fox suppose I was goose enough to go into such a trap? Verily, he relied too much on "the stupidity of the African race." I did not return the family of Flints any thanks for their cordial invitation—a remissness for which I was, no doubt, charged with base ingratitude.

Not long afterwards I received a letter from one of my friends at the south, informing me that Dr. Flint was about to visit the north. The letter had been delayed, and I supposed he might be already on the way. Mrs. Bruce did not know I was a fugitive. I told her that important business called me to Boston, where my brother then was, and asked permission to bring a friend to supply my place as nurse, for a fortnight. I started on my journey immediately; and as soon as I arrived, I wrote to my grandmother that if Benny came, he must be sent to Boston. I knew she was only waiting for a good chance to send him north, and, fortunately, she had the legal power to do so, without asking leave of any body. She was a free woman; and when my children were purchased,

Mr. Sands preferred to have the bill of sale drawn up in her name. It was conjectured that he advanced the money, but it was not known. At the south, a gentleman may have a shoal of colored children without any disgrace; but if he is known to purchase them, with the view of setting them free, the example is thought to be dangerous to their "peculiar institution," and he becomes unpopular.

There was a good opportunity to send Benny in a vessel coming directly to New York. He was put on board with a letter to a friend, who was requested to see him off to Boston. Early one morning, there was a loud rap at my door, and in rushed Benjamin, all out of breath. "O mother!" he exclaimed, "here I am! I run all the way; and I come all alone. How d'you do?"

O reader, can you imagine my joy? No, you cannot, unless you have been a slave mother. Benjamin rattled away as fast as his tongue could go. "Mother, why don't you bring Ellen here? I went over to Brooklyn to see her, and she felt very bad when I bid her good by. She said, 'O Ben, I wish I was going too.' I thought she'd know ever so much; but she don't know so much as I do; for I can read, and she can't. And, mother, I lost all my clothes coming. What can I do to get some more? I 'spose free boys can get along here at the north as well as white boys."

I did not like to tell the sanguine, happy little fellow how much he was mistaken. I took him to a tailor, and procured a change of clothes. The rest of the day was spent in mutual asking and answering of questions, with the wish constantly repeated that the good old grandmother was with us, and frequent injunctions from Benny to write to her immediately, and be sure to tell her every thing about his voyage, and his journey to Boston.

Dr. Flint made his visit to New York, and made every exertion to call upon me, and invite me to return with him, but not being able to ascertain where I was, his hospitable intentions were frustrated, and the affectionate family, who were waiting for me with "open arms," were doomed to disappointment.

As soon as I knew he was safely at home, I placed Benjamin in the care of my brother William, and returned to Mrs. Bruce. There I remained through the winter and spring, endeavoring to perform my duties faithfully, and finding a good degree of happiness in the attractions of baby Mary, the considerate kindness of her excellent mother, and occasional interviews with my darling daughter.

But when summer came, the old feeling of insecurity haunted me. It was necessary for me to take little Mary out daily, for exercise and fresh air, and the city was swarming with Southerners, some of whom might recognize me. Hot weather brings out snakes and slaveholders, and I like one class of the venomous creatures as little as I do the other. What a comfort it is, to be free to say so!

# XXXV. PREJUDICE AGAINST COLOR.

It was a relief to my mind to see preparations for leaving the city. We went to Albany in the steamboat Knickerbocker. When the gong sounded for tea, Mrs. Bruce said, "Linda, it is late, and you and baby had better come to the table with me." I replied, "I know it is time baby had her supper, but I had rather not go with you, if you please. I am afraid of being insulted." "O no, not if you are with me," she said. I saw several white nurses go with their ladies, and I ventured to do the same. We were at the extreme end of the table. I was no sooner seated, than a gruff voice said, "Get up! You know you are not allowed to sit here." I looked up, and, to my astonishment and indignation, saw that the speaker was a colored man. If his office required him to enforce the by-laws of the boat, he might, at least, have done it politely. I replied, "I shall not get up, unless the captain comes and takes me up." No cup of tea was offered me, but Mrs. Bruce handed me hers and called for another. I looked to see whether the other nurses were treated in a similar manner. They were all properly waited on.

Next morning, when we stopped at Troy for breakfast, every body was making a rush for the table. Mrs. Bruce said, "Take my arm, Linda, and we'll go in together." The landlord heard her, and said, "Madam, will you allow your nurse and baby to take breakfast with my family?" I knew this was to be attributed to my complexion; but he spoke courteously, and therefore I did not mind it.

At Saratoga we found the United States Hotel crowded, and Mr. Bruce took one of the cottages belonging to the hotel. I had thought, with gladness, of going to the quiet of the country, where I should meet few people, but here I found myself in the midst of a swarm of Southerners. I looked round me with fear and trembling, dreading to see some one who would recognize me. I was rejoiced to find that we were to stay but a short time.

We soon returned to New York, to make arrangements for spending the remainder of the summer at Rockaway. While the laundress was putting the clothes in order, I took an opportunity to go over to Brooklyn to see Ellen. I met her going to a grocery store, and the first words she said, were, "O, mother, don't go to Mrs. Hobbs's. Her brother, Mr. Thorne, has come from the south, and may be he'll tell where you are." I accepted the warning. I told her I was going away with Mrs. Bruce the next day, and would try to see her when I came back.

Being in servitude to the Anglo-Saxon race, I was not put into a "Jim Crow car," on our way to Rockaway, neither was I invited to ride through the streets on the top of trunks in a truck; but every where I found the same manifestations of that cruel prejudice, which so discourages the feelings, and represses the energies of the colored people. We reached Rockaway before dark, and put up at the Pavilion—a large hotel, beautifully situated by the sea-side—a great resort of the fashionable world. Thirty or forty nurses were there, of a great variety of nations. Some of the ladies had colored waiting-maids and coachmen, but I was the only nurse tinged with the blood of Africa. When the tea bell rang, I took little Mary and followed the other nurses. Supper was served in a long hall. A young man, who had the ordering of things, took the circuit of the table two or three times, and finally pointed me to a seat at the lower end of it. As there was but one chair, I sat down and took the child in my lap. Whereupon the young man came to me and said, in the blandest manner possible, "Will you please to seat the little girl in the chair, and stand behind it and feed her? After they have done, you will be shown to the kitchen, where you will have a good supper."

This was the climax! I found it hard to preserve my self-control, when I looked round, and saw women who were nurses, as I was, and only one shade lighter in complexion, eyeing me with a defiant look, as if my presence were a contamination. However, I said nothing. I quietly took the child in my arms, went to our room, and refused to go to the table again. Mr. Bruce ordered meals to be sent to the room for little Mary and I. This answered for a few days; but the waiters of the establishment were white, and they soon began to complain, saying they were not hired to wait on negroes. The landlord requested Mr. Bruce to send me down to my meals, because his servants rebelled against bringing them up, and the colored servants of other boarders were dissatisfied because all were not treated alike.

My answer was that the colored servants ought to be dissatisfied with themselves, for not having too much self-respect to submit to such treatment; that there was no difference in the price of board for colored and white servants, and there was no justification for difference of treatment. I staid a month after this, and finding I was resolved to stand up for my rights, they concluded to treat me well. Let every colored man and woman do this, and eventually we shall cease to be trampled under foot by our oppressors.

# XXXVI. THE HAIRBREADTH ESCAPE.

After we returned to New York, I took the earliest opportunity to go and see Ellen. I asked to have her called down stairs; for I supposed Mrs. Hobbs's southern brother might still be there, and I was desirous to avoid seeing him, if possible. But Mrs. Hobbs came to the kitchen, and insisted on my going up stairs. "My brother wants to see you," said she, "and he is sorry you seem to shun him. He knows you are living in New York. He told me to say to you that he owes thanks to good old aunt Martha for too many little acts of kindness for him to be base enough to betray her grandchild."

This Mr. Thorne had become poor and reckless long before he left the south, and such persons had much rather go to one of the faithful old slaves to borrow a dollar, or get a good dinner, than to go to one whom they consider an equal. It was such acts of kindness as these for which he professed to feel grateful to my grandmother. I wished he had kept at a distance, but as he was here, and knew where I was, I concluded there was nothing to be gained by trying to avoid him; on the contrary, it might be the means of exciting his ill will. I followed his sister up stairs. He met me in a very friendly manner, congratulated me on my escape from slavery, and hoped I had a good place, where I felt happy.

I continued to visit Ellen as often as I could. She, good thoughtful child, never forgot my hazardous situation, but always kept a vigilant lookout for my safety. She never made any complaint about her own inconveniences and troubles; but a mother's observing eye easily perceived that she was not happy. On the occasion of one of my visits I found her unusually serious. When I asked her what was the matter, she said nothing was the matter. But I insisted upon knowing what made her look so very grave. Finally, I ascertained that she felt troubled about the dissipation that was continually going on in the house. She was sent to the store very often for rum and brandy, and she felt ashamed to ask for it so often; and Mr. Hobbs and Mr. Thorne drank a great deal, and their hands trembled so that they had to call her to pour out the liquor for them. "But for all that," said she, "Mr. Hobbs is good to me, and I can't help liking him. I feel sorry for him." I tried to comfort her, by telling her that I had laid up a hundred dollars, and that before long I hoped to be able to give her and Benjamin a home, and send them to school. She was always desirous not to add to my troubles more than she could help, and I did not discover till years afterwards that Mr. Thorne's intemperance was not the only annoyance she suffered from him. Though he professed too much gratitude to my grandmother to injure any of her descendants, he had poured vile language into the ears of her innocent great-grandchild.

I usually went to Brooklyn to spend Sunday afternoon. One Sunday, I found Ellen anxiously waiting for me near the house. "O, mother," said she, "I've been waiting for you this long time. I'm afraid Mr. Thorne has written to tell Dr. Flint where you are. Make haste and come in. Mrs. Hobbs will tell you all about it!"

The story was soon told. While the children were playing in the grape-vine arbor, the day before, Mr. Thorne came out with a letter in his hand, which he tore up and scattered about. Ellen was sweeping the yard at the time, and having her mind full of suspicions of him, she picked up the pieces and carried them to the children, saying, "I wonder who Mr. Thorne has been writing to."

"I'm sure I don't know, and don't care," replied the oldest of the children; "and I don't see how it concerns you."

"But it does concern me," replied Ellen; "for I'm afraid he's been writing to the south about my mother."

They laughed at her, and called her a silly thing, but good-naturedly put the fragments of writing together, in order to read them to her. They were no sooner arranged, than the little girl exclaimed, "I declare, Ellen, I believe you are right."

The contents of Mr. Thorne's letter, as nearly as I can remember, were as follows: "I have seen your slave, Linda, and conversed with her. She can be taken very easily, if you manage prudently. There are enough of us here to swear to her identity as your property. I am a patriot, a lover of my country, and I do this as an act of justice to the laws." He concluded by informing the doctor of the street and number where I lived. The children carried the pieces to Mrs. Hobbs, who immediately went to her brother's room for an explanation. He was not to be found. The servants said they saw him go out with a letter in his hand, and they supposed he had gone to the post office. The natural inference was, that he had sent to Dr. Flint a copy of those fragments. When he returned, his sister accused him of it, and he did not deny the charge. He went immediately to his room, and the next morning he was missing. He had gone over to New York, before any of the family were astir.

It was evident that I had no time to lose; and I hastened back to the city with a heavy heart. Again I was to be torn from a comfortable home, and all my plans for the welfare of my children were to be frustrated by that demon Slavery! I now regretted that I never told Mrs. Bruce my story. I had not concealed it merely on account of being a fugitive; that would have made her anxious, but it would have excited sympathy in her kind heart. I valued her good opinion, and I was afraid of losing it, if I told her all the particulars of my sad story. But now I felt that it was necessary for her to know how I was situated. I had once left her abruptly, without explaining the reason, and it would not be proper to do it again. I went home resolved to tell her in the morning. But the sadness of my face attracted her attention, and, in answer to her kind inquiries, I poured out my full heart to her, before bed time. She listened with true womanly sympathy, and told me she would do all she could to protect me. How my heart blessed her!

Early the next morning, Judge Vanderpool and Lawyer Hopper were consulted. They said I had better leave the city at once, as the risk would be great if the case came to trial. Mrs. Bruce took me in a carriage to the house of one of her friends, where she assured me I should be safe until my brother could arrive, which would be in a few days. In the interval my thoughts were much occupied with Ellen. She was mine by birth, and she was also mine by Southern law, since my grandmother held the bill of sale that made her so. I did not feel that she was safe unless I had her with me. Mrs. Hobbs, who felt badly about her brother's treachery, yielded to my entreaties, on condition that she should return in ten days. I avoided making any promise. She came to me clad in very thin garments, all outgrown, and with a school satchel on her arm, containing a few articles. It was late in October, and I knew the child must suffer; and not daring to go out in the streets to purchase any thing, I took off my own flannel skirt and converted it into one for her. Kind Mrs. Bruce came to bid me good by, and when she saw that I had taken off my clothing for my child, the tears came to her eyes. She said, "Wait for me, Linda," and went out. She soon returned with a nice warm shawl and hood for Ellen. Truly, of such souls as hers are the kingdom of heaven.

My brother reached New York on Wednesday. Lawyer Hopper advised us to go to Boston by the Stonington route, as there was less Southern travel in that direction. Mrs. Bruce directed her servants to tell all inquirers that I formerly lived there, but had gone from the city. We reached the steamboat Rhode Island in safety. That boat employed colored hands, but I knew that colored passengers were not admitted to the cabin. I was very desirous for the seclusion of the cabin, not only on account of exposure to the night air, but also to avoid observation. Lawyer Hopper was waiting on board for us. He spoke to the stewardess, and asked, as a particular favor, that she would treat us well. He said to me, "Go and speak to the captain yourself by and by. Take your little girl with you, and I am sure that he will not let her sleep on deck." With these kind words and a shake of the hand he departed.

The boat was soon on her way, bearing me rapidly from the friendly home where I had hoped to find security and rest. My brother had left me to purchase the tickets, thinking that I might have better success than he would. When the stewardess came to me, I paid what she asked, and she gave me three tickets with clipped corners. In the most unsophisticated manner I said, "You have made a mistake; I asked you for cabin tickets. I cannot possibly consent to sleep on deck with my little daughter." She assured me there was no mistake. She said on some of the routes colored people were allowed to sleep in the cabin, but not on this route, which was much travelled by the wealthy. I asked her to show me to the captain's office, and she said she would after tea. When the time came, I took Ellen by the hand and went to the captain, politely requesting him to change our tickets, as we should be very uncomfortable on deck. He said it was contrary to their custom, but he would see that we had berths below; he would also try to obtain comfortable seats for us in the cars; of that he was not certain, but he would speak to the conductor about it, when the boat arrived. I thanked him, and returned to the ladies' cabin. He came afterwards and told me that the conductor of the cars was on board, that he had spoken to him, and he had promised to take care of us. I was very much surprised at receiving so much kindness. I don't know whether the pleasing face of my little girl had won his heart, or whether the stewardess inferred from Lawyer Hopper's manner that I was a fugitive, and had pleaded with him in my behalf.

When the boat arrived at Stonington, the conductor kept his promise, and showed us to seats in the first car, nearest the engine. He asked us to take seats next the door, but as he passed through, we ventured to move on toward the other end of the car. No incivility was offered us, and we reached Boston in safety.

The day after my arrival was one of the happiest of my life. I felt as if I was beyond the reach of the bloodhounds; and, for the first time during many years, I had both my children together with me. They greatly enjoyed their reunion, and laughed and chatted merrily. I watched them with a swelling heart. Their every motion delighted me.

I could not feel safe in New York, and I accepted the offer of a friend, that we should share expenses and keep house together. I represented to Mrs. Hobbs that Ellen must have some schooling, and must remain with me for that purpose. She felt ashamed of being unable to read or spell at her age, so instead of sending her to school with Benny, I instructed her myself till she was fitted to enter an intermediate school. The winter passed pleasantly, while I was busy with my needle, and my children with their books.

# XXXVII. A VISIT TO ENGLAND

In the spring, sad news came to me. Mrs. Bruce was dead. Never again, in this world, should I see her gentle face, or hear her sympathizing voice. I had lost an excellent friend, and little Mary had lost a tender mother. Mr. Bruce wished the child to visit some of her mother's relatives in England, and he was desirous that I should take charge of her. The little motherless one was accustomed to me, and attached to me, and I thought she would be happier in my care than in that of a stranger. I could also earn more in this way than I could by my needle. So I put Benny to a trade, and left Ellen to remain in the house with my friend and go to school.

We sailed from New York, and arrived in Liverpool after a pleasant voyage of twelve days. We proceeded directly to London, and took lodgings at the Adelaide Hotel. The supper seemed to me less luxurious than those I had seen in American hotels; but my situation was indescribably more pleasant. For the first time in my life I was in a place where I was treated according to my deportment, without reference to my complexion. I felt as if a great millstone had been lifted from my breast. Ensconced in a pleasant room, with my dear little charge, I laid my head on my pillow, for the first time, with the delightful consciousness of pure, unadulterated freedom.

As I had constant care of the child, I had little opportunity to see the wonders of that great city; but I watched the tide of life that flowed through the streets, and found it a strange contrast to the stagnation in our Southern towns. Mr. Bruce took his little daughter to spend some days with friends in Oxford Crescent, and of course it was necessary for me to accompany her. I had heard much of the systematic method of English education, and I was very desirous that my dear Mary should steer straight in the midst of so much propriety. I closely observed her little playmates and their nurses, being ready to take any lessons in the science of good management. The children were more rosy than American children, but I did not see that they differed materially in other respects. They were like all children—sometimes docile and sometimes wayward.

We next went to Steventon, in Berkshire. It was a small town, said to be the poorest in the county. I saw men working in the fields for six shillings, and seven shillings, a week, and women for sixpence, and sevenpence, a day, out of which they boarded themselves. Of course they lived in the most primitive manner; it could not be otherwise, where a woman's wages for an entire day were not sufficient to buy a pound of meat. They paid very low rents, and their clothes were made of the cheapest fabrics, though much better than could have been procured in the United States for the same money. I had heard much about the oppression of the poor in Europe. The people I saw around me were, many of them, among the poorest poor. But when I visited them in their little thatched cottages, I felt that the condition of even the meanest and most ignorant among them was vastly superior to the condition of the most favored slaves in America. They labored hard; but they were not ordered out to toil while the stars were in the sky, and driven and slashed by an overseer, through heat and cold, till the stars shone out again. Their homes were very humble; but they were protected by law. No insolent patrols could come, in the dead of night, and flog them at their pleasure. The father, when he closed his cottage door, felt safe with his family around him. No master or overseer could come and take from him his wife, or his daughter. They must separate to earn their living; but the parents knew where their children were going, and could communicate with them by letters. The relations of husband and wife, parent and child, were too sacred for the richest noble in the land to violate with impunity. Much was being done to enlighten these poor people. Schools were established among them, and benevolent societies were active in efforts to ameliorate their condition. There was no law forbidding them to learn to read and write; and if they helped each other in spelling out the Bible, they were in no danger of thirty-nine lashes, as was the case with myself and poor, pious, old uncle Fred. I repeat that the most ignorant and the most destitute of these peasants was a thousand fold better off than the most pampered American slave.

I do not deny that the poor are oppressed in Europe. I am not disposed to paint their condition so rose-colored as the Hon. Miss Murray paints the condition of the slaves in the United States. A small portion of my experience would enable her to read her own pages with anointed eyes. If she were to lay aside her title, and, instead of visiting among the fashionable, become domesticated, as a poor governess, on some plantation in Louisiana or Alabama, she would see and hear things that would make her tell quite a different story.

My visit to England is a memorable event in my life, from the fact of my having there received strong religious impressions. The contemptuous manner in which the communion had been administered to colored people, in my native place; the church membership of Dr. Flint, and others like him; and the buying and selling of slaves, by professed ministers of the gospel, had given me a prejudice against the Episcopal church. The whole service seemed to me a mockery and a sham. But my home in Steventon was in the family of a clergyman, who was a true disciple of Jesus. The beauty of his daily life inspired me with faith in the genuineness of Christian professions. Grace entered my heart, and I knelt at the communion table, I trust, in true humility of soul.

I remained abroad ten months, which was much longer than I had anticipated. During all that time, I never saw the slightest symptom of prejudice against color. Indeed, I entirely forgot it, till the time came for us to return to America.

# XXXVIII. RENEWED INVITATIONS TO GO SOUTH.

We had a tedious winter passage, and from the distance spectres seemed to rise up on the shores of the United States. It is a sad feeling to be afraid of one's native country. We arrived in New York safely, and I hastened to Boston to look after my children. I found Ellen well, and improving at her school; but Benny was not there to welcome me. He had been left at a good place to learn a trade, and for several months every thing worked well. He was liked by the master, and was a favorite with his fellow-apprentices; but one day they accidentally discovered a fact they had never before suspected—that he was colored! This at once transformed him into a different being. Some of the apprentices were Americans, others American-born Irish; and it was offensive to their dignity to have a "nigger" among them, after they had been told that he was a "nigger." They began by treating him with silent scorn, and finding that he returned the same, they resorted to insults and abuse. He was too spirited a boy to stand that, and he went off. Being desirous to do something to support himself, and having no one to advise him, he shipped for a whaling voyage. When I received these tidings I shed many tears, and bitterly reproached myself for having left him so long. But I had done it for the best, and now all I could do was to pray to the heavenly Father to guide and protect him.

Not long after my return, I received the following letter from Miss Emily Flint, now Mrs. Dodge:—

> In this you will recognize the hand of your friend and mistress. Having heard that you had gone with a family to Europe, I have waited to hear of your return to write to you. I should have answered the letter you wrote to me long since, but as I could not then act independently of my father, I knew there could be nothing done satisfactory to you. There were persons here who were willing to buy you and run the risk of getting you. To this I would not consent. I have always been attached to you, and would not like to see you the slave of another, or have unkind treatment. I am married now, and can protect you. My husband expects to move to Virginia this spring, where we think of settling. I am very anxious that you should come and live with me. If you are not willing to come, you may purchase yourself; but I should prefer having you live with me. If you come, you may, if you like, spend a month with your grandmother and

friends, then come to me in Norfolk, Virginia. Think this over, and write as soon as possible, and let me know the conclusion. Hoping that your children are well, I remain your friend and mistress.

Of course I did not write to return thanks for this cordial invitation. I felt insulted to be thought stupid enough to be caught by such professions.

"Come up into my parlor," said the spider to the fly;
"Tis the prettiest little parlor that ever you did spy."

It was plain that Dr. Flint's family were apprised of my movements, since they knew of my voyage to Europe. I expected to have further trouble from them; but having eluded them thus far, I hoped to be as successful in future. The money I had earned, I was desirous to devote to the education of my children, and to secure a home for them. It seemed not only hard, but unjust, to pay for myself. I could not possibly regard myself as a piece of property. Moreover, I had worked many years without wages, and during that time had been obliged to depend on my grandmother for many comforts in food and clothing. My children certainly belonged to me; but though Dr. Flint had incurred no expense for their support, he had received a large sum of money for them. I knew the law would decide that I was his property, and would probably still give his daughter a claim to my children; but I regarded such laws as the regulations of robbers, who had no rights that I was bound to respect.

The Fugitive Slave Law had not then passed. The judges of Massachusetts had not then stooped under chains to enter her courts of justice, so called. I knew my old master was rather skittish of Massachusetts. I relied on her love of freedom, and felt safe on her soil. I am now aware that I honored the old Commonwealth beyond her deserts.

# XXXIX. THE CONFESSION.

For two years my daughter and I supported ourselves comfortably in Boston. At the end of that time, my brother William offered to send Ellen to a boarding school. It required a great effort for me to consent to part with her, for I had few near ties, and it was her presence that made my two little rooms seem home-like. But my judgment prevailed over my selfish feelings. I made preparations for her departure. During the two years we had lived together I had often resolved to tell her something about her father; but I had never been able to muster sufficient courage. I had a shrinking dread of diminishing my child's love. I knew she must have curiosity on the subject, but she had never asked a question. She was always very careful not to say any thing to remind me of my troubles. Now that she was going from me, I thought if I should die before she returned, she might hear my story from some one who did not understand the palliating circumstances; and that if she were entirely ignorant on the subject, her sensitive nature might receive a rude shock.

When we retired for the night, she said, "Mother, it is very hard to leave you alone. I am almost sorry I am going, though I do want to improve myself. But you will write to me often; won't you, mother?"

I did not throw my arms round her. I did not answer her. But in a calm, solemn way, for it cost me great effort, I said, "Listen to me, Ellen; I have something to tell you!" I recounted my early sufferings in slavery, and told her how nearly they had crushed me. I began to tell her how they had driven me into a great sin, when she clasped me in her arms, and exclaimed, "O, don't, mother! Please don't tell me any more."

I said, "But, my child, I want you to know about your father."

"I know all about it, mother," she replied; "I am nothing to my father, and he is nothing to me. All my love is for you. I was with him five months in Washington, and he never cared for me. He never spoke to me as he did to his little Fanny. I knew all the time he was my father, for Fanny's nurse told me so, but she said I must never tell any body, and I never did. I used to wish he would take me in his arms and kiss me, as he did Fanny; or that he would sometimes smile at me, as he did at her. I thought if he was my own father, he ought to love me. I was a little girl then, and didn't know any better. But now I never think any thing about my father. All my love is for you." She hugged me closer as she spoke, and I thanked God that the knowledge I had so much dreaded to impart had not diminished the affection of my child. I had not the slightest idea she knew that portion of my history. If I had, I should have spoken to her long before; for my pent-up feelings had often longed to pour themselves out to some one I could trust. But I loved the dear girl better for the delicacy she had manifested towards her unfortunate mother.

The next morning, she and her uncle started on their journey to the village in New York, where she was to be placed at school. It seemed as if all the sunshine had gone away. My little room was dreadfully lonely. I was thankful when a message came from a lady, accustomed to employ me, requesting me to come and sew in her family for several weeks. On my return, I found a letter from brother William. He thought of opening an anti-slavery reading room in Rochester, and combining with it the sale of some books and stationery; and he wanted me to unite with him. We tried it, but it was not successful. We found warm anti-slavery friends there, but the feeling was not general enough to support such an establishment. I passed nearly a year in the family of Isaac and Amy Post, practical believers in the Christian doctrine of human brotherhood. They measure a man's worth by his character, not by his complexion. The memory of those beloved and honored friends will remain with me to my latest hour.

# XL. THE FUGITIVE SLAVE LAW.

My brother, being disappointed in his project, concluded to go to California; and it was agreed that Benjamin should go with him. Ellen liked her school, and was a great favorite there. They did not know her history, and she did not tell it, because she had no desire to make capital out of their sympathy. But when it was accidentally discovered that her mother was a fugitive slave, every method was used to increase her advantages and diminish her expenses.

I was alone again. It was necessary for me to be earning money, and I preferred that it should be among those who knew me. On my return from Rochester, I called at the house of Mr. Bruce, to see Mary, the darling little babe that had thawed my heart, when it was freezing into a cheerless distrust of all my fellow-beings. She was growing a tall girl now, but I loved her always. Mr. Bruce had married again, and it was proposed that I should become nurse to a new infant. I had but one hesitation, and that was feeling of insecurity in New York, now greatly increased by the passage of the Fugitive Slave Law. However, I resolved to try the experiment. I was again fortunate in my employer. The new Mrs. Bruce was an American, brought up under aristocratic influences, and still living in the midst of them; but if she had any prejudice against color, I was never made aware of it; and as for the system of slavery, she had a most hearty dislike of it. No sophistry of Southerners could blind her to its enormity. She was a person of excellent principles and a noble heart. To me, from that hour to the present, she has been a true and sympathizing friend. Blessings be with her and hers!

About the time that I reentered the Bruce family, an event occurred of disastrous import to the colored people. The slave Hamlin, the first fugitive that came under the new law, was given up by the bloodhounds of the north to the bloodhounds of the south. It was the beginning of a reign of terror to the colored population. The great city rushed on in its whirl of excitement, taking no note of the "short and simple annals of the poor." But while fashionables were listening to the thrilling voice of Jenny Lind in Metropolitan Hall, the thrilling voices of poor hunted colored people went up, in an agony of supplication, to the Lord, from Zion's church. Many families, who had lived in the city for twenty years, fled from it now. Many a poor washerwoman, who, by hard labor, had made herself a comfortable home, was obliged to sacrifice her furniture, bid a hurried farewell to friends, and seek her fortune among strangers in Canada. Many a wife discovered a secret she had never known before—that her husband was a fugitive, and must leave her to insure his own safety. Worse still, many a husband discovered that his wife had fled from slavery years ago, and as "the child follows the condition of its mother," the children of his love were liable to be seized and carried into slavery. Every where, in those humble homes, there was consternation and anguish. But what cared the legislators of the "dominant race" for the blood they were crushing out of trampled hearts?

When my brother William spent his last evening with me, before he went to California, we talked nearly all the time of the distress brought on our oppressed people by the passage of this iniquitous law; and never had I seen him manifest such bitterness of spirit, such stern hostility to our oppressors. He was himself free from the operation of the law; for he did not run from any Slaveholding State, being brought into the Free States by his master. But I was subject to it; and so were hundreds of intelligent and industrious people all around us. I seldom ventured into the streets; and when it was necessary to do an errand for Mrs. Bruce, or any of the family, I went as much as possible through back streets and by-ways. What a disgrace to a city calling itself free, that inhabitants, guiltless of offence, and seeking to perform their duties conscientiously, should be condemned to live in such incessant fear, and have nowhere to turn for protection! This state of things, of course, gave rise to many impromptu vigilance committees. Every colored person, and every friend of their persecuted race, kept their eyes wide open. Every evening I examined the newspapers carefully, to see what Southerners had put up at the hotels. I did this for my own sake, thinking my young mistress and her husband might be among the list; I wished also to give information to others, if necessary; for if many were "running to and fro," I resolved that "knowledge should be increased."

This brings up one of my Southern reminiscences, which I will here briefly relate. I was somewhat acquainted with a slave named Luke, who belonged to a wealthy man in our vicinity. His master died, leaving a son and daughter heirs to his large fortune. In the division of the slaves, Luke was included in the son's portion. This young man became a prey to the vices he went to the north, to complete his education, he carried his vices with him. He was brought home, deprived of the use of his limbs, by excessive dissipation. Luke was appointed to wait upon his bed-ridden master, whose despotic habits were greatly increased by exasperation at his own helplessness. He kept a cowhide beside him, and, for the most trivial occurrence, he would order his attendant to bare his back, and kneel beside the couch, while he whipped him till his strength was exhausted. Some days he was not allowed to wear any thing but his shirt, in order to be in readiness to be flogged. A day seldom passed without his receiving more or less blows. If the slightest resistance was offered, the town constable was sent for to execute the punishment, and Luke learned from experience how much more the constable's strong arm was to be dreaded than the comparatively feeble one of his master. The arm of his tyrant grew weaker, and was finally palsied; and then the constable's services were in constant requisition. The fact that he was entirely dependent on Luke's care, and was obliged to be tended like an infant, instead of inspiring any gratitude or compassion towards his poor slave, seemed only to increase his irritability and cruelty. As he lay there on his bed, a mere degraded wreck of manhood, he took into his head the strangest freaks of despotism; and if Luke hesitated to submit to his orders, the constable was immediately sent for. Some of these freaks were of a nature too filthy to be repeated. When I fled from the house of bondage, I left poor Luke still chained to the bedside of this cruel and disgusting wretch.

One day, when I had been requested to do an errand for Mrs. Bruce, I was hurrying through back streets, as usual, when I saw a young man approaching, whose face was familiar to me. As he came nearer, I recognized Luke. I always rejoiced to see or hear of any one who had escaped from the black pit; I was peculiarly glad to see him on Northern soil, though I no longer called it free soil. I well remembered what a desolate feeling it was to be alone among strangers, and I went up to him and greeted him cordially. At first, he did not know me; but when I mentioned my name, he remembered all about me. I told him of the Fugitive Slave Law, and asked him if he did not know that New York was a city of kidnappers.

He replied, "De risk ain't so bad for me, as 'tis fur you. 'Cause I runned away from de speculator, and you runned away from de massa. Dem speculators vont spen dar money to come here fur a runaway, if dey ain't sartin sure to put dar hans right on him. An I tell you I's tuk good car 'bout dat. I had too hard times down dar, to let 'em ketch dis nigger."

He then told me of the advice he had received, and the plans he had laid. I asked if he had money enough to take him to Canada. "'Pend upon it, I hab," he replied. "I tuk car fur dat. I'd bin workin all my days fur dem cussed whites, an got no pay but kicks and cuffs. So I tought dis nigger had a right to money nuff to bring him to de Free States. Massa Henry he lib till ebery body vish him dead; an ven he did die, I knowed de debbil would hab him, an vouldn't vant him to bring his money 'long too. So I tuk some of his bills, and put 'em in de pocket of his ole trousers. An ven he was buried, dis nigger ask fur dem ole trousers, an dey gub 'em to me." With a low, chuckling laugh, he added, "You see I didn't steal it; dey gub it to me. I tell you, I had mighty hard time to keep de speculator from findin it; but he didn't git it."

This is a fair specimen of how the moral sense is educated by slavery. When a man has his wages stolen from him, year after year, and the laws sanction and enforce the theft, how can he be expected to have more regard to honesty than has the man who robs him? I have become somewhat enlightened, but I confess that I agree with poor, ignorant, much-abused Luke, in thinking he had a right to that money, as a portion of his unpaid wages. He went to Canada forthwith, and I have not since heard from him.

All that winter I lived in a state of anxiety. When I took the children out to breathe the air, I closely observed the countenances of all I met. I dreaded the approach of summer, when snakes and slaveholders make their appearance. I was, in fact, a slave in New York, as subject to slave laws as I had been in a Slave State. Strange incongruity in a State called free!

Spring returned, and I received warning from the south that Dr. Flint knew of my return to my old place, and was making preparations to have e caught. I learned afterwards that my dress, and that of Mrs. Bruce's children, had been described to him by some of the Northern tools, which slaveholders employ for their base purposes, and then indulge in sneers at their cupidity and mean servility.

I immediately informed Mrs. Bruce of my danger, and she took prompt measures for my safety. My place as nurse could not be supplied immediately, and this generous, sympathizing lady proposed that I should carry her baby away. It was a comfort to me to have the child with me; for the heart is reluctant to be torn away from every object it loves. But how few mothers would have consented to have one of their own babes become a fugitive, for the sake of a poor, hunted nurse, on whom the legislators of the country had let loose the bloodhounds! When I spoke of the sacrifice she was making, in depriving herself of her dear baby, she replied, "It is better for you to have baby with you, Linda; for if they get on your track, they will be obliged to bring the child to me; and then, if there is a possibility of saving you, you shall be saved."

This lady had a very wealthy relative, a benevolent gentleman in many respects, but aristocratic and pro-slavery. He remonstrated with her for harboring a fugitive slave; told her she was violating the laws of her country; and asked her if she was aware of the penalty. She replied, "I am very well aware of it. It is imprisonment and one thousand dollars fine. Shame on my country that it is so! I am ready to incur the penalty. I will go to the state's prison, rather than have any poor victim torn from my house, to be carried back to slavery."

The noble heart! The brave heart! The tears are in my eyes while I write of her. May the God of the helpless reward her for her sympathy with my persecuted people!

I was sent into New England, where I was sheltered by the wife of a senator, whom I shall always hold in grateful remembrance. This honorable gentleman would not have voted for the Fugitive Slave Law, as did the senator in "Uncle

Tom's Cabin;" on the contrary, he was strongly opposed to it; but he was enough under its influence to be afraid of having me remain in his house many hours. So I was sent into the country, where I remained a month with the baby. When it was supposed that Dr. Flint's emissaries had lost track of me, and given up the pursuit for the present, I returned to New York.

# XLI. FREE AT LAST.

Mrs. Bruce, and every member of her family, were exceedingly kind to me. I was thankful for the blessings of my lot, yet I could not always wear a cheerful countenance. I was doing harm to no one; on the contrary, I was doing all the good I could in my small way; yet I could never go out to breathe God's free air without trepidation at my heart. This seemed hard; and I could not think it was a right state of things in any civilized country.

From time to time I received news from my good old grandmother. She could not write; but she employed others to write for her. The following is an extract from one of her last letters:—

> Dear Daughter: I cannot hope to see you again on earth; but I pray to God to unite us above, where pain will no more rack this feeble body of mine; where sorrow and parting from my children will be no more. God has promised these things if we are faithful unto the end. My age and feeble health deprive me of going to church now; but God is with me here at home. Thank your brother for his kindness. Give much love to him, and tell him to remember the Creator in the days of his youth, and strive to meet me in the Father's kingdom. Love to Ellen and Benjamin. Don't neglect him. Tell him for me, to be a good boy. Strive, my child, to train them for God's children. May he protect and provide for you, is the prayer of your loving old mother.

These letters both cheered and saddened me. I was always glad to have tidings from the kind, faithful old friend of my unhappy youth; but her messages of love made my heart yearn to see her before she died, and I mourned over the fact that it was impossible. Some months after I returned from my flight to New England, I received a letter from her, in which she wrote, "Dr. Flint is dead. He has left a distressed family. Poor old man! I hope he made his peace with God."

I remembered how he had defrauded my grandmother of the hard earnings she had loaned; how he had tried to cheat her out of the freedom her mistress had promised her, and how he had persecuted her children; and I thought to myself that she was a better Christian than I was, if she could entirely forgive him. I cannot say, with truth, that the news of my old master's death softened my feelings towards him. There are wrongs which even the grave does not bury. The man was odious to me while he lived, and his memory is odious now.

His departure from this world did not diminish my danger. He had threatened my grandmother that his heirs should hold me in slavery after he was gone; that I never should be free so long as a child of his survived. As for Mrs. Flint, I had seen her in deeper afflictions than I supposed the loss of her husband would be, for she had buried several children; yet I never saw any signs of softening in her heart. The doctor had died in embarrassed circumstances, and had little to will to his heirs, except such property as he was unable to grasp. I was well aware what I had to expect from the family of Flints; and my fears were confirmed by a letter from the south, warning me to be on my guard, because Mrs. Flint openly declared that her daughter could not afford to lose so valuable a slave as I was.

I kept close watch of the newspapers for arrivals; but one Saturday night, being much occupied, I forgot to examine the Evening Express as usual. I went down into the parlor for it, early in the morning, and found the boy about to kindle a fire with it. I took it from him and examined the list of arrivals. Reader, if you have never been a slave, you cannot imagine the acute sensation of suffering at my heart, when I read the names of Mr. and Mrs. Dodge, at a hotel in Courtland Street. It was a third-rate hotel, and that circumstance convinced me of the truth of what I had heard, that they were short of funds and had need of my value, as they valued me; and that was by dollars and cents. I hastened with the paper to Mrs. Bruce. Her heart and hand were always open to every one in distress, and she always warmly sympathized with mine. It was impossible to tell how near the enemy was. He might have passed and repassed the house while we were sleeping. He might at that moment be waiting to pounce upon me if I ventured out of doors. I had never seen the husband of my young mistress, and therefore I could not distinguish him from any other stranger. A carriage was hastily ordered; and, closely veiled, I followed Mrs. Bruce, taking the baby again with me into exile. After various turnings and crossings, and returnings, the carriage stopped at the house of one of Mrs. Bruce's friends, where I was kindly received. Mrs. Bruce returned immediately, to instruct the domestics what to say if any one came to inquire for me.

It was lucky for me that the evening paper was not burned up before I had a chance to examine the list of arrivals. It was not long after Mrs. Bruce's return to her house, before several people came to inquire for me. One inquired for me, another asked for my daughter Ellen, and another said he had a letter from my grandmother, which he was requested to deliver in person.

They were told, "She has lived here, but she has left."

"How long ago?"

"I don't know, sir."

"Do you know where she went?"

"I do not, sir." And the door was closed.

This Mr. Dodge, who claimed me as his property, was originally a Yankee pedler in the south; then he became a merchant, and finally a slaveholder. He managed to get introduced into what was called the first society, and married Miss Emily Flint. A quarrel arose between him and her brother, and the brother cowhided him. This led to a family feud, and he proposed to remove to Virginia. Dr. Flint left him no property, and his own means had become circumscribed, while a wife and children depended upon him for support. Under these circumstances, it was very natural that he should make an effort to put me into his pocket.

I had a colored friend, a man from my native place, in whom I had the most implicit confidence. I sent for him, and told him that Mr. and Mrs. Dodge had arrived in New York. I proposed that he should call upon them to make inquiries about his friends at the south, with whom Dr. Flint's family were well acquainted. He thought there was no impropriety in his doing so, and he consented. He went to the hotel, and knocked at the door of Mr. Dodge's room, which was opened by the gentleman himself, who gruffly inquired, "What brought you here? How came you to know I was in the city?"

"Your arrival was published in the evening papers, sir; and I called to ask Mrs. Dodge about my friends at home. I didn't suppose it would give any offence."

"Where's that negro girl, that belongs to my wife?"

"What girl, sir?"

"You know well enough. I mean Linda, that ran away from Dr. Flint's plantation, some years ago. I dare say you've seen her, and know where she is."

"Yes, sir, I've seen her, and know where she is. She is out of your reach, sir."

"Tell me where she is, or bring her to me, and I will give her a chance to buy her freedom."

"I don't think it would be of any use, sir. I have heard her say she would go to the ends of the earth, rather than pay any man or woman for her freedom, because she thinks she has a right to it. Besides, she couldn't do it, if she would, for she has spent her earnings to educate her children."

This made Mr. Dodge very angry, and some high words passed between them. My friend was afraid to come where I was; but in the course of the day I received a note from him. I supposed they had not come from the south, in the winter, for a pleasure excursion; and now the nature of their business was very plain.

Mrs. Bruce came to me and entreated me to leave the city the next morning. She said her house was watched, and it was possible that some clew to me might be obtained. I refused to take her advice. She pleaded with an earnest tenderness, that ought to have moved me; but I was in a bitter, disheartened mood. I was weary of flying from pillar to post. I had been chased during half my life, and it seemed as if the chase was never to end. There I sat, in that great city, guiltless of crime, yet not daring to worship God in any of the churches. I heard the bells ringing for afternoon service, and, with contemptuous sarcasm, I said, "Will the preachers take for their text, 'Proclaim liberty to the captive, and the opening of prison doors to them that are bound'? or will they preach from the text, 'Do unto others as ye would they should do unto you'?" Oppressed Poles and Hungarians could find a safe refuge in that city; John Mitchell was free to proclaim in the City Hall his desire for "a plantation well stocked with slaves;" but there I sat, an oppressed American, not daring to show my face. God forgive the black and bitter thoughts I indulged on that Sabbath day! The Scripture says, "Oppression makes even a wise man mad;" and I was not wise.

I had been told that Mr. Dodge said his wife had never signed away her right to my children, and if he could not get me, he would take them. This it was, more than any thing else, that roused such a tempest in my soul. Benjamin was with his uncle William in California, but my innocent young daughter had come to spend a vacation with me. I thought of what I had suffered in slavery at her age, and my heart was like a tiger's when a hunter tries to seize her young.

Dear Mrs. Bruce! I seem to see the expression of her face, as she turned away discouraged by my obstinate mood. Finding her expostulations unavailing, she sent Ellen to entreat me. When ten o'clock in the evening arrived and Ellen had not returned, this watchful and unwearied friend became anxious. She came to us in a carriage, bringing a well-filled trunk for my journey—trusting that by this time I would listen to reason. I yielded to her, as I ought to have done before.

The next day, baby and I set out in a heavy snow storm, bound for New England again. I received letters from the City of Iniquity, addressed to me under an assumed name. In a few days one came from Mrs. Bruce, informing me that my new master was still searching for me, and that she intended to put an end to this persecution by buying my freedom. I felt grateful for the kindness that prompted this offer, but the idea was not so pleasant to me as might have been expected. The more my mind had become enlightened, the more difficult it was for me to consider myself an article of property; and to pay money to those who had so grievously oppressed me seemed like taking from my sufferings the glory of triumph. I wrote to Mrs. Bruce, thanking her, but saying that being sold from one owner to another seemed too much like slavery; that such a great obligation could not be easily cancelled; and that I preferred to go to my brother in California.

Without my knowledge, Mrs. Bruce employed a gentleman in New York to enter into negotiations with Mr. Dodge. He proposed to pay three hundred dollars down, if Mr. Dodge would sell me, and enter into obligations to relinquish all claim to me or my children forever after. He who called himself my master said he scorned so small an offer for such a valuable servant. The gentleman replied, "You can do as you choose, sir. If you reject this offer you will never get any thing; for the woman has friends who will convey her and her children out of the country."

Mr. Dodge concluded that "half a loaf was better than no bread," and he agreed to the proffered terms. By the next mail I received this brief letter from Mrs. Bruce: "I am rejoiced to tell you that the money for your freedom has been paid to Mr. Dodge. Come home to-morrow. I long to see you and my sweet babe."

My brain reeled as I read these lines. A gentleman near me said, "It's true; I have seen the bill of sale." "The bill of sale!" Those words struck me like a blow. So I was sold at last! A human being sold in the free city of New York! The bill of sale is on record, and future generations will learn from it that women were articles of traffic in New York, late in the nineteenth century of the Christian religion. It may hereafter prove a useful document to antiquaries, who are seeking to measure the progress of civilization in the United States. I well know the value of that bit of paper; but much as I love freedom, I do not like to look upon it. I am deeply grateful to the generous friend who procured it, but I despise the miscreant who demanded payment for what never rightfully belonged to him or his.

I had objected to having my freedom bought, yet I must confess that when it was done I felt as if a heavy load had been lifted from my weary shoulders. When I rode home in the cars I was no longer afraid to unveil my face and look at people as they passed. I should have been glad to have met Daniel Dodge himself; to have had him seen me and known me, that he might have mourned over the untoward circumstances which compelled him to sell me for three hundred dollars.

When I reached home, the arms of my benefactress were thrown round me, and our tears mingled. As soon as she could speak, she said, "O Linda, I'm so glad it's all over! You wrote to me as if you thought you were going to be transferred from one owner to another. But I did not buy you for your services. I should have done just the same, if you had been going to sail for California to-morrow. I should, at least, have the satisfaction of knowing that you left me a free woman."

My heart was exceedingly full. I remembered how my poor father had tried to buy me, when I was a small child, and how he had been disappointed. I hoped his spirit was rejoicing over me now. I remembered how my good old grandmother had laid up her earnings to purchase me in later years, and how often her plans had been frustrated. How that faithful, loving old heart would leap for joy, if she could look on me and my children now that we were free! My relatives had been foiled in all their efforts, but God had raised me up a friend among strangers, who had bestowed on me the precious, long-desired boon. Friend! It is a common word, often lightly used. Like other good and beautiful things, it may be tarnished by careless handling; but when I speak of Mrs. Bruce as my friend, the word is sacred.

My grandmother lived to rejoice in my freedom; but not long after, a letter came with a black seal. She had gone "where the wicked cease from troubling, and the weary are at rest."

Time passed on, and a paper came to me from the south, containing an obituary notice of my uncle Phillip. It was the only case I ever knew of such an honor conferred upon a colored person. It was written by one of his friends, and contained these words: "Now that death has laid him low, they call him a good man and a useful citizen; but what are eulogies to the black man, when the world has faded from his vision? It does not require man's praise to obtain rest in God's kingdom." So they called a colored man a citizen! Strange words to be uttered in that region!

Reader, my story ends with freedom; not in the usual way, with marriage. I and my children are now free! We are as free from the power of slaveholders as are the white people of the north; and though that, according to my ideas, is not saying a great deal, it is a vast improvement in my condition. The dream of my life is not yet realized. I do not sit with my children in a home of my own, I still long for a hearthstone of my own, however humble. I wish it for my children's sake far more than for my own. But God so orders circumstances as to keep me with my friend Mrs. Bruce. Love, duty, gratitude, also bind me to her side. It is a privilege to serve her who pities my oppressed people, and who has bestowed the inestimable boon of freedom on me and my children.

It has been painful to me, in many ways, to recall the dreary years I passed in bondage. I would gladly forget them if I could. Yet the retrospection is not altogether without solace; for with those gloomy recollections come tender memories of my good old grandmother, like light, fleecy clouds floating over a dark and troubled sea.

# APPENDIX.

The following statement is from Amy Post, a member of the Society of Friends in the State of New York, well known and highly respected by friends of the poor and the oppressed. As has been already stated, in the preceding pages, the author of this volume spent some time under her hospitable roof.

L.M.C.

The author of this book is my highly-esteemed friend. If its readers knew her as I know her, they could not fail to be deeply interested in her story. She was a beloved inmate of our family nearly the whole of the year 1849. She was introduced to us by her affectionate and conscientious brother, who had previously related to us some of the almost incredible events in his sister's life. I immediately became much interested in Linda; for her appearance was prepossessing, and her deportment indicated remarkable delicacy of feeling and purity of thought.

As we became acquainted, she related to me, from time to time some of the incidents in her bitter experiences as a slave-woman. Though impelled by a natural craving for human sympathy, she passed through a baptism of suffering, even in recounting her trials to me, in private confidential conversations. The burden of these memories lay heavily upon her spirit—naturally virtuous and refined. I repeatedly urged her to consent to the publication of her narrative; for I felt that it would arouse people to a more earnest work for the disinthralment of millions still remaining in that soul-crushing condition, which was so unendurable to her. But her sensitive spirit shrank from publicity. She said, "You know a woman can whisper her cruel wrongs in the ear of a dear friend much easier than she can record them for the world to read." Even in talking with me, she wept so much, and seemed to suffer such mental agony, that I felt her story was too sacred to be drawn from her by inquisitive questions, and I left her free to tell as much, or as little, as she chose. Still, I urged upon her the duty of publishing her experience, for the sake of the good it might do; and, at last, she undertook the task.

Having been a slave so large a portion of her life, she is unlearned; she is obliged to earn her living by her own labor, and she has worked untiringly to procure education for her children; several times she has been obliged to leave her employments, in order to fly from the man-hunters and woman-hunters of our land; but she pressed through all these obstacles and overcame them. After the labors of the day were over, she traced secretly and wearily, by the midnight lamp, a truthful record of her eventful life.

This Empire State is a shabby place of refuge for the oppressed; but here, through anxiety, turmoil, and despair, the freedom of Linda and her children was finally secured, by the exertions of a generous friend. She was grateful for the boon; but the idea of having been bought was always galling to a spirit that could never acknowledge itself to be a chattel. She wrote to us thus, soon after the event: "I thank you for your kind expressions in regard to my freedom; but the freedom I had before the money was paid was dearer to me. God gave me that freedom; but man put God's image in the scales with the paltry sum of three hundred dollars. I served for my liberty as faithfully as Jacob served for Rachel. At the end, he had large possessions; but I was robbed of my victory; I was obliged to resign my crown, to rid myself of a tyrant."

Her story, as written by herself, cannot fail to interest the reader. It is a sad illustration of the condition of this country, which boasts of its civilization, while it sanctions laws and customs which make the experiences of the present more strange than any fictions of the past.

Amy Post. Rochester, N.Y., Oct. 30th, 1859.
The following testimonial is from a man who is now a highly respectable colored citizen of Boston.

L.M.C.

This narrative contains some incidents so extraordinary, that, doubtless, many persons, under whose eyes it may chance to fall, will be ready to believe that it is colored highly, to serve a special purpose. But, however it may be regarded by the incredulous, I know that it is full of living truths. I have been well acquainted with the author from my boyhood. The circumstances recounted in her history are perfectly familiar to me. I knew of her treatment from her master; of the imprisonment of her children; of their sale and redemption; of her seven years' concealment; and of her subsequent escape to the North. I am now a resident of Boston, and am a living witness to the truth of this interesting narrative.

George W. Lowther.

# THE HISTORY OF MARY PRINCE, A WEST INDIAN SLAVE. RELATED BY HERSELF.

WITH A SUPPLEMENT BY THE EDITOR.

To which is added,
THE NARRATIVE OF ASA-ASA, A CAPTURED AFRICAN.

"By our sufferings, since ye brought us
To the man-degrading mart,—
All sustain'd by patience, taught us
Only by a broken heart,—
Deem our nation brutes no longer,
Till some reason ye shall find
Worthier of regard, and stronger
Than the colour of our kind."

- Cowper.

LONDON:
PUBLISHED BY F. WESTLEY AND A. H. DAVIS,
Stationers' Hall Court;
And by WAUGH & INNES, EDINBURGH.
1831.

# CONTENTS

PREFACE 283

THE HISTORY OF MARY PRINCE,
A WEST INDIAN SLAVE 285

SUPPLEMENT TO THE HISTORY OF
MARY PRINCE. BY THE EDITOR 309

FOOTNOTES 328

NARRATIVE OF LOUIS ASA-ASA,
A CAPTURED AFRICAN 334

# PREFACE.

The idea of writing Mary Prince's history was first suggested by herself. She wished it to be done, she said, that good people in England might hear from a slave what a slave had felt and suffered; and a letter of her late master's, which will be found in the Supplement, induced me to accede to her wish without farther delay. The more immediate object of the publication will afterwards appear.

The narrative was taken down from Mary's own lips by a lady who happened to be at the time residing in my family as a visitor. It was written out fully, with all the narrator's repetitions and prolixities, and afterwards pruned into its present shape; retaining, as far as was practicable, Mary's exact expressions and peculiar phraseology. No fact of importance has been omitted, and not a single circumstance or sentiment has been added. It is essentially her own, without any material alteration farther than was requisite to exclude redundancies and gross grammatical errors, so as to render it clearly intelligible.

After it had been thus written out, I went over the whole, carefully examining her on every fact and circumstance detailed; and in all that relates to her residence in Antigua I had the advantage of being assisted in this scrutiny by Mr. Joseph Phillips, who was a resident in that colony during the same period, and had known her there.

The names of all the persons mentioned by the narrator have been printed in full, except those of Capt. I—— and his wife, and that of Mr. D——, to whom conduct of peculiar atrocity is ascribed. These three individuals are now gone to answer at a far more awful tribunal than that of public opinion, for the deeds of which their former bondwoman accuses them; and to hold them up more openly to human reprobation could no longer affect themselves, while it might deeply lacerate the feelings of their surviving and perhaps innocent relatives, without any commensurate public advantage.

Without detaining the reader with remarks on other points which will be adverted to more conveniently in the Supplement, I shall here merely notice farther, that the Anti-Slavery Society have no concern whatever with this publication, nor are they in any degree responsible for the statements it contains. I have published the tract, not as their Secretary, but in my private capacity; and any profits that may arise from the sale will be exclusively appropriated to the benefit of Mary Prince herself.

THO. PRINGLE.

7, Solly Terrace, Claremont Square,

January 25, 1831.

P. S. Since writing the above, I have been furnished by my friend Mr. George Stephen, with the interesting narrative of Asa-Asa, a captured African, now under his protection; and have printed it as a suitable appendix to this little history.

T. P.

# THE HISTORY OF MARY PRINCE, A WEST INDIAN SLAVE.
## (Related by herself.)

I was born at Brackish-Pond, in Bermuda, on a farm belonging to Mr. Charles Myners. My mother was a household slave; and my father, whose name was Prince, was a sawyer belonging to Mr. Trimmingham, a ship-builder at Crow-Lane. When I was an infant, old Mr. Myners died, and there was a division of the slaves and other property among the family. I was bought along with my mother by old Captain Darrel, and given to his grandchild, little Miss Betsey Williams. Captain Williams, Mr. Darrel's son-in-law, was master of a vessel which traded to several places in America and the West Indies, and he was seldom at home long together.

Mrs. Williams was a kind-hearted good woman, and she treated all her slaves well. She had only one daughter, Miss Betsey, for whom I was purchased, and who was about my own age. I was made quite a pet of by Miss Betsey, and loved her very much. She used to lead me about by the hand, and call me her little nigger. This was the happiest period of my life; for I was too young to understand rightly my condition as a slave, and too thoughtless and full of spirits to look forward to the days of toil and sorrow.

My mother was a household slave in the same family. I was under her own care, and my little brothers and sisters were my play-fellows and companions. My mother had several fine children after she came to Mrs. Williams,—three girls and two boys. The tasks given out to us children were light, and we used to play together with Miss Betsey, with as much freedom almost as if she had been our sister.

My master, however, was a very harsh, selfish man; and we always dreaded his return from sea. His wife was herself much afraid of him; and, during his stay at home, seldom dared to shew her usual kindness to the slaves. He often left her, in the most distressed circumstances, to reside in other female society, at some place in the West Indies of which I have forgot the name. My poor mistress bore his ill-treatment with great patience, and all her slaves loved and pitied her. I was truly attached to her, and, next to my own mother, loved her better than any creature in the world. My obedience to her commands was cheerfully given: it sprung solely from the affection I felt for her, and not from fear of the power which the white people's law had given her over me.

I had scarcely reached my twelfth year when my mistress became too poor to keep so many of us at home; and she hired me out to Mrs. Pruden, a lady who lived about five miles off, in the adjoining parish, in a large house near the sea. I cried bitterly at parting with my dear mistress and Miss Betsey, and when I kissed my mother and brothers and sisters, I thought my young heart would break, it pained me so. But there was no help; I was forced to go. Good Mrs. Williams comforted me by saying that I should still be near the home I was about to quit, and might come over and see her and my kindred whenever I could obtain leave of absence from Mrs. Pruden. A few hours after this I was taken to a strange house, and found myself among strange people. This separation seemed a sore trial to me then; but oh! 'twas light, light to the trials I have since endured!—'twas nothing—nothing to be mentioned with them; but I was a child then, and it was according to my strength.

I knew that Mrs. Williams could no longer maintain me; that she was fain to part with me for my food and clothing; and I tried to submit myself to the change. My new mistress was a passionate woman; but yet she did not treat me very unkindly. I do not remember her striking me but once, and that was for going to see Mrs. Williams when I heard she was sick, and staying longer than she had given me leave to do. All my employment at this time was nursing a sweet baby, little Master Daniel; and I grew so fond of my nursling that it was my greatest delight to walk out with him by the sea-shore, accompanied by his brother and sister, Miss Fanny and Master James.—Dear Miss Fanny! She was a sweet, kind young lady, and so fond of me that she wished me to learn all that she knew herself; and her method of teaching me was as follows:—Directly she had said her lessons to her grandmamma, she used to come running to me, and make me repeat them one by one after her; and in a few months I was able not only to say my letters but to spell many small words. But this happy state was not to last long. Those days were too pleasant to last. My heart always softens when I think of them.

At this time Mrs. Williams died. I was told suddenly of her death, and my grief was so great that, forgetting I had the baby in my arms, I ran away directly to my poor mistress's house; but reached it only in time to see the corpse carried out. Oh, that was a day of sorrow,—a heavy day! All the slaves cried. My mother cried and lamented her sore; and I (foolish creature!) vainly entreated them to bring my dear mistress back to life. I knew nothing rightly about death then, and it seemed a hard thing to bear. When I thought about my mistress I felt as if the world was all gone wrong; and for many days and weeks I could think of nothing else. I returned to Mrs. Pruden's; but my sorrow was too great to be comforted, for my own dear mistress was always in my mind. Whether in the house or abroad, my thoughts were always talking to me about her.

I staid at Mrs. Pruden's about three months after this; I was then sent back to Mr. Williams to be sold. Oh, that was a sad sad time! I recollect the day well.

Mrs. Pruden came to me and said, "Mary, you will have to go home directly; your master is going to be married, and he means to sell you and two of your sisters to raise money for the wedding." Hearing this I burst out a crying,—though I was then far from being sensible of the full weight of my misfortune, or of the misery that waited for me. Besides, I did not like to leave Mrs. Pruden, and the dear baby, who had grown very fond of me. For some time I could scarcely believe that Mrs. Pruden was in earnest, till I received orders for my immediate return.—Dear Miss Fanny! how she cried at parting with me, whilst I kissed and hugged the baby, thinking I should never see him again. I left Mrs. Pruden's, and walked home with a heart full of sorrow. The idea of being sold away from my mother and Miss Betsey was so frightful, that I dared not trust myself to think about it. We had been bought of Mr. Myners, as I have mentioned, by Miss Betsey's grandfather, and given to her, so that we were by right her property, and I never thought we should be separated or sold away from her.

When I reached the house, I went in directly to Miss Betsey. I found her in great distress; and she cried out as soon as she saw me, "Oh, Mary! my father is going to sell you all to raise money to marry that wicked woman. You are my slaves, and he has no right to sell you; but it is all to please her." She then told me that my mother was living with her father's sister at a house close by, and I went there to see her. It was a sorrowful meeting; and we lamented with a great and sore crying our unfortunate situation. "Here comes one of my poor picaninnies!" she said, the moment I came in, "one of the poor slave-brood who are to be sold to-morrow."

Oh dear! I cannot bear to think of that day,—it is too much.—It recalls the great grief that filled my heart, and the woeful thoughts that passed to and fro through my mind, whilst listening to the pitiful words of my poor mother, weeping for the loss of her children. I wish I could find words to tell you all I then felt and suffered. The great God above alone knows the thoughts of the poor slave's heart, and the bitter pains which follow such separations as these. All that we love taken away from us—Oh, it is sad, sad! and sore to be borne!—I got no sleep that night for thinking of the morrow; and dear Miss Betsey was scarcely less distressed. She could not bear to part with her old playmates, and she cried sore and would not be pacified.

The black morning at length came; it came too soon for my poor mother and us. Whilst she was putting on us the new osnaburgs in which we were to be sold, she said, in a sorrowful voice, (I shall never forget it!) "See, I am shrouding my poor children; what a task for a mother!"—She then called Miss Betsey to take leave of us. "I am going to carry my little chickens to market," (these were her very words,) "take your last look of them; may be you will see them no more." "Oh, my poor slaves! my own slaves!" said dear Miss Betsey, "you belong to me; and it grieves my heart to part with you."—Miss Betsey kissed us all, and, when she left us, my mother called the rest of the slaves to bid us good bye. One of them, a woman named Moll, came with her infant in her arms. "Ay!" said my mother, seeing her turn away and look at her child with the tears in her eyes, "your turn will come next." The slaves could say nothing to comfort us; they could only weep and lament with us. When I left my dear little brothers and the house in which I had been brought up, I thought my heart would burst.

Our mother, weeping as she went, called me away with the children Hannah and Dinah, and we took the road that led to Hamble Town, which we reached about four o'clock in the afternoon. We followed my mother to the market-place, where she placed us in a row against a large house, with our backs to the wall and our arms folded across our breasts. I, as the eldest, stood first, Hannah next to me, then Dinah; and our mother stood beside, crying over us. My heart throbbed with grief and terror so violently, that I pressed my hands quite tightly across my breast, but I could not keep it still, and it continued to leap as though it would burst out of my body. But who cared for that? Did one of the many by-standers, who were looking at us so carelessly, think of the pain that wrung the hearts of the negro woman and her young ones? No, no! They were not all bad, I dare say; but slavery hardens white people's hearts towards the blacks; and many of them were not slow to make their remarks upon us aloud, without regard to our grief—though their light words fell like cayenne on the fresh wounds of our hearts. Oh those white people have small hearts who can only feel for themselves.

At length the vendue master, who was to offer us for sale like sheep or cattle, arrived, and asked my mother which was the eldest. She said nothing, but pointed to me. He took me by the hand, and led me out into the middle of the street, and, turning me slowly round, exposed me to the view of those who attended the vendue. I was soon surrounded by strange men, who examined and handled me in the same manner that a butcher would a calf or a lamb he was about to purchase, and who talked about my shape and size in like words—as if I could no more understand their meaning than the dumb beasts. I was then put up to sale. The bidding commenced at a few pounds, and gradually rose to fifty-seven,[1] when I was knocked down to the highest bidder; and the people who stood by said that I had fetched a great sum for so young a slave.

I then saw my sisters led forth, and sold to different owners; so that we had not the sad satisfaction of being partners in bondage. When the sale was over, my mother hugged and kissed us, and mourned over us, begging of us to keep up a good heart, and do our duty to our new masters. It was a sad parting; one went one way, one another, and our poor mammy went home with nothing.[2]

My new master was a Captain I——, who lived at Spanish Point. After parting with my mother and sisters, I followed him to his store, and he gave me into the charge of his son, a lad about my own age, Master Benjy, who took me to my new home. I did not know where I was going, or what my new master would do with me. My heart was quite broken with grief, and my thoughts went back continually to those from whom I had been so suddenly parted. "Oh, my mother! my mother!" I kept saying to myself, "Oh, my mammy and my sisters and my brothers, shall I never see you again!"

Oh, the trials! the trials! they make the salt water come into my eyes when I think of the days in which I was afflicted—the times that are gone; when I mourned and grieved with a young heart for those whom I loved.

It was night when I reached my new home. The house was large, and built at the bottom of a very high hill; but I could not see much of it that night. I saw too much of it afterwards. The stones and the timber were the best things in it; they were not so hard as the hearts of the owners.[3]

Before I entered the house, two slave women, hired from another owner, who were at work in the yard, spoke to me, and asked who I belonged to? I replied, "I am come to live here." "Poor child, poor child!" they both said; "you must keep a good heart, if you are to live here."—When I went in, I stood up crying in a corner. Mrs. I—— came and took off my hat, a little black silk hat Miss Pruden made for me, and said in a rough voice, "You are not come here to stand up in corners and cry, you are come here to work." She then put a child into my arms, and, tired as I was, I was forced instantly to take up my old occupation of a nurse.—I could not bear to look at my mistress, her countenance was so stern. She was a stout tall woman with a very dark complexion, and her brows were always drawn together into a frown. I thought of the words of the two slave women when I saw Mrs. I——, and heard the harsh sound of her voice.

The person I took the most notice of that night was a French Black called Hetty, whom my master took in privateering from another vessel, and made his slave. She was the most active woman I ever saw, and she was tasked to her utmost. A few minutes after my arrival she came in from milking the cows, and put the sweet-potatoes on for supper. She then fetched home the sheep, and penned them in the fold; drove home the cattle, and staked them about the pond side;[4] fed and rubbed down my master's horse, and gave the hog and the fed cow[5] their suppers; prepared the beds, and undressed the children, and laid them to sleep. I liked to look at her and watch all her doings, for hers was the only friendly face I had as yet seen, and I felt glad that she was there. She gave me my supper of potatoes and milk, and a blanket to sleep upon, which she spread for me in the passage before the door of Mrs. I——'s chamber.

I got a sad fright, that night. I was just going to sleep, when I heard a noise in my mistress's room; and she presently called out to inquire if some work was finished that she had ordered Hetty to do. "No, Ma'am, not yet," was Hetty's answer from below. On hearing this, my master started up from his bed, and just as he was, in his shirt, ran down stairs with a long cow-skin[6] in his hand. I heard immediately after, the cracking of the thong, and the house rang to the shrieks of poor Hetty, who kept crying out, "Oh, Massa! Massa! me dead. Massa! have mercy upon me—don't kill me outright."—This was a sad beginning for me. I sat up upon my blanket, trembling with terror, like a frightened hound, and thinking that my turn would come next. At length the house became still, and I forgot for a little while all my sorrows by falling fast asleep.

The next morning my mistress set about instructing me in my tasks. She taught me to do all sorts of household work; to wash and bake, pick cotton and wool, and wash floors, and cook. And she taught me (how can I ever forget it!) more things than these; she caused me to know the exact difference between the smart of the rope, the cart-whip, and the cow-skin, when applied to my naked body by her own cruel hand. And there was scarcely any punishment more dreadful than the blows I received on my face and head from her hard heavy fist. She was a fearful woman, and a savage mistress to her slaves.

There were two little slave boys in the house, on whom she vented her bad temper in a special manner. One of these children was a mulatto, called Cyrus, who had been bought while an infant in his mother's arms; the other, Jack, was an African from the coast of Guinea, whom a sailor had given or sold to my master. Seldom a day passed without these boys receiving the most severe treatment, and often for no fault at all. Both my master and mistress seemed to think that they had a right to ill-use them at their pleasure; and very often accompanied their commands with blows, whether the children were behaving well or ill. I have seen their flesh ragged and raw with licks.—Lick—lick—they were never secure one moment from a blow, and their lives were passed in continual fear. My mistress was not contented with using the whip, but often pinched their cheeks and arms in the most cruel manner. My pity for these poor boys was soon transferred to myself; for I was licked, and flogged, and pinched by her pitiless fingers in the neck and arms, exactly as they were. To strip me naked—to hang me up by the wrists and lay my flesh open with the cow-skin, was an ordinary punishment for even a slight offence. My mistress often robbed me too of the hours that belong to sleep. She used to sit up very late, frequently even until morning; and I had then to stand at a bench and wash during the greater part of the night, or pick wool and cotton; and often I have dropped down overcome by sleep and fatigue, till roused from a state of stupor by the whip, and forced to start up to my tasks.

Poor Hetty, my fellow slave, was very kind to me, and I used to call her my Aunt; but she led a most miserable life, and her death was hastened (at least the slaves all believed and said so,) by the dreadful chastisement she received from my master during her pregnancy. It happened as follows. One of the cows had dragged the rope away from the stake to which Hetty had fastened it, and got loose. My master flew into a terrible passion, and ordered the poor creature to be stripped quite naked, notwithstanding her pregnancy, and to be tied up to a tree in the yard. He then flogged her as hard as he could lick, both with the whip and cow-skin, till she was all over streaming with blood. He rested, and then beat her again and again. Her shrieks were terrible. The consequence was that poor Hetty was brought to bed before her time, and was delivered after severe labour of a dead child. She appeared to recover after her confinement, so far that she was repeatedly flogged by both master and mistress afterwards; but her former strength never returned to her. Ere long her body and limbs swelled to a great size; and she lay on a mat in the kitchen, till the water burst out of her body and she died. All the slaves said that death was a good thing for poor Hetty; but I cried very much for her death. The manner of it filled me with horror. I could not bear to think about it; yet it was always present to my mind for many a day.

After Hetty died all her labours fell upon me, in addition to my own. I had now to milk eleven cows every morning before sunrise, sitting among the damp weeds; to take care of the cattle as well as the children; and to do the work of the house. There was no end to my toils—no end to my blows. I lay down at night and rose up in the morning in fear and sorrow; and often wished that like poor Hetty I could escape from this cruel bondage and be at rest in the grave. But the hand of that God whom then I knew not, was stretched over me; and I was mercifully preserved for better things. It was then, however, my heavy lot to weep, weep, weep, and that for years; to pass from one misery to another, and from one cruel master to a worse. But I must go on with the thread of my story.

One day a heavy squall of wind and rain came on suddenly, and my mistress sent me round the corner of the house to empty a large earthen jar. The jar was already cracked with an old deep crack that divided it in the middle, and in turning it upside down to empty it, it parted in my hand. I could not help the accident, but I was dreadfully frightened, looking forward to a severe punishment. I ran crying to my mistress, "O mistress, the jar has come in two." "You have broken it, have you?" she replied; "come directly here to me." I came trembling; she stripped and flogged me long and severely with the cow-skin; as long as she had strength to use the lash, for she did not give over till she was quite tired.—When my master came home at night, she told him of my fault; and oh, frightful! how he fell a swearing. After abusing me with every ill name he could think of, (too, too bad to speak in England,) and giving me several heavy blows with his hand, he said, "I shall come home to-morrow morning at twelve, on purpose to give you a round hundred." He kept his word—Oh sad for me! I cannot easily forget it. He tied me up upon a ladder, and gave me a hundred lashes with his own hand, and master Benjy stood by to count them for him. When he had licked me for some time he sat down to take breath; then after resting, he beat me again and again, until he was quite wearied, and so hot (for the weather was very sultry), that he sank back in his chair, almost like to faint. While my mistress went to bring him drink, there was a dreadful earthquake. Part of the roof fell down, and every thing in the house went—clatter, clatter, clatter. Oh I thought the end of all things near at hand; and I was so sore with the flogging, that I scarcely cared whether I lived or died. The earth was groaning and shaking; every thing tumbling about; and my mistress and the slaves were shrieking and crying out, "The earthquake! the earthquake!" It was an awful day for us all.

During the confusion I crawled away on my hands and knees, and laid myself down under the steps of the piazza, in front of the house. I was in a dreadful state—my body all blood and bruises, and I could not help moaning piteously. The other slaves, when they saw me, shook their heads and said, "Poor child! poor child!"—I lay there till the morning, careless of what might happen, for life was very weak in me, and I wished more than ever to die. But when we are very young, death always seems a great way off, and it would not come that night to me. The next morning I was forced by my master to rise and go about my usual work, though my body and limbs were so stiff and sore, that I could not move without the greatest pain.—Nevertheless, even after all this severe punishment, I never heard the last of that jar; my mistress was always throwing it in my face.

Some little time after this, one of the cows got loose from the stake, and eat one of the sweet-potatoe slips. I was milking when my master found it out. He came to me, and without any more ado, stooped down, and taking off his heavy boot, he struck me such a severe blow in the small of my back, that I shrieked with agony, and thought I was killed; and I feel a weakness in that part to this day. The cow was frightened at his violence, and kicked down the pail and spilt the milk all about. My master knew that this accident was his own fault, but he was so enraged that he seemed glad of an excuse to go on with his ill usage. I cannot remember how many licks he gave me then, but he beat me till I was unable to stand, and till he himself was weary.

After this I ran away and went to my mother, who was living with Mr. Richard Darrel. My poor mother was both grieved and glad to see me; grieved because I had been so ill used, and glad because she had not seen me for a long, long while. She dared not receive me into the house, but she hid me up in a hole in the rocks near, and brought me food at night, after every body was asleep. My father, who lived at Crow-Lane, over the salt-water channel, at last heard of my being hid up in the cavern, and he came and took me back to my master. Oh I was loth, loth to go back; but as there was no remedy, I was obliged to submit.

When we got home, my poor father said to Capt. I— —, "Sir, I am sorry that my child should be forced to run away from her owner; but the treatment she has received is enough to break her heart. The sight of her wounds has nearly broke mine.—I entreat you, for the love of God, to forgive her for running away, and that you will be a kind master to her in future." Capt. I— — said I was used as well as I deserved, and that I ought to be punished for running away. I then took courage and said that I could stand the floggings no longer; that I was weary of my life, and therefore I had run away to my mother; but mothers could only weep and mourn over their children, they could not save them from cruel masters—from the whip, the rope, and the cow-skin. He told me to hold my tongue and go about my work, or he would find a way to settle me. He did not, however, flog me that day.

For five years after this I remained in his house, and almost daily received the same harsh treatment. At length he put me on board a sloop, and to my great joy sent me away to Turk's Island. I was not permitted to see my mother or father, or poor sisters and brothers, to say good bye, though going away to a strange land, and might never see them again. Oh the Buckra people who keep slaves think that black people are like cattle, without natural affection. But my heart tells me it is far otherwise.

We were nearly four weeks on the voyage, which was unusually long. Sometimes we had a light breeze, sometimes a great calm, and the ship made no way; so that our provisions and water ran very low, and we were put upon short allowance. I should almost have been starved had it not been for the kindness of a black man called Anthony, and his wife, who had brought their own victuals, and shared them with me.

When we went ashore at the Grand Quay, the captain sent me to the house of my new master, Mr. D— —, to whom Captain I— —had sold me. Grand Quay is a small town upon a sandbank; the houses low and built of wood. Such was my new master's. The first person I saw, on my arrival, was Mr. D— —, a stout sulky looking man, who carried me through the hall to show me to his wife and children. Next day I was put up by the vendue master to know how much I was worth, and I was valued at one hundred pounds currency.

My new master was one of the owners or holders of the salt ponds, and he received a certain sum for every slave that worked upon his premises, whether they were young or old. This sum was allowed him out of the profits arising from the salt works. I was immediately sent to work in the salt water with the rest of the slaves. This work was perfectly new to me. I was given a half barrel and a shovel, and had to stand up to my knees in the water, from four o'clock in the morning till nine, when we were given some Indian corn boiled in water, which we were obliged to swallow as fast as we could for fear the rain should come on and melt the salt. We were then called again to our tasks, and worked through the heat of the day; the sun flaming upon our heads like fire, and raising salt blisters in those parts which were not completely covered. Our feet and legs, from standing in the salt water for so many hours, soon became full of dreadful boils, which eat down in some cases to the very bone, afflicting the sufferers with great torment. We came home at twelve; ate our corn soup, called blawly, as fast as we could, and went back to our employment till dark at night. We then shovelled up the salt in large heaps, and went down to the sea, where we washed the pickle from our limbs, and cleaned the barrows and shovels from the salt. When we returned to the house, our master gave us each our allowance of raw Indian corn, which we pounded in a mortar and boiled in water for our suppers.

We slept in a long shed, divided into narrow slips, like the stalls used for cattle. Boards fixed upon stakes driven into the ground, without mat or covering, were our only beds. On Sundays, after we had washed the salt bags, and done other work required of us, we went into the bush and cut the long soft grass, of which we made trusses for our legs and feet to rest upon, for they were so full of the salt boils that we could get no rest lying upon the bare boards.

Though we worked from morning till night, there was no satisfying Mr. D——. I hoped, when I left Capt. I——, that I should have been better off, but I found it was but going from one butcher to another. There was this difference between them: my former master used to beat me while raging and foaming with passion; Mr. D—— was usually quite calm. He would stand by and give orders for a slave to be cruelly whipped, and assist in the punishment, without moving a muscle of his face; walking about and taking snuff with the greatest composure. Nothing could touch his hard heart—neither sighs, nor tears, nor prayers, nor streaming blood; he was deaf to our cries, and careless of our sufferings. Mr. D—— has often stripped me naked, hung me up by the wrists, and beat me with the cow-skin, with his own hand, till my body was raw with gashes. Yet there was nothing very remarkable in this; for it might serve as a sample of the common usage of the slaves on that horrible island.

Owing to the boils in my feet, I was unable to wheel the barrow fast through the sand, which got into the sores, and made me stumble at every step; and my master, having no pity for my sufferings from this cause, rendered them far more intolerable, by chastising me for not being able to move so fast as he wished me. Another of our employments was to row a little way off from the shore in a boat, and dive for large stones to build a wall round our master's house. This was very hard work; and the great waves breaking over us continually, made us often so giddy that we lost our footing, and were in danger of being drowned.

Ah, poor me!—my tasks were never ended. Sick or well, it was work—work—work!—After the diving season was over, we were sent to the South Creek, with large bills, to cut up mangoes to burn lime with. Whilst one party of slaves were thus employed, another were sent to the other side of the island to break up coral out of the sea.

When we were ill, let our complaint be what it might, the only medicine given to us was a great bowl of hot salt water, with salt mixed with it, which made us very sick. If we could not keep up with the rest of the gang of slaves, we were put in the stocks, and severely flogged the next morning. Yet, not the less, our master expected, after we had thus been kept from our rest, and our limbs rendered stiff and sore with ill usage, that we should still go through the ordinary tasks of the day all the same.—Sometimes we had to work all night, measuring salt to load a vessel; or turning a machine to draw water out of the sea for the salt-making. Then we had no sleep—no rest—but were forced to work as fast as we could, and go on again all next day the same as usual. Work—work—work—Oh that Turk's Island was a horrible place! The people in England, I am sure, have never found out what is carried on there. Cruel, horrible place!

Mr. D—— had a slave called old Daniel, whom he used to treat in the most cruel manner. Poor Daniel was lame in the hip, and could not keep up with the rest of the slaves; and our master would order him to be stripped and laid down on the ground, and have him beaten with a rod of rough briar till his skin was quite red and raw. He would then call for a bucket of salt, and fling upon the raw flesh till the man writhed on the ground like a worm, and screamed aloud with agony. This poor man's wounds were never healed, and I have often seen them full of maggots, which increased his torments to an intolerable degree. He was an object of pity and terror to the whole gang of slaves, and in his wretched case we saw, each of us, our own lot, if we should live to be as old.

Oh the horrors of slavery!—How the thought of it pains my heart! But the truth ought to be told of it; and what my eyes have seen I think it is my duty to relate; for few people in England know what slavery is. I have been a slave—I have felt what a slave feels, and I know what a slave knows; and I would have all the good people in England to know it too, that they may break our chains, and set us free.

Mr. D—— had another slave called Ben. He being very hungry, stole a little rice one night after he came in from work, and cooked it for his supper. But his master soon discovered the theft; locked him up all night; and kept him without food till one o'clock the next day. He then hung Ben up by his hands, and beat him from time to time till the slaves came in at night. We found the poor creature hung up when we came home; with a pool of blood beneath him, and our master still licking him. But this was not the worst. My master's son was in the habit of stealing the rice and rum. Ben had seen him do this, and thought he might do the same, and when master found out that Ben had stolen the rice and swore to punish him, he tried to excuse himself by saying that Master Dickey did the same thing every night. The lad denied it to his father, and was so angry with Ben for informing against him, that out of revenge he ran and got a bayonet, and whilst the poor wretch was suspended by his hands and writhing under his wounds, he run it quite through his foot. I was not by when he did it, but I saw the wound when I came home, and heard Ben tell the manner in which it was done.

I must say something more about this cruel son of a cruel father.—He had no heart—no fear of God; he had been brought up by a bad father in a bad path, and he delighted to follow in the same steps. There was a little old woman among the slaves called Sarah, who was nearly past work; and, Master Dickey being the overseer of the slaves just then, this poor creature, who was subject to several bodily infirmities, and was not quite right in her head, did not wheel the barrow fast enough to please him. He threw her down on the ground, and after beating her severely, he took her up in his arms and flung her among the prickly-pear bushes, which are all covered over with sharp venomous prickles. By this her naked flesh was so grievously wounded, that her body swelled and festered all over, and she died a few days after. In telling my own sorrows, I cannot pass by those of my fellow-slaves—for when I think of my own griefs, I remember theirs.

I think it was about ten years I had worked in the salt ponds at Turk's Island, when my master left off business, and retired to a house he had in Bermuda, leaving his son to succeed him in the island. He took me with him to wait upon his daughters; and I was joyful, for I was sick, sick of Turk's Island, and my heart yearned to see my native place again, my mother, and my kindred.

I had seen my poor mother during the time I was a slave in Turk's Island. One Sunday morning I was on the beach with some of the slaves, and we saw a sloop come in loaded with slaves to work in the salt water. We got a boat and went aboard. When I came upon the deck I asked the black people, "Is there any one here for me?" "Yes," they said, "your mother." I thought they said this in jest—I could scarcely believe them for joy; but when I saw my poor mammy my joy was turned to sorrow, for she had gone from her senses. "Mammy," I said, "is this you?" She did not know me. "Mammy," I said, "what's the matter?" She began to talk foolishly, and said that she had been under the vessel's bottom. They had been overtaken by a violent storm at sea. My poor mother had never been on the sea before, and she was so ill, that she lost her senses, and it was long before she came quite to herself again. She had a sweet child with her—a little sister I had never seen, about four years of age, called Rebecca. I took her on shore with me, for I felt I should love her directly; and I kept her with me a week. Poor little thing! her's has been a sad life, and continues so to this day. My mother worked for some years on the island, but was taken back to Bermuda some time before my master carried me again thither.[7]

After I left Turk's Island, I was told by some negroes that came over from it, that the poor slaves had built up a place with boughs and leaves, where they might meet for prayers, but the white people pulled it down twice, and would not allow them even a shed for prayers. A flood came down soon after and washed away many houses, filled the place with sand, and overflowed the ponds: and I do think that this was for their wickedness; for the Buckra men[8] there were very wicked. I saw and heard much that was very very bad at that place.

I was several years the slave of Mr. D—— after I returned to my native place. Here I worked in the grounds. My work was planting and hoeing sweet-potatoes, Indian corn, plantains, bananas, cabbages, pumpkins, onions, &c. I did all the household work, and attended upon a horse and cow besides,—going also upon all errands. I had to curry the horse—to clean and feed him—and sometimes to ride him a little. I had more than enough to do—but still it was not so very bad as Turk's Island.

My old master often got drunk, and then he would get in a fury with his daughter, and beat her till she was not fit to be seen. I remember on one occasion, I had gone to fetch water, and when I Was coming up the hill I heard a great screaming; I ran as fast as I could to the house, put down the water, and went into the chamber, where I found my master beating Miss D—— dreadfully. I strove with all my strength to get her away from him; for she was all black and blue with bruises. He had beat her with his fist, and almost killed her. The people gave me credit for getting her away. He turned round and began to lick me. Then I said, "Sir, this is not Turk's Island." I can't repeat his answer, the words were too wicked—too bad to say. He wanted to treat me the same in Bermuda as he had done in Turk's Island.

He had an ugly fashion of stripping himself quite naked, and ordering me then to wash him in a tub of water. This was worse to me than all the licks. Sometimes when he called me to wash him I would not come, my eyes were so full of shame. He would then come to beat me. One time I had plates and knives in my hand, and I dropped both plates and knives, and some of the plates were broken. He struck me so severely for this, that at last I defended myself, for I thought it was high time to do so. I then told him I would not live longer with him, for he was a very indecent man—very spiteful, and too indecent; with no shame for his servants, no shame for his own flesh. So I went away to a neighbouring house and sat down and cried till the next morning, when I went home again, not knowing what else to do.

After that I was hired to work at Cedar Hills, and every Saturday night I paid the money to my master. I had plenty of work to do there—plenty of washing; but yet I made myself pretty comfortable. I earned two dollars and a quarter a week, which is twenty pence a day.

During the time I worked there, I heard that Mr. John Wood was going to Antigua. I felt a great wish to go there, and I went to Mr. D——, and asked him to let me go in Mr. Wood's service. Mr. Wood did not then want to purchase me; it was my own fault that I came under him, I was so anxious to go. It was ordained to be, I suppose; God led me there. The truth is, I did not wish to be any longer the slave of my indecent master.

Mr. Wood took me with him to Antigua, to the town of St. John's, where he lived. This was about fifteen years ago. He did not then know whether I was to be sold; but Mrs. Wood found that I could work, and she wanted to buy me. Her husband then wrote to my master to inquire whether I was to be sold? Mr. D—— wrote in reply, "that I should not be sold to any one that would treat me ill." It was strange he should say this, when he had treated me so ill himself. So I was purchased by Mr. Wood for 300 dollars, (or £100 Bermuda currency.)[9]

My work there was to attend the chambers and nurse the child, and to go down to the pond and wash clothes. But I soon fell ill of the rheumatism, and grew so very lame that I was forced to walk with a stick. I got the Saint Anthony's fire, also, in my left leg, and became quite a cripple. No one cared much to come near me, and I was ill a long long time; for several months I could not lift the limb. I had to lie in a little old out-house, that was swarming with bugs and other vermin, which tormented me greatly; but I had no other place to lie in. I got the rheumatism by catching cold at the pond side, from washing in the fresh water; in the salt water I never got cold. The person who lived in next yard, (a Mrs. Greene,) could not bear to hear my cries and groans. She was kind, and used to send an old slave woman to help me, who sometimes brought me a little soup. When the doctor found I was so ill, he said I must be put into a bath of hot water. The old slave got the bark of some bush that was good for the pains, which she boiled in the hot water, and every night she came and put me into the bath, and did what she could for me: I don't know what I should have done, or what would have become of me, had it not been for her.—My mistress, it is true, did send me a little food; but no one from our family came near me but the cook, who used to shove my food in at the door, and say, "Molly, Molly, there's your dinner." My mistress did not care to take any trouble about me; and if the Lord had not put it into the hearts of the neighbours to be kind to me, I must, I really think, have lain and died.

It was a long time before I got well enough to work in the house. Mrs. Wood, in the meanwhile, hired a mulatto woman to nurse the child; but she was such a fine lady she wanted to be mistress over me. I thought it very hard for a coloured woman to have rule over me because I was a slave and she was free. Her name was Martha Wilcox; she was a saucy woman, very saucy; and she went and complained of me, without cause, to my mistress, and made her angry with me. Mrs. Wood told me that if I did not mind what I was about, she would get my master to strip me and give me fifty lashes: "You have been used to the whip," she said, "and you shall have it here." This was the first time she threatened to have me flogged; and she gave me the threatening so strong of what she would have done to me, that I thought I should have fallen down at her feet, I was so vexed and hurt by her words. The mulatto woman was rejoiced to have power to keep me down. She was constantly making mischief; there was no living for the slaves—no peace after she came.

I was also sent by Mrs. Wood to be put in the Cage one night, and was next morning flogged, by the magistrate's order, at her desire; and this all for a quarrel I had about a pig with another slave woman. I was flogged on my naked back on this occasion: although I was in no fault after all; for old Justice Dyett, when we came before him, said that I was in the right, and ordered the pig to be given to me. This was about two or three years after I came to Antigua.

When we moved from the middle of the town to the Point, I used to be in the house and do all the work and mind the children, though still very ill with the rheumatism. Every week I had to wash two large bundles of clothes, as much as a boy could help me to lift; but I could give no satisfaction. My mistress was always abusing and fretting after me. It is not possible to tell all her ill language.—One day she followed me foot after foot scolding and rating me. I bore in silence a great deal of ill words: at last my heart was quite full, and I told her that she ought not to use me so;—that when I was ill I might have lain and died for what she cared; and no one would then come near me to nurse me, because they were afraid of my mistress. This was a great affront. She called her husband and told him what I had said. He flew into a passion: but did not beat me then; he only abused and swore at me; and then gave me a note and bade me go and look for an owner. Not that he meant to sell me; but he did this to please his wife and to frighten me. I went to Adam White, a cooper, a free black, who had money, and asked him to buy me. He went directly to Mr. Wood, but was informed that I was not to be sold. The next day my master whipped me.

Another time (about five years ago) my mistress got vexed with me, because I fell sick and I could not keep on with my work. She complained to her husband, and he sent me off again to look for an owner. I went to a Mr. Burchell, showed him the note, and asked him to buy me for my own benefit; for I had saved about 100 dollars, and hoped, with a little help, to purchase my freedom. He accordingly went to my master:—"Mr. Wood," he said, "Molly has brought me a note that she wants an owner. If you intend to sell her, I may as well buy her as another." My master put him off and said that he did not mean to sell me. I was very sorry at this, for I had no comfort with Mrs. Wood, and I wished greatly to get my freedom.

The way in which I made my money was this.—When my master and mistress went from home, as they sometimes did, and left me to take care of the house and premises, I had a good deal of time to myself, and made the most of it. I took in washing, and sold coffee and yams and other provisions to the captains of ships. I did not sit still idling during the absence of my owners; for I wanted, by all honest means, to earn money to buy my freedom. Sometimes I bought a hog cheap on board ship, and sold it for double the money on shore; and I also earned a good deal by selling coffee. By this means I by degrees acquired a little cash. A gentleman also lent me some to help to buy my freedom—but when I could not get free he got it back again. His name was Captain Abbot.

My master and mistress went on one occasion into the country, to Date Hill, for change of air, and carried me with them to take charge of the children, and to do the work of the house. While I was in the country, I saw how the field negroes are worked in Antigua. They are worked very hard and fed but scantily. They are called out to work before daybreak, and come home after dark; and then each has to heave his bundle of grass for the cattle in the pen. Then, on Sunday morning, each slave has to go out and gather a large bundle of grass; and, when they bring it home, they have all to sit at the manager's door and wait till he come out: often have they to wait there till past eleven o'clock, without any breakfast. After that, those that have yams or potatoes, or fire-wood to sell, hasten to market to buy a dog's worth[10] of salt fish, or pork, which is a great treat for them. Some of them buy a little pickle out of the shad barrels, which they call sauce, to season their yams and Indian corn. It is very wrong, I know, to work on Sunday or go to market; but will not God call the Buckra men to answer for this on the great day of judgment—since they will give the slaves no other day?

While we were at Date Hill Christmas came; and the slave woman who had the care of the place (which then belonged to Mr. Roberts the marshal), asked me to go with her to her husband's house, to a Methodist meeting for prayer, at a plantation called Winthorps. I went; and they were the first prayers I ever understood. One woman prayed; and then they all sung a hymn; then there was another prayer and another hymn; and then they all spoke by turns of their own griefs as sinners. The husband of the woman I went with was a black driver. His name was Henry. He confessed that he had treated the slaves very cruelly; but said that he was compelled to obey the orders of his master. He prayed them all to forgive him, and he prayed that God would forgive him. He said it was a horrid thing for a ranger[11] to have sometimes to beat his own wife or sister; but he must do so if ordered by his master.

I felt sorry for my sins also. I cried the whole night, but I was too much ashamed to speak. I prayed God to forgive me. This meeting had a great impression on my mind, and led my spirit to the Moravian church; so that when I got back to town, I went and prayed to have my name put down in the Missionaries' book; and I followed the church earnestly every opportunity. I did not then tell my mistress about it; for I knew that she would not give me leave to go. But I felt I must go. Whenever I carried the children their lunch at school, I ran round and went to hear the teachers.

The Moravian ladies (Mrs. Richter, Mrs. Olufsen, and Mrs. Sauter) taught me to read in the class; and I got on very fast. In this class there were all sorts of people, old and young, grey headed folks and children; but most of them were free people. After we had done spelling, we tried to read in the Bible. After the reading was over, the missionary gave out a hymn for us to sing. I dearly loved to go to the church, it was so solemn. I never knew rightly that I had much sin till I went there. When I found out that I was a great sinner, I was very sorely grieved, and very much frightened. I used to pray God to pardon my sins for Christ's sake, and forgive me for every thing I had done amiss; and when I went home to my work, I always thought about what I had heard from the missionaries, and wished to be good that I might go to heaven. After a while I was admitted a candidate for the holy Communion.—I had been baptized long before this, in August 1817, by the Rev. Mr. Curtin, of the English Church, after I had been taught to repeat the Creed and the Lord's Prayer. I wished at that time to attend a Sunday School taught by Mr. Curtin, but he would not receive me without a written note from my master, granting his permission. I did not ask my owner's permission, from the belief that it would be refused; so that I got no farther instruction at that time from the English Church.[12]

Some time after I began to attend the Moravian Church, I met with Daniel James, afterwards my dear husband. He was a carpenter and cooper to his trade; an honest, hard-working, decent black man, and a widower. He had purchased his freedom of his mistress, old Mrs. Baker, with money he had earned whilst a slave. When he asked me to marry him, I took time to consider the matter over with myself, and would not say yes till he went to church with me and joined the Moravians. He was very industrious after he bought his freedom; and he had hired a comfortable house, and had convenient things about him. We were joined in marriage, about Christmas 1826, in the Moravian Chapel at Spring Gardens, by the Rev. Mr. Olufsen. We could not be married in the English Church. English marriage is not allowed to slaves; and no free man can marry a slave woman.

When Mr. Wood heard of my marriage, he flew into a great rage, and sent for Daniel, who was helping to build a house for his old mistress. Mr. Wood asked him who gave him a right to marry a slave of his? My husband said, "Sir, I am a free man, and thought I had a right to choose a wife; but if I had known Molly was not allowed to have a husband, I should not have asked her to marry me." Mrs. Wood was more vexed about my marriage than her husband. She could not forgive me for getting married, but stirred up Mr. Wood to flog me dreadfully with the horsewhip. I thought it very hard to be whipped at my time of life for getting a husband—I told her so. She said that she would not have nigger men about the yards and premises, or allow a nigger man's clothes to be washed in the same tub where hers were washed. She was fearful, I think, that I should lose her time, in order to wash and do things for my husband: but I had then no time to wash for myself; I was obliged to put out my own clothes, though I was always at the wash-tub.

I had not much happiness in my marriage, owing to my being a slave. It made my husband sad to see me so ill-treated. Mrs. Wood was always abusing me about him. She did not lick me herself, but she got her husband to do it for her, whilst she fretted the flesh off my bones. Yet for all this she would not sell me. She sold five slaves whilst I was with her; but though she was always finding fault with me, she would not part with me. However, Mr. Wood afterwards allowed Daniel to have a place to live in our yard, which we were very thankful for.

After this, I fell ill again with the rheumatism, and was sick a long time; but whether sick or well, I had my work to do. About this time I asked my master and mistress to let me buy my own freedom. With the help of Mr. Burchell, I could have found the means to pay Mr. Wood; for it was agreed that I should afterwards, serve Mr. Burchell a while, for the cash he was to advance for me. I was earnest in the request to my owners; but their hearts were hard—too hard to consent. Mrs. Wood was very angry—she grew quite outrageous—she called me a black devil, and asked me who had put freedom into my head. "To be free is very sweet," I said: but she took good care to keep me a slave. I saw her change colour, and I left the room.

About this time my master and mistress were going to England to put their son to school, and bring their daughters home; and they took me with them to take care of the child. I was willing to come to England: I thought that by going there I should probably get cured of my rheumatism, and should return with my master and mistress, quite well, to my husband. My husband was willing for me to come away, for he had heard that my master would free me,—and I also hoped this might prove true; but it was all a false report.

The steward of the ship was very kind to me. He and my husband were in the same class in the Moravian Church. I was thankful that he was so friendly, for my mistress was not kind to me on the passage; and she told me, when she was angry, that she did not intend to treat me any better in England than in the West Indies—that I need not expect it. And she was as good as her word.

When we drew near to England, the rheumatism seized all my limbs worse than ever, and my body was dreadfully swelled. When we landed at the Tower, I shewed my flesh to my mistress, but she took no great notice of it. We were obliged to stop at the tavern till my master got a house; and a day or two after, my mistress sent me down into the wash-house to learn to wash in the English way. In the West Indies we wash with cold water—in England with hot. I told my mistress I was afraid that putting my hands first into the hot water and then into the cold, would increase the pain in my limbs. The doctor had told my mistress long before I came from the West Indies, that I was a sickly body and the washing did not agree with me. But Mrs. Wood would not release me from the tub, so I was forced to do as I could. I grew worse, and could not stand to wash. I was then forced to sit down with the tub before me, and often through pain and weakness was reduced to kneel or to sit down on the floor, to finish my task. When I complained to my mistress of this, she only got into a passion as usual, and said washing in hot water could not hurt any one;—that I was lazy and insolent, and wanted to be free of my work; but that she would make me do it. I thought her very hard on me, and my heart rose up within me. However I kept still at that time, and went down again to wash the child's things; but the English washerwomen who were at work there, when they saw that I was so ill, had pity upon me and washed them for me.

After that, when we came up to live in Leigh Street, Mrs. Wood sorted out five bags of clothes which we had used at sea, and also such as had been worn since we came on shore, for me and the cook to wash. Elizabeth the cook told her, that she did not think that I was able to stand to the tub, and that she had better hire a woman. I also said myself, that I had come over to nurse the child, and that I was sorry I had come from Antigua, since mistress would work me so hard, without compassion for my rheumatism. Mr. and Mrs. Wood, when they heard this, rose up in a passion against me. They opened the door and bade me get out. But I was a stranger, and did not know one door in the street from another, and was unwilling to go away. They made a dreadful uproar, and from that day they constantly kept cursing and abusing me. I was obliged to wash, though I was very ill. Mrs. Wood, indeed once hired a washerwoman, but she was not well treated, and would come no more.

My master quarrelled with me another time, about one of our great washings, his wife having stirred him up to do so. He said he would compel me to do the whole of the washing given out to me, or if I again refused, he would take a short course with me: he would either send me down to the brig in the river, to carry me back to Antigua, or he would turn me at once out of doors, and let me provide for myself. I said I would willingly go back, if he would let me purchase my own freedom. But this enraged him more than all the rest: he cursed and swore at me dreadfully, and said he would never sell my freedom—if I wished to be free, I was free in England, and I might go and try what freedom would do for me, and be d——d. My heart was very sore with this treatment, but I had to go on. I continued to do my work, and did all I could to give satisfaction, but all would not do.

Shortly after, the cook left them, and then matters went on ten times worse. I always washed the child's clothes without being commanded to do it, and any thing else that was wanted in the family; though still I was very sick—very sick indeed. When the great washing came round, which was every two months, my mistress got together again a great many heavy things, such as bed-ticks, bed-coverlets, &c. for me to wash. I told her I was too ill to wash such heavy things that day. She said, she supposed I thought myself a free woman, but I was not; and if I did not do it directly I should be instantly turned out of doors. I stood a long time before I could answer, for I did not know well what to do. I knew that I was free in England, but I did not know where to go, or how to get my living; and therefore, I did not like to leave the house. But Mr. Wood said he would send for a constable to thrust me out; and at last I took courage and resolved that I would not be longer thus treated, but would go and trust to Providence. This was the fourth time they had threatened turn me out, and, go where I might, I was determined now to take them at their word; though I thought it very hard, after I had lived with them for thirteen years, and worked for them like a horse, to be driven out in this way, like a beggar. My only fault was being sick, and therefore unable to please my mistress, who thought she never could get work enough out of her slaves; and I told them so: but they only abused me and drove me out. This took place from two to three months, I think, after we came to England.

When I came away, I went to the man (one Mash) who used to black the shoes of the family, and asked his wife to get somebody to go with me to Hatton Garden to the Moravian Missionaries: these were the only persons I knew in England. The woman sent a young girl with me to the mission house, and I saw there a gentleman called Mr. Moore. I told him my whole story, and how my owners had treated me, and asked him to take in my trunk with what few clothes I had. The missionaries were very kind to me—they were sorry for my destitute situation, and gave me leave to bring my things to be placed under their care. They were very good people, and they told me to come to the church.

When I went back to Mr. Wood's to get my trunk, I saw a lady, Mrs. Pell, who was on a visit to my mistress. When Mr. and Mrs. Wood heard me come in, they set this lady to stop me, finding that they had gone too far with me. Mrs. Pell came out to me, and said, "Are you really going to leave, Molly? Don't leave, but come into the country with me." I believe she said this because she thought Mrs. Wood would easily get me back again. I replied to her, "Ma'am, this is the fourth time my master and mistress have driven me out, or threatened to drive me—and I will give them no more occasion to bid me go. I was not willing to leave them, for I am a stranger in this country, but now I must go—I can stay no longer to be so used." Mrs. Pell then went up stairs to my mistress, and told that I would go, and that she could not stop me. Mrs. Wood was very much hurt and frightened when she found I was determined to go out that day. She said, "If she goes the people will rob her, and then turn her adrift." She did not say this to me, but she spoke it loud enough for me to hear; that it might induce me not to go, I suppose. Mr. Wood also asked me where I was going to. I told him where I had been, and that I should never have gone away had I not been driven out by my owners. He had given me a written paper some time before, which said that I had come with them to England by my own desire; and that was true. It said also that I left them of my own free will, because I was a free woman in England; and that I was idle and would not do my work—which was not true. I gave this paper afterwards to a gentleman who inquired into my case.[13]

I went into the kitchen and got my clothes out. The nurse and the servant girl were there, and I said to the man who was going to take out my trunk, "Stop, before you take up this trunk, and hear what I have to say before these people. I am going out of this house, as I was ordered; but I have done no wrong at all to my owners, neither here nor in the West Indies. I always worked very hard to please them, both by night and day; but there was no giving satisfaction, for my mistress could never be satisfied with reasonable service. I told my mistress I was sick, and yet she has ordered me out of doors. This is the fourth time; and now I am going out."

And so I came out, and went and carried my trunk to the Moravians. I then returned back to Mash the shoe-black's house, and begged his wife to take me in. I had a little West Indian money in my trunk; and they got it changed for me. This helped to support me for a little while. The man's wife was very kind to me. I was very sick, and she boiled nourishing things up for me. She also sent for a doctor to see me, and he sent me medicine, which did me good, though I was ill for a long time with the rheumatic pains. I lived a good many months with these poor people, and they nursed me, and did all that lay in their power to serve me. The man was well acquainted with my situation, as he used to go to and fro to Mr. Wood's house to clean shoes and knives; and he and his wife were sorry for me.

About this time, a woman of the name of Hill told me of the Anti-Slavery Society, and went with me to their office, to inquire if they could do any thing to get me my freedom, and send me back to the West Indies. The gentlemen of the Society took me to a lawyer, who examined very strictly into my case; but told me that the laws of England could do nothing to make me free in Antigua[14]. However they did all they could for me: they gave me a little money from time to time to keep me from want; and some of them went to Mr. Wood to try to persuade him to let me return a free woman to my husband; but though they offered him, as I have heard, a large sum for my freedom, he was sulky and obstinate, and would not consent to let me go free.

This was the first winter I spent in England, and I suffered much from the severe cold, and from the rheumatic pains, which still at times torment me. However, Providence was very good to me, and I got many friends—especially some Quaker ladies, who hearing of my case, came and sought me out, and gave me good warm clothing and money. Thus I had great cause to bless God in my affliction.

When I got better I was anxious to get some work to do, as I was unwilling to eat the bread of idleness. Mrs. Mash, who was a laundress, recommended me to a lady for a charwoman. She paid me very handsomely for what work I did, and I divided the money with Mrs. Mash; for though very poor, they gave me food when my own money was done, and never suffered me to want.

In the spring, I got into service with a lady, who saw me at the house where I sometimes worked as a charwoman. This lady's name was Mrs. Forsyth. She had been in the West Indies, and was accustomed to Blacks, and liked them. I was with her six months, and went with her to Margate. She treated me well, and gave me a good character when she left London.[15]

After Mrs. Forsyth went away, I was again out of place, and went to lodgings, for which I paid two shillings a week, and found coals and candle. After eleven weeks, the money I had saved in service was all gone, and I was forced to go back to the Anti-Slavery office to ask a supply, till I could get another situation. I did not like to go back—I did not like to be idle. I would rather work for my living than get it for nothing. They were very good to give me a supply, but I felt shame at being obliged to apply for relief whilst I had strength to work.

At last I went into the service of Mr. and Mrs. Pringle, where I have been ever since, and am as comfortable as I can be while separated from my dear husband, and away from my own country and all old friends and connections. My dear mistress teaches me daily to read the word of God, and takes great pains to make me understand it. I enjoy the great privilege of being enabled to attend church three times on the Sunday; and I have met with many kind friends since I have been here, both clergymen and others. The Rev. Mr. Young, who lives in the next house, has shown me much kindness, and taken much pains to instruct me, particularly while my master and mistress were absent in Scotland. Nor must I forget, among my friends, the Rev. Mr. Mortimer, the good clergyman of the parish, under whose ministry I have now sat for upwards of twelve months. I trust in God I have profited by what I have heard from him. He never keeps back the truth, and I think he has been the means of opening my eyes and ears much better to understand the word of God. Mr. Mortimer tells me that he cannot open the eyes of my heart, but that I must pray to God to change my heart, and make me to know the truth, and the truth will make me free.

I still live in the hope that God will find a way to give me my liberty, and give me back to my husband. I endeavour to keep down my fretting, and to leave all to Him, for he knows what is good for me better than I know myself. Yet, I must confess, I find it a hard and heavy task to do so.

I am often much vexed, and I feel great sorrow when I hear some people in this country say, that the slaves do not need better usage, and do not want to be free.[16] They believe the foreign people,[17] who deceive them, and say slaves are happy. I say, Not so. How can slaves be happy when they have the halter round their neck and the whip upon their back? and are disgraced and thought no more of than beasts?—and are separated from their mothers, and husbands, and children, and sisters, just as cattle are sold and separated? Is it happiness for a driver in the field to take down his wife or sister or child, and strip them, and whip them in such a disgraceful manner?—women that have had children exposed in the open field to shame! There is no modesty or decency shown by the owner to his slaves; men, women, and children are exposed alike. Since I have been here I have often wondered how English people can go out into the West Indies and act in such a beastly manner. But when they go to the West Indies, they forget God and all feeling of shame, I think, since they can see and do such things. They tie up slaves like hogs—moor[18] them up like cattle, and they lick them, so as hogs, or cattle, or horses never were flogged;—and yet they come home and say, and make some good people believe, that slaves don't want to get out of slavery. But they put a cloak about the truth. It is not so. All slaves want to be free—to be free is very sweet. I will say the truth to English people who may read this history that my good friend, Miss S——, is now writing down for me. I have been a slave myself—I know what slaves feel—I can tell by myself what other slaves feel, and by what they have told me. The man that says slaves be quite happy in slavery—that they don't want to be free—that man is either ignorant or a lying person. I never heard a slave say so. I never heard a Buckra man say so, till I heard tell of it in England. Such people ought to be ashamed of themselves. They can't do without slaves, they say. What's the reason they can't do without slaves as well as in England? No slaves here—no whips—no stocks—no punishment, except for wicked people. They hire servants in England; and if they don't like them, they send them away: they can't lick them. Let them work ever so hard in England, they are far better off than slaves. If they get a bad master, they give warning and go hire to another. They have their liberty. That's just what we want. We don't mind hard work, if we had proper treatment, and proper wages like English servants, and proper time given in the week to keep us from breaking the Sabbath. But they won't give it: they will have work—work—work, night and day, sick or well, till we are quite done up; and we must not speak up nor look amiss, however much we be abused. And then when we are quite done up, who cares for us, more than for a lame horse? This is slavery. I tell it, to let English people know the truth; and I hope they will never leave off to pray God, and call loud to the great King of England, till all the poor blacks be given free, and slavery done up for evermore.

# SUPPLEMENT TO THE HISTORY OF MARY PRINCE.
# BY THE EDITOR.

Leaving Mary's narrative, for the present, without comment to the reader's reflections, I proceed to state some circumstances connected with her case which have fallen more particularly under my own notice, and which I consider it incumbent now to lay fully before the public.

About the latter end of November, 1828, this poor woman found her way to the office of the Anti-Slavery Society in Aldermanbury, by the aid of a person who had become acquainted with her situation, and had advised her to apply there for advice and assistance. After some preliminary examination into the accuracy of the circumstances related by her, I went along with her to Mr. George Stephen, solicitor, and requested him to investigate and draw up a statement of her case, and have it submitted to counsel, in order to ascertain whether or not, under the circumstances, her freedom could be legally established on her return to Antigua. On this occasion, in Mr. Stephen's presence and mine, she expressed, in very strong terms, her anxiety to return thither if she could go as a free person, and, at the same time, her extreme apprehensions of the fate that would probably await her if she returned as a slave. Her words were, "I would rather go into my grave than go back a slave to Antigua, though I wish to go back to my husband very much—very much—very much! I am much afraid my owners would separate me from my husband, and use me very hard, or perhaps sell me for a field negro;—and slavery is too too bad. I would rather go into my grave!"

The paper which Mr. Wood had given her before she left his house, was placed by her in Mr. Stephen's hands. It was expressed in the following terms:—

"I have already told Molly, and now give it her in writing, in order that there may be no misunderstanding on her part, that as I brought her from Antigua at her own request and entreaty, and that she is consequently now free, she is of course at liberty to take her baggage and go where she pleases. And, in consequence of her late conduct, she must do one of two things—either quit the house, or return to Antigua by the earliest opportunity, as she does not evince a disposition to make herself useful. As she is a stranger in London, I do not wish to turn her out, or would do so, as two female servants are sufficient for my establishment. If after this she does remain, it will be only during her good behaviour: but on no consideration will I allow her wages or any other remuneration for her services.

"JOHN A. WOOD."

"London, August 18, 1828."

This paper, though not devoid of inconsistencies, which will be apparent to any attentive reader, is craftily expressed; and was well devised to serve the purpose which the writer had obviously in view, namely, to frustrate any appeal which the friendless black woman might make to the sympathy of strangers, and thus prevent her from obtaining an asylum, if she left his house, from any respectable family. As she had no one to refer to for a character in this country except himself, he doubtless calculated securely on her being speedily driven back, as soon as the slender fund she had in her possession was expended, to throw herself unconditionally upon his tender mercies; and his disappointment in this expectation appears to have exasperated his feelings of resentment towards the poor woman, to a degree which few persons alive to the claims of common justice, not to speak of christianity or common humanity, could easily have anticipated. Such, at least, seems the only intelligible inference that can be drawn from his subsequent conduct.

The case having been submitted, by desire of the Anti-Slavery Committee, to the consideration of Dr. Lushington and Mr. Sergeant Stephen, it was found that there existed no legal means of compelling Mary's master to grant her manumission; and that if she returned to Antigua, she would inevitably fall again under his power, or that of his attorneys, as a slave. It was, however, resolved to try what could be effected for her by amicable negotiation; and with this view Mr. Ravenscroft, a solicitor, (Mr. Stephen's relative,) called upon Mr. Wood, in order to ascertain whether he would consent to Mary's manumission on any reasonable terms, and to refer, if required, the amount of compensation for her value to arbitration. Mr. Ravenscroft with some difficulty obtained one or two interviews, but found Mr. Wood so full of animosity against the woman, and so firmly bent against any arrangement having her freedom for its object, that the negotiation was soon broken off as hopeless. The angry slave-owner declared "that he would not move a finger about her in this country, or grant her manumission on any terms whatever; and that if she went back to the West Indies, she must take the consequences."

This unreasonable conduct of Mr. Wood, induced the Anti-Slavery Committee, after several other abortive attempts to effect a compromise, to think of bringing the case under the notice of Parliament. The heads of Mary's statement were accordingly engrossed in a Petition, which Dr. Lushington offered to present, and to give notice at the same time of his intention to bring in a Bill to provide for the entire emancipation of all slaves brought to England with the owner's consent. But before this step was taken, Dr. Lushington again had recourse to negotiation with the master; and, partly through the friendly intervention of Mr. Manning, partly by personal conference, used every persuasion in his power to induce Mr. Wood to relent and let the bondwoman go free. Seeing the matter thus seriously taken up, Mr. Wood became at length alarmed,—not relishing, it appears, the idea of having the case publicly discussed in the House of Commons; and to avert this result he submitted to temporize—assumed a demeanour of unwonted civility, and even hinted to Mr. Manning (as I was given to understand) that if he was not driven to utter hostility by the threatened exposure, he would probably meet our wishes "in his own time and way." Having gained time by these manœuvres, he adroitly endeavoured to cool the ardour of Mary's new friends, in her cause, by representing her as an abandoned and worthless woman, ungrateful towards him, and undeserving of sympathy from others; allegations which he supported by the ready affirmation of some of his West India friends, and by one or two plausible letters procured from Antigua. By these and like artifices he appears completely to have imposed on Mr. Manning, the respectable West India merchant whom Dr. Lushington had asked to negotiate with him; and he prevailed so far as to induce Dr. Lushington himself (actuated by the benevolent view of thereby best serving Mary's cause,) to abstain from any remarks upon his conduct when the petition was at last presented in Parliament. In this way he dextrously contrived to neutralize all our efforts, until the close of the Session of 1829; soon after which he embarked with his family for the West Indies.

Every exertion for Mary's relief having thus failed; and being fully convinced from a twelvemonth's observation of her conduct, that she was really a well-disposed and respectable woman; I engaged her, in December 1829, as a domestic servant in my own family. In this capacity she has remained ever since; and I am thus enabled to speak of her conduct and character with a degree of confidence I could not have otherwise done. The importance of this circumstance will appear in the sequel.

From the time of Mr. Wood's departure to Antigua, in 1829, till June or July last, no farther effort was attempted for Mary's relief. Some faint hope was still cherished that this unconscionable man would at length relent, and "in his own time and way," grant the prayer of the exiled negro woman. After waiting, however, nearly twelve months longer, and seeing the poor woman's spirits daily sinking under the sickening influence of hope deferred, I resolved on a final attempt in her behalf, through the intervention of the Moravian Missionaries, and of the Governor of Antigua. At my request, Mr. Edward Moore, agent of the Moravian Brethren in London, wrote to the Rev. Joseph Newby, their Missionary in that island, empowering him to negotiate in his own name with Mr. Wood for Mary's manumission, and to procure his consent, if possible, upon terms of ample pecuniary compensation. At the same time the excellent and benevolent William Allen, of the Society of Friends, wrote to Sir Patrick Ross, the Governor of the Colony, with whom he was on terms of friendship, soliciting him to use his influence in persuading Mr. Wood to consent: and I confess I was sanguine enough to flatter myself that we should thus at length prevail. The result proved, however, that I had not yet fully appreciated the character of the man we had to deal with.

Mr. Newby's answer arrived early in November last, mentioning that he had done all in his power to accomplish our purpose, but in vain; and that if Mary's manumission could not be obtained without Mr. Wood's consent, he believed there was no prospect of its ever being effected.

A few weeks afterwards I was informed by Mr. Allen, that he had received a letter from Sir Patrick Ross, stating that he also had used his best endeavours in the affair, but equally without effect. Sir Patrick at the same time inclosed a letter, addressed by Mr. Wood to his Secretary, Mr. Taylor, assigning his reasons for persisting in this extraordinary course. This letter requires our special attention. Its tenor is as follows:—

"My dear Sir,

"In reply to your note relative to the woman Molly, I beg you will have the kindness to oblige me by assuring his Excellency that I regret exceedingly my inability to comply with his request, which under other circumstances would afford me very great pleasure.

"There are many and powerful reasons for inducing me to refuse my sanction to her returning here in the way she seems to wish. It would be to reward the worst species of ingratitude, and subject myself to insult whenever she came in my way. Her moral character is very bad, as the police records will shew; and she would be a very troublesome character should she come here without any restraint. She is not a native of this country, and I know of no relation she has here. I induced her to take a husband, a short time before she left this, by providing a comfortable house in my yard for them, and prohibiting her going out after 10 to 12 o'clock (our bed-time) without special leave. This she considered the greatest, and indeed the only, grievance she ever complained of, and all my efforts could not prevent it. In hopes of inducing her to be steady to her husband, who was a free man, I gave him the house to occupy during our absence; but it appears the attachment was too loose to bind her, and he has taken another wife: so on that score I do her no injury.—In England she made her election, and quitted my family. This I had no right to object to; and I should have thought no more of it, but not satisfied to leave quietly, she gave every trouble and annoyance in her power, and endeavoured to injure the character of my family by the most vile and infamous falsehoods, which was embodied in a petition to the House of Commons, and would have been presented, had not my friends from this island, particularly the Hon. Mr. Byam and Dr. Coull, come forward, and disproved what she had asserted.

"It would be beyond the limits of an ordinary letter to detail her baseness, though I will do so should his Excellency wish it; but you may judge of her depravity by one circumstance, which came out before Mr. Justice Dyett, in a quarrel with another female.

"Such a thing I could not have believed possible.[19]

"Losing her value as a slave in a pecuniary point of view I consider of no consequence; for it was our intention, had she conducted herself properly and returned with us, to have given her freedom. She has taken her freedom; and all I wish is, that she would enjoy it without meddling with me.

"Let me again repeat, if his Excellency wishes it, it will afford me great pleasure to state such particulars of her, and which will be incontestably proved by numbers here, that I am sure will acquit me in his opinion of acting unkind or ungenerous towards her. I'll say nothing of the liability I should incur, under the Consolidated Slave Law, of dealing with a free person as a slave.

"My only excuse for entering so much into detail must be that of my anxious wish to stand justified in his Excellency's opinion.

"I am, my dear Sir,
Yours very truly,
John A. Wood.

"20th Oct. 1830."

"Charles Taylor, Esq.
&c. &c. &c.

"I forgot to mention that it was at her own special request that she accompanied me to England—and also that she had a considerable sum of money with her, which she had saved in my service. I knew of £36 to £40, at least, for I had some trouble to recover it from a white man, to whom she had lent it.

"J. A. W."

Such is Mr. Wood's justification of his conduct in thus obstinately refusing manumission to the Negro-woman who had escaped from his "house of bondage."

Let us now endeavour to estimate the validity of the excuses assigned, and the allegations advanced by him, for the information of Governor Sir Patrick Ross, in this deliberate statement of his case.

1. To allow the woman to return home free, would, he affirms "be to reward the worst species of ingratitude."

He assumes, it seems, the sovereign power of pronouncing a virtual sentence of banishment, for the alleged crime of ingratitude. Is this then a power which any man ought to possess over his fellow-mortal? or which any good man would ever wish to exercise? And, besides, there is no evidence whatever, beyond Mr. Wood's mere assertion, that Mary Prince owed him or his family the slightest mark of gratitude. Her account of the treatment she received in his service, may be incorrect; but her simple statement is at least supported by minute and feasible details, and, unless rebutted by positive facts, will certainly command credence from impartial minds more readily than his angry accusation, which has something absurd and improbable in its very front. Moreover, is it not absurd to term the assertion of her natural rights by a slave,—even supposing her to have been kindly dealt with by her "owners," and treated in every respect the reverse of what Mary affirms to have been her treatment by Mr. Wood and his wife,—"the worst species of ingratitude?" This may be West Indian ethics, but it will scarcely be received as sound doctrine in Europe.

2. To permit her return would be "to subject himself to insult whenever she came in his way."

This is a most extraordinary assertion. Are the laws of Antigua then so favourable to the free blacks, or the colonial police so feebly administered, that there are no sufficient restraints to protect a rich colonist like Mr. Wood,—a man who counts among his familiar friends the Honourable Mr. Byam, and Mr.

Taylor the Government Secretary,—from being insulted by a poor Negro-woman? It is preposterous.

3. Her moral character is so bad, that she would prove very troublesome should she come to the colony "without any restraint."

"Any restraint?" Are there no restraints (supposing them necessary) short of absolute slavery to keep "troublesome characters" in order? But this, I suppose, is the argumentum ad gubernatorem—to frighten the governor. She is such a termagant, it seems, that if she once gets back to the colony free, she will not only make it too hot for poor Mr. Wood, but the police and courts of justice will scarce be a match for her! Sir Patrick Ross, no doubt, will take care how he intercedes farther for so formidable a virago! How can one treat such arguments seriously?

4. She is not a native of the colony, and he knows of no relation she has there.

True: But was it not her home (so far as a slave can have a home) for thirteen or fourteen years? Were not the connexions, friendships, and associations of her mature life formed there? Was it not there she hoped to spend her latter years in domestic tranquillity with her husband, free from the lash of the taskmaster? These considerations may appear light to Mr. Wood, but they are every thing to this poor woman.

5. He induced her, he says, to take a husband, a short time before she left Antigua, and gave them a comfortable house in his yard, &c. &c.

This paragraph merits attention. He "induced her to take a husband?" If the fact were true, what brutality of mind and manners does it not indicate among these slave-holders? They refuse to legalize the marriages of their slaves, but induce them to form such temporary connexions as may suit the owner's conveniency, just as they would pair the lower animals; and this man has the effrontery to tell us so! Mary, however, tells a very different story, (see page 17;) and her assertion, independently of other proof, is at least as credible as Mr. Wood's. The reader will judge for himself as to the preponderance of internal evidence in the conflicting statements.

6. He alleges that she was, before marriage, licentious, and even depraved in her conduct, and unfaithful to her husband afterwards.

These are serious charges. But if true, or even partially true, how comes it that a person so correct in his family hours and arrangements as Mr. Wood professes to be, and who expresses so edifying a horror of licentiousness, could reconcile it to his conscience to keep in the bosom of his family so depraved, as well as so troublesome a character for at least thirteen years, and confide to her for long periods too the charge of his house and the care of his children—for such I shall shew to have been the facts? How can he account for not having rid himself with all speed, of so disreputable an inmate—he who values her loss so little "in a pecuniary point of view?" How can he account for having sold five other slaves in that period, and yet have retained this shocking woman—nay, even have refused to sell her, on more than one occasion, when offered her full value? It could not be from ignorance of her character, for the circumstance which he adduces as a proof of her shameless depravity, and which I have omitted on account of its indecency, occurred, it would appear, not less than ten years ago. Yet, notwithstanding her alleged ill qualities and habits of gross immorality, he has not only constantly refused to part with her; but after thirteen long years, brings her to England as an attendant on his wife and children, with the avowed intention of carrying her back along with his maiden daughter, a young lady returning from school! Such are the extraordinary facts; and until Mr. Wood shall reconcile these singular inconsistencies between his actions and his allegations, he must not be surprised if we in England prefer giving credit to the former rather than the latter; although at present it appears somewhat difficult to say which side of the alternative is the more creditable to his own character.

7. Her husband, he says, has taken another wife; "so that on that score," he adds, "he does her no injury."

Supposing this fact be true, (which I doubt, as I doubt every mere assertion from so questionable a quarter,) I shall take leave to put a question or two to Mr. Wood's conscience. Did he not write from England to his friend Mr. Darrel, soon after Mary left his house, directing him to turn her husband, Daniel James, off his premises, on account of her offence; telling him to inform James at the same time that his wife had taken up with another man, who had robbed her of all she had—a calumny as groundless as it was cruel? I further ask if the person who invented this story (whoever he may be,) was not likely enough to impose similar fabrications on the poor negro man's credulity, until he may have been induced to prove false to his marriage vows, and to "take another wife," as Mr. Wood coolly expresses it? But withal, I strongly doubt the fact of Daniel James' infidelity; for there is now before me a letter from himself to

Mary, dated in April 1830, couched in strong terms of conjugal affection; expressing his anxiety for her speedy return, and stating that he had lately "received a grace" (a token of religious advancement) in the Moravian church, a circumstance altogether incredible if the man were living in open adultery, as Mr. Wood's assertion implies.

8. Mary, he says, endeavoured to injure the character of his family by infamous falsehoods, which were embodied in a petition to the House of Commons, and would have been presented, had not his friends from Antigua, the Hon. Mr. Byam, and Dr. Coull, disproved her assertions.

I can say something on this point from my own knowledge. Mary's petition contained simply a brief statement of her case, and, among other things, mentioned the treatment she had received from Mr. and Mrs. Wood. Now the principal facts are corroborated by other evidence, and Mr. Wood must bring forward very different testimony from that of Dr. Coull before well-informed persons will give credit to his contradiction. The value of that person's evidence in such cases will be noticed presently. Of the Hon. Mr. Byam I know nothing, and shall only at present remark that it is not likely to redound greatly to his credit to appear in such company. Furthermore, Mary's petition was presented, as Mr. Wood ought to know; though it was not discussed, nor his conduct exposed as it ought to have been.

9. He speaks of the liability he should incur, under the Consolidated Slave Law, of dealing with a free person as a slave.

Is not this pretext hypocritical in the extreme? What liability could he possibly incur by voluntarily resigning the power, conferred on him by an iniquitous colonial law, of re-imposing the shackles of slavery on the bondwoman from whose limbs they had fallen when she touched the free soil of England?—There exists no liability from which he might not have been easily secured, or for which he would not have been fully compensated.

He adds in a postscript that Mary had a considerable sum of money with her,—from £36 to £40 at least, which she had saved in his service. The fact is, that she had at one time 113 dollars in cash; but only a very small portion of that sum appears to have been brought by her to England, the rest having been partly advanced, as she states, to assist her husband, and partly lost by being lodged in unfaithful custody.

Finally, Mr. Wood repeats twice that it will afford him great pleasure to state for the governor's satisfaction, if required, such particulars of "the woman Molly," upon incontestable evidence, as he is sure will acquit him in his Excellency's opinion "of acting unkind or ungenerous towards her."

This is well: and I now call upon Mr. Wood to redeem his pledge;—to bring forward facts and proofs fully to elucidate the subject;—to reconcile, if he can, the extraordinary discrepancies which I have pointed out between his assertions and the actual facts, and especially between his account of Mary Prince's character and his own conduct in regard to her. He has now to produce such a statement as will acquit him not only in the opinion of Sir Patrick Ross, but of the British public. And in this position he has spontaneously placed himself, in attempting to destroy, by his deliberate criminatory letter, the poor woman's fair fame and reputation,—an attempt but for which the present publication would probably never have appeared.

Here perhaps we might safely leave the case to the judgment of the public; but as this negro woman's character, not the less valuable to her because her condition is so humble, has been so unscrupulously blackened by her late master, a party so much interested and inclined to place her in the worst point of view,—it is incumbent on me, as her advocate with the public, to state such additional testimony in her behalf as I can fairly and conscientiously adduce.

My first evidence is Mr. Joseph Phillips, of Antigua. Having submitted to his inspection Mr. Wood's letter and Mary Prince's narrative, and requested his candid and deliberate sentiments in regard to the actual facts of the case, I have been favoured with the following letter from him on the subject:—

"London, January 18, 1831.

"Dear Sir,

"In giving you my opinion of Mary Prince's narrative, and of Mr. Wood's letter respecting her, addressed to Mr. Taylor, I shall first mention my opportunities of forming a proper estimate of the conduct and character of both parties.

"I have known Mr. Wood since his first arrival in Antigua in 1803. He was then a poor young man, who had been brought up as a ship carpenter in Bermuda. He was afterwards raised to be a clerk in the Commissariat department, and realised sufficient capital to commence business as a merchant. This last profession he has followed successfully for a good many years, and is understood to have accumulated very considerable wealth. After he entered into trade, I had constant intercourse with him in the way of business; and in 1824 and 1825, I was regularly employed on his premises as his clerk; consequently, I had opportunities of seeing a good deal of his character both as a merchant, and as a master of slaves. The former topic I pass over as irrelevant to the present subject: in reference to the latter, I shall merely observe that he was not, in regard to ordinary matters, more severe than the ordinary run of slave owners; but, if seriously offended, he was not of a disposition to be easily appeased, and would spare no cost or sacrifice to gratify his vindictive feelings. As regards the exaction of work from domestic slaves, his wife was probably more severe than himself—it was almost impossible for the slaves ever to give her entire satisfaction.

"Of their slave Molly (or Mary) I know less than of Mr. and Mrs. Wood; but I saw and heard enough of her, both while I was constantly employed on Mr. Wood's premises, and while I was there occasionally on business, to be quite certain that she was viewed by her owners as their most respectable and trustworthy female slave. It is within my personal knowledge that she had usually the charge of the house in their absence, was entrusted with the keys, &c.; and was always considered by the neighbours and visitors as their confidential household servant, and as a person in whose integrity they placed unlimited confidence,—although when Mrs. Wood was at home, she was no doubt kept pretty closely at washing and other hard work. A decided proof of the estimation in which she was held by her owners exists in the fact that Mr. Wood uniformly refused to part with her, whereas he sold five other slaves while she was with them. Indeed, she always appeared to me to be a slave of superior intelligence and respectability; and I always understood such to be her general character in the place.

"As to what Mr. Wood alleges about her being frequently before the police, &c. I can only say I never heard of the circumstance before; and as I lived for twenty years in the same small town, and in the vicinity of their residence, I think I could scarcely have failed to become acquainted with it, had such been the fact. She might, however, have been occasionally before the magistrate in consequence of little disputes among the slaves, without any serious imputation on her general respectability. She says she was twice summoned to appear as a witness on such occasions; and that she was once sent by her mistress to be confined in the Cage, and was afterwards flogged by her desire. This cruel practice is very common in Antigua; and, in my opinion, is but little creditable to the slave owners and magistrates by whom such arbitrary punishments are inflicted, frequently for very trifling faults. Mr. James Scotland is the only magistrate in the colony who invariably refuses to sanction this reprehensible practice.

"Of the immoral conduct ascribed to Molly by Mr. Wood, I can say nothing further than this—that I have heard she had at a former period (previous to her marriage) a connexion with a white person, a Capt. — —, which I have no doubt was broken off when she became seriously impressed with religion. But, at any rate, such connexions are so common, I might almost say universal, in our slave colonies, that except by the missionaries and a few serious persons, they are considered, if faults at all, so very venial as scarcely to deserve the name of immorality. Mr. Wood knows this colonial estimate of such connexions as well as I do; and, however false such an estimate must be allowed to be, especially When applied to their own conduct by persons of education, pretending to adhere to the pure Christian rule of morals,—yet when he ascribes to a negro slave, to whom legal marriage was denied, such great criminality for laxity of this sort, and professes to be so exceedingly shocked and amazed at the tale he himself relates, he must, I am confident, have had a farther object in view than the information of Mr. Taylor or Sir Patrick Ross. He must, it is evident, have been aware that his letter would be sent to Mr. Allen, and accordingly adapted it, as more important documents from the colonies are often adapted, for effect in England. The tale of the slave Molly's immoralities, be assured, was not intended for Antigua so much as for Stoke Newington, and Peckham, and Aldermanbury.

"In regard to Mary's narrative generally, although I cannot speak to the accuracy of the details, except in a few recent particulars, I can with safety declare that I see no reason to question the truth of a single fact stated by her, or even to suspect her in any instance of intentional exaggeration. It bears in my judgment the genuine stamp of truth and nature. Such is my unhesitating opinion, after a residence of twenty-seven years in the West Indies.

"I remain, &c.

"Joseph Phillips."
To T. Pringle, Esq.

"P.S. As Mr. Wood refers to the evidence of Dr. T. Coull in opposition to Mary's assertions, it may be proper to enable you justly to estimate the worth of that person's evidence in cases connected with the condition and treatment of slaves. You are aware that in 1829, Mr. M'Queen of Glasgow, in noticing a Report of the "Ladies' Society of Birmingham for the relief of British Negro Slaves," asserted with his characteristic audacity, that the statement which it contained respecting distressed and deserted slaves in Antigua was "an abominable falsehood." Not contented with this, and with insinuating that I, as agent of the society in the distribution of their charity in Antigua, had fraudulently duped them out of their money by a fabricated tale of distress, Mr. M'Queen proceeded to libel me in the most opprobrious terms, as "a man of the most worthless and abandoned character."[20] Now I know from good authority that it was upon Dr. Coull's information that Mr. M'Queen founded this impudent contradiction of notorious facts, and this audacious libel of my personal character. From this single circumstance you may judge of the value of his evidence in the case of Mary Prince. I can furnish further information respecting Dr. Coull's colonial proceedings, both private and judicial, should circumstances require it."

"J. P."

I leave the preceding letter to be candidly weighed by the reader in opposition to the inculpatory allegations of Mr. Wood—merely remarking that Mr. Wood will find it somewhat difficult to impugn the evidence of Mr. Phillips, whose "upright," "unimpeached," and "unexceptionable" character, he has himself vouched for in unqualified terms, by affixing his signature to the testimonial published in the Weekly Register of Antigua in 1825. (See Note below.)

The next testimony in Mary's behalf is that of Mrs. Forsyth, a lady in whose service she spent the summer of 1829.—(See page 21.) This lady, on leaving London to join her husband, voluntarily presented Mary with a certificate, which, though it relates only to a recent and short period of her history, is a strong corroboration of the habitual respectability of her character. It is in the following terms:—

"Mrs. Forsyth states, that the bearer of this paper (Mary James,) has been with her for the last six months; that she has found her an excellent character, being honest, industrious, and sober; and that she parts with her on no other account than this—that being obliged to travel with her husband, who has lately come from abroad in bad health, she has no farther need of a servant. Any person Wishing to engage her, can have her character in full from Miss Robson, 4, Keppel Street, Russel Square, whom Mrs. Forsyth has requested to furnish particulars to any one desiring them.

"4, Keppel Street, 28th Sept. 1829."

In the last place, I add my own testimony in behalf of this negro woman. Independently of the scrutiny, which, as Secretary of the Anti-Slavery Society,

I made into her case when she first applied for assistance, at 18, Aldermanbury, and the watchful eye I kept upon her conduct for the ensuing twelvemonths, while she was the occasional pensioner of the Society, I have now had the opportunity of closely observing her conduct for fourteen months, in the situation of a domestic servant in my own family; and the following is the deliberate opinion of Mary's character, formed not only by myself, but also by my wife and sister-in-law, after this ample period of observation. We have found her perfectly honest and trustworthy in all respects; so that we have no hesitation in leaving every thing in the house at her disposal. She had the entire charge of the house during our absence in Scotland for three months last autumn, and conducted herself in that charge with the utmost discretion and fidelity. She is not, it is true, a very expert housemaid, nor capable of much hard work, (for her constitution appears to be a good deal broken,) but she is careful, industrious, and anxious to do her duty and to give satisfaction. She is capable of strong attachments, and feels deep, though unobtrusive, gratitude for real kindness shown her. She possesses considerable natural sense, and has much quickness of observation and discrimination of character. She is remarkable for decency and propriety of conduct—and her delicacy, even in trifling minutiæ, has been a trait of special remark by the females of my family. This trait, which is obviously quite unaffected, would be a most inexplicable anomaly, if her former habits had been so indecent and depraved as Mr. Wood alleges. Her chief faults, so far as we have discovered them, are, a somewhat violent and hasty temper, and a considerable share of natural pride and self-importance; but these defects have been but rarely and transiently manifested, and have scarcely occasioned an hour's uneasiness at any time in our household. Her religious knowledge, notwithstanding the pious care of her Moravian instructors in Antigua, is still but very limited, and her views of christianity indistinct; but her profession, whatever it may have of imperfection, I am convinced, has nothing of insincerity. In short, we consider her on the whole as respectable and well-behaved a person in her station, as any domestic, white or black, (and we have had ample experience of both colours,) that we have ever had in our service.

But after all, Mary's character, important though its exculpation be to her, is not really the point of chief practical interest in this case. Suppose all Mr. Wood's defamatory allegations to be true—suppose him to be able to rake up against her out of the records of the Antigua police, or from the veracious testimony of his brother colonists, twenty stories as bad or worse than what he insinuates—suppose the whole of her own statement to be false, and even the whole of her conduct since she came under our observation here to be a tissue of hypocrisy;—suppose all this—and leave the negro woman as black in character as in complexion,[21] —yet it would affect not the main facts—which are these.—1. Mr. Wood, not daring in England to punish this woman arbitrarily, as he would have done in the West Indies, drove her out of his house, or left her, at least, only the alternative of returning instantly to Antigua, with the certainty of severe treatment there, or submitting in silence to what she considered intolerable usage in his household. 2. He has since obstinately persisted in refusing her manumission, to enable her to return home in security, though repeatedly offered more than ample compensation for her value as a slave; and this on various frivolous pretexts, but really, and indeed not unavowedly, in order to punish her for leaving his service in England, though he himself had professed to give her that option. These unquestionable facts speak volumes.[22]

The case affords a most instructive illustration of the true spirit of the slave system, and of the pretensions of the slave-holders to assert, not merely their claims to a "vested right" in the labour of their bondmen, but to an indefeasible property in them as their "absolute chattels." It furnishes a striking practical comment on the assertions of the West Indians that self-interest is a sufficient check to the indulgence of vindictive feelings in the master; for here is a case where a man (a respectable and benevolent man as his friends aver,) prefers losing entirely the full price of the slave, for the mere satisfaction of preventing a poor black woman from returning home to her husband! If the pleasure of thwarting the benevolent wishes of the Anti-Slavery Society in behalf of the deserted negro, be an additional motive with Mr. Wood, it will not much mend his wretched plea.

I may here add a few words respecting the earlier portion of Mary Prince's narrative. The facts there stated must necessarily rest entirely,—since we have no collateral evidence,—upon their intrinsic claims to probability, and upon the reliance the reader may feel disposed, after perusing the foregoing pages, to place on her veracity. To my judgment, the internal evidence of the truth of her narrative appears remarkably strong. The circumstances are related in a tone of natural sincerity, and are accompanied in almost every case with characteristic and minute details, which must, I conceive, carry with them full conviction to every candid mind that this negro woman has actually seen, felt, and suffered all that she so impressively describes; and that the picture she has given of West Indian slavery is not less true than it is revolting.

But there may be some persons into whose hands this tract may fall, so imperfectly acquainted with the real character of Negro Slavery, as to be shocked into partial, if not absolute incredulity, by the acts of inhuman oppression and brutality related of Capt. I—— and his wife, and of Mr. D——, the salt manufacturer of Turk's Island. Here, at least, such persons may be disposed to think, there surely must be some exaggeration; the facts are too shocking to be credible. The facts are indeed shocking, but unhappily not the less credible on that account. Slavery is a curse to the oppressor scarcely less than to the oppressed: its natural tendency is to brutalize both. After a residence myself of six years in a slave colony, I am inclined to doubt whether, as regards its demoralizing influence, the master is not even a greater object of compassion than his bondman. Let those who are disposed to doubt the atrocities related in this narrative, on the testimony of a sufferer, examine the details of many cases of similar barbarity that have lately come before the public, on unquestionable evidence. Passing over the reports of the Fiscal of Berbice,[23] and the Mauritius horrors recently unveiled,[24] let them consider the case of Mr. and Mrs. Moss, of the Bahamas, and their slave Kate, so justly denounced by the Secretary for the Colonies;[25]—the cases of Eleanor Mead,[26]— of Henry Williams,[27]—and of the Rev. Mr. Bridges and Kitty Hylton,[28] in Jamaica. These cases alone might suffice to demonstrate the inevitable tendency of slavery as it exists in our colonies, to brutalize the master to a truly frightful degree—a degree which would often cast into the shade even the atrocities related in the narrative of Mary Prince; and which are sufficient to prove, independently of all other evidence, that there is nothing in the revolting character of the facts to affect their credibility; but that on the contrary, similar deeds are at this very time of frequent occurrence in almost every one of our slave colonies. The system of coercive labour may vary in different places; it may be more destructive to human life in the cane culture of Mauritius and Jamaica, than in the predial and domestic bondage of Bermuda or the Bahamas,—but the spirit and character of slavery are every where the same, and cannot fail to produce similar effects. Wherever slavery prevails, there will inevitably be found cruelty and oppression. Individuals who have preserved humane, and amiable, and tolerant dispositions towards their black dependents, may doubtless be found among slave-holders; but even where a happy instance of this sort occurs, such as Mary's first mistress, the kind-hearted Mrs. Williams, the favoured condition of the slave is still as precarious as it is rare: it is every moment at the mercy of events; and must always be held by a tenure so proverbially uncertain as that of human prosperity, or human life. Such examples, like a feeble and flickering streak of light in a gloomy picture, only serve by contrast to exhibit the depth of the prevailing shades. Like other exceptions, they only prove the general rule: the unquestionable tendency of the system is to vitiate the best tempers, and to harden the most feeling hearts. "Never be kind, nor speak kindly to a slave," said an accomplished English lady in South Africa to my wife: "I have now," she added, "been for some time a slave-owner, and have found, from vexatious experience in my own household, that nothing but harshness and hauteur will do with slaves."

I might perhaps not inappropriately illustrate this point more fully by stating many cases which fell under my own personal observation, or became known to me through authentic sources, at the Cape of Good Hope—a colony where slavery assumes, as it is averred, a milder aspect than in any other dependency of the empire where it exists; and I could shew, from the judicial records of that colony, received by me within these few weeks, cases scarcely inferior in barbarity to the worst of those to which I have just specially referred; but to do so would lead me too far from the immediate purpose of this pamphlet, and extend it to an inconvenient length. I shall therefore content myself with quoting a single short passage from the excellent work of my friend Dr. Walsh, entitled "Notices of Brazil,"—a work which, besides its other merits, has vividly illustrated the true spirit of Negro Slavery, as it displays itself not merely in that country, but wherever it has been permitted to open its Pandora's box of misery and crime.

Let the reader ponder on the following just remarks, and compare the facts stated by the Author in illustration of them, with the circumstances related at pages 6 and 7 of Mary's narrative:—

"If then we put out of the question the injury inflicted on others, and merely consider the deterioration of feeling and principle with which it operates on ourselves, ought it not to be a sufficient, and, indeed, unanswerable argument, against the permission of Slavery?

"The exemplary manner in which the paternal duties are performed at home, may mark people as the most fond and affectionate parents; but let them once go abroad, and come within the contagion of slavery, and it seems to alter the very nature of a man; and the father has sold, and still sells, the mother and his children, with as little compunction as he would a sow and her litter of pigs; and he often disposes of them together.

"This deterioration of feeling is conspicuous in many ways among the Brazilians. They are naturally a people of a humane and good-natured disposition, and much indisposed to cruelty or severity of any kind. Indeed, the manner in which many of them treat their slaves is a proof of this, as it is really gentle and considerate; but the natural tendency to cruelty and oppression in the human heart, is continually evolved by the impunity and uncontrolled licence in which they are exercised. I never walked through the streets of Rio, that some house did not present to me the semblance of a bridewell, where the moans and the cries of the sufferers, and the sounds of whips and scourges within, announced to me that corporal punishment was being inflicted. Whenever I remarked this to a friend, I was always answered that the refractory nature of the slave rendered it necessary, and no house could properly be conducted unless it was practised. But this is certainly not the case; and the chastisement is constantly applied in the very wantonness of barbarity, and would not, and dared not, be inflicted on the humblest wretch in society, if he was not a slave, and so put out of the pale of pity.

"Immediately joining our house was one occupied by a mechanic, from which the most dismal cries and moans constantly proceeded. I entered the shop one day, and found it was occupied by a saddler, who had two negro boys working at his business. He was a tawny, cadaverous-looking man, with a dark aspect; and he had cut from his leather a scourge like a Russian knout, which he held in his hand, and was in the act of exercising on one of the naked children in an inner room: and this was the cause of the moans and cries we heard every day, and almost all day long.

"In the rear of our house was another, occupied by some women of bad character, who kept, as usual, several negro slaves. I was awoke early one morning by dismal cries, and looking out of the window, I saw in the back yard of the house, a black girl of about fourteen years old; before her stood her mistress, a white woman, with a large stick in her hand. She was undressed except her petticoat and chemise, which had fallen down and left her shoulders and bosom bare. Her hair was streaming behind, and every fierce and malevolent passion was depicted in her face. She too, like my hostess at Governo [another striking illustration of the dehumanizing effects of Slavery,] was the very representation of a fury. She was striking the poor girl, whom she had driven up into a corner, where she was on her knees appealing for mercy. She shewed her none, but continued to strike her on the head and thrust the stick into her face, till she was herself exhausted, and her poor victim covered with blood. This scene was renewed every morning, and the cries and moans of the poor suffering blacks, announced that they were enduring the penalty of slavery, in being the objects on which the irritable and malevolent passions of the whites are allowed to vent themselves with impunity; nor could I help deeply deploring that state of society in which the vilest characters in the community are allowed an almost uncontrolled power of life and death, over their innocent, and far more estimable fellow-creatures."—(Notices of Brazil, vol. ii. p. 354-356.)

In conclusion, I may observe that the history of Mary Prince furnishes a corollary to Lord Stowell's decision in the case of the slave Grace, and that it is most valuable on this account. Whatever opinions may be held by some readers on the grave question of immediately abolishing Colonial Slavery, nothing assuredly can be more repugnant to the feelings of Englishmen than that the system should be permitted to extend its baneful influence to this country. Yet such is the case, when the slave landed in England still only possesses that qualified degree of freedom, that a change of domicile will determine it. Though born a British subject, and resident within the shores of England, he is cut off from his dearest natural rights by the sad alternative of regaining them at the expence of liberty, and the certainty of severe treatment. It is true that he has the option of returning; but it is a cruel mockery to call it a voluntary choice, when upon his return depend his means of subsistence and his re-union with all that makes life valuable. Here he has tasted "the sweets of freedom," to quote the words of the unfortunate Mary Prince; but if he desires to restore himself to his family, or to escape from suffering and destitution, and the other evils of a climate uncongenial to his constitution and habits, he must abandon the enjoyment of his late-acquired liberty, and again subject himself to the arbitrary power of a vindictive master.

The case of Mary Prince is by no means a singular one; many of the same kind are daily occurring: and even if the case were singular, it would still loudly call for the interference of the legislature. In instances of this kind no injury can possibly be done to the owner by confirming to the slave his resumption of his natural rights. It is the master's spontaneous act to bring him to this country; he knows when he brings him that he divests himself of his property; and it is, in fact, a minor species of slave trading, when he has thus enfranchised his slave, to re-capture that slave by the necessities of his condition, or by working upon the better feelings of his heart. Abstractedly from all legal technicalities, there is no real difference between thus compelling the return of the enfranchised negro, and trepanning a free native of England by delusive hopes into perpetual slavery. The most ingenious casuist could not point out any essential distinction between the two cases. Our boasted liberty is the dream of imagination, and no longer the characteristic of our country, if its bulwarks can thus be thrown down by colonial special pleading. It would well become the character of the present Government to introduce a Bill into the Legislature making perpetual that freedom which the slave has acquired by his passage here, and thus to declare, in the most ample sense of the words, (what indeed we had long fondly believed to be the fact, though it now appears that we have been mistaken,) that no slave can exist within the shores of Great Britain.

# FOOTNOTES:

[1] Bermuda currency; about £38 sterling.

[2] Let the reader compare the above affecting account, taken down from the mouth of this negro woman, with the following description of a vendue of slaves at the Cape of Good Hope, published by me in 1826, from the letter of a friend,—and mark their similarity in several characteristic circumstances. The resemblance is easily accounted for: slavery wherever it prevails produces similar effects.—"Having heard that there was to be a sale of cattle, farm stock, &c. by auction, at a Veld-Cornet's in the vicinity, we halted our waggon one day for the purpose of procuring a fresh spann of oxen. Among the stock of the farm sold, was a female slave and her three children. The two eldest children were girls, the one about thirteen years of age, and the other about eleven; the youngest was a boy. The whole family were exhibited together, but they were sold separately, and to different purchasers. The farmers examined them as if they had been so many head of cattle. While the sale was going on, the mother and her children were exhibited on a table, that they might be seen by the company, which was very large. There could not have been a finer subject for an able painter than this unhappy group. The tears, the anxiety, the anguish of the mother, while she met the gaze of the multitude, eyed the different countenances of the bidders, or cast a heart-rending look upon the children; and the simplicity and touching sorrow of the young ones, while they clung to their distracted parent, wiping their eyes, and half concealing their faces,—contrasted with the marked insensibility and jocular countenances of the spectators and purchasers,—furnished a striking commentary on the miseries of slavery, and its debasing effects upon the hearts of its abettors. While the woman was in this distressed situation she was asked, 'Can you feed sheep?' Her reply was so indistinct that it escaped me; but it was probably in the negative, for her purchaser rejoined, in a loud and harsh voice, 'Then I will teach you with the sjamboc,' (a whip made of the rhinoceros' hide.) The mother and her three children were sold to three separate purchasers; and they were literally torn from each other."—Ed.

[3] These strong expressions, and all of a similar character in this little narrative, are given verbatim as uttered by Mary Prince.—Ed.

[4] The cattle on a small plantation in Bermuda are, it seems, often thus staked or tethered, both night and day, in situations where grass abounds.

[5] A cow fed for slaughter.

[6] A thong of hard twisted hide, known by this name in the West Indies.

[7] Of the subsequent lot of her relatives she can tell but little. She says, her father died while she and her mother were at Turk's Island; and that he had been long dead and buried before any of his children in Bermuda knew of it, they being slaves on other estates. Her mother died after Mary went to Antigua. Of the fate of the rest of her kindred, seven brothers and three sisters, she knows nothing further than this—that the eldest sister, who had several children to her master, was taken by him to Trinidad; and that the youngest, Rebecca, is still alive, and in slavery in Bermuda. Mary herself is now about forty-three years of age.—Ed.

[8] Negro term for white people.

[9] About £67. 10s. sterling.

[10] A dog is the 72nd part of a dollar.

[11] The head negro of an estate—a person who has the chief superintendence under the manager.

[12] She possesses a copy of Mrs. Trimmer's "Charity School Spelling Book," presented to her by the Rev. Mr. Curtin, and dated August 30, 1817. In this book her name is written "Mary, Princess of Wales"—an appellation which, she says, was given her by her owners. It is a common practice with the colonists to give ridiculous names of this description to their slaves; being, in fact, one of the numberless modes of expressing the habitual contempt with which they regard the negro race.—In printing this narrative we have retained Mary's paternal name of Prince.—Ed.

[13] See page 24.

[14] She came first to the Anti-Slavery Office in Aldermanbury, about the latter end of November 1828; and her case was referred to Mr. George Stephen to be investigated. More of this hereafter.—Ed.

[15] She refers to a written certificate which will be inserted afterwards.

[16] The whole of this paragraph especially, is given as nearly as was possible in Mary's precise words.

[17] She means West Indians.

[18] A West Indian phrase: to fasten or tie up.

[19] I omit the circumstance here mentioned, because it is too indecent to appear in a publication likely to be perused by females. It is, in all probability, a vile calumny; but even if it were perfectly true, it would not serve Mr. Wood's case one straw.—Any reader who wishes it, may see the passage referred to, in the autograph letter in my possession. T. P.

[20] In elucidation of the circumstances above referred to, I subjoin the following extracts from the Report of the Birmingham Ladies' Society for 1830:—

"As a portion of the funds of this association has been appropriated to assist the benevolent efforts of a society which has for fifteen years afforded relief to distressed and deserted slaves in Antigua, it may not be uninteresting to our friends to learn the manner in which the agent of this society has been treated for simply obeying the command of our Saviour, by ministering, like the good Samaritan, to the distresses of the helpless and the desolate. The society's proceedings being adverted to by a friend of Africa, at one of the public meetings held in this country, a West Indian planter, who was present, wrote over to his friends in Antigua, and represented the conduct of the distributors of this charity in such a light, that it was deemed worthy of the cognizance of the House of Assembly. Mr. Joseph Phillips, a resident of the island, who had most kindly and disinterestedly exerted himself in the distribution of the money from England among the poor deserted slaves, was brought before the Assembly, and most severely interrogated: on his refusing to deliver up his private correspondence with his friends in England, he was thrown into a loathsome jail, where he was kept for nearly five months; while his loss of business, and the oppressive proceedings instituted against him, were involving him in poverty and ruin. On his discharge by the House of Assembly, he was seized in their lobby for debt, and again imprisoned."

"In our report for the year 1826, we quoted a passage from the 13th Report of the Society for the relief of deserted Slaves in the island of Antigua, in reference to a case of great distress. This statement fell into the hands of Mr. M'Queen, the Editor of the Glasgow Courier. Of the consequences resulting from this circumstance we only gained information through the Leicester Chronicle, which had copied an article from the Weekly Register of Antigua, dated St. John's, September 22, 1829. We find from this that Mr. M'Queen affirms, that 'with the exception of the fact that the society is, as it deserves to be, duped out of its money, the whole tale' (of the distress above referred to) 'is an abominable falsehood.' This statement, which we are informed has appeared in many of the public papers, is completely refuted in our Appendix, No. 4, to which we refer our readers. Mr. M'Queen's statements, we regret to say, would lead many to believe that there are no deserted Negroes to assist; and that the case mentioned was a perfect fabrication. He also distinctly avers, that the disinterested and humane agent of the society, Mr. Joseph Phillips, is 'a man of the most worthless and abandoned character.' In opposition to this statement, we learn the good character of Mr. Phillips from those who have long been acquainted with his laudable exertions in the cause of humanity, and from the Editor of the Weekly Register of Antigua, who speaks, on his own knowledge, of more than twenty years back; confidently appealing at the same time to the inhabitants of the colony in which he resides for the truth of his averments, and producing a testimonial to Mr. Phillips's good character signed by two members of the Antigua House of Assembly, and by Mr. Wyke, the collector of his Majesty's customs, and by Antigua merchants, as follows—'that they have been acquainted with him the last four years and upwards, and he has always conducted himself in an upright becoming manner—his character we know to be unimpeached, and his morals unexceptionable.'

(Signed) "Thomas Saunderson     John D. Taylor
John A. Wood     George Wyke
Samuel L. Darrel     Giles S. Musson
Robert Grant."

"St. John's, Antigua, June 28, 1825."

In addition to the above testimonies, Mr. Phillips has brought over to England with him others of a more recent date, from some of the most respectable persons in Antigua—sufficient to cover with confusion all his unprincipled calumniators. See also his account of his own case in the Anti-Slavery Reporter, No. 74, p. 69.

[21] If it even were so, how strong a plea of palliation might not the poor negro bring, by adducing the neglect of her various owners to afford religious instruction or moral discipline, and the habitual influence of their evil example

(to say the very least,) before her eyes? What moral good could she possibly learn—what moral evil could she easily escape, while under the uncontrolled power of such masters as she describes Captain I— — and Mr. D— — of Turk's Island? All things considered, it is indeed wonderful to find her such as she now is. But as she has herself piously expressed it, "that God whom then she knew not mercifully preserved her for better things."

[22] Since the preceding pages were printed off, I have been favoured with a communication from the Rev. J. Curtin, to whom among other acquaintances of Mr. Wood's in this country, the entire proof sheets of this pamphlet had been sent for inspection. Mr. Curtin corrects some omissions and inaccuracies in Mary Prince's narrative (see page 17,) by stating, 1. That she was baptized, not in August, but on the 6th of April, 1817; 2. That sometime before her baptism, on her being admitted a catechumen, preparatory to that holy ordinance, she brought a note from her owner, Mr. Wood, recommending her for religious instruction, &c.; 3. That it was his usual practice, when any adult slaves came on week days to school, to require their owners' permission for their attendance; but that on Sundays the chapel was open indiscriminately to all.— Mary, after a personal interview with Mr. Curtin, and after hearing his letter read by me, still maintains that Mr. Wood's note recommended her for baptism merely, and that she never received any religious instruction whatever from Mr. and Mrs. Wood, or from any one else at that period beyond what she has stated in her narrative. In regard to her non-admission to the Sunday school without permission from her owners, she admits that she may possibly have mistaken the clergyman's meaning on that point, but says that such was certainly her impression at the time, and the actual cause of her non-attendance.

Mr. Curtin finds in his books some reference to Mary's connection with a Captain — —, (the individual, I believe, alluded to by Mr. Phillips at page 32); but he states that when she attended his chapel she was always decently and becomingly dressed, and appeared to him to be in a situation of trust in her mistress's family.

Mr. Curtin offers no comment on any other part of Mary's statement; but he speaks in very favourable, though general terms of the respectability of Mr. Wood, whom he had known for many years in Antigua; and of Mrs. Wood, though she was not personally known to him, he says, that he had "heard her spoken of by those of her acquaintance, as a lady of very mild and amiable manners."

Another friend of Mr. and Mrs. Wood, a lady who had been their guest both in Antigua and England, alleges that Mary has grossly misrepresented them in her narrative; and says that she "can vouch for their being the most benevolent, kind-hearted people that can possibly live." She has declined, however, to furnish me with any written correction of the misrepresentations she complains of, although I offered to insert her testimony in behalf of her friends, if sent to me in time. And having already kept back the publication a fortnight waiting for communications of this sort, I will not delay it longer. Those who have withheld their strictures have only themselves to blame.

Of the general character of Mr. and Mrs. Wood, I would not designedly give any unfair impression. Without implicitly adopting either the ex parte view of Mary Prince, or the unmeasured encomiums of their friends, I am willing to believe them to be, on the whole, fair, perhaps favourable, specimens of colonial character. Let them even be rated, if you will, in the very highest and most benevolent class of slave-holders; and, laying everything else entirely out of view, let Mr. Wood's conduct in this affair be tried exclusively by the facts established beyond dispute, and by his own statement of the case in his letter to Mr. Taylor. But then, I ask, if the very best and mildest of your slave-owners can act as Mr. Wood is proved to have acted, what is to be expected of persons whose mildness, or equity, or common humanity no one will dare to vouch for? If such things are done in the green tree, what will be done in the dry?—And what else then can Colonial Slavery possibly be, even in its best estate, but a system incurably evil and iniquitous?—I require no other data—I need add no further comment.

[23] See Anti-Slavery Reporter, Nos. 5 and 16.

[24] Ibid, No. 44.

[25] Ibid, No. 47.

[26] Ibid, No. 64, p. 345; No. 71, p. 481.

[27] Ibid, No. 65, p. 356; No. 69, p. 431.

[28] Anti-Slavery Reporter, Nos. 66, 69, and 76.

# NARRATIVE OF LOUIS ASA-ASA, A CAPTURED AFRICAN.

The following interesting narrative is a convenient supplement to the history of Mary Prince. It is given, like hers, as nearly as possible in the narrator's words, with only so much correction as was necessary to connect the story, and render it grammatical. The concluding passage in inverted commas, is entirely his own.

While Mary's narrative shews the disgusting character of colonial slavery, this little tale explains with equal force the horrors in which it originates.

It is necessary to explain that Louis came to this country about five years ago, in a French vessel called the Pearl. She had lost her reckoning, and was driven by stress of weather into the port of St. Ives, in Cornwall. Louis and his four companions were brought to London upon a writ of Habeas Corpus at the instance of Mr. George Stephen; and, after some trifling opposition on the part of the master of the vessel, were discharged by Lord Wynford. Two of his unfortunate fellow-sufferers died of the measles at Hampstead; the other two returned to Sierra Leone; but poor Louis, when offered the choice of going back to Africa, replied, "Me no father, no mother now; me stay with you." And here he has ever since remained; conducting himself in a way to gain the good will and respect of all who know him. He is remarkably intelligent, understands our language perfectly, and can read and write well. The last sentences of the following narrative will seem almost too peculiar to be his own; but it is not the first time that in conversation with Mr. George Stephen, he has made similar remarks. On one occasion in particular, he was heard saying to himself in the kitchen, while sitting by the fire apparently in deep thought, "Me think,—me think——" A fellow-servant inquired what he meant; and he added, "Me think what a good thing I came to England! Here, I know what God is, and read my Bible; in my country they have no God, no Bible."

How severe and just a reproof to the guilty wretches who visit his country only with fire and sword! How deserved a censure upon the not less guilty men, who dare to vindicate the state of slavery, on the lying pretext, that its victims are of an inferior nature! And scarcely less deserving of reprobation are those who have it in their power to prevent these crimes, but who remain inactive from indifference, or are dissuaded from throwing the shield of British power over the victim of oppression, by the sophistry, and the clamour, and the avarice of the oppressor. It is the reproach and the sin of England. May God avert from our country the ruin which this national guilt deserves!

We lament to add, that the Pearl which brought these negroes to our shore, was restored to its owners at the instance of the French Government, instead of being condemned as a prize to Lieut. Rye, who, on his own responsibility, detained her, with all her manacles and chains and other detestable proofs of her piratical occupation on board. We trust it is not yet too late to demand investigation into the reasons for restoring her.

## The Negro Boy's Narrative.

My father's name was Clashoquin; mine is Asa-Asa. He lived in a country called Bycla, near Egie, a large town. Egie is as large as Brighton; it was some way from the sea. I had five brothers and sisters. We all lived together with my father and mother; he kept a horse, and was respectable, but not one of the great men. My uncle was one of the great men at Egie: he could make men come and work for him: his name was Otou. He had a great deal of land and cattle. My father sometimes worked on his own land, and used to make charcoal. I was too little to work; my eldest brother used to work on the land; and we were all very happy.

A great many people, whom we called Adinyés, set fire to Egie in the morning before daybreak; there were some thousands of them. They killed a great many, and burnt all their houses. They staid two days, and then carried away all the people whom they did not kill.

They came again every now and then for a month, as long as they could find people to carry away. They used to tie them by the feet, except when they were taking them off, and then they let them loose; but if they offered to run away, they would shoot them. I lost a great many friends and relations at Egie; about a dozen. They sold all they carried away, to be slaves. I know this because I afterwards saw them as slaves on the other side of the sea. They took away brothers, and sisters, and husbands, and wives; they did not care about this. They were sold for cloth or gunpowder, sometimes for salt or guns; sometimes they got four or five guns for a man: they were English guns, made like my master's that I clean for his shooting. The Adinyés burnt a great many places besides Egie. They burnt all the country wherever they found villages; they used to shoot men, women, and children, if they ran away.

They came to us about eleven o'clock one day, and directly they came they set our house on fire. All of us had run away. We kept together, and went into the woods, and stopped there two days. The Adinyés then went away, and we returned home and found every thing burnt. We tried to build a little shed, and were beginning to get comfortable again. We found several of our neighbours lying about wounded; they had been shot. I saw the bodies of four or five little children whom they had killed with blows on the head. They had carried away their fathers and mothers, but the children were too small for slaves, so they killed them. They had killed several others, but these were all that I saw. I saw them lying in the street like dead dogs.

In about a week after we got back, the Adinyés returned, and burnt all the sheds and houses they had left standing. We all ran away again; we went to the woods as we had done before.—They followed us the next day. We went farther into the woods, and staid there about four days and nights; we were half starved; we only got a few potatoes. My uncle Otou was with us. At the end of this time, the Adinyés found us. We ran away. They called my uncle to go to them; but he refused, and they shot him immediately: they killed him. The rest of us ran on, and they did not get at us till the next day. I ran up into a tree: they followed me and brought me down. They tied my feet. I do not know if they found my father and mother, and brothers and sisters: they had run faster than me, and were half a mile farther when I got up into the tree: I have never seen them since.—There was a man who ran up into the tree with me: I believe they shot him, for I never saw him again.

They carried away about twenty besides me. They carried us to the sea. They did not beat us: they only killed one man, who was very ill and too weak to carry his load: they made all of us carry chickens and meat for our food; but this poor man could not carry his load, and they ran him through the body with a sword.—He was a neighbour of ours. When we got to the sea they sold all of us, but not to the same person. They sold us for money; and I was sold six times over, sometimes for money, sometimes for cloth, and sometimes for a gun. I was about thirteen years old. It was about half a year from the time I was taken, before I saw the white people.

We were taken in a boat from place to place, and sold at every place we stopped at. In about six months we got to a ship, in which we first saw white people: they were French. They bought us. We found here a great many other slaves; there were about eighty, including women and children. The Frenchmen sent away all but five of us into another very large ship. We five staid on board till we got to England, which was about five or six months. The slaves we saw on board the ship were chained together by the legs below deck, so close they could not move. They were flogged very cruelly: I saw one of them flogged till he died; we could not tell what for. They gave them enough to eat. The place they were confined in below deck was so hot and nasty I could not bear to be in it. A great many of the slaves were ill, but they were not attended to. They used to flog me very bad on board the ship: the captain cut my head very bad one time.

"I am very happy to be in England, as far as I am very well;—but I have no friend belonging to me, but God, who will take care of me as he has done already. I am very glad I have come to England, to know who God is. I should like much to see my friends again, but I do not now wish to go back to them: for if I go back to my own country, I might be taken as a slave again. I would rather stay here, where I am free, than go back to my country to be sold. I shall stay in England as long as (please God) I shall live. I wish the King of England could know all I have told you. I wish it that he may see how cruelly we are used. We had no king in our country, or he would have stopt it. I think the king of England might stop it, and this is why I wish him to know it all. I have heard say he is good; and if he is, he will stop it if he can. I am well off myself, for I am well taken care of, and have good bed and good clothes; but I wish my own people to be as comfortable."

"LOUIS ASA-ASA."

"London, January 31, 1831."

# THE STORY OF
# Mattie J. Jackson;

Her Parentage—Experience of Eighteen Years in Slavery—Incidents During the War—Her Escape from Slavery.

A TRUE STORY.

WRITTEN AND ARRANGED BY
DR. L. S. THOMPSON,
(FORMERLY MRS. SCHUYLER,)
AS GIVEN BY MATTIE.

LAWRENCE:
PRINTED AT SENTINEL OFFICE, 123 ESSEX STREET.
1866.

# CONTENTS

| | |
|---|---|
| PREFACE | 343 |
| MATTIE'S STORY | 344 |
| THEIR ATTEMPT TO MAKE THEIR ESCAPE | 347 |
| THE SOLDIERS, AND OUR TREATMENT DURING THE WAR | 350 |
| MR. LEWIS CALLS AT THE BOARDING HOUSE | 353 |
| RELEASED FROM THE TRADER'S YARD AND TAKEN TO HER NEW MASTER | 355 |
| CAPT. TIRRELL REMOVES THE FAMILY— ANOTHER STRATEGY | 356 |
| THE FARE AT THEIR NEW HOMES | 360 |
| MATTIE IN INDIANAPOLIS—THE GLORY OF FREEDOM— PRESIDENT LINCOLN'S | 362 |
| SISTER LOST—MOTHER'S ESCAPE | 365 |
| MOTHER'S MARRIAGE | 366 |
| MATTIE MEETS HER OLD MASTER—GOES TO SERVICE —IS SENT FOR BY HER | 367 |
| SUMMARY | 370 |
| CHRISTIANITY | 372 |

# PREFACE

The object in publishing this book is to gain sympathy from the earnest friends of those who have been bound down by a dominant race in circumstances over which they had no control—a butt of ridicule and a mark of oppression; over whom weary ages of degradation have passed. As the links have been broken and the shackles fallen from them through the unwearied efforts of our beloved martyr President Lincoln, as one I feel it a duty to improve the mind, and have ever had a thirst for education to fill that vacuum for which the soul has ever yearned since my earliest remembrance.

Thus I ask you to buy my little book to aid me in obtaining an education, that I may be enabled to do some good in behalf of the elevation of my emancipated brothers and sisters. I have now arrived at the age of twenty. As the first dawn of morning has passed, and the meridian of life is approaching, I know of no other way to speedily gain my object than through the aid and patronage of the friends of humanity.

NOTE: Miss Jackson sustains a high moral character—has been much respected since she has been in Lawrence. She is from St. Louis, Missouri, and arrived here on the 11th of April, 1866. To gain the wish of the heart is utterly impossible without more means than she can obtain otherwise. Her friends have borne her expenses to Lawrence, and have and are still willing to render her aid as far their limited means will allow. She was in the same condition of all the neglected and oppressed. Her personal requirements are amply supplied. She now only craves the means to clothe and qualify the intellect. My humble prayer is that she may meet with unlimited success.

This young lady is highly worthy of all the aid our kind friends feel a duty to bestow upon her. She purposes lecturing and relating her story; and I trust she may render due satisfaction and bear some humble part in removing doubts indulged by the prejudices against the natural genius and talent of our race. May God give her grace and speed her on her way.

Respectfully yours,
L. S. T.

# MATTIE'S STORY

My ancestors were transported from Africa to America at the time the slave trade flourished in the Eastern States. I cannot give dates, as my progenitors, being slaves, had no means of keeping them. By all accounts my great grandfather was captured and brought from Africa. His original name I never learned. His master's name was Jackson, and he resided in the State of New York. My grandfather was born in the same State, and also remained a slave for some length of time, when he was emancipated, his master presenting him with quite an amount of property. He was true, honest and responsible, and this present was given him as a reward. He was much encouraged by the cheering prospect of better days. A better condition of things now presented itself. As he possessed a large share of confidence, he came to the conclusion, as he was free, that he was capable of selecting his own residence and manage his own affairs with prudence and economy. But, alas, his hopes were soon blighted. More heart rending sorrow and degradation awaited him. He was earnestly invited by a white decoyer to relinquish his former design and accompany him to Missouri and join him in speculation and become wealthy. As partners, they embarked on board a schooner for St. Charles, Mo. On the passage, my grandfather was seized with a fever, and for a while was totally unconscious. When he regained his reason he found himself, near his journey's end, divested of his free papers and all others. On his arrival at St. Charles he was seized by a huge, surly looking slaveholder who claimed him as his property. The contract had previously been concluded by his Judas-like friend, who had received the bounty. Oh, what a sad disappointment. After serving for thirty years to be thrust again into bondage where a deeper degradation and sorrow and hopeless toil were to be his portion for the remaining years of his existence. In deep despair and overwhelmed with grief, he made his escape to the woods, determined to put an end to his sorrows by perishing with cold and hunger. His master immediately pursued him, and in twenty-four hours found him with hands and feet frost-bitten, in consequence of which he lost the use of his fingers and toes, and was thenceforth of little use to his new master. He remained with him, however, and married a woman in the same station in life. They lived as happily as their circumstances would permit. As Providence allotted, they only had one son, which was my father, Westly Jackson. He had a deep affection for his family, which the slave ever cherishes for his dear ones. He had no other link to fasten him to the human family but his fervent love for those who were bound to him by love and sympathy in their wrongs and sufferings. My grandfather remained in the same family until his death. My father, Westly Jackson, married, at the age of twenty-two, a girl owned by James Harris, named Ellen Turner. Nothing of importance occurred until three years after their marriage, when her master, Harris failed through the extravagance and mismanagement of his wife, who was a great spendthrift and a dreaded terror to the poor slaves and all others with whom she associated in common circumstances, consequently the entire stock was sold by the sheriff to a trader residing in Virginia. On account of the good reputation my mother sustained as a worthy servant and excellent cook, a tyrannical and much dreaded slaveholder watched for an opportunity to purchase her, but fortunately arrived a few moments too late, and she was bid off in too poor a condition of health to remain long a subject of banter and speculation. Her husband was allowed to carefully lift her down from the block and accompany her to her new master's, Charles Canory, who treated her very kindly while she remained in his family. Mr. Canory resided in St. Charles County for five years after he purchased my mother. During that time my father and mother were in the same neighborhood, but a short distance from each other. But another trial awaited them. Her master removed twenty miles away to a village called Bremen, near St. Louis, Mo. My father, thereafter, visited my mother once a week, walking the distance every Saturday evening and returning on Sunday evening. But through all her trials and deprivations her trust and confidence was in Him who rescued his faithful followers from the fiery furnace and the lion's den, and led Moses through the Red Sea. Her trust and confidence was in Jesus. She relied on His precious promises, and ever found Him a present help in every time of need. Two years after this separation my father was sold and separated from us, but previous to his delivery to his new master he made his escape to a free State. My mother was then left with two children. She had three during the time they were permitted to remain together, and buried one. Their names were Sarah Ann, Mattie Jane and Esther J. When my father left I was about three years of age, yet I can well remember the little kindnesses my father used to bestow upon us, and the deep affection and fondness he manifested for us. I shall never forget the bitter anguish of my parents' hearts, the sighs they uttered or the profusion of tears which coursed down their sable cheeks. O, what a horrid scene, but he was not her's, for cruel hands had separated them.

> The strongest tie of earthly joy that bound the aching heart—
> His love was e'er a joyous light that o'er the pathway shone—
> A fountain gushing ever new amid life's desert wild—
> His slightest word was a sweet tone of music round her heart—
> Their lives a streamlet blent in one. O, Father, must they part?

> They tore him from her circling arms, her last and fond embrace—
> O never again can her sad eyes gaze upon his mournful face.
> It is not strange these bitter sighs are constant bursting forth.
> Amid mirth and glee and revelry she never took a part,
> She was a mother left alone with sorrow in her heart.

But my mother was conscious some time previous of the change that was to take place with my father, and if he was sold in the immediate vicinity he would be likely to be sold again at their will, and she concluded to assist him to make his escape from bondage. Though the parting was painful, it afforded her solace in the contemplation of her husband becoming a free man, and cherishing a hope that her little family, through the aid of some angel of mercy, might be enabled to make their escape also, and meet to part no more on earth. My father came to spend the night with us, according to his usual custom. It was the last time, and sadness brooded upon his brow. It was the only opportunity he had to make his escape without suspicion and detection, as he was immediately to fall into the hands of a new master. He had never been sold from the place of his birth before, and was determined never to be sold again if God would verify his promise. My father was not educated, but was a preacher, and administered the Word of God according to the dictation and revelation of the spirit. His former master had allowed him the privilege of holding meetings in the village within the limits of his pass on the Sundays when he visited my mother. But on this Saturday evening he arrived and gave us all his farewell kiss, and hurried away. My mother's people were aware of my father's intention, but rather than spare my mother, and for fear she might be detected, they secreted his escape. His master called a number of times and enquired for him and strongly pressed my mother to give him an account of my father, but she never gave it. We waited patiently, hoping to learn if he succeeded in gaining his freedom. Many anxious weeks and months passed before we could get any tidings from him, until at length my mother heard that he was in Chicago, a free man and preaching the Gospel. He made every effort to get his family, but all in vain. The spirit of slavery so strongly existed that letters could not reach her; they were all destroyed. My parents had never learned the rescuing scheme of the underground railroad which had borne so many thousands to the standard of freedom and victories. They knew no other resource than to depend upon their own chance in running away and secreting themselves. If caught they were in a worse condition than before.

# THEIR ATTEMPT TO MAKE THEIR ESCAPE

Two years after my father's departure, my mother, with her two children, my sister and myself, attempted to make her escape. After traveling two days we reached Illinois. We slept in the woods at night. I believe my mother had food to supply us but fasted herself. But the advertisement had reached there before us, and loafers were already in search of us, and as soon as we were discovered on the brink of the river one of the spies made enquiries respecting her suspicious appearance. She was aware that she was arrested, consequently she gave a true account of herself—that she was in search of her husband. We were then destitute of any articles of clothing excepting our wearing apparel. Mother had become so weary that she was compelled to leave our package of clothing on the way. We were taken back to St. Louis and committed to prison and remained there one week, after which they put us in Linch's trader's yard, where we remained about four weeks. We were then sold to William Lewis. Mr. Lewis was a very severe master, and inflicted such punishment upon us as he thought proper. However, I only remember one severe contest Mr. Lewis had with my mother. For some slight offence Mrs. Lewis became offended and was tartly and loudly reprimanding her, when Mr. L. came in and rashly felled her to the floor with his fist. But his wife was constantly pulling our ears, snapping us with her thimble, rapping us on the head and sides of it. It appeared impossible to please her. When we first went to Mr. L.'s they had a cowhide which she used to inflict on a little slave girl she previously owned, nearly every night. This was done to learn the little girl to wake early to wait on her children. But my mother was a cook, as I before stated, and was in the habit of roasting meats and toasting bread. As they stinted us for food my mother roasted the cowhide. It was rather poor picking, but it was the last cowhide my mother ever had an opportunity to cook while we remained in his family. Mr. L. soon moved about six miles from the city, and entered in partnership with his brother-in-law. The servants were then divided and distributed in both families. It unfortunately fell to my lot to live with Mrs. Larry, my mistress' sister, which rendered my condition worse than the first. My master even disapproved of my ill treatment and took me to another place; the place my mother resided before my father's escape. After a short time Mr. Lewis again returned to the city. My mother still remained as cook in his family. After six years' absence of my father my mother married again a man by the name of George Brown, and lived with her second husband about four years, and had two children, when he was sold for requesting a different kind and enough food. His master considered it a great insult, and declared he would sell him. But previous to this insult, as he called it, my step-father was foreman in Mr. L.'s tobacco factory. He was trusty and of good moral habits, and was calculated to bring the highest price in the human market; therefore the excuse to sell him for the above offence was only a plot. The morning this offence occurred, Mr. L. bid my father to remain in the kitchen till he had taken his breakfast. After pulling his ears and slapping his face bade him come to the factory; but instead of going to the factory he went to Canada. Thus my poor mother was again left alone with two more children added to her misery and sorrow to toil on her weary pilgrimage.

> Racked with agony and pain she was left alone again,
> With a purpose nought could move
> And the zeal of woman's love,
> Down she knelt in agony
> To ask the Lord to clear the way.
> True she said O gracious Lord,
> True and faithful is thy word;
> But the humblest, poorest, may
> Eat the crumbs they cast away.
> Though nine long years had passed
> Without one glimmering light of day
> She never did forget to pray
> And has not yet though whips and chains are cast away.
> For thus said the blessed Lord,
> I will verify my word;
> By the faith that has not failed,
> Thou hast asked and shall prevail.

We remained but a short time at the same residence when Mr. Lewis moved again to the country. Soon after, my little brother was taken sick in consequence of being confined in a box in which my mother was obliged to keep him. If permitted to creep around the floor her mistress thought it would take too much time to attend to him. He was two years old and never walked. His limbs were perfectly paralyzed for want of exercise. We now saw him gradually failing, but was not allowed to render him due attention. Even the morning he died she was compelled to attend to her usual work. She watched over him for three months by night and attended to her domestic affairs by day. The night previous to his death we were aware he could not survive through the approaching day, but it made no impression on my mistress until she came into the kitchen and saw his life fast ebbing away, then she put on a sad countenance for fear of being exposed, and told my mother to take the child to her room, where he only lived one hour. When she found he was dead she ordered grave clothes to be brought and gave my mother time to bury him. O that morning, that solemn morning. It appears to me that when that little spirit departed as though all heaven rejoiced and angels veiled their faces.

   My mother too in concert joined,—
Her mingled praise with them combined.
Her little saint had gone to God
Who saved him with his precious blood.
Who said "Suffer little children to come unto me and forbid them not."

# THE SOLDIERS, AND OUR TREATMENT DURING THE WAR

Soon after the war commenced the rebel soldiers encamped near Mr. Lewis' residence, and remained there one week. They were then ordered by General Lyons to surrender, but they refused. There were seven thousand Union and seven hundred rebel soldiers. The Union soldiers surrounded the camp and took them and exhibited them through the city and then confined them in prison. I told my mistress that the Union soldiers were coming to take the camp. She replied that it was false, that it was General Kelly coming to re-enforce Gen. Frost. In a few moments the alarm was heard. I told Mrs. L. the Unionists had fired upon the rebels. She replied it was only the salute of Gen. Kelly. At night her husband came home with the news that Camp Jackson was taken and all the soldiers prisoners. Mrs. Lewis asked how the Union soldiers could take seven hundred men when they only numbered the same. Mr. L. replied they had seven thousand. She was much astonished, and cast her eye around to us for fear we might hear her. Her suspicion was correct; there was not a word passed that escaped our listening ears. My mother and myself could read enough to make out the news in the papers. The Union soldiers took much delight in tossing a paper over the fence to us. It aggravated my mistress very much. My mother used to sit up nights and read to keep posted about the war. In a few days my mistress came down to the kitchen again with another bitter complaint that it was a sad affair that the Unionists had taken their delicate citizens who had enlisted and made prisoners of them—that they were babes. My mother reminded her of taking Fort Sumpter and Major Anderson and serving them the same and that turn about was fair play. She then hastened to her room with the speed of a deer, nearly unhinging every door in her flight, replying as she went that the Niggers and Yankees were seeking to take the country. One day, after she had visited the kitchen to superintend some domestic affairs, as she pretended, she became very angry without a word being passed, and said—"I think it has come to a pretty pass, that old Lincoln, with his long legs, an old rail splitter, wishes to put the Niggers on an equality with the whites; that her children should never be on an equal footing with a Nigger. She had rather see them dead." As my mother made no reply to her remarks, she stopped talking, and commenced venting her spite on my companion servant. On one occasion Mr. Lewis searched my mother's room and found a picture of President Lincoln, cut from a newspaper, hanging in her room. He asked her what she was doing with old Lincoln's picture. She replied it was there because she liked it. He then knocked her down three times, and sent her to the trader's yard for a month as punishment. My mistress indulged some hopes till the victory of New Orleans, when she heard the famous Union song sang to the tune of Yankee Doodle:

> The rebels swore that New Orleans never should be taken,
> But if the Yankees came so near they should not save their bacon.
> That's the way they blustered when they thought they were so handy,
> But Farragut steamed up one day and gave them Doodle Dandy.
> Ben Butler then was ordered down to regulate the city;
> He made the rebels walk a chalk, and was not that a pity?
> That's the way to serve them out—that's the way to treat them,
> They must not go and put on airs after we have beat them.
> He made the rebel banks shell out and pay the loyal people,
> He made them keep the city clean from pig's sty to church steeple.
> That's the way Columbia speaks, let all men believe her;
> That's the way Columbia speaks instead of yellow fever.
> He sent the saucy women up and made them treat us well
> He helped the poor and snubbed the rich; they thought he was the devil,
> Bully for Ben. Butler, then, they thought he was so handy;
> Bully for Ben Butler then,—Yankee Doodle Dandy.

The days of sadness for mistress were days of joy for us. We shouted and laughed to the top of our voices. My mistress was more enraged than ever—nothing pleased her. One evening, after I had attended to my usual duties, and I supposed all was complete, she, in a terrible range, declared I should be punished that night. I did not know the cause, neither did she. She went immediately and selected a switch. She placed it in the corner of the room to await the return of her husband at night for him to whip me. As I was not pleased with the idea of a whipping I bent the switch in the shape of W, which was the first letter of his name, and after I had attended to the dining room my fellow servant and myself walked away and stopped with an aunt of mine during the night. In the morning we made our way to the Arsenal, but could gain no admission. While we were wandering about seeking protection, the girl's father overtook us and persuaded us to return home. We finally complied. All was quiet. Not a word was spoken respecting our sudden departure. All went on as usual. I was permitted to attend to my work without interruption until three weeks after. One morning I entered Mrs. Lewis' room, and she was in a room adjoining, complaining of something I had neglected. Mr. L. then enquired if I had done my work. I told him I had. She then flew into a rage and told him I was saucy, and to strike me, and he immediately gave me a severe blow with a stick of wood, which inflicted a deep wound upon my head. The blood ran over my clothing, which gave me a frightful appearance. Mr. Lewis then ordered me to change my clothing immediately. As I did not obey he became more enraged, and pulled me into another room and threw me on the floor, placed his knee on my stomach, slapped me on the face and beat me with his fist, and would have punished me more had not my mother interfered. He then told her to go away or he would compel her to, but she remained until he left me. I struggled mightily, and stood him a good test for a while, but he was fast conquering me when my mother came. He was aware my mother could usually defend herself against one man, and both of us would overpower him, so after giving his wife strict orders to take me up stairs and keep me there, he took his carriage and drove away. But she forgot it, as usual. She was highly gratified with my appropriate treatment, as she called it, and retired to her room, leaving me to myself. I then went to my mother and told her I was going away. She bid me go, and added "May the Lord help you." I started for the Arsenal again and succeeded in gaining admittance and seeing the Adjutant. He ordered me to go to another tent, where there was a woman in similar circumstances, cooking. When the General found I was there he sent me to the boarding house. I remained there three weeks, and when I went I wore the same stained clothing as when I was so severely punished, which has left a mark on my head which will ever remind me of my treatment while in slavery. Thanks be to God, though tortured by wrong and goaded by oppression, the hearts that would madden with misery have broken the iron yoke.

# MR. LEWIS CALLS AT THE BOARDING HOUSE

At the expiration of three weeks Mr. Lewis called at my boarding house, accompanied by his brother-in-law, and enquired for me, and the General informed him where I was. He then told me my mother was very anxious for me to come home, and I returned. The General had ordered Mr. Lewis to call at headquarters, when he told him if he had treated me right I would not have been compelled to seek protection of him; that my first appearance was sufficient proof of his cruelty. Mr. L. promised to take me home and treat me kindly. Instead of fulfilling his promise he carried me to the trader's yard, where, to my great surprise, I found my mother. She had been there during my absence, where she was kept for fear she would find me and take my brother and sister and make her escape. There was so much excitement at that time, (1861), by the Union soldiers rendering the fugitives shelter and protection, he was aware that if she applied to them, as he did not fulfill his promise in my case, he would stand a poor chance. If my mother made application to them for protection they would learn that he did not return me home, and immediately detect the intrigue. After I was safely secured in the trader's yard, Mr. L. took my mother home. I remained in the yard three months. Near the termination of the time of my confinement I was passing by the office when the cook of the Arsenal saw and recognized me and informed the General that Mr. L. had disobeyed his orders, and had put me in the trader's yard instead of taking me home. The General immediately arrested Mr. L. and gave him one hundred lashes with the cowhide, so that they might identify him by a scarred back, as well as his slaves. My mother had the pleasure of washing his stained clothes, otherwise it would not have been known. My master was compelled to pay three thousand dollars and let me out. He then put me to service, where I remained seven months, after which he came in great haste and took me into the city and put me into the trader's yard again. After he received the punishment he treated my mother and the children worse than ever, which caused her to take her children and secrete themselves in the city, and would have remained undetected had it not been for a traitor who pledged himself to keep the secret. But King Whiskey fired up his brain one evening, and out popped the secret. My mother and sister were consequently taken and committed to the trader's yard. My little brother was then eight years of age, my sister sixteen, and myself eighteen. We remained there two weeks, when a rough looking man, called Capt. Tirrell, came to the yard and enquired for our family. After he had examined us he remarked that we were a fine looking family, and bid us retire. In about two hours he returned, at the edge of the evening, with a covered wagon, and took my mother and brother and sister and left me. My mother refused to go without me, and told him she would raise an alarm. He advised her to remain as quiet as possible. At length she was compelled to go. When she entered the wagon there was a man standing behind with his hands on each side of the wagon to prevent her from making her escape. She sprang to her feet and gave this man a desperate blow, and leaping to the ground she made an alarm. The watchmen came to her assistance immediately, and there was quite a number of Union policemen guarding the city at that time, who rendered her due justice as far as possible. This was before the emancipation proclamation was issued. After she leaped from the wagon they drove on, taking her children to the boat. The police questioned my mother. She told them that Capt. Tirrell had put her children on board the boat, and was going to take them to Memphis and sell them into hard slavery. They accompanied her to the boat, and arrived just as they were casting off. The police ordered them to stop and immediately deliver up the children, who had been secreted in the Captain's private apartment. They were brought forth and returned. Slave speculation was forbidden in St. Louis at that time. The Union soldiers had possession of the city, but their power was limited to the suppression of the selling of slaves to got out of the city. Considerable smuggling was done, however, by pretending Unionism, which was the case with our family.

# RELEASED FROM THE TRADER'S YARD AND TAKEN TO HER NEW MASTER

Immediately after dinner my mother called for me to accompany her to our new home, the residence of the Captain, together with my brother and sister. We fared very well while we were there. Mrs. Tirrell was insane, and my mother had charge of the house. We remained there four months. The Captain came home only once a week and he never troubled us for fear we might desert him. His intention was to smuggle us away before the State became free. That was the understanding when he bought us of Mr. Lewis, as it was not much of an object to purchase slaves while the proclamation was pending, and they likely to lose all their property; but they would, for a trifle purchase a whole family of four or five persons to send out of the State. Kentucky paid as much, or more than ever, for slaves. As they pretended to take no part in the rebellion they supposed they would be allowed to keep them without interference. Consequently the Captain's intention was to keep as quiet as possible till the excitement concerning us was over, and he could get us off without detection. Mr. Lewis would rather have disposed of us for nothing than have seen us free. He hated my mother in consequence of her desire for freedom, and her endeavors to teach her children the right way as far as her ability would allow. He also held a charge against her for reading the papers and understanding political affairs. When he found he was to lose his slaves he could not bear the idea of her being free. He thought it too hard, as she had raised so many tempests for him, to see her free and under her own control. He had tantalized her in every possible way to humiliate and annoy her; yet while he could demand her services he appreciated and placed perfect confidence in mother and family. None but a fiendish slaveholder could have rended an honest Christian heart in such a manner as this.

> Though it was her sad and weary lot to toil in slavery
> But one thing cheered her weary soul
> When almost in despair
> That she could gain a sure relief in attitude of prayer

# CAPT. TIRRELL REMOVES THE FAMILY— ANOTHER STRATEGY

One day the Captain commenced complaining of the expense of so large a family, and proposed to my mother that we should work out and he take part of the pay. My mother told him she would need what she earned for my little brother's support. Finally the Captain consented, and I was the first to be disposed of. The Captain took me in his buggy and carried me to the Depot, and I was put into a Union family, where I remained five months. Previous to my leaving, however, my mother and the Captain entered into a contract—he agreeing not to sell us, and mother agreeing not to make her escape. While she was carrying out her promise in good faith, he was plotting to separate us. We were all divided except mother and my little brother, who remained together. My sister remained with one of the rebels, but was tolerably treated. We all fared very well; but it was only the calm before the rending tornado. Captain T. was Captain of the boat to Memphis, from which the Union soldiers had rescued us. He commenced as a deck hand on the boat, then attained a higher position, and continued to advance until he became her Captain. At length he came in possession of slaves. Then his accomplishments were complete. He was a very severe slave master. Those mushroom slaveholders are much dreaded, as their severity knows no bounds

> Bondage and torture, scourges and chains
> Placed on our backs indelible stains.

I stated previously, in relating a sketch of my mother's history, that she was married twice, and both husbands were to be sold and made their escape. They both gained their freedom. One was living,—the other died before the war. Both made every effort to find us, but to no purpose. It was some years before we got a correct account of her second husband, and he had no account of her, except once he heard that mother and children had perished in the woods while endeavoring to make their escape. In a few years after his arrival in the free States he married again.

When about sixteen years of age, while residing with her original master, my mother became acquainted with a young man, Mr. Adams, residing in a neighboring family, whom she much respected; but he was soon sold, and she lost trace of him entirely, as was the common occurrence with friends and companions though united by the nearest ties. When my mother arrived at

Captain Tirrell's, after leaving the boat, in her excitement she scarce observed anything except her little group so miraculously saved from perhaps a final separation in this world. She at length observed that the servant who was waiting to take her to the Captain's residence in the country was the same man with whom she formed the acquaintance when sixteen years old, and they again renewed their acquaintance. He had been married and buried his wife. It appeared that his wife had been in Captain Tirrell's family many years, and he also, for some time. They had a number of children, and Capt. Tirrell had sold them down South. This cruel blow, assisted by severe flogging and other ill treatment, rendered the mother insane, and finally caused her death.

> In agony close to her bosom she pressed,
> The life of her heart, the child of her breast—
> Oh love from its tenderness gathering might
> Had strengthed her soul for declining age.
> But she is free. Yes, she has gone from the land of the slave;
> The hand of oppression must rest in the grave.
> The blood hounds have missed the scent of her way,
> The hunter is rifled and foiled of his prey.

After my mother had left the Captain to take care of herself and child, according to agreement with the Captain, she became engaged to Mr. Adams. He had bought himself previously for a large price. After they became acquainted, the Captain had an excellent opportunity of carrying out his stratagem. He commenced bestowing charity upon Mr. Adams. As he had purchased himself, and Capt. T. had agreed not to sell my mother, they had decided to marry at an early day. They hired a house in the city and were to commence housekeeping immediately. The Captain made him a number of presents and seemed much pleased with the arrangement. The day previous to the one set for the marriage, while they were setting their house in order, a man called and enquired for a nurse, pretending he wanted one of us. Mother was absent; he said he would call again, but he never came. On Wednesday evening we attended a protracted meeting. After we had returned home and retired, a loud rap was heard at the door. My Aunt enquired who was there. The reply was, "Open the door or I will break it down." In a moment in rushed seven men, four watchmen and three traders, and ordered mother to take my brother and me and follow them, which she hastened to do as fast as possible, but we were not allowed time to put on our usual attire. They thrust us into a close carriage. For fear of my mother alarming the citizens they threw her to the ground and choked her until she was nearly strangled, then pushed her into a coach. The night was dark and dreary; the stars refused to shine, the moon to shed her light.

> 'Tis not strange the heavenly orbs
> In silence blushed neath Nature's sable garb
> When woman's gagged and rashly torn away
> Without blemish and without crime.
> Unheeded by God's holy word:—
> Unloose the fetters, break the chain,
> And make my people free again,
> And let them breath pure freedom's air
> And her rich bounty freely share.
> Let Eutopia stretch her bleeding hands abroad;
> Her cry of anguish finds redress from God.

We were hurried along the streets. The inhabitants heard our cries and rushed to their doors, but our carriage being perfectly tight, and the alarm so sudden, that we were at the jail before they could give us any relief. There were strong Union men and officers in the city, and if they could have been informed of the human smuggling they would have released us. But oh, that horrid, dilapidated prison, with its dim lights and dingy walls, again presented itself to our view. My sister was there first, and we were thrust in and remained there until three o'clock the following afternoon. Could we have notified the police we should have been released, but no opportunity was given us. It appears that this kidnapping had been in contemplation from the time we were before taken and returned; and Captain Tirrell's kindness to mother,—his benevolence towards Mr. Adams in assisting him to furnish his house,—his generosity in letting us work for ourselves,—his approbation in regard to the contemplated marriage was only a trap. Thus instead of a wedding Thursday evening, we were hurled across the ferry to Albany Court House and to Kentucky through the rain and without our outer garments. My mother had lost her bonnet and shawl in the struggle while being thrust in the coach, consequently she had no protection from the storm, and the rest of us were in similar circumstances. I believe we passed through Springfield. I think it was the first stopping place after we left East St. Louis, and we were put on board the cars and secreted in the gentlemen's smoking car, in which there were only a few rebels. We arrived in Springfield about twelve o'clock at night. When we took the cars it was dark, bleak and cold. It was the 18th of March, and as we were without bonnets and clothing to shield us from the sleet and wind, we suffered intensely. The old trader, for fear that mother might make her escape, carried my brother, nine years of age, from one train to the other. We then took the cars for Albany, and arrived at eight o'clock in the morning. We were then carried on the ferry in a wagon. There was another family in the wagon, in the same condition. We landed at Portland, from thence to Louisville, and were put into John Clark's trader's yard, and sold out separately, except my mother and little brother, who were sold together. Mother remained in the trader's yard two weeks, my sister six, myself four.

# THE FARE AT THEIR NEW HOMES

Mother was sold to Captain Plasio. My sister to Benj. Board, and myself to Capt. Ephraim Frisbee. The man who bought my mother was a Spaniard. After she had been there a short time he tried to have my mother let my brother stop at his saloon, a very dissipated place, to wait upon his miserable crew, but my mother objected. In spite of her objections he took him down to try him, but some Union soldiers called at the saloon, and noticing that he was very small, they questioned him, and my brother, child like, divulged the whole matter. The Captain, fearful of being betrayed and losing his property, let him continue with my mother. The Captain paid eight hundred dollars for my mother and brother. We were all sold for extravagant prices. My sister, aged sixteen, was sold for eight hundred and fifty dollars; I was sold for nine hundred dollars. This was in 1863. My mother was cook and fared very well. My sister was sold to a single gentleman, whose intended took charge of her until they were married, after which they took her to her home. She was her waiter, and fared as well as could be expected. I fared worse than either of the family. I was not allowed enough to eat, exposed to the cold, and not allowed through the cold winter to thoroughly warm myself once a month. The house was very large, and I could gain no access to the fire. I was kept constantly at work of the heaviest kind,—compelled to move heavy trunks and boxes,—many times to wash till ten and twelve o'clock at night. There were three deaths in the family while I remained there, and the entire burden was put upon me. I often felt to exclaim as the Children of Israel did: "O Lord, my burden is greater than I can bear." I was then seventeen years of age. My health has been impaired from that time to the present. I have a severe pain in my side by the slightest over exertion. In the Winter I suffer intensely with cold, and cannot get warm unless in a room heated to eighty degrees. I am infirm and burdened with the influence of slavery, whose impress will ever remain on my mind and body. For six months I tried to make my escape. I used to rise at four o'clock in the morning to find some one to assist me, and at last I succeeded. I was allowed two hours once in two weeks to go and return three miles. I could contrive no other way than to improve one of these opportunities, in which I was finally successful. I became acquainted with some persons who assisted slaves to escape by the underground railroad. They were colored people. I was to pretend going to church, and the man who was to assist and introduce me to the proper parties was to linger on the street opposite the house, and I was to follow at a short distance. On Sunday evening I begged leave to attend church, which was reluctantly granted if I completed all my work, which was no easy task. It appeared as if my mistress used every possible exertion to delay me from church, and I concluded that her old cloven-footed companion had impressed his intentions on her mind. Finally, when I was ready to start, my mistress took a notion to go out to ride, and desired me to dress her little boy, and then get ready for church. Extensive hoops were then worn, and as I had attached my whole wardrobe under mine by a cord around my waist, it required considerable dexterity and no small amount of maneuvering to hide the fact from my mistress. While attending to the child I had managed to stand in one corner of the room, for fear she might come in contact with me and thus discover that my hoops were not so elastic as they usually are. I endeavored to conceal my excitement by backing and edging very genteelly out of the door. I had nine pieces of clothing thus concealed on my person, and as the string which fastened them was small it caused me considerable discomfort. To my great satisfaction I at last passed into the street, and my master and mistress drove down the street in great haste and were soon out of sight. I saw my guide patiently awaiting me. I followed him at a distance until we arrived at the church, and there met two young ladies, one of whom handed me a pass and told me to follow them at a square's distance. It was now twilight. There was a company of soldiers about to take passage across the ferry, and I followed. I showed my pass, and proceeded up the stairs on the boat. While thus ascending the stairs, the cord which held my bundle of clothing broke, and my feet became entangled in my wardrobe, but by proceeding, the first step released one foot and the next the other. This was observed only by a few soldiers, who were too deeply engaged in their own affairs to interfere with mine. I seated myself in a remote corner of the boat, and in a few moments I landed on free soil for the first time in my life, except when hurled through Albany and Springfield at the time of our capture. I was now under my own control. The cars were waiting in Jefferson City for the passengers for Indianapolis, where we arrived about nine o'clock.

# MATTIE IN INDIANAPOLIS—THE GLORY OF FREEDOM—PRESIDENT LINCOLN'S REMAINS EXHIBITED

My first business, after my arrival at Indianapolis was to find a boarding place in which I at once succeeded, and in a few hours thereafter was at a place of service of my own choice. I had always been under the yoke of oppression, compelled to submit to its laws, and not allowed to advance a rod from the house, or even out of call, without a severe punishment. Now this constant fear and restless yearning was over. It appeared as though I had emerged into a new world, or had never lived in the old one before. The people I lived with were Unionists, and became immediately interested in teaching and encouraging me in my literary advancement and all other important improvements, which precisely met the natural desires for which my soul had ever yearned since my earliest recollection. I could read a little, but was not allowed to learn in slavery. I was obliged to pay twenty-five cents for every letter written for me. I now began to feel that as I was free I could learn to write, as well as others; consequently Mrs. Harris, the lady with whom I lived, volunteered to assist me. I was soon enabled to write quite a legible hand, which I find a great convenience. I would advise all, young, middle aged or old, in a free country to learn to read and write. If this little book should fall into the hands of one deficient of the important knowledge of writing, I hope they will remember the old maxim:—"Never too old to learn." Manage your own secrets, and divulge them by the silent language of your own pen. Had our blessed President considered it too humiliating to learn in advanced years, our race would yet have remained under the galling yoke of oppression. After I had been with Mrs. Harris seven months, the joyful news came of the surrender of Lee's army and the capture of Richmond.

> Whilst the country's hearts were throbbing,
> Filled with joy for victories won;
> Whilst the stars and stripes were waving
> O'er each cottage, ship and dome,
> Came upon like winged lightning
> Words that turned each joy to dread,
> Froze with horror as we listened:
> Our beloved chieftain, Lincoln's dead
> War's dark clouds has long held o'er us,

They have rolled their gloomy fold's away,
And all the world is anxious, waiting
For that promised peaceful day.
But that fearful blow inflicted,
Fell on his devoted head,
And from every town and hamlet
Came the cry our Chieftain's dead.
Weep, weep, O bleeding nation
For the patriot spirit fled,
All untold our country's future—
Buried with the silent dead.
God of battles, God of nations to our country send relief
Turn each lamentation into joy whilst we mourn our murdered chief.

On the Saturday after the assassination of the President there was a meeting held on the Common, and a vote taken to have the President's body brought through Indianapolis, for the people to see his dear dead face. The vote was taken by raising the hands, and when the question was put in favor of it a thousand black hands were extended in the air, seemingly higher and more visible than all the rest. Nor were their hands alone raised, for in their deep sorrow and gloom they raised their hearts to God, for well they knew that He, through martyred blood, had made them free. It was some time before the remains reached Indianapolis, as it was near the last of the route. The body was placed in the centre of the hall of the State House, and we marched in by fours, and divided into two on each side of the casket, and passed directly through the hall. It was very rainy,—nothing but umbrellas were to be seen in any direction. The multitude were passing in and out from eight o'clock in the morning till four o'clock in the afternoon. His body remained until twelve o'clock in the evening, many distinguished persons visiting it, when amid the booming of cannon, it moved on its way to Springfield, its final resting-place. The death of the President was like an electric shock to my soul. I could not feel convinced of his death until I gazed upon his remains, and heard the last roll of the muffled drum and the farewell boom of the cannon. I was then convinced that though we were left to the tender mercies of God, we were without a leader.

Gone, gone is our chieftain,
The tried and the true;
The grief of our nation the world never knew.
We mourn as a nation has never yet mourned;

The foe to our freedom more deeply has scorned.
In the height of his glory in manhood's full prime,
Our country's preserver through darkest of time;
A merciful being, whose kindness all shared
Shown mercy to others. Why was he not spared?
The lover of Justice, the friend of the slave,
He struck at oppression and made it a grave;
He spoke for our bond-men, and chains from them fell,
By making them soldiers they served our land well.
Because he had spoken from sea unto sea
Glad tidings go heavenward, our country is free,
And angels I'm thinking looked down from above,
With sweet smiles approving his great works of love.
His name with the honor forever will live,
And time to his laurels new lustre will give;
He lived so unselfish, so loyal and true,
That his deeds will shine brighter at every view.
Then honor and cherish the name of the brave,
The champion of freedom, the friend to the slave,
The far-sighted statesman who saw a fair end,
When north land and south land one flag shall defend.
Rest, rest, fallen chieftain, thy labors are o'er,
For thee mourns a nation as never before;
Farewell honored chieftain whom millions adore,
Farewell gentle spirit, whom heaven has won.

# SISTER LOST — MOTHER'S ESCAPE

In two or three weeks after the body of the President was carried through, my sister made her escape, but by some means we entirely lost trace of her. We heard she was in a free State. In three months my mother also escaped. She rose quite early in the morning, took my little brother, and arrived at my place of service in the afternoon. I was much surprised, and asked my mother how she came there. She could scarcely tell me for weeping, but I soon found out the mystery. After so many long years and so many attempts, for this was her seventh, she at last succeeded, and we were now all free. My mother had been a slave for more than forty-three years, and liberty was very sweet to her. The sound of freedom was music in our ears; the air was pure and fragrant; the genial rays of the glorious sun burst forth with a new lustre upon us, and all creation resounded in responses of praise to the author and creator of him who proclaimed life and freedom to the slave. I was overjoyed with my personal freedom, but the joy at my mother's escape was greater than anything I had ever known. It was a joy that reaches beyond the tide and anchors in the harbor of eternal rest. While in oppression, this eternal life-preserver had continually wafted her toward the land of freedom, which she was confident of gaining, whatever might betide. Our joy that we were permitted to mingle together our earthly bliss in glorious strains of freedom was indescribable. My mother responded with the children of Israel, — "The Lord is my strength and my song. The Lord is a man of war, and the Lord is his name." We left Indianapolis the day after my mother arrived, and took the cars at eleven o'clock the following evening for St. Louis, my native State. We were then free, and instead of being hurried along, bare headed and half naked, through cars and boats, by a brutal master with a bill of sale in his pocket, we were our own, comfortably clothed, and having the true emblems of freedom.

# MOTHER'S MARRIAGE

It appeared to me that the city presented an entirely new aspect. The reader will remember that my mother was engaged to be married on the evening after we were kidnapped, and that Mr. Adams, her intended, had prepared the house for the occasion. We now went in search of him. He had moved about five miles into the country. He had carefully preserved his furniture and was patiently awaiting our return. We were gone two years and four months. The clothing and furniture which we had collected were all destroyed. It was over a year after we left St. Louis before we heard from there. We went immediately from the cars to my aunt's, and from there went to Mr. Adams' residence and took him by surprise. They were married in a week after our return. My mother is comfortably situated on a small farm with a kind and affectionate companion, with whom she had formed an early acquaintance, and from whom she had been severed by the ruthless hand of Wrong; but by the divine hand of Justice they were now reunited forever.

# MATTIE MEETS HER OLD MASTER—GOES TO SERVICE—IS SENT FOR BY HER STEP-FATHER IN LAWRENCE, MASS.

In a short time I had selected a place of service, and was improving my studies in a small way. The place I engaged was in the family where I was born, where my mother lived when my father Jackson made his escape. Although Mr. Canory's family were always kind to us, I felt a great difference between freedom and slavery. After I had been there a short time my step-father sent for me and my half brother to come to Lawrence. He had been waiting ever since the State was free, hoping to get some account of us. He had been informed, previously, that mother, in trying to make her escape, had perished by the way, and the children also, but he was never satisfied. He was aware that my aunt was permanently in St. Louis, as her master had given her family their freedom twenty years previous. She was formerly owned by Major Howe, harness and leather dealer, yet residing in St. Louis. And long may he live and his good works follow him and his posterity forever. My father well knew the deception of the rebels, and was determined to persevere until he had obtained a satisfactory account of his family. A gentleman moved directly from Lawrence to St. Louis, who made particular enquiries for us, and even called at my aunt's. We then heard directly from my father, and commenced correspondence. He had not heard directly from us since he made his escape, which was nine years. He had never heard of his little son who my mother was compelled by Mrs. Lewis to confine in a box. He was born eight months after he left. As soon as possible after my mother consented to let my little brother go to his father he sent means to assist us to make preparations for our journey to the North. At first he only sent for his little son. My mother was anxious about sending him alone. He was only eleven years old, and perfectly unused to traveling, and had never been away from his mother. Finally my father came to the conclusion that, as my mother had endured such extreme hardships and sufferings during the nine years he was not permitted to participate or render her any assistance, that it would afford him much pleasure in sending for us both, bearing our expenses and making us as comfortable as his means would allow. Money was sent us, and our kind friend, Mr. Howe, obtained our tickets and voluntarily assisted us in starting. We left for the North on Monday, April 9th, and arrived safe and sound, on the 11th. We found my step-father's residence about six o'clock in the evening. He was not expecting us till the next day. Our meeting is better imagined than told. I cannot describe it. His little son was only two years old when he left, and I was eleven, and we never expected to meet him again this side of eternity. It was Freedom that brought us together. My father was comfortably situated in a nice white cottage, containing some eight rooms, all well furnished, and attached to it was a fine garden. His wife, who is a physician, was absent, but returned on the following day. The people were kind and friendly. They informed me there was no other colored family in the city, but my step-mother was continually crowded with friends and customers without distinction. My step-mother had buried her only son, who returned from the war in a decline. The white friends were all in deep sympathy with them. I felt immediately at home among such kind and friendly people, and have never felt homesick, except when I think of my poor mother's farewell embrace when she accompanied us to the cars. As soon as my step-mother had arrived, and our excitement was over, they commenced calculating upon placing me in the Sabbath school at the church where my mother belonged. On the next Sabbath I accompanied her and joined the Sabbath school, she occupying a side seat about middle way up the house. I was not reminded of my color except by an occasional loafer or the Irish, usually the colored man's enemy. I was never permitted to attend a white church before, or ride in any public conveyance without being placed in a car for the especial purpose; and in the street cars we were not permitted to ride at all, either South or West. Here I ride where I please, without the slightest remark, except from the ignorant. Many ask me if I am contented. They can imagine by the above contrast. My brother and myself entered the public school, and found a host of interested friends and formed many dear acquaintances whom I shall never forget. After attending school a month the term closed. I advanced in my studies as fast as could be expected. I never attended school but one month before. I needed more attention than my kind teacher could possibly bestow upon me, encumbered as she was by so many small children. Mother then proposed my entering some select school and placing myself entirely under its discipline and influence. I was much pleased with the idea, but as they had already been to so much expense for me, I could not wish to place them under any heavier contribution. I had previously told my step-mother my story, and how often my own mother had wished she could have it published. I did not imagine she could find time to write and arrange it, but she immediately proposed writing and publishing the entire story, by the sale of which I might obtain the aid towards completing my studies. I am glad I came to the old Bay State, the people of which the rebels hate with an extreme hatred. I found it just such a place as I had imagined by the appearance of the soldiers and the kindness they manifested.

New England, that blessed land,
All in a happy Union band;
They with the needy share their bread
And teach the weak the Word of God.

We never heard from my sister Hester, who made her escape from Kentucky, except when she was on the cars, though we have no doubt she succeeded in gaining her freedom.

# SUMMARY

On my return to St. Louis I met my old master, Lewis, who strove so hard to sell us away that he might avoid seeing us free, on the street. He was so surprised that before he was aware of it he dropped a bow. My mother met Mrs. Lewis, her old mistress, with a large basket on her arm, trudging to market. It appeared she had lived to see the day when her children had to wait upon themselves, and she likewise. The Yankees had taken possession, and her posterity were on an equality with the black man. Mr. Lewis despised the Irish, and often declared he would board at the hotel before he would employ Irish help, but he now has a dissipated Irish cook. When I was his slave I was obliged to keep away every fly from the table, and not allow one to light on a person. They are now compelled to brush their own flies and dress themselves and children. Mr. Lewis' brother Benjamin was a more severe slave master than the one who owned me. He was a tobacconist and very wealthy. As soon as the war commenced he turned Unionist to save his property. He was very severe in his punishments. He used to extend his victim, fastened to a beam, with hands and feet tied, and inflict from fifty to three hundred lashes, laying their flesh entirely open, then bathe their quivering wounds with brine, and, through his nose, in a slow rebel tone he would tell them "You'd better walk a fair chalk line or else I'll give yer twice as much." His former friends, the guerrillas, were aware he only turned Union to save his cash, and they gave those persons he had abused a large share of his luxury. They then, in the presence of his wife and another distinguished lady, tortured him in a most inhuman manner. For pretending Unionism they placed him on a table and threatened to dissect him alive if he did not tell them where he kept his gold. He immediately informed them. They then stood him against the house and fired over his head. From that, they changed his position by turning him upside down, and raising him two feet from the floor, letting him dash his head against the floor until his skull was fractured, after which he lingered awhile and finally died. There was a long piece published in the paper respecting his repentance, benevolence, &c. All the slaves who ever lived in his family admit the Lord is able to save to the uttermost. He saved the thief on the cross, and perhaps he saved him.

When I made my escape from slavery I was in a query how I was to raise funds to bear my expenses. I finally came to the conclusion that as the laborer was worthy of his hire, I thought my wages should come from my master's pocket. Accordingly I took twenty-five dollars. After I was safe and had learned to write, I sent him a nice letter, thanking him for the kindness his pocket bestowed to me in time of need. I have never received any answer to it.

When I complete my education, if my life is spared, I shall endeavor to publish further details of our history in another volume from my own pen.

# CHRISTIANITY

Christianity is a system claiming God for its author, and the welfare of man for its object. It is a system so uniform, exalted and pure, that the loftiest intellects have acknowledged its influence, and acquiesced in the justness of its claims. Genius has bent from his erratic course to gather fire from her altars, and pathos from the agony of Gethsemane and the sufferings of Calvary. Philosophy and science have paused amid their speculative researches and wonderous revelations, to gain wisdom from her teachings and knowledge from her precepts. Poetry has culled her fairest flowers and wreathed her softest, to bind her Author's "bleeding brow." Music has strung her sweetest lyres and breathed her noblest strains to celebrate His fame; whilst Learning has bent from her lofty heights to bow at the lowly cross. The constant friend of man, she has stood by him in his hour of greatest need. She has cheered the prisoner in his cell, and strengthened the martyr at the stake. She has nerved the frail and sinking heart of woman for high and holy deeds. The worn and weary have rested their fainting heads upon her bosom, and gathered strength from her words and courage from her counsels. She has been the staff of decrepit age, and the joy of manhood in its strength. She has bent over the form of lovely childhood, and suffered it to have a place in the Redeemer's arms. She has stood by the bed of the dying, and unveiled the glories of eternal life; gilding the darkness of the tomb with the glory of the resurrection.

Christianity has changed the moral aspect of nations. Idolatrous temples have crumbled at her touch, and guilt owned its deformity in her presence. The darkest habitations of earth have been irradiated with heavenly light, and the death shriek of immolated victims changed for ascriptions of praise to God and the Lamb. Envy and Malice have been rebuked by her contented look, and fretful Impatience by her gentle and resigned manner.

At her approach, fetters have been broken, and men have risen redeemed from dust, and freed from chains. Manhood has learned its dignity and worth, its kindred with angels, and alliance to God.

To man, guilty, fallen and degraded man, she shows a fountain drawn from the Redeemer's veins; there she bids him wash and be clean. She points him to "Mount Zion, the city of the living God, to an innumerable company of angels, to the spirits of just men made perfect, and to Jesus the Mediator of the new Covenant," and urges him to rise from the degradation of sin, renew his nature and join with them. She shows a pattern so spotless and holy, so elevated and pure, that he might shrink from it discouraged, did she not bring with her a promise from the lips of Jehovah, that he would give power to the faint, and might to those who have no strength. Learning may bring her ample pages and her ponderous records, rich with the spoils of every age, gathered from every land, and gleaned from every source. Philosophy and science may bring their abstruse researches and wonderous revelations—Literature her elegance, with the toils of the pen, and the labors of the pencil—but they are idle tales compared to the truths of Christianity. They may cultivate the intellect, enlighten the understanding, give scope to the imagination, and refine the sensibilities; but they open not, to our dim eyes and longing vision, the land of crystal founts and deathless flowers. Philosophy searches earth; Religion opens heaven. Philosophy doubts and trembles at the portals of eternity; Religion lifts the veil, and shows us golden streets, lit by the Redeemer's countenance, and irradiated by his smile. Philosophy strives to reconcile us to death; Religion triumphs over it. Philosophy treads amid the pathway of stars, and stands a delighted listener to the music of the spheres; but Religion gazes on the glorious palaces of God, while the harpings of the blood-washed, and the songs of the redeemed, fall upon her ravished ear. Philosophy has her place; Religion her important sphere; one is of importance here, the other of infinite and vital importance both here and hereafter.

Amid ancient lore the Word of God stands unique and pre-eminent. Wonderful in its construction, admirable in its adaptation, it contains truths that a child may comprehend, and mysteries into which angels desire to look. It is in harmony with that adaptation of means to ends which pervades creation, from the polypus tribes, elaborating their coral homes, to man, the wonderous work of God. It forms the brightest link of that glorious chain which unites the humblest work of creation with the throne of the infinite and eternal Jehovah. As light, with its infinite particles and curiously blended colors, is suited to an eye prepared for the alterations of day; as air, with its subtle and invisible essence, is fitted for the delicate organs of respiration; and, in a word, as this material world is adapted to man's physical nature; so the word of eternal truth is adapted to his moral nature and mental constitution. It finds him wounded, sick and suffering, and points him to the balm of Gilead and the Physician of souls. It finds him stained by transgressions and defiled with guilt, and directs him to the "blood that cleanseth from all unrighteousness and sin." It finds him athirst and faint, pining amid the deserts of life, and shows him the wells of salvation and the rivers of life. It addresses itself to his moral and spiritual nature, makes provision for his wants and weaknesses, and meets his yearnings and aspirations. It is adapted to his mind in its earliest stages of progression, and its highest state of intellectuality. It provides light for his darkness, joy for his anguish, a solace for his woes, balm for his wounds, and heaven for his hopes. It unveils the unseen world, and reveals him who is the light of creation, and the joy of the universe, reconciled through the death of His Son. It promises the faithful a blessed re-union in a land undimmed with tears, undarkened by sorrow. It affords a truth for the living and a refuge for the dying. Aided by the Holy Spirit, it guides us through life, points out the shoals, the quicksands and hidden rocks which endanger our path, and at last leaves us with the eternal God for our refuge, and his everlasting arms for our protection.

Printed in Great Britain
by Amazon